How Different Religions View Death & Afterlife

Second Edition

Edited by

Christopher Jay Johnson, PhD
and Marsha G. McGee, PhD

The Charles Press, Publishers
Philadelphia

The Charles Press, Publishers
Post Office Box 15715
Philadelphia, PA 19103
(215) 545-8933 Telephone
(215) 545-8937 Telefax
sales@charlespresspub.com
http://www.charlespresspub.com

Library of Congress Cataloging-in-Publication Data

How different religions view death and afterlife / edited by
Christopher Jay Johnson and Marsha G. McGee. – 2nd ed.
p. cm.
Rev. ed. of Encounters with eternity.
Includes bibliographical references and index.
ISBN 0-914783-85-8 (alk. paper)
1. Death – Religious Aspects – Comparative studies.
2. Future life – Comparative studies
I. Johnson, Christopher Jay. II. McGee, Marsha G.
III. Encounters with eternity.
BL504.E53 1998
291.2'3 – dc21

CIP
98-12743

Printed in the United States of America

ISBN 0-914783-85-8

Preface

When the first edition of this book was published in 1991, society was riding the crest of a new wave of interest in the subject of death and dying. Much of this interest was instigated by the fact that the unrelenting and overwhelming progress of modern technology had created a massive spiritual void in the minds of millions of thoughtful people. People had begun to realize that certain things — issues of great significance to our lives — could not be "answered" by science and medical technology. Furthermore, modern technology seemed to have offered certain ideas that were especially troublesome — such as the idea that everything is over and done with the moment we die — that is, the moment our bodies experience clinical death.

As a result of this dissatisfaction, the closing decade of the millennium has witnessed an unmistakable movement back to the roots of religious tradition, at least throughout the technologically developed world and most notably in the United States. People from all walks of life are now embracing a new search for spiritual answers to questions about life and death. We realized that now seemed an appropriate time for an expanded and updated second edition of this book.

The goal of this book is to aid readers in their search for spiritual answers by offering the information needed to explore a wide range of views on death and afterlife presented by theologians and experts from many different religious groups. Even though one would think that this information would be readily available, surprisingly, this is not the case. There are many books on death and many books on religion, but few have managed to integrate these subjects thoughtfully and effectively. Here, in a single volume, is all the information necessary for obtaining a solid understanding of the thoughts, doctrines and customs regarding death and afterlife of many of the world's religions, presented in a fact-based, objective and nonproselytizing manner. The result is a unique exploration of comparative ideas on death and afterlife — straightforward, concise and fact-filled.

We have included chapters from authors who represent the largest and fastest-growing Christian groups, Christian groups that are smaller but growing and the largest non-Christian groups in North America. We asked the authors to outline the main beliefs and backgrounds of their faith and then to address their approach to the subject of death and afterlife as specifically as possible. We fully realize that the authors have expressed their own personal interpretation of the beliefs of their faith and therefore we have made sure that their views are acceptable to a broad range of members of their denomination.

In this new edition, we have added four religious groups to the 15 religions that were in the first edition. These are Christian Science, the Quakers, the Unity Church and Zoroastrianism. We have also replaced the old chapter on Hinduism with a new, more detailed chapter. Although we have not been able to include a chapter on every religious group in the spiritual spectrum, we believe the groups we have included offer a wide cross section of different beliefs and should provide the reader with a good deal of food for thought. Please bear with us in our necessarily simplified treatment of these great religions. This book is meant as an introduction to religious points of view and we could not do justice to the richness and depth of these faiths in a single volume such as this. By providing only the most salient information about the death and afterlife beliefs and practices of each faith, we hope to whet your appetite without overburdening your digestive system.

This book will be of enormous value to a wide range of readers for many reasons. Readers who are seeking a better comprehension of the beliefs of their own faith and those who want to investigate the belief systems of other faiths will be able to obtain all the information they need for a solid, if basic, understanding of the general teachings and death and afterlife beliefs of each religion. Teachers and students of comparative religion, death education and gerontology will appreciate that this book not only offers objective and factual information, but also that it has synthesized a tremendous amount of information and placed it into a logical and directly comparative format that facilitates easy comprehension. Healthcare professionals who work with the terminally ill and the dying will find practical information that will help them offer greater understanding and sensitivity to their patients of different faiths. Pastoral and grief counselors, clergy and chaplains will be able to obtain information about the death practices and beliefs of 19 faiths in one book. Funeral directors will find thoroughly practical and specific direction about the funeral, burial and grieving practices of each religion. Finally, all readers will appreciate the fact that the contributing authors present their information objectively and without an overbearing amount of theological language.

Because beliefs about death and afterlife have wide implications for life, we encourage you to join us in our search for greater understanding of these subjects. We sincerely hope this book will expand your horizons and will help you in your journey.

Christopher Jay Johnson, PhD
Marsha G. McGee, PhD

Contributors

Jamsheed K. Choksy, PhD is Associate Professor of Near Eastern, Iranian and Central Eurasian Studies at Indiana University. He is the author of several books, including *An Introduction to Zoroastrianism, Earliest Zoroastrianism, Purity and Pollution in Zoroastrianism* and *The Avesta: A New Translation of the Zoroastrian Scriptures.*

Rev. Francis X. Cleary, SJ is Professor of Theology at St. Louis University and scripture columnist for the *St. Louis Review*. He holds a doctorate in sacred theology from the Gregorian University and a licentiate in sacred scripture from the Pontifical Biblical Institute. A group and seminar leader in the St. Louis area, Fr. Cleary is also a regional and national lecturer.

Richard M. Eyre, a management consultant and writer based in Salt Lake City, holds degrees from Utah State, Brigham Young and Harvard Universities. A prolific author and lecturer, he served as a missionary in New York City and later as a Mormon Mission President in London.

Elaine R. Follis, PhD is Jeanne and George Todd Professor of Religious Studies and Associate Dean of Faculty at Principia College in Elsah, Illinois. She is a contributor to *The Anchor Bible Dictionary*, writes frequently for Christian Science periodicals and is a practicing Christian Scientist. Dr. Follis is currently researching the history of Christian Science in Germany during the Third Reich.

Rev. James Gaither, MA is an ordained Unity minister and Chair of the Department of Metaphysical Studies and Skills at the Unity School of Christianity in Unity Village, Missouri. Ordained in 1979, he came to Unity School in 1984 after serving a congregation in Collinsville, Illinois.

John S. Hatcher, PhD is Professor of English Literature at the University of South Florida. He is the author of *The Ocean of His Words: A Reader's Guide to the Art of Baha'u'llah, The Law of Love Enshrined, The Purpose of Physical Reality* and *The Arc of Ascent*, as well as a children's book, a novel and collections of poetry.

William L. Hendricks, PhD, ThD is Director of Baptist Studies and Lecturer in Theology at Brite Divinity School. Formerly Senior Professor of Christian Theology at Southern Baptist Theological Seminary, he is the author of *The Doctrine of Man, A Theology for Aging* and *Who is Jesus Christ?* among other books on scripture.

Stanley M. Horton, ThD, a leading Pentecostal scholar, is Distinguished Professor Emeritus of Bible and Theology at the Assemblies of God Theological Seminary and the General Editor at Logion Press, Springfield, Missouri. He is the author of numerous books, including *What the Bible Says About the Holy Spirit, The Ultimate Victory* and a major study on the Book of Acts.

Robert M. Johnston, PhD is Professor of New Testament and Christian Origins at the Seventh-day Adventist Theological Seminary at Andrews University. An Adventist missionary for 12 years in Korea and the Philippines, he has traveled extensively in the Far East and is the author of numerous articles in scholarly journals and religious publications.

Anne C. Klein, PhD is Professor and Chair of the Department of Religious Studies at Rice University. She is the author of four books, including *Meeting the Great Bliss Queen: Buddhists, Feminists and the Art of the Self* and *Knowledge and Liberation: An Epistemological Analysis in Support of Transformative Religious Experience*. Dr. Klein is co-director of Dawn Mountain, a Tibetan Buddhist community center and research institute in Houston.

Daniel E. Lee, PhD, a leading Lutheran scholar, is Professor of Religion at Augustana College. His books include *Death and Dying: Ethical Choices in a Caring Community, On the Porch and on the Trail, Hope is Where We Least Expect to Find It* and *Generations and the Challenge of Justice.*

George N. Marshall, PhD, DD, former minister and Religious Editor at the Church of the Larger Fellowship in Boston, has served a number of Unitarian-Universalist congregations during his long career. He is the author of many books and articles, most notably *Challenge of a Liberal Faith* and *Facing Death and Grief.*

Thomas H. Olbricht, PhD is Distinguished Professor of Religion, Emeritus, at Pepperdine University. His books include *Power to Be, He Loves Forever, The Message of Ephesians and Colossians*, and *Hearing God's Voice: My Life with Scriptures in the Churches of Christ*. Dr. Olbricht is the Founder and Director of the Christian Scholars Conference.

Anne Mackenzie Pearson, PhD is Lecturer in Religious Studies at McMaster University in Hamilton, Ontario, where she teaches courses in Indian religion and culture, world religions and women's role in religion. Dr. Pearson is the author of *Because It Gives Me Peace of Mind: Ritual Fasts in the Lives of Hindu Women.*

Rabbi Alan L. Ponn, a graduate of Columbia University and Hebrew Union College, has served congregations in several states, including Temple Beth Shalom in Danville, Virginia. During his rabbinical career he has also worked as a chaplain and a religious columnist.

Arthur O. Roberts, PhD is Professor-at-Large at George Fox University in Newberg, Oregon. He is editor of the journal, *Quaker Religious Thought* and is the author of *Tomorrow is Growing Old: Stories of Quakers in Alaska* and *Messengers of God: The Sensuous Side of Spirituality* as well as a theologically reflective autobiography, *Drawn by the Light.*

Ben Lacy Rose, ThD, DD has served as an Army chaplain and as the pastor of several Presbyterian congregations. A distinguished emeritus professor at the Union Theological Seminary in Richmond, Dr. Rose has served in positions of national leadership in the Presbyterian Church. He is also a prolific author and a well-known leader of religious seminars.

Jane Idleman Smith, PhD is Professor of the History of Religions at Hartford Seminary. A former Lecturer in Comparative Religion at Harvard Divinity School, she is the author of *The Concept of Islam in the History of Qur'anic Studies*, the co-author of *Islamic Understanding of Death and Resurrection*, and the editor of the journal, *Women in Contemporary Muslim Society.*

James Ivey Warren, Jr., PhD, a graduate of Duke and Glasgow Universities, has served as a Methodist minister and chaplain in Scotland and has had a distinguished teaching career, most notably as Cadwallader Professor of Global Evangelism and the Mission of the Church at Scarritt Graduate School in Nashville. Dr. Warren is the author of *Workbook on Vital Evangelism.*

Contents

Assemblies of God

Stanley M. Horton, ThD

BACKGROUND OF THE FAITH

With over 14 million members worldwide, the Assemblies of God form the largest of the Pentecostal or charismatic churches. The charismatic churches arose from a tremendous Pentecostal revival that began early in the 20th century.

> The United States in the years between the Civil War and the close of the century was in social and religious ferment. Moral, political and economic corruption increased the stresses occasioned by urbanization, industrialization and immigration. The great denominations, successful in Christianizing the frontier, had become complacent and sophisticated, lacking the vision and vitality to meet the changing needs of a distressed populace. Varying degrees of accommodation to popular ideas, newly imported from Europe, which assaulted orthodox Evangelicalism, further weakened the great communions. Against the erosion in the church world arose the Fundamentalist and Holiness movements. It was largely out of the spiritual concern generated in this segment of the church that the yearning for a new Pentecost was born. Prior to 1900 there were charismatic manifestations, but these were isolated and episodic in nature. But the stage was being set for a great outpouring of the Holy Spirit which would quickly encircle the earth, bringing a great refreshing in the Latter Days.[1]

Books such as *The Twofold Life* by the Baptist, A.J. Gordon (founder of Gordon College, Wenham, Massachusetts), as well as the teaching and writings of men such as Reuben A. Torrey, helped stimulate interest and stir a sense of need for the power of the Holy Spirit. However, there was little agreement about how to obtain the Holy Spirit's power or baptism in the late 1800s.

New interest arose when a revival began at Bethel Bible College in Topeka, Kansas, on January 1, 1901. From their studies of the Bible, the students came to the conclusion that speaking in tongues, as recorded in Acts 2:4, is evidence that a person has received the baptism in the Holy Spirit. Miss Agnes Ozman, one of the students, described the experience "as though rivers of living water were proceeding from my innermost being."[2]

From Kansas, the revival spread to Missouri, to Texas and then to Los Angeles. There, in 1906, a black holiness preacher, W.J. Seymour, found a response among both whites and blacks and secured an old two-story frame building, a former Methodist church, at 312 Azusa Street. Soon the Azusa Street Revival caught the attention of the newspapers. People began coming from all over the United States and Canada, even from overseas. Rich and poor, black and white, educated and uneducated joined together as one in worshipping and seeking God. Services ran almost continuously every day from 10 A.M. to midnight. W.J. Seymour, the leader, in simplicity and humility kept a low profile and let the Holy Spirit direct the services. "The meeting did not depend on the human leader. God's presence became more and more wonderful.... All was spontaneous...in testimony, praise, and worship."[3]

The Azusa Street Revival lasted three years. Most of those who received the Pentecostal experience of the baptism in the Holy Spirit took the message and spread it. As a result, a number of Pentecostal groups and denominations soon emerged. Some of these followed a "holiness," a view in which they called for a definite experience of "sanctification" by grace to cleanse the believer from "inbred sin" as a preparation for the baptism in the Holy Spirit. Others taught sanctification as a continuous process involving spiritual growth rather than a crisis experience. These saw faith as the only prerequisite for the baptism in the Holy Spirit. The Assemblies of God eventually became the largest group to hold to the latter position.

> After the Pentecostal outpourings began, numerous publications appeared advocating its teachings and serving as channels for teaching, information, and support of missionaries overseas. One of these publications, the *Word and Witness,* edited by Eudorus N. Bell, issued a call in 1913 for a conference of Pentecostal believers to convene in Hot Springs, Arkansas, the following year. This became the founding meeting of the General Council of the Assemblies of God.[4]

Over 300 persons responded. Twelve men were elected to serve as executive presbyters to provide leadership and direct the missionary work of what was termed "a voluntary, cooperative fellowship." E.N. Bell was chosen as chairman (later, superintendent). T.K. Leonard offered his printing plant and school in Findlay, Ohio, as a publishing house and headquarters for the new fellowship. In 1915, this "Gospel Publishing House" was moved to St. Louis and in 1918 to Springfield, Missouri, "The Queen City of the Ozarks." Springfield has remained the international headquarters of the Assemblies of God.

Due to controversy over the nature of the divine Trinity, a "Statement of Fundamental Truths" as a basis of fellowship was prepared in 1916.

> "The Statement of Fundamental Truths" was chiefly the work of one man, Daniel Warren Kerr of Cleveland, Ohio. Kerr did not fit the popular conception of a powerful defender of the faith. A rather shy individual, a man of few words, seldom indulging in laughter, but able to light up the whole room with his smile. His dry wit was a help, too, in lightening the tension of debate and in taking the starch out of his opponents.[5]

During the years 1915 to 1925, John W. Welch, known as "Daddy" Welch, provided a father image and was a strong, wise, steadying influence on the growing movement. J. Roswell Flower, as General Secretary for 27 years, also provided leadership through his organizational ability and literary skills. A small, alert man with a farsighted view for the development of the Assemblies of God, he did much to inspire the fellowship as it continued to grow. By 1927 the Assemblies of God in the United States had a membership of 72,143. By 1941, this had grown to 209,549, with nearly 400 missionaries in 34 countries.

Growth continued after the second World War. In 1959, Thomas F. Zimmerman was elected General Superintendent. His skill as an administrator and spiritual leader consolidated the gains made. In 1984 there were nearly 25,000 ministers of the Assemblies of God in the United States, with over a million members. Missionaries minister in more than 90 fields to over 10 million members.

MAIN BELIEFS

The sole source and authority for our beliefs is the Bible. We believe that both the Old and New Testaments are verbally inspired by God and are the unique revelation of God to man, the one authoritative rule of faith and conduct. In the Bible we see that the one true God has revealed Himself as eternally self-existent, the creator of the heavens and earth and the redeemer of mankind. He has further revealed Himself as embodying three distinct persons that are expressed in specific terms of relationship as Father, Son and Holy Spirit. Through His Son, our Lord Jesus Christ, He has revealed Himself in a special and supreme way to mankind. Through the Holy Spirit this revelation is made real to us in a vital, personal way.

God created mankind in His image or likeness. Because God is spirit, it means we were created capable of reflecting God's holiness, righteousness and love and also capable of sharing fellowship with God with understanding and intelligence. So that this fellowship might be on the highest level, God also gave us freedom of choice. Mankind, however, freely chose to sin. The result was spiritual death (separation from God), physical death, a curse on the natural world and the inheritance by all mankind of the tendency to sin, so that all are sinners.

God, however, did not give up. He began to carry out a plan to bring salvation and restoration to all who would respond to Him in faith. Central to that plan, in the Old Testament times, was the promise given to Abraham that through him and through his descendants, all the peoples of the earth would be blessed. The New Testament shows that this blessing comes through Jesus Christ. In Him, God became man, identifying Himself with us from birth to death, taking our place to die on a cruel cross, bearing the guilt and penalty of our sins, then rising from the dead that we might share eternal life with Him and share His glory when He returns to earth again.

Forty days after His resurrection Jesus ascended to the right hand of God's throne in heaven. There He remains the God-Man, our divine Helper. But He has not left us orphaned here on earth. He and the Father have sent us the Holy Spirit as another Helper to be with us always. He helps us to show our love and faith toward God through faithful, obedient worship and by loving acts to all. He imparts gifts, ministries and graces to help us do the work God wants us to do.

We recognize we are in a world still dominated by sinful men and by the activity of Satan. The devil, or Satan, usurped authority in this world. He was once an angel (messenger) of God, but fell through rebellion. Evil and sickness are in the world, not only because of man's wrong choices, but because of Satan's activity. Though he is a spirit being, he is a limited being. He cannot be present everywhere and much of his activity is carried out by evil spirits (demons). He is also limited in that he cannot go beyond what God allows.

We are not helpless against Satan's attacks, however. Our faith in God and Christ shields us. The Holy Spirit uses God's Word to give us victories. Through the baptism in the Holy Spirit, with its initial outward evidence of speaking in tongues, we receive power and gifts to help us against the devil and to help us in our worship and service of God as we build up the Church and serve mankind.

Because for centuries the Holy Spirit was neglected, even ignored by the Christian Church as a whole, we have felt a special calling to proclaim the whole gospel, fully, not just in part. We emphasize Jesus as Savior, Baptizer in the Holy Spirit, Healer and Coming King. Christ is central in our preaching and teaching. But we endeavor to give the Holy Spirit His proper place as revealed in the New Testament. We encourage believers to enter into the fullness of a new relationship with the Holy Spirit through the baptism in the Holy Spirit and by seeking His gifts and ministries for the blessings they bring to us all.

We find that the Holy Spirit uses God's written Word and spiritual, charismatic gifts to challenge us, encourage us and comfort us in every situation of life. He gives moral courage in the midst of difficulty and suffering. He provides gracious gifts of healing for minds, souls and bodies. Many have joined our churches because they have experienced healing, even healing of "incurable" conditions and diseases. The Holy Spirit also gives us comfort and assurance of God's goodness even in the presence of unexplainable death. He makes us know that death is not the end, for God's promise of our resurrection is real.

Our pastors report that, though many Christians have doubts concerning their faith when they face death, this never happens with our Assemblies of God people who have been baptized in the Holy Spirit. Through the experience of this baptism, the Holy Spirit indwells every part of our inner being, including the subconscious. I personally have observed many dying with peace in their hearts and the praises of God on their lips. Instead of the fear of death, there is anticipation of blessings on the other side with Christ.

We differ from non-Pentecostal churches in that we emphasize that the baptism in the Holy Spirit with the accompanying evidence of speaking in other tongues (languages) is the normal experience God intends every believer in Christ to enjoy. We expect the Holy Spirit to help us in our prayers. In public worship, we pray aloud all at once, each in his own way, with much praise and thanks to God and to our Lord Jesus Christ. In private prayers, we are encouraged to use the gift of speaking in other tongues (Holy Spirit-given languages unknown to the speaker) as a prayer language to pour out our love to Christ and to express feelings beyond the power of human speech to express. The Spirit helps us as we pray in our own language as well. Our desire is to see the spiritual life and love seen in the New Testament restored in our own experience. We invite others to join us who want something more than religious forms and ceremonies, however meaningful these might be. Repentance toward God and faith toward the Lord Jesus Christ are the basic conditions for membership, though local assemblies may ask members to agree to definite standards of Christian living that are biblical.

We do observe two ordinances of the Church: baptism in water by immersion and the Lord's Supper or Holy Communion. In America the latter is observed using unleavened bread and unfermented wine as solemn emblems or symbols of Christ's broken body and shed blood. We expect our pastors and other ministers to experience God's personal call to their ministry. We ordain them only after they have demonstrated that the Holy Spirit has indeed given them a ministry and blessed it.

Because the Bible is our standard, we try to take the teachings of the Bible as a whole. Thus, we see that premarital sex, homosexuality and abortion are wrong. Yet we encourage all to seek the forgiveness and restoration that is freely available through the death and resurrection of Christ. We recognize that God hates divorce. Yet Jesus allowed it where one partner had become habitually immoral. The Apostle Paul also allowed it when an unbelieving (non-Christian) partner did not want to live faithfully with the believer. On the other hand, we seek to strengthen marriages in order to prevent divorce.

We have always discouraged the use of alcoholic beverages and tobacco in any form. Our Teen Challenge ministry has a record of about 80 percent of those who go through their program still staying off drugs when contacted after five years. This has been accomplished through the work and power of the Holy Spirit. In general we discourage extremes in clothing, makeup and deportment. We accept all types of nutritious food as God's good gifts to us. But we put more emphasis on our need of spiritual food (teaching) and on the necessity of doing the will of God joyfully. The Holy Spirit helps us in this by making God's will real through His written Word, the Bible.

DEATH AND THE AFTERLIFE

Though death is in the world because of sin, in the case of believers we do not look at death as punishment. Jesus took all our penalty on the Cross. Death for us is simply transition into the presence of our Lord Jesus where we will share the joys of heaven. When death comes we normally follow the customs practiced by the majority of the Protestant churches in the community or the part of the country or the world where we live. Our ministers consider the conducting of funeral services as one of their most important opportunities for helping families and serving people. Hymns, often the favorite hymns of the deceased, are sung, usually by a soloist, but sometimes by the congregation. Passages from the Bible are read. A eulogy is given. Always there is a sermon intended to encourage the faith and hope of the family and friends. Tears are common, but a sense of joy in the hope of the resurrection is encouraged. Sometimes the funeral of a godly believer will be triumphant.

At the close of the service, unless the family requests otherwise, those present pass by the open coffin to pay their last respects to the deceased. Then the pastor and the family join to do the same, often with much emotion. Then the coffin is closed and escorts (pallbearers) carry it out. A committal service at the cemetery follows. It is usually brief and includes the reading of a passage from the Bible and a prayer. Then those present line up and go past family members to shake their hands or hug them and offer words of comfort.

Normally, burial takes place about three days after death unless the funeral is delayed to allow family members to come from a distance. Embalming of the body is expected. Most feel there is precedent for this in the Bible. The delay of the decay of the body that embalming brings also fits in with our respect for the body and with our hope of the resurrection. It is also an expression of a love that wishes to do everything that should be done for the deceased. On the other hand, we believe that decay, fire or destruction of the body by whatever other means will not hinder God from bringing together whatever is necessary for the resurrection of the body. We also believe the body will be swallowed up by a new God-prepared body at the resurrection, a new body that is immortal, not subject to decay or death anymore, a body like Christ's resurrected, glorified body.

With this in mind we feel free to donate body parts for transplant, though the choice is left up to the individual. For this reason also we can allow autopsy if it is deemed necessary. Cremation is discouraged because burial was the normal method used in the Bible. However, Because God is the one who resurrects the body and brings it together, we do not forbid cremation, especially in countries where disease or climate calls for it. Normally, the body is displayed at the funeral home for at least a day before funeral services, though some prefer to have it remain in the home of the deceased and others prefer to have it brought to the church sanctuary.

We have no prayer book, for we expect prayer to come spontaneously from the heart. Nor do we have any specified mourning rituals. In some parts of the country the family spends an evening before the funeral at the funeral home with the casket open. Friends are expected to come by and express their condolences. In other parts of the country the family does not gather until the funeral service. Friends and relatives are expected to send flowers to the funeral home, though the family may request that donations be given to a charity, a church organization or a college instead. In many parts of the country concerned members of the Assembly will plan together and bring food to the home of the deceased to provide a meal for the family after the funeral. Members of the Assembly are expected to give further help and comfort to the family in whatever way they see it is needed.

The services of our pastors are always available whether the deceased is a member of our faith or not. Our pastors consider the conducting of a funeral service as an opportunity to show Christian love, to bring the message of Christ and to comfort the living by the help of the Holy Spirit. Pastors are willing to assist the family and give them advice concerning the type of service to whatever extent the family wishes. No fee is ever charged for these or any other pastoral services related to the funeral. Most pastors will accept a small honorarium from those outside our faith if it is offered, but most will not accept one from members of their own congregation.

We draw our greatest comfort from the Bible. We have seen its historical truth confirmed again and again by archaeological discoveries. We have had its spiritual truth confirmed to our own hearts and minds by the same Holy Spirit who inspired it. Therefore, we receive its truths and endeavor to apply them in our lives. We recognize that death is inevitable until Jesus returns to earth, for our bodies are all gradually dying. Yet our inner selves are renewed day by day (II Corinthians 4:16). This gives us courage to keep going no matter what our circumstances or physical condition might be. We have the assurance that God guides us in this life and afterward receives us to glory (Psalm 73:24). The Bible also tells us that to be absent from the body is to be present with the Lord Jesus (II Corinthians 5:8). Thus, we need not fear death, for it is only an entrance into His presence in the glories of heaven.

When we speak of heaven, we are referring to what the Bible calls the third heaven where the throne of God is and where Paradise is. We understand the first heaven to be the atmospheric heavens, the second heaven to be the starry heavens and the third heaven to be the place where God (who is everywhere present) manifests His presence in a special way. We take literally the description of the heavenly Jerusalem given in the Book of Revelation. But we see it as the eternal headquarters for Israel and the Church after the final judgment, for it is part of a new creation of the heavens and the earth.

We also recognize that there is much about heaven that cannot be put into our present human language, for our language grows out of our human experience. Even the Apostle Paul was not able to describe in human words what he experienced when he was caught away in vision to the third heaven and Paradise. Isaiah and Paul both let us know that "Eye has not seen, nor ear heard, neither have entered into the heart [including the mind and imagination] of man, the things which God has prepared for them that love Him." But the Bible does not stop there, for "God has revealed them unto us by His Spirit" (I Corinthians 2:9:10). That is, the joys, gifts and blessings we now receive through the Holy Spirit are a foretaste or first installment of what we shall receive in greater fullness in heaven after death as well as in the age to come. Thus we can look forward to wonderful fellowship with Christ in heaven as well as with our loved ones and with the departed men and women of past ages who shared the biblical faith.

We believe that the opportunity to prepare for the joys of heaven is available in this life only. Only in this life are we confronted with God's promises and with the opportunity to accept and follow Christ as Savior and Lord. The Bible teaches that it is appointed unto mankind once to die and after death comes God's judgment (Hebrews 9:27). We see that God can make an exception and take prophets like Enoch and Elijah to heaven without dying. But the Bible's main point here is that there is no second chance for salvation after death, nor is there any further opportunity to prepare for the joys of heaven. From this we understand also that there is no reincarnation. The believer who accepts and follows Christ is saved for eternity and retains his same personal identity. The unbeliever who rejects or disregards the Bible's way of salvation through Christ also retains his identity forever, but in a place of punishment.

Because all have sinned through unbelief, disobedience to God, rebellion against God's will, mistreatment of other people or through exalting ourselves and seeking to please ourselves without regard to others, we all deserve punishment. But the believer who accepts Christ's death on the cross as his substitute and believes God resurrected Jesus from the dead, receives cleansing and forgiveness. Jesus bore all our sins and guilt. He therefore sets us free to walk in newness of life with Christ. Yet the believer is still in this present body and must continue to make choices for the right. Thus, there will be a judgment day for the believer as well as for the unbeliever.

We also understand the Bible to teach that all faithful believers who have maintained a living faith relationship with Christ in this life will be resurrected from the dead and given new immortal bodies when Jesus returns to earth. Those who are still alive at that time will be caught away suddenly to join them for a meeting with Christ in the air (I Thessalonians 4:17). Their bodies will also be changed, transformed in an instant to new immortal bodies. This resurrection will include only those who have committed their lives to Christ as the divine Son of God and only Savior. It will not include those who in their teachings have reduced Christ to the status of an ordinary human being, even though they, like theological liberals, may consider Him a good man, or like the Muslims, may consider Him a prophet.

After the resurrection of these believers they must come before the judgment seat (throne) of Christ. He will judge us all according to our works. But the Bible makes it clear that the judgment of believers will be primarily based on our motives. If we give all our goods to feed the poor but do not have a real, self-giving love for them, it will bring us no reward (I Corinthians 12:3). If we have done good deeds primarily to win the praise of people, build up our own reputation or build a little kingdom for ourselves, there will be no reward, even though our faith in Christ will save us and allow us to enter heaven.

The Bible does not tell us where heaven is. We believe it may be beyond the created universe, or perhaps within it, but in a different order of existence. That is, heaven may be all around us, but on a different wavelength. All who continue faithful to Christ will attain it, no matter what church they belong to.

God's holiness and justice demand that sin be dealt with. Because all have sinned, we must accept the provision of God's love for the forgiveness of our sins through the blood Jesus shed in His violent, sacrificial death on the cross. If we reject or disregard His love, our sins demand that at death we are transported to the place of punishment the Bible calls Hell or Hades. The Bible does not say where it is. It says only that there is a great, impassable gulf between it and the place where those who died with their faith in our Lord are enjoying His presence. Those in hell are aware that faithful believers in the true God and in His promises are enjoying fellowship with other believers such as Abraham, Moses, the prophets of the Old Testament and the apostles, prophets and saints (dedicated believers) of the New Testament.

Hell (Hades) is described both as a place of fire and of darkness. Its inhabitants are full of remorse and frustration. They are cut off from faith, hope and love. Human language cannot adequately describe what hell's awful sufferings are really like. But it is not the final state. After the final judgment of the unbelievers, death and hell will be absorbed into an eternal state of punishment outside the new heaven and the new earth, a place called the lake of fire. It will be the final separation from all the good God has planned for mankind.

The final judgment of unbelievers, including all who have failed to commit themselves by faith to follow Jesus as Lord and Savior, will not take place until after Jesus returns to earth to bring a total end to the present world system and to establish the reign of God over all the earth for 1000 years.

We accept literally the New Testament teaching that at the time of Christ's return, believers from all past ages will rise from the dead, clothed with new bodies prepared for them by God. Believers who are still alive will rise with them to meet Jesus and will be transformed instantaneously into their new bodies. These new bodies will be real, tangible, yet immortal, never to be touched again by decay, corruption or death.[6] They will share in Christ's rule for 1000 years. Christ's return and the work of the Holy Spirit will rid the earth of pollution and restore it to ideal conditions. Before this happens there must be the defeat of a false christ referred to in the Bible as Antichrist and as the man of sin or lawlessness. He and his false prophet will be cast into the lake of fire. The lake of fire will be prepared for the devil and his angels. But men who follow Satan will thus choose to go to Satan's place.

The Bible is concerned about the justice of God. When Jesus administers judgment on the earth, no one can say He deserves judgment too, for He lived totally without sin. Nor can anyone point a finger at Him and say He did not do enough to save them from coming judgment. He gave His life. Some might say that if people knew how wonderful the reign of Christ will be they would all follow Him; yet after 1000 years of Christ's reign Satan will be released for a short time and many will follow him as soon as they have opportunity, even though they have enjoyed the blessings of the thousand-year reign. Thus, the Bible shows they are rebels. God can do nothing with them but separate them off from His new heavens and earth forever in the lake of fire, the "second death." Death here means separation. So the lake of fire will be a final separation from all that is good, righteous, holy, just and loving.[7]

Before being sent to the lake of fire, the wicked and all unbelievers will be resurrected and brought before God's Great White Throne of Judgment. At the appearance of God's presence and glory in this judgment, the present heavens and earth will go out of existence. Because God the Father has given all judgment to the Son (John 5:22), the one we will see on the throne will be Jesus. He will judge those who are resurrected at this time by their works and the verdict will be eternal punishment in the lake of fire. After that God will create a brand new heaven and earth. (Some believe the new earth is simply the present earth renovated by fire.)

The new earth will be of a different order. There will be no more seas or oceans. There will be no need of the sun, for Christ will be its light and His glory will be everywhere present. Thus there will be no night. Many elements will be of a different order. Gold will be as transparent as glass and so common that streets will be paved with it. Christ will mediate His life and energy to us directly, so we shall never be weak or tired. At the outset, the New Jerusalem will come down out of heaven to the new earth. God's throne will be in it. That is, God's "headquarters," the place of His special manifestation, will no longer be in heaven but on the new earth. God and mankind will be united in a new degree of fellowship for all eternity. Then, Because God is infinite, there will always be new joys, new things to learn about Him and undoubtedly, more of the new heaven to explore. But the New Jerusalem on the new earth will be our home and headquarters forever.

Our most important responsibility in this present life is to proclaim the New Testament teaching that salvation is by grace through faith in Christ alone. It is necessary to understand also that faith is more than a mental acceptance of a body of belief. It involves personal trust in Jesus as Savior, receiving His sacrifice on the cross as sufficient penalty for our sins, Because He had no sin of His own and thus could bear ours. It means also that we believe God accepted Christ's sacrifice on our behalf and demonstrated His acceptance by raising Jesus from the dead, thus making His resurrection the guarantee of ours, just as Jesus promised.

We also declare our faith by water baptism by immersion. This is our testimony that we, through faith, have died to the old life and have risen to a new life in Christ. We do not believe the water of baptism has any value in itself. Baptism is merely a picture symbolizing what has already happened. Peter compared it in the Bible to the faith of Noah. The fact that Noah came through the waters of the great flood was a testimony to the faith he had before the flood, a faith expressed in obedience as he built the ark. So the water of baptism does not cleanse us, nor does it convey salvation. It is simply the testimony of a good conscience that has already been cleansed by Christ.

Our salvation also includes our inheritance, our new bodies and our eternal reign with Christ. Thus we must continue to express our faith through faithfulness in worship and service to God, by obeying His Word, by doing His will and by showing His love through acts of love to others. This means that like our Heavenly Father we must forgive those who mistreat us and reach out in love to those who do not deserve our love. Thus, we are saved because Christ died and rose again, not because of our good works. But we are saved in order that we might do good works that will bring glory to God.

Then, because Christ's death was accepted by God the Father as a sufficient sacrifice for all our sins, we cannot add to His provision. Because of Christ's sufficient sacrifice also, we do not need to make further sacrifice or pay further penalty for our sins. At death we go directly to heaven. Thus we reject totally the idea of purgatory. Nor do we see any need for limbo. Jesus blessed the little children. He did not ask them to repent. Nor do we see any evidence in the Bible for the baptism of infants. The Bible teaches the baptism of believers. The Book of Acts shows that when the household of the Philippian jailer was baptized, they all first heard the word of God, the gospel and afterward they all rejoiced. No infants were included. God does not hold accountable children who are too young to understand the gospel. Thus His grace provides salvation for children who die as well as for all who are mentally incapable of understanding the requirements of the gospel. God will mature and perfect them in heaven.

Because faith is the key, we accept all believers of all denominations as children of God and heirs of salvation. We do not believe God holds the members of the Assemblies of God faith in any higher favor than He does other believers in Christ as Lord and only Savior. God's favor is grace, "unmerited favor," and God makes it available to all mankind, to whoever will accept it. We believe that our hope is a sure hope, a hope without any sense of contingency on God's part. Even if we fail, God will find some who will respond and He will bring the fulfillment of all His promises.

All of the Bible has a forward look. Thus, we live enjoying what God has provided us in the present life and at the same time expecting and looking forward to the future life. God's Word is a lamp to guide us here and now. It is also a star to give direction and meaning to our lives. We look ahead to enjoying the presence of Christ in heaven. From the Bible we see also that we will recognize each other there. We shall know our friends and relatives. We shall enjoy fellowship with the saints of old time.

In heaven, however, our primary relationship will always be to Christ and then to all other believers as part of the family of God. Other relationships will still be valued but will be less important. The relationship of a small child in the present life centers around his parents. When the child grows up and marries, the relationship to the marriage partner becomes central. The relationship to the parents is still valued, but it drops somewhat into the background. In heaven our relationship with God through Christ will be central. Other relationships, including the marriage relationship, will drop somewhat into the background. We shall all be in a unity of fellowship with Christ and with one another.

Finally, we understand that the Bible does not tell us about the afterlife simply to satisfy our curiosity. The Bible wants us to see God has a plan. It shows us also that God has the intelligence, power, love and faithfulness necessary to carry out His plan. As a part of His great overall plan He has a plan for each of us, both in this life and in the afterlife. But He has created us creatures with the responsibility for making choices and it is up to us to accept His plan for our lives. If we fail, He will not fail. He will find a way to carry out His plan. He tells us of the future in the Bible to encourage us to live for Him and be the kind of person we ought to be now.

The major emphasis of Assemblies of God teaching is on what God does for us now through Christ and through the Holy Spirit and His gifts. At the same time we know the Holy Spirit is preparing us to receive the fullness of our salvation, which includes the inheritance God has for us: our new bodies, our full privileges as heirs of God and our ruling and reigning with Christ, not only through the 1000 years of the Millennium, but also throughout all eternity.

The same Holy Spirit who brings us Christ's salvation, help and healing now will bring about our resurrection and cause us to rise to meet Jesus in the air when He comes. The same Christ, who is still the God-Man in heaven, is now at the right hand of God the Father. That is, He is at the place of power and authority. There He is interceding for us, waiting for the time when He will come and receive us to Himself.

We are confident that Christ in the afterlife will bring us light and beauty, fullness of knowledge and freedom from all the weariness, pain, strife, grief and sorrow of this present life.[8] Above all, the promise is "So shall we ever be with the Lord" (I Thessalonians 4:17).[9]

Notes

1. William W. Menzies, *Anointed to Serve: The Story of the Assemblies of God* (Springfield, MO: Gospel Publishing House, 1971), p. 33.
2. Stanley H. Frodsham, *With Signs Following* (Springfield, MO: Gospel Publishing House, 1946), p. 20.
3. Frank Bartleman, *How Pentecost Came to Los Angeles* (Los Angeles, by the author, 1928), p. 58.
4. Gary B. McGee, "A Brief History of the Modern Pentecostal Outpouring," *Paraclete,* Vol. 18, no. 2, Spring 1984, p. 22.
5. Carl Brumback, *Like a River* (Springfield, MO: Gospel Publishing House, 1977), p. 55.
6. Myer Pearlman, *Knowing the Doctrines of the Bible* (Springfield, MO: Gospel Publishing House, 6th ed., 1945), pp. 373-377.
7. Pearlman, op. cit., pp. 387-394.
8. Ibid., p. 383.
9. Bible passages supporting Assemblies of God views can be found in the *Minutes of the 40th Session of the General Council of the Assemblies of God, with Revised Constitution and Bylaws,* pp. 90-95. They can also be found in P.C. Nelson, *Bible Doctrines* (Springfield, MO: Gospel Publishing House, 1948).

Baha'i Faith

John S. Hatcher, PhD

BACKGROUND OF THE FAITH

The word *Baha'i* means "a follower of Baha'u'llah," the prophet-founder of the Baha'i Faith whose title means "the Glory of God." Baha'u'llah (Mirza Husayn-'Ali) was a Persian of noble lineage who was born in Teheran in 1817 and died in Akka, Palestine (now Israel), in 1892 after four successive exiles from His native Persia. The Faith itself dates from May 23, 1844, when the Bab ("the Gate"), a young merchant from Shiraz by the name of Mirza 'Ali Muhammad, announced that He was the Promised Qa'im whose mission it was to prepare the way for the coming of "Him Whom God Shall Make Manifest," a prophet from God whose revelation would usher in world peace and a world civilization as promised in the holy scriptures of all world religions.

The Bab and His followers were immediately persecuted by the Islamic clergy in collusion with government officials because they viewed the Bab's religion as heretical and a threat to their authority. Some of the most prominent Islamic scholars became followers of the Bab, but at the height of the persecution of the Babis, over 20,000 followers were cruelly tortured and slaughtered when they refused to recant their beliefs. The Bab Himself was executed by firing squad in the town square of Tabriz under miraculous circumstances. After telling the guards He had not finished dictating His final instructions, He was suspended by ropes from a barracks wall. Thousands of citizens watched in amazement as 750 rifles fired — when the smoke had cleared, the Bab had vanished from sight. He was later found completing his instructions, after which He consented to be taken again before another firing squad and the execution was carried out.

In the bloody persecution that followed, most of the Babi leaders were killed except for Baha'u'llah, whom the Bab had indicated as the very prophet whose coming He had foretold. Baha'u'llah's own revelation began in 1852 when He was imprisoned in the dreaded Siyyah Chal, an underground prison in which were placed the most grievous criminals, their feet in stocks, their necks strung together by a weighty chain. It was in these circumstances that Baha'u'llah received the first intimation of His mission. For a number of years He withheld this information from the other Babis, choosing instead to reorganize the bewildered community.

In 1853 the Shah exiled Baha'u'llah to Baghdad in neighboring Iraq so that the religion would die out in Persia. In Baghdad, however, Baha'u'llah revitalized the disheartened believers, disseminated the teachings of the Bab, as well as the first works of His own revelation and attracted admirers from various religions far and wide.

Over the next 10 years (1853-63) the community rapidly increased in size and acquired renown for its honesty and kindliness. But as the reputation of Baha'u'llah and His followers spread, the jealousy of the Islamic clergy was once more aroused. Through a barrage of petitions to the Shah, some of these mullahs managed to have Baha'u'llah exiled even further from His homeland and, they hoped, from any further influence. Before His departure in 1863, however, Baha'u'llah officially announced to the believers what most had already surmised — that He was "Him Whom God Shall Make Manifest," the prophet alluded to in prophecies of all the world's major religions. Shortly afterwards, the community of believers began to call themselves "Baha'is" as a sign of their recognition of His revelation.

Once again, in 1868, Baha'u'llah was exiled, this time to the prison city of Akka, Palestine, where He was expected to die along with the Baha'i Faith itself. For nine years He remained a prisoner within the city walls, though He managed, with the help of His son 'Abdu'l-Baha, to maintain contact with His followers and to write His most important work, *The Most Holy Book*, the book of Baha'i laws and institutions, what Baha'is view as a blueprint for world civilization. After His release from strict confinement in 1877, He took a residence outside Akka where He continued to write and direct the affairs of the religion. By the end of His ministry He had revealed over 100 volumes on every subject from kindness to animals to world government.

Upon Baha'u'llah's death in 1892, 'Abdu'l-Baha assumed authority over the Baha'i Faith, in compliance with the explicit dictates of Baha'u'llah's will, and He began to organize the religion worldwide according to the plan set forth in His father's writings. In 1912 He visited the West, traveling across the United States to meet with the members of the various Baha'i communities. Upon His death in 1921, Shoghi Effendi, 'Abdu'l-Baha's grandson, assumed guardianship of the Baha'i Faith, in accordance with the will and testament of 'Abdu'l-Baha. Gradually He guided construction of the worldwide administrative institutions of the Baha'i Faith as designed by Baha'u'llah. After His death in 1957 the final part of that design was completed with the election in 1963 of the Universal House of Justice, a nine-membered body elected every five years to guide the affairs of the Baha'i Faith. The House of Justice resides in Haifa, Israel, the world center for the religion. As of 1998, the Baha'i faith had over 5 million adherents in some 230 countries and dependencies. In the United States, there are over 100,000 Baha'is who reside in over 7,300 localities and comprise 1,750 organized communities.

MAJOR BELIEFS

The Baha'i Faith is not a cult, a sect, not an offshoot of Islam, but an independent world religion. Neither is it manmade (eclectic or syncretic), but a revealed religion following in a progression of revelation derived from the eternal or ancient covenant between God and man — that God will never leave man without guidance and that man will strive both to recognize the divine Manifestations when they appear and to follow their teachings. This is the pivotal teaching of Baha'u'llah, that God's purpose for man, collectively and individually, is spiritual education and transformation and that to assist man in this endeavor, God has periodically sent exemplary beings to advance further mankind's understanding of His spiritual nature and to incorporate more completely that knowledge in action. In short, the Baha'i Faith affirms the oneness of God, the oneness of religion and the oneness of mankind.

From the Baha'i perspective, these successive Manifestations or Prophets are like perfect mirrors, each reflecting in his life and teachings the reality of God. Each is endowed by God with a capacity far beyond that of human beings, but each reveals only what is appropriate to the capacities of mankind for the historical period in which he appears. In this sense all the world religions are one religion revealed in successive stages, inasmuch as all the Manifestations are equal in capacity, fully coordinated in their efforts and willing agents in this eternal plan of spiritual evolution.

At the center of this divinely ordained education system is the student, mankind, because only the human being is endowed with a soul and is, therefore, uniquely capable of recognizing and acquiring spiritual attributes. According to the Baha'i teachings, the soul takes its beginning at conception, develops according to man's free will during its association with the physical body and continues its development in the next life. From this view, there is no source of evil in creation, no Satanic force except the willful rejection of spiritual growth. The purpose of mankind in this life is a two-fold process of coming to understand the spiritual perfections of God through these Manifestations and of reflecting that knowledge in every aspect of daily life (prayer, vocation, good works, etc.).

In general, therefore, the Baha'i writings portray the physical experience as the first stage in an eternal process whereby each individual soul is exhorted and assisted to strive toward perfection. Clearly not every soul encounters the same experience, the same opportunities, but the Baha'i writings explain that because this is only a beginning and because God is just and merciful, all that seems unjust or inequitable from our limited terrestrial perspective (unjust suffering, infant mortality, natural disasters, etc.) is taken care of in the successive stages of our existence in the afterlife.

Such a belief does not imply a passive acceptance of injustice or the status quo. At the heart of the Baha'i life is the daily striving to put into physical and social form the spiritual principles that Baha'u'llah has revealed for this stage in the spiritual advancement of the planet. Among the most significant principles are the recognition of the essential unity of mankind and the abolition of all forms of prejudice — whether racial, national or religious — the recognition of the harmony of science and religion, of the equality of men and women and of the necessity for each individual to investigate truth independently. Some of the measures which Baha'u'llah elucidates for bringing about these conditions are the establishment of a universal auxiliary language, a universal system of weights and measures, universal compulsory education, the abolition of the extremes of poverty and wealth and the founding of a world federation of governments to ensure a universal and lasting peace. In short, the "Revelation proclaimed by Baha'u'llah, His followers believe, is divine in origin, all-embracing in scope, broad in its outlook, scientific in its method, humanitarian in its principles and dynamic in the influence it exerts on the hearts and minds of men."[1]

DEATH ISSUES

Funerals

The Baha'i writings state, "I have made death a messenger of joy to thee. Wherefore dost thou grieve?"[2] Since the Baha'i teachings affirm the continuation of the individual soul after its association with the body, the focus of a Baha'i funeral or memorial service is on commemorating the spiritual contributions the deceased has rendered. In grieving, the family and fellow believers lament the loss of that association, not the condition of the departed. And even this separation is viewed as temporary. In consoling a bereaved widow, 'Abdu'l-Baha stated, "This separation is temporal; this remoteness and sorrow is counted only by days. Thou shalt find him in the Kingdom of God and thou wilt attain to the everlasting union."[3]

The Baha'i funeral or memorial service itself is largely devoid of ritual. It consists primarily of prayers and other appropriate readings from the Baha'i sacred scriptures. There may be music, a eulogy, whatever the family desires. Likewise, the casket may be open or closed. Finally, since there is no clergy in the Baha'i Faith, the service may be conducted by the family itself or by whomever the family chooses. The only required part of the funeral service is the Prayer for the Dead revealed by Baha'u'llah, which is to be "recited by one believer while all present stand."[4]

Treatment and Interment of the Body

While there are relatively few regulations regarding the service, there are important Baha'i laws concerning the treatment and interment of the body. First, embalming is prohibited unless it is required by law. Second, the body must not be transported more than one hour's journey from the place of death, not even for purposes of interment. Third, the body must not be cremated. The Baha'i is free to donate his body to science, provided that the body is treated with respect and the laws prohibiting cremation and removal of the body more than one hour's journey from the place of death are observed.[5] According to Shoghi Effendi, guardian of the Baha'i Faith, "The spirit has no more connection with the body after it departs, but as the body was once the temple of the spirit, we Baha'is are taught that it must be treated with respect."[6]

The appropriate symbols for the grave marker are the nine-pointed star, the word Baha'i, or a nine-pointed star or rosette with the word Baha'i in the center, the number nine being associated in the Arabic language with the name of Baha'u'llah. The wording on the gravestone is "left to the discretion of the relatives of the deceased"[7] and any appropriate quote from Baha'i writings may be used.

Responding to the Bereaved

The Baha'i Faith has no mourning rituals nor is there any recommended response to the bereaved, though there are myriad passages in the Baha'i writings that deal pointedly and poignantly with this subject. Most generally, the Baha'i writings make it quite clear that the physical life is but the initial portion of an eternal existence that begins with the soul's association with the body at conception. From the Baha'i perspective, the soul continues its development after this life and retains its awareness of identity — "thou wilt not forget (there) the life that thou hast had in the material world."[8] Furthermore, Baha'u'llah states that "the soul, after its separation from the body, will continue to progress until it attaineth the presence of God, in a state and condition which neither the revolution of ages and centuries, nor the changes and chances of this world, can alter."[9]

But in addition to these assurances that the soul continues and that the separation is temporary, because souls will recognize each other in the spiritual world,"[10] Abdu'l-Baha offers several comforting analogies that explain the relationship between the body and the soul. In one, analogy, for example, he compares the soul to a bird and the body to a cage:

> To consider that after the death of the body the spirit perishes is like imagining that a bird in a cage will be destroyed if the cage is broken, though the bird has nothing to fear from the destruction of the cage.

> Our body is like the cage and the spirit is like the bird...if the cage becomes broken, the bird will continue and exist. Its feelings will be even more powerful, its perceptions greater and its happiness increased.[11]

From the Baha'i view, death marks the beginning of another and greater stage in the spiritual education of the soul. Because the soul does not enter the body, but temporarily associates with it, it will not be hampered in its development when that relationship terminates. 'Abdu'l-Baha explains this in another analogy when he compares the soul to a light and the body to a mirror:

> The spirit never entered this body, so in quitting it, it will not be in need of an abiding-place: no, the spirit is connected with the body, as this light is with this mirror. When the mirror is clear and perfect, the light of the lamp will be apparent in it and when the mirror becomes covered with dust or breaks, the light will disappear.[12]

The grief we feel, then, results from the fact that we are prevented for a time from seeing the lights because the mirror has been shattered. But if earthly companionship is ultimately destined for separation, the "heavenly association is eternal."[13] 'Abdu'l-Baha states, "Whenever thou rememberest the eternal and never-ending union, thou wilt be comforted and blissful."[14]

Burial of Nonbelievers

While Baha'is or Baha'i institutions may conduct services for non-Baha'is, the laws incumbent on a Baha'i would not be binding (in other words, that there be no cremation or removal of the body over one hour's journey from the place of death and no embalming, unless required by law, etc.). In this sense, the burial would not be, strictly speaking, a Baha'i funeral. But inasmuch as the Baha'i service itself has no ritual, certainly the prayers and readings that comprise such a service can be used for anyone.

LIFE AFTER DEATH

General Beliefs

On the one hand, it is clear in the Baha'i writings that we can only hazily understand the nature of the soul and its progress in the afterlife. Baha'u'llah states, for example, that the "nature of the soul after death can never be described, nor is it meet and permissible to reveal its whole character to the eyes of men."[15] In like manner, Baha'u'llah states, "The world beyond is as different from this world as this world is different from that of the child while still in the womb of its mother."[16] On the other hand, the essential reality and purpose of this life, as it relates to our progress in the next life, is delineated with clarity in the Baha'i writings.

First of all, the Baha'i writings teach that the awareness, identity and reality of all human beings is the soul, a spiritual entity, unique in creation, that has a beginning but no end. Baha'is believe that the soul begins with its association with the body at conception, develops by means of education and noble effort in the physical reality and continues its progress after its association with the corporeal world. Thus, as the period of gestation is a preparation of the physical man for its entrance into a reality where senses and all the bodily capacities are essential to human advancement and learning, so the earthly life is a period of preparation for the new life wherein spiritual faculties and perceptions are essential. Viewed from this perspective, the physical life is not detrimental to the soul's continuation; used properly, the physical reality is a divinely ordained training for life after death, which is but another stage in a process begun in this reality, not a separate existence:

> The Prophets and Messengers of God have been sent down for the sole purpose of guiding mankind to the straight Path of Truth. The purpose underlying their revelation hath been to educate all men, that they may, at the hour of death, ascend, in the utmost purity and sanctity and with absolute detachment, to the throne of the Most High.[17]

More specifically, the Baha'i writings teach that, in death, each person retains his identity, recalls his past life in the physical realm and recognizes his deceased companions. As here, the purpose in the next life is the spiritual progress of the soul. 'Abdu'l-Baha notes, "as the perfections of humanity are endless, man can also make progress in perfections after leaving this world."[18]

Reincarnation

Baha'u'llah states that "the worlds of God are countless in their number and infinite in their range."[19] Likewise, it is clear that the stages in the spiritual evolution of a single human soul are quite beyond our temporal comprehension. At the same time, it is abundantly clear that there is, from a Baha'i view, but one physical experience for each soul — Baha'is do not believe in transmigration or reincarnation. The physical experience is not viewed as unimportant — the Baha'i perceives physical reality as a unique beginning to an endless spiritual journey, a reality in which we are challenged to perceive the essential spiritual reality underlying the physical metaphors and symbols that comprise this life: "Know thou that every created thing is a sign of the revelation of God."[20] However, it is also clear that the physical world is only a beginning, that progress of the soul after this life is not finally conditioned by one's earthly experience and that divine justice for the individual is not contingent solely on its expression in the physical world.

Heaven and Hell

The Baha'i Faith recognizes the importance of the relationship between one's efforts at spiritual development in the physical world and one's experience after death. However, Baha'is do not believe in heaven and hell as physical places nor as eternally fixed conditions of the soul. Baha'u'llah describes the use of these terms by previous Manifestations as the attempt to explain an abstract or spiritual condition in symbolic or metaphorical terms — thus, proximity to God is portrayed as Heaven, remoteness as Hell and Baha'u'llah employs these terms Himself.[21] Likewise, the figure of Satan is not a literal being or demi-god, but a personification of the sort of selfishness and willfulness that deters spiritual growth.

This does not mean that the Baha'i does not believe in reward and punishment in the afterlife. In a number of places, Baha'u'llah emphatically delineates the relationship between one's earthly life and the experience after death:

> They that are the followers of the one true God shall, the moment they depart out of this life, experience such joy and gladness as would be impossible to describe, while they that live in error shall be seized with such fear and trembling and shall be filled with such consternation, as nothing can exceed.[22]

But because the next stages in our development also involve change and growth, the initial experience after death may become altered so that the understanding and faith of the righteous may become heightened and "the condition of those who have died in sin and unbelief may become changed...."[23] This principle of spiritual development after death is, in the Baha'i writings, not a vague notion. It is clear, for example, that understanding and learning are achieved through means such as conversing with "the Prophet and His chosen ones."[24] "The mysteries of which man is heedless in this earthly world, those he will discover in the heavenly world and there will he be informed of the secret of truth...."[25] Some of the other means by which the soul progresses are "through the intercession and the sincere prayers of other human souls, or through the charities and important good works which are performed in its name," and "through the bounty and grace of the Lord alone,"[26] a grace that includes the opportunity to pray for forgiveness: "Through their own prayers and supplications they can also progress, more especially when they are the object of the intercession of the holy manifestations."[27]

From such a view, it is possible to conceive of a soul becoming so willfully perverted that it could be devoid of the capacity for progress, but whether or not a soul in the next life is ever beyond hope we cannot know from the limited perspective of this life. However, it is clear that our actions have consequence in both this life and in the next and that no formulaic act can alter that process. Thus, while Baha'u'llah exhorts all mankind to recognize the truth of this revelation, He does not describe the rewards in the next life as confined to those who call themselves Baha'is. Instead, Baha'u'llah uses such terms as "Every pure, every refined and sanctified soul,"[28] and "Every soul that walketh humbly with its God, in this Day and cleaveth unto Him."[29]

From the Baha'i point of view, it is clear that the next world is quite beyond our comprehension except in these broad terms. Part of our inability to understand is the result of our not having a frame of reference. Also, the concealment of that reality from us is part of divinely ordained training for understanding and growth. Still another reason the next life is concealed is that if we were fully aware of it, we would not be able to restrain ourselves from attaining it:

> If any man be told that which hath been ordained for such a soul in the worlds of God, the Lord of the throne on high and of earth below, his whole being will instantly blaze out in his great longing to attain that most exalted, that sanctified and resplendent station....[30]

The Time of the End

Just as Baha'is believe that the literalistic Pharasaic Jews failed to understand the symbolic and metaphoric nature of the prophesies regarding the Messiah (that He would come from an unknown place, would rule with a rod of iron and would sit upon the throne of David, etc.), so Baha'is believe that the signs regarding the "Day of Judgment" and the "Time of the End" are likewise figurative.[31] More specifically, Baha'is believe that the time of the end is alluding to the process of progressive revelation by which man is evolving on this planet, a process that is cyclical in nature and marked by certain leaps forward in mankind's understanding of his spiritual nature. According to the Baha'i writings, mankind is currently in an immense transition, not simply from the Islamic dispensation to the Baha'i dispensation, but from one era of development to another, a transition, in effect, from adolescence to adulthood. From this perspective, Muhammad was the "Seal of the Prophets" because He was the last Manifestation in the Adamic or prophetic cycle; and the Bab was the first Manifestation in the new era of man's development, the Baha'i Era, which is destined to endure for not less 500,000 years. As Baha'u'llah Himself states, this "Day," this period in the history of mankind, has been longingly awaited by every previous Manifestation:

> "It is evident," He explains in another passage, "that every age in which a Manifestation of God hath lived is divinely ordained and may, in a sense, be characterized as God's appointed Day. This Day, however, is unique and is to be distinguished from those that have preceded it. The designation 'Seal of the Prophets' fully revealeth its high station. The

> Prophetic Cycle hath verily ended. The Eternal Truth is now come.... In this most mighty Revelation," He declares in categorical language, "all the Dispensations of the past have attained their highest, their final consummation."[32]

Thus, the "Time of the End," Baha'is believe, refers not to the end of the earth, but the end of one era and the beginning of another, an era of mankind's fulfillment. But as with the coming of any new Manifestation, the followers of the previous Prophets are tested, are judged, as were the Jews with the coming of Christ. One of these tests is the challenge to discern in prophesies the hidden or inner significance regarding this period. One of Baha'u'llah's most weighty tablets, *The Book of Certitude*, is, among other things, virtually a casebook study of such signs as the trumpet call, the day of judgment, coming "in the clouds," the sun becoming darkened and the stars falling from heaven.[33] In one sense, then, the events prophesied have already occurred. However, inasmuch as mankind is yet unaware of these events and their significance and since the transition to a new awareness is still taking place, we are still living in that period and some of the prophesies are yet to be fulfilled.

Bodily Resurrection

In keeping with the Baha'i belief regarding the essentially spiritual nature of man, the Baha'i writings view the "resurrection" as a symbol of a spiritual condition, a state of revitalized spirituality. 'Abdu'l-Baha explains that the Resurrection of Christ was significant as a spiritual analogue, not as a physical fact:

> It is clear, then, that when it is said that the Son of man is come from heaven, this has not an outward but an inward signification; it is a spiritual, not a material, fact.... And as it has become evident that Christ came from the spiritual heaven of the Divine Kingdom, therefore His disappearance under the earth for three days has an inner signification and is not an outward fact. In the same way, His resurrection from the interior of the earth is also symbolical; it is a spiritual and divine fact and not material; and likewise His ascension to heaven is a spiritual and not material ascension.[34]

Christ himself did not mention the bodily resurrection of the believers as a characteristic of the coming of the Son of man and when Paul discusses the subject in the first letter to the Corinthians, chapter 15, he speaks of an imperishable "spiritual body" to replace the physical one. As Baha'u'llah explains in *The Book of Certitude*, the term "resurrection" is often used as figurative expression of spiritual revivification, just as the condition of sleep or death is a common symbol in the scriptures for spiritual obliviousness.[35] Thus the resurrection of mankind alluded to by both Christians and Muslims alike as a sign of this period is understood by Baha'is to refer to the spiritual transformation of the planet, which is about to occur and which will result in the eventual establishment of world peace, a world commonwealth and an advancement in learning and civilization as has not occurred before in the history of this planet.

Purgatory or Limbo

As already mentioned, the Baha'i writings reject the idea of physical places or conditions in an existence that is by nature a spiritual reality, although physical descriptions may sometimes be used to portray figuratively a metaphysical experience. Baha'u'llah indicates that the worlds of God and presumably the experiences of the soul within those worlds are infinite in variety: "Know thou of a truth that the worlds of God are countless in their number and infinite in their range."[36] It is no doubt possible that there is a spiritual condition in the next world which the figurative concept of Purgatory or Limbo attempts to depict, a state in which the soul accomplishes a purgation or transition to a higher condition. But clearly the details of such a process, which have been portrayed often by artists and theologians alike, are something we can only guess at from our limited understanding of the next life.

Concept of Salvation

While the concept of "salvation" varies greatly among the world religions, the term as used by many Western religions has come to signify a dramatic turning point in one's spiritual life. This transformation, or doctrinally based belief that one is secure, most generally involves a profession of faith, an inductive leap of some sort, which is largely independent of deeds or merit; one is "saved" by grace, by theological technicalities that conform to the structures of particular religious belief.

For the most part, the Baha'i concept of salvation is quite different. First of all, in the Baha'i Faith there is no particular point in one's spiritual progress where growth and development is finalized or eternally secure; the most abysmal failure can suddenly ascend and the most elite of men is capable of rejecting his belief. Clearly, however, the Baha'i does not believe that faith and salvation are capricious or whimsical — the Baha'i writings carefully delineate the means by which one can daily ensure spiritual progress so that gradually doubt is replaced by certitude and one's daily life becomes a clear reflection of one's spiritual conviction. The point is that this is an ongoing process, whether in this life or the next, and that the exertion of free will in seeking salvation, from a Baha'i point of view, involves not merely a single act of determination but daily assessment and effort.

Underlying this general concept of salvation as a continuous evolution of the soul are several significant ingredients. First, the Baha'i writings teach that each human soul is capable of infinite growth or perfectability; therefore at no point is that evolution finalized:

> Know that nothing which exists remains in a state of repose — that is to say, all things are in motion. Everything is either growing or declining....[37]
>
> There is no other being higher than a perfect man. But man when he has reached this state can still make progress in perfections but not in state because there is no state higher than that of a perfect man to which he can transfer himself....
>
> Hence, as the perfections of humanity are endless, man can also make progress in perfections after leaving this world.[38]

Secondly, faith or belief, from a Baha'i view, is not a matter of blind affirmation or acceptance, but independent investigation of truth, a belief grounded in the confirmation and corroboration of evidence:

> If religious beliefs and opinions are found contrary to the standards of science they are mere superstitions and imaginations; for the antithesis of knowledge is ignorance and the child of ignorance is superstition.... If a question be found contrary to reason, faith and belief in it are impossible and there is no outcome but wavering and vacillation.[39]

Thirdly, religious conviction or faith is not the mere statement of belief; salvation or spiritual evolution must be achieved by putting that belief in action. 'Abdu'l-Baha states, "By faith is meant, first, conscious knowledge and second, the practice of good deeds."[40] While this does not imply that one precisely earns salvation, it does indicate that belief without action is hollow and worthless.

But while the spiritual progress of the soul is a continuum, the Baha'i writings do describe stages of development in which one is relatively secure. For example, Baha'u'llah frequently uses the metaphor "the City of Certitude" to represent a condition wherein one is confirmed in his belief:

> When the channel of the human soul is cleansed of all worldly and impeding attachments, it will unfailingly perceive the breath of the Beloved across immeasurable distances and will, led by its perfume, attain and enter the City of Certitude.[41]

Nevertheless, Baha'u'llah exhorts all people regardless of how meritorious their deeds or firm their faith to "bring thyself to account each day ere thou art summoned to a reckoning; for death, unheralded, shall come upon thee and thou shalt be called to give account for thy deeds."[42]

There is no distinction, then, between the salvation of a Baha'i and a non-

Baha'i in the sense that a just and loving God no doubt takes into account how each soul responds to his opportunities and capacities. In effect, one is not saved by the name he bears. Many people who call themselves Baha'is may not follow the guidance revealed by Baha'u'llah and many who have never heard of the Baha'i Faith may live spiritual lives. But it is clear that, from a Baha'i view, it is the plan of God that mankind as a whole recognize this most recent Manifestation, Baha'u'llah, and follow His teachings for this period in the spiritual evolution of mankind. This concept of the eternal covenant as the source of salvation of mankind is expressed throughout the Baha'i writings. It is expressed in religious history in terms of the literal ark of Noah, which was a source of salvation for the faithful, and by the Ark of the Covenant, which was the chest containing the Ten Commandments which, as God's revealed law, were a source of salvation for the Jews. Thus, from a Baha'i view, the surest source of salvation for mankind in this day, the "ark of salvation," as 'Abdu'l-Baha describes it,[43] is in the teachings of Baha'u'llah and in the institutions He established as the most recent expression of this ancient covenant.

By becoming a Baha'i, one is not necessarily assured of salvation or of becoming more spiritual than someone who is not a Baha'i. But Baha'is believe that God has designated Baha'u'llah's teachings as the source of salvation of mankind for this dispensation, a period which shall endure for at least 1000 years. Therefore Baha'is also believe that the best means for the transformation and ascent of the human soul can presently be found in recognizing the station of Baha'u'llah and in following the guidance He has revealed.

Recognition of Friends and Family in the Next World

'Abdu'l-Baha states: "As to thy question whether the souls will recognize each other in the spiritual world: This fact is certain; for the Kingdom is the world of vision where all the concealed realities will become disclosed. How much more the well-known souls will become manifest. The mysteries of which man is heedless in the earthly world, those he will discover in the heavenly world and there will he be informed of the secret of truth; how much more will he recognize or discover persons with whom he hath been associated."[44] On another occasion, 'Abdu'l-Baha wrote to a bereaved widow, "a love that one may have entertained for any one will not be forgotten in the world of the Kingdom. Likewise, thou wilt not forget [there] the life that thou hast had in the material world."[45] This association is not confined to friends and family, however; Baha'u'llah states that the soul will "freely converse" with the prophets and the "chosen ones" and will "recount unto them that which it hath been made to endure in the path of God, the Lord of all worlds."[46]

The Sequence of Events at the Moment of Death

On the one hand, considerations of time are obviously irrelevant in the next life, which is eternal. Yet Baha'u'llah indicates that the sense of reward or punishment occurs even before death itself. For example, Baha'u'llah states that those who have rejected spiritual development "shall...when breathing their last be made aware of the good things that have escaped them and shall bemoan their plight and shall humble themselves before God. They shall continue doing so after the separation of their souls from their bodies."[47]

We can understand in only a limited way the nature of this experience, but it is common to all souls that "all men shall, after their physical death, estimate the worth of their deeds and realize all that their hands have wrought."[48] Obviously those who have lived good lives will be immediately "rewarded" by a feeling of "joy and gladness as would be impossible to describe."[49] Whereas those who have lived "in error" shall "be seized with such fear and trembling and shall be filled with such consternation, as nothing can exceed."[50] How long these conditions last, or what sequence of events or what spiritual process succeeds them, we can only imagine. But the sense of reward and punishment represented by the scriptural symbols of "Heaven" and "Hell" is experienced immediately.

Related to this question is the matter of whether or not "every soul without exception" will "achieve life everlasting."[51] In a response to this, 'Abdu'l-Baha has stated:

> Know thou that immortality belongeth to those souls in whom hath been breathed the spirit of life from God. All save these are lifeless — they are the dead, even as Christ hath explained in the Gospel text. He whose eyes the Lord hath opened will see the souls of men in the stations they will occupy after their release from the body. He will find the living ones thriving within the precincts of their Lord and the dead sunk down in the lowest abyss of perdition.[52]

The Second Coming of Christ

Because Baha'is believe in the continuous succession of prophets throughout history, each Manifestation is the return of the same spirit that the previous Manifestation reflected and each Manifestation affirms this by alluding to the previous prophets and prophesying the future prophets. Thus, Christ stated:

> Therefore I send you prophets and wise men and scribes, some of whom you will kill and crucify and some you will scourge in your synagogues and persecute from town to town.... O Jerusalem, Jerusalem, killing the prophets and stoning those who are sent to you![53]

Likewise in the Qur'an, Muhammad stated:

> Moreover, to Moses gave we "the Book," and we raised up apostles after

> him; and to Jesus, son of Mary, gave we clear proofs of his mission and strengthened him by the Holy Spirit. So oft then as an apostle cometh to you with that which your souls desire not, swell ye with pride and treat some as imposters and slay others?[54]

When Christ alluded to the Manifestations who would succeed Him, He used various appellations — the Counselor, the Holy Spirit, the Son of Man. Likewise, on several occasions, Christ described various conditions that would accompany the advent of this figure. What is generally referred to as "The Second Coming," then, is the appearance that Christ described in such passages as Matthew, chapter 24; Mark, chapter 13; Luke, chapters 17 and 21; and John, chapter 16. These all seem to allude to a particularly significant return that would be accompanied by historically momentous circumstances. Likewise, various passages in the Old Testament allude to the appearance of Christ, but others, like the description of the "Desolation" in the book of Daniel, seem to prophesy a later point in history.

From the Baha'i view, Muhammad was the return of Christ, since He was the next Manifestation in history and Christ was sometimes alluding to that appearance. The particular return that will usher in a universal transformation of mankind, however, the return commonly referred to as "The Second Coming," this Baha'is believe to be the appearance of Baha'u'llah. Likewise the historical events that are prefigured in the veiled metaphors and symbols of the scriptures have taken place, are currently taking place, or will shortly occur in the future.

There are numerous passages in the writings of Baha'u'llah and 'Abdu'l-Baha that discuss this matter in detail,[55] and William Sears has written a most readable analysis of these prophesies regarding The Second Coming in his book *Thief in the Night: The Case of the Missing Millennium*.[56] A major theme in all of these is that while all the prophets have come to educate mankind "to carry forward an ever-advancing civilization,"[57] this particular point in the spiritual evolution of mankind signals the fruition of all the previous stages of development:

> Great indeed is this Day! The allusions made to it in all the sacred Scriptures as the Day of God attest its greatness. The soul of every Prophet of God, of every Divine Messenger, hath thirsted for this wondrous Day. All the divers kindreds of the earth have, likewise, yearned to attain it.[58]

EDITOR'S NOTES

Called the world's most racially integrated faith, the Baha'i faith is second only to Christianity in its diffusion of believers worldwide. Baha'is reside in over 200 countries and comprise more than 5 million believers. It is interesting to compare the life of Baha'u'llah to biblical prophecy. Baha'u'llah was imprisoned for most of his life while he was on earth, was banished from country to country, and was finally sent to Israel where He pitched His tent on Mount Carmel (cf. Micah 7:12-15). Thus, from the beginning of His mission to the end, there were 40 years exactly according to the "days of thy coming out of the land of Egypt." Baha'u'llah claimed to be the promised world redeemer of all major religions. During His time on earth, He wrote over 100 books in Arabic and Persian languages, a good number of which are currently being translated. For extensive treatments of Judeo-Christian prophecy, see William Sears' *Thief in the Night* and Gary L. Matthew's *He Cometh with the Clouds*.

Notes

1. Shoghi Effendi, *The World Order of Baha'u'llah* (Wilmette, Ill: Baha'i Publishing Trust, 1955), p. xi.
2. Baha'u'llah, *The Hidden Worlds of Baha'u'llah*, translated by Shoghi Effendi, rev. ed. (Wilmette, Ill.: Baha'i Publishing Trust, 1939), p. 11.
3. Quoted in *The Open Door* (Wilmette, Ill.: Baha'i Publishing Trust), pp. 6-7.
4. *A Synopsis and Codification of "The Kitab-i-Aqdas"* (Haifa, Israel: Baha'i World Centre, 1973), p. 58.
5. *National Bahai Review*, No. 121 (1983), p. 6.
6. Ibid.
7. The Universal House of Justice, Letter 23, April 1969.
8. Quoted in *The Open Door*, pp. 8-9.
9. *Gleanings from the Writings of Baha'u'llah*, translated by Shoghi Effendi, 2nd rev. ed. (Wilmette, Ill.: Baha'i Publishing Trust, 1976), p. 155.
10. *The Open Door*, p. 7.
11. *Some Answered Questions*, compiled by Laura Clifford Barney, rev. ed. (Wilmette, Ill.: Baha'i Publishing Trust, 1981), p. 228.
12. Ibid., p. 239.
13. *The Open Door*, p. 7.
14. Ibid.
15. *Gleanings*, p. 156.
16. Ibid., p. 157.
17. Ibid., pp. 156-157.
18. *Some Answered Questions*, p. 237.
19. *Gleanings*, pp. 151-152.
20. Ibid., p. 184.
21. Ibid., p. 158.
22. Ibid., p. 171.
23. *Some Answered Questions*, p. 232.
24. *The Open Door*, p. 9.
25. Ibid., pp. 7-8.
26. *Some Answered Questions*, p. 240.
27. Ibid., p. 232.
28. *Gleanings*, p. 154.

29. Ibid., p. 159.
30. *Gleanings*, p. 156.
31. See *Some Answered Questions*, pp. 110-112; J.E. Esslemont, *Baha'u'llah and the New Era* (Wilmette, Ill., 1980), pp. 6-7; Baha'u'llah, *The Book of Certitude* (Wilmette, Ill.: Baha'i Publishing Trust, 1950), p. 143ff; William Sears, *Thief in the Night* (Oxford: George Ronald, 1977), pp. 74-75.
32. Quoted by Shoghi Effendi in *World Order of Baha'u'llah*, p. 167.
33. The whole of Part One of *The Book of Certitude* focuses importantly on explaining the prophesies of Christianity and Islam.
34. *Some Answered Questions*, pp. 103-104.
35. *The Book of Certitude*, p. 117ff.
36. *Gleanings*, pp. 151-152.
37. *Some Answered Questions*, p. 233.
38. Ibid., p. 237.
39. 'Abdu'l-Baha in *Bahai World Faith: Selected Writings of Baha'u'llah and 'Abdu'l-Baha*, rev. ed. (Wilmette, Ill.: Baha'i Publishing Trust, 1976), p. 240.
40. Ibid., p. 383.
41. *Gleanings*, p. 268.
42. *The Hidden Worlds of Baha'u'llah*, p. 11.
43. *Selections from the Writings of 'Abdu'l-Baha* (Haifa: Baha'i World Centre, 1978), p. 187.
44. *The Open Door*, pp. 7-8.
45. Ibid., pp. 8-9.
46. Ibid., p. 9.
47. *Gleanings*, pp. 170-171.
48. Ibid., p. 171.
49. Ibid.
50. Ibid.
51. Selections from the *Writings of 'Abdu'l-Baha*, p. 189.
52. Ibid., pp. 189-190.
53. Matthew 23:34-37.
54. Muhammad, *The Koran*, translated by J. M. Rodwell (London: J.M. Dent, 1953), p. 346 (Sura "The Cow," verse 81).
55. See note 31.
56. See note 31.
57. *Gleanings*, p. 215.
58. Ibid., p. 11.

A Baptist Perspective

William L. Hendricks, PhD, ThD

BACKGROUND OF THE FAITH

This chapter must be entitled *a* Baptist perspective, because there is no such thing as *the* Baptist perspective. There are at least 52 kinds of Baptists in the United States ranging from the small (less than 200) two-seed-in-the-Spirit predestinarian Baptists to the large (nearly 16 million) Southern Baptist Convention. One of the general characteristics of Baptists is their fierce independence of viewpoint. Never trust a Baptist who says "All Baptists believe...."

Most Baptists are born again. All Baptists die. They don't die because they are born again. They die because they are born. Death is a universal phenomenon and obviously religious preference doesn't change the biological inevitability of death. Yet religious beliefs can and do shape how one looks at death. In the first part of the chapter, I will articulate a Baptist belief system that is drawn from Baptist sources. The theory of death that I will discuss is extrapolated from my experiences as a Baptist minister and seminary professor. In the second part of the chapter, I will discuss how theory fits practice, how Baptists relate to the reality of death, what positions they prefer in matters of life and death and how they face the "technocracy of death" medically available in contemporary society.

The problem of sources is acute. As previously indicated, there is no Baptist dogma, i.e., an officially accepted doctrine that must be believed by all adherents of a religious community. There are generally accepted beliefs among Baptists, chief of which is the authority and integrity of Scripture.[1] Baptists are often called a people of the Book. And it was generally the case in the frontier life of our country that a second book completed the library of every farm house, namely a hymn book. Baptists began, and continue, both as biblicists (despite the scholars' aversion to the term) and as a singing people. The primary sources for this chapter are the Bible and Baptist hymnody.

Baptists have drawn up formal, but not binding, statements about what they believe. These are called confessions of faith rather than creeds.[2] Contrary to popular opinion, Baptists have an honorable intellectual and academic heritage and there are Baptist scholars who have written theologies from a Baptist perspective. These theologies have somewhat influenced Baptist ministers who were taught these sources, and these ministers have, in turn, molded the thinking of Baptist congregations. It must be acknowledged (to my regret) that the formal theological instruction plays only a minor part in shaping the beliefs of the Baptist in the pew.[3] All of these sources — Scripture, hymnody, confessions of faith and Baptist systematic theologies — will be cited in this chapter because they have affected popular beliefs about death among some Baptists.

THE THEORY OF DEATH

Aristotle is not the only one who used his powers of perception to see that death is an inevitable part of life (see his *Generation and Corruption*). Generations of Baptists, rural farming folk, have also observed and given rudimentary philosophical explanations of the cycles of birth and death in the world around us. Crops are planted so they may be harvested. Animals are raised to be used for food. These truisms were naturally adopted by rural people. Death as a phenomenon in nature and of the subhuman species required no explanation beyond the obvious; and the agrarian saying of Jesus, "Truly, truly I say to you, unless a grain of wheat falls into the earth and dies, it remains by itself alone; but if it dies it bears much fruit" (John, 12:24), embodies a self-evident, natural principle.

But the question of human death with its emotional entailments and its existential Angst is quite another matter. Most Baptists, aware of Aristotle or not, would accept his naturalist assumptions about death in nature. Few Baptists would emulate Aristotle's pupil, Alexander the Great, and be awakened each morning with the less than cheerful news, "Alexander, someday you must die." But when it becomes apparent that one must die and that one's loved ones must die, then it is time to think theologically. The question arises, Why must we die?

THE DOUBLE VIEW OF DEATH

When the question of death as a human phenomenon arises and becomes, in fact, the boundary question that calls life and meaning into question, then one must have recourse to the sources of faith.[4] The first place a Baptist would look for a theological rationale for death would be the Bible. And the first place in the Bible a Baptist would look for his theology would be the New Testament. And, within the New Testament, the first source of things theological would be Paul. And, within the writings of Paul, a universally known and frequently quoted passage is Romans 6:23: "For the wages of sin is death, but the free gift of God is eternal life in Christ Jesus our Lord." Most Baptists would take this terse expression as the basis for their double view about death. That double view is on the one hand that death is evil and a punishment for sin and on the other hand, that because of the death of Jesus Christ, death may be the gate to another, better life.

Whereas other groups of classical Christians tend to come to a theological focus for death sequentially through the Old Testament to the New, most Baptists would come at death consequentially and work back to Adam from the New Testament focus. This is especially true among those Baptists who have not been so greatly influenced by Calvinism and who do not have a formal doctrine of original sin. Most Baptists would say death came because of sin. All persons sin. Therefore, all die. Adam was the first of the line and just as he sinned, we also will sin, therefore we must die (see Romans 3, 5; I Corinthians 15). The average Baptist is oblivious to, and unconcerned with, theories of transmission of original sin (see A.H. Strong's elaborate chart in *Systematic Theology*, p. 628). Most Baptists are certain that Adam was a historical figure, the first human. But most are certain that it is personal guilt and not any inherited guilt that brings about individual death. Corporate and covenantal ideas, so prominent in Reformed theology, have carried the day with some Baptists, but not many. For most Baptists, there are no ready academic answers as to why all people do sin, but there is solid biblical evidence (Romans 3:23, 6:23; I Corinthians 15:1-3); and any additional corroboration required may be found on the evening news, in the uneasy conscience of modern man or by a long look in the mirror. This does not mean mankind is worthless, just ornery. Beyond the inevitable fact of sin and its ineluctable consequence of death, there is an inherent worth in mankind and a resolution of the dilemma posed by death. About the nature of mankind and the murky relationship to Adam, the *Baptist Faith and Message* says:

> Man was created by the special act of God, in His own image, and is the crowning work of His creation. In the beginning man was innocent of sin and was endowed by His Creator with freedom of choice. By his free choice man sinned against God and brought sin into the human race. Through the temptation of Satan, man transgressed the command of God, and fell from his original innocence; whereby his posterity inherit a nature and an environment inclined toward sin, and as soon as they are capable of moral action become transgressors and are under condemnation. Only the grace of God can bring man into His holy fellowship and enable man to fulfill the creative purpose of God. The sacredness of human personality is evident in that God created man in His own image, and in that Christ died for man; therefore every man possesses dignity and is worthy of respect and Christian love.[5]

The unambiguous, if unexplained, first affirmation of Baptists as to death's cause is that death is a result of sin. Therefore, death is evil and is a woe that sinful mankind must face.

If death is the last enemy (I Corinthians 15:26), what possible good can come from it? Must not we lose loved ones and grieve? Do we not all go down into the pit, gathered to our fathers echoing David's logical sentence, "The child cannot come to me, but I can go to him" (referring to his dead son by Bathsheba). Grief is intense enough by virtue of the loss of those loved; it is intensified when death is viewed as related to sin. If sorrow joined with evil is Baptists' first expression about death, the negative aspect, what is the second?

The second way that Baptists view death is as a cure and a release. Of course, this insight of faith is maintained Christologically. Because of Christ's death, death has been overcome. By assuming the curse of death, Christ removes death's curses for us. And by virtue of Christ's resurrection, we who believe in Him may have a resurrected life with Him in the world to come. "Truly, truly I say to you, he who hears my word, and believes Him who sent Me, has eternal life, and does not come into judgment but has passed out of death into life" (John 5:24). "Truly, truly, I say to you, if anyone keeps my word he shall never see death" (John 8:51). Baptists, like other Christians, affirm that the purpose of God has been revealed in Christ "who abolished death, and brought life and immortality to light through the Gospel" (II Timothy 1:10).

Obviously, this abolition of death and the affirmation that Christ has overcome death are forensic declarations of faith. Baptists believe they will have to die biologically. The reality of biological death is incontrovertible. What the positive focus of faith assures is that God is with us in death, through it and beyond it. I Corinthians 15 is the great Christian manifesto that death, the enemy of mankind, has been defeated by Christ in his resurrection. The double determination about death is that it is connected with sin and with salvation. It is obvious that theological value judgments and faith affirmation have heightened biological death by relating it to both the source of man's weakness and the possibility of his ultimate destiny. This double determination is a quasi-metaphorical use of the term death — a use that is related to other more strictly metaphorical uses of death.

DEATH AS METAPHOR

Baptists know (no less than Alexander the Great) that someday they must die biologically. Furthermore, the dread of death is compounded because death is theologically related to sin: "the sting of death is sin" (I Corinthians 15:56a). But death has been overcome, "swallowed up in victory" (I Corinthians 15:54c). For the Christian, these theological additions add grandeur, awe and resolution to the dilemma. When one has faith that the ultimate dimension of life involves more than the physical and psychological expressions of human reality, then the resources of this faith dimension become the "real" or motivational springs of human existence. It may be metaphorical from a biological or psychological viewpoint that death is a result of sin and is overcome by Christ's death and resurrection, but from the believer's perspective, these affirmations are just as "real" as the pragmatic fact of death.

When the believer says death is overcome, he means that he is "not alone" in death and that through and beyond death there is a resolution to what otherwise seems a definitive closure to his existence. Rhapsodic singing expresses this metaphorical overcoming of death in the spiritual, "I Won't Have to Cross Jordan Alone," and in the old gospel song, "My Savior First of All." The first verse of the latter says:

When life on earth is ended
And I cross the swelling tide
And the glory of His resurrection share,
I shall know my Redeemer
Over on the other side,
And His face will be
The first to greet me there.

Refrain

I shall know Him, I shall know Him
As redeemed by His side I shall stand.
I shall know Him, I shall know Him
By the prints of the nails in His hand.

In addition to the affirmations about faith, which speak of death as the result of sin and death as overcome, there is a metaphorical use of death that Baptists often use in relation to the ethical and devotional expressions of their lives here and now.

This present-focused use of death as metaphor begins with conversion. Baptists espouse a conversionist theology. This view, which speaks with the birth metaphor of being born again (John 3), also speaks of a death metaphor of "dying to the old self." "For the mind set on the flesh is death, but the mind set on the Spirit is life and peace. And if Christ is in you, though the body is dead because of sin, yet the spirit is alive because of righteousness. But if the Spirit of Him who raised Jesus from the dead dwells in you, He who raised Christ Jesus from the dead will also give life to your mortal bodies through His Spirit who indwells you" (Romans 8:6, 10-11). Baptists believe all were once dead in "sins and trespasses" (Ephesians 2:1). There is therefore, theologically, a spiritual death from which one enters into new life at conversion. The symbol of this is baptism: "we have been buried with Him through the baptism into death, in order that as Christ was raised from the dead through the glory of the Father, so we too might walk in newness of life" (Romans 6:4). Furthermore the characteristics of a baptized convert are that "our old self was crucified with Him, that our body of sin might be done away with, that we should no longer be slaves to sin; for he who has died is freed from sin" (Romans 6:6-7). Baptists usually understand this "dying to the old self" and "dying to sin" as a dynamic process rather than a forensic announcement or an instantaneous achievement. Gospel songs such as "Must Jesus Bear the Cross Alone?" "More Like the Master" and "Higher Ground" are typical expressions of this process of dying to one way of life or a lower nature while struggling to attain new life. Defining the Christian life as a type of dying and the ethical struggle as the "overcoming" of death is a metaphorical usage that gives a more sustained and experiential flavor to the idea of death. Without these metaphorical uses death would remain an unresolved absolute. These metaphorical uses of death are of great value to Baptists in relativizing and relating to biological death.

By metaphorical extension, death is not merely biological termination. It is also: (1) a spiritual state of unbelief, (2) that is overcome by a new life, being born again; (3) and this overcoming of death is symbolized by being buried in the waters of baptism; (4) these experiences lead to a new way of life which is daily overcoming and "putting to death" the old person by desirable ethical actions. This rich metaphorical use of death makes the term a part of the ongoing process of life and tends to relativize, for the believer, the idea of death as only a final, punctiliar act.

One final metaphorical use of death is important in a Baptist perspective of death, namely, the "second death." The biblical foundation for the concept of "second death" is in the Book of Revelation (2:11, 20:14, 21:8). "Second death" is a theological term for the undesirable and irrevocable state of the wicked in the world to come. Baptists feel they have escaped this second death and are obliged to help others do likewise. The idea of a "second death" as a final state of the wicked is an impetus to Baptist evangelism. The "second death" is not death in the sense of ceasing to be or a passing into non-existence. It is a final confirmation of spiritual death, the "first death" of unbelievers. Second death is the negative pole of the two-fold inevitability that mankind faces.

THE TWO-FOLD INEVITABILITY

Baptists would add a third sure thing to the two-fold inevitabilities of life and death — judgment. "And inasmuch as it is appointed for men to die once, and after this comes judgment" (Hebrews 9:27). The inevitability of judgment is, for Baptists, as certain as the inevitability of death. In an annotated edition of the Bible published by Broadman Press, the section on judgment includes the following biblical references: I Chronicles 16:33; Job 21:30; Psalm 9:7; Psalm 50:3; Psalm 96:13; Ecclesiastes 12:14; Matthew 3:12, 11:22, 12:36, 16:27 (and parallels); II Corinthians 5:10; II Timothy 4:1; and Hebrews 9:27. All world religions have concepts of the afterlife. Most world religions have a perspective of judgment with a resultant system of rewards and punishments. Classical Christianity is no exception. In some areas of contemporary Christian theology the idea of a judgment in the world to come has diminished and in even more circles, the reality of punishment and/or a place for it has declined in belief systems. Among a majority of Baptists these doctrines are still firmly held.

The theological, two-fold inevitability for mankind is death and judgment and the two-fold, inevitable results of judgment are heaven or hell. Heaven and hell are conceived of as places where the redeemed and the damned either receive their rewards and undergo eternal felicity or are alienated from God. In one there is the fellowship with God; in the other, the possibility of fellowship does not exist. The one is characterized by mansions, golden streets, home and reunion with loved ones; the other by outer darkness, fire, torment and isolation. Scriptures that corroborate these pictures of heaven are: Matthew 6:20, 25:34; Luke 15:7, 16; John 5:28-29, 14; II Peter 3:13; and Revelation 2:7, 20-22. Scriptures concerning hell are: Matthew 3:12, 5:29, 7:13-14, 8:11, 10:28, 13:49-50, 18:9, 23:15; Mark 9:43; James 3:6; II Peter 2:4; and Revelation 9:1, 20:10, 21:8. Whereas formerly both the concepts of heaven and hell were believed with equal intensity, in contemporary practical church life, heaven is stressed more than hell. The accent is on the positive rather than the negative. The older Baptist theologies of Strong and Mullins give equal space to hell and to heaven; in fact, Strong gives considerably more space to hell. Conner has more about heaven than hell. Moody, a more recent author of a major Baptist systematic theology, has no discussion of hell. The American Baptist, Langdon Gilkey, affirms that the redemptive love of God will overcome all opposition.[6]

Baptist hymnody demonstrates this preference for the positive in such hymns and gospel songs as "O Love That Will Not Let Me Go," "In the Sweet By and By," "Ring the Bells of Heaven" and, in some circles, the still much-used funeral song, "I'll Fly Away, O Glory." The *Baptist Faith and Message* has two brief sentences about the fate of the dead: "The unrighteous will be consigned to Hell, the place of everlasting punishment. The righteous in their resurrected and glorified bodies will dwell forever in Heaven with the Lord."[7]

Given the inevitability of death and the inescapability of judgment with its indubitable results of heaven or hell, Baptists have a theology that places significant weight on death as a final door to destiny. This heightened status of death as gate to eternal felicity or damnation has pastoral and psychological consequences. What happens in death and after death? Since the inevitable comes upon us, curiosity about the particulars of what happens at death and beyond is natural.

THE WAY IT HAPPENS

What happens when you die? That's a question asked by eight- and eighty-year-olds and by people of all ages in between. Understandably, Baptists are not too specific about these matters. The reason they are not is because the biblical sources do not provide details. The old Reformation dictum "where the Bible speaks we speak" and its concomitant principle "where it is silent, so are we" is invoked.

The outline of a personal eschatology (doctrine of last things) would involve the following elements: At the "appointed time" one dies. There is a strong Calvinist undercurrent of providence in setting the boundaries of individual existence. The dead go immediately into the presence of God in a conscious state. The parable of Dives and Lazarus (Luke 16) is often used as a proof-text for this assertion. The dead are in heaven or hell in some intermediate form (II Corinthians 5:1-5). Baptists do not, on the one hand, espouse the doctrine of soul sleep until the general resurrection of the dead; nor, on the other hand, do they affirm that the final, general resurrection of all persons takes place at death. Consequently, some type of conscious intermediate form is required. The dead are "souls" awaiting the resurrection of the body. (No amount of Baptist scholarly holism about the totality of the person seems able to shake the Platonic notion of the flight of a soul from a body — an idea held by most Baptists.) At the end of the age, Christ comes, ushers in the new age and confirms by final judgment what is already *de facto,* namely the reward of the righteous and the punishment of the wicked. Judgment is preceded by the resurrection of the body. Judgment is followed by, or simultaneous with, the formation of a new heaven and a new earth with all wickedness shut away so that corruption and destruction cannot continue. This outline of things to come is pieced together from various portions of the New Testament: Matthew 16:27, 18:8-9, 19:28, 24:27, 30, 36, 44, 24:31-46, 26:64; Mark 8:38, 9:43-48; Luke 12:40, 48, 16:19-26, 17:22-37, 21:27-28; John 14:1-3; Acts 1:11; 17:31; Romans 14:10; I Corinthians 4:5, 15:24-28, 35-58; II Corinthians 5:10; Philemon 3:20-21; Colossians 1:5, 3:4; I Thessalonians 4:14-18, 5:1ff.; II Thessalonians 1:7ff., 2; I Timothy 6:14; II Timothy 4:1, 8; Titus 2:13; Hebrews 9:27-28; James 5:8; II Peter 3:7ff.; I John 2:28, 3:2; Jude 14; and Revelation 1:18, 3:11, 20:1 to 22:13. An overview is drawn especially from Revelation 21:1-5:

> Then I saw a new heaven and a new earth; for the first heaven and the first earth had passed away, and the sea was no more. And I saw the holy city, new Jerusalem, coming down out of heaven from God, prepared as a bride adorned for her husband; and I heard a great voice from the throne saying, "Behold, the dwelling of God is with men. He will dwell with them, and they shall be his people, and God himself will be with them; he will wipe away every tear from their eyes, and death shall be no more, neither shall there be mourning nor crying nor pain any more, for the former things have passed away." And he who sat upon the throne said, "Behold, I make all things new." Also he said, "Write this,

for these words are trustworthy and true."

Songs expressing the joy and blessings of the final condition of mankind abound: "There's a New Name Written Down in Glory," "When They Ring Those Golden Bells for You and Me," "Victory in Jesus" and the choral work, "The King Is Coming." I recall only one gospel song used to any extent in Baptist congregations that refers to the terrors of hell and that reference is found in the middle verses of the Appalachian gospel song, "Brethren, We Have Met to Worship," in which one sees his father, mother, brothers and sisters "sinking down, trembling on the brink of woe." He is advised that "death is coming, hell is moving" and is asked, "Can you bear to see them go?"

The features of the afterlife are, for the most part, sketchy. What is certain is that one is in God's presence, one is conscious, one is resurrected. Death is overcome. Life goes on. The last enemy has been defeated. Absent loved ones are "with the Lord." And that same Lord who came to earth at Bethlehem will come at the end of the age to judge, reward and punish. The destiny of those who trust in Christ is secure, for the "friend we have in Jesus" is the guarantor of these promises.

When one accents the positive all seems to the good, but there are two grim realities that persist: the fact of physical death and the biblical teaching that evil intensifies "in the last days," which means that there will be increased suffering and trials even for, and perhaps especially for, Christians. All could be corrected if there were some possibilities of escaping either death and/or suffering and crisis at the end of the age. Some Baptists hold to such a possibility.

AN ESCAPIST POSSIBILITY

In some of Paul's earliest correspondence there is comfort given about believers who have "fallen asleep." Then he says," then [at Christ's coming] we who are alive and remain shall be caught up together with them in the clouds to meet the Lord in the air, and thus we shall always be with the Lord. Therefore comfort one another with these words" (I Thessalonians 4:17-18).

What a comfort it would be if we could escape physical death! And it is with this intent that modern interpreters read the passage. The original intention of the passage was to give some word of well-being about those who had died before Christ came back. And that is still, in my opinion, the basic intention of the biblical writer. Yet the question intrudes, Does the Bible say some people will not have to face physical death? If so, wouldn't this be the ultimate panacea and a splendid "selling point" for Christianity? The answer is yes, but it is a highly qualified yes, which must be accompanied by the full expression of Paul's teaching. The full expression is that only those alive when Christ does terminate the age will be "translated," for want of a better term, and will not undergo physical death.

A more recent, less documentable, view is held by some Baptists, via dispensational theology, that Christians will be taken away from any suffering and trauma that precedes the final days.[8] This refinement provides a double protection against suffering and death. The two things are not of equal certainty on the basis of biblical teaching. The first possibility of escape from death is a possibility only if one is living at the end of the age. The second possibility is also dependent upon being in the last days. But it seems contrary to the New Testament pattern of suffering as a necessary part of the Christian pilgrimage.

Certainly ours is an age that is apocalyptic in outlook. Furthermore, those individuals and groups, and there are many Baptists among them, who see signs of the end of the times are certainly making a large appeal and a good "selling point" out of a theological system that promises actual escape from death and probable escape from suffering. The dilemma of these escapist possibilities is time. The more of it that passes and the greater the number of people who die and suffer, the more diminishing are the returns of a system that capitalizes on these special escape clauses.

The above section has dealt with theory and belief systems of Baptists. How are these theological beliefs related to life and death in the actual experience of Baptists today? How does theology affect life and, in particular, how does a theology of death affect the life of one who takes it seriously?

FORGING THEORY TO FACT

These boundary situations of life and death are lonely and momentous occasions. This is especially true of death, for the birthing is a cooperative, participatory process ordinarily accompanied by joy and sustained caring of an individual whose thought processes are, as yet, unformed. Whereas death is individual, possibly surrounded by pain and Angst and amid grieving persons, or worse, without them in sterile medical facilities. It is very difficult to know how one relates a faith theory to dying for several reasons: (1) Until the 1950s and the early Kübler-Ross research, people did not speak openly of death; (2) the ministers, priests and rabbis who were charged with "comforting the dying" and the grieving interpreted what the theological theory of death was supposed to mean to persons *in extremis,* rather than listening for how those undergoing the experience were relating faith and fact; (3) properly speaking, one does not experience death, only dying; and (4) modern medical science has attenuated "life" to such a degree that the boundaries between life and death are controversial medically and legally.

Despite these factors, and in part because of them, "death" has become a significant topic in the last half of the 20th century. Religious communities, due to technological possibilities and the shifting of social mores, have been obliged to make formal statements about matters of life and death. The sources for this second section, for want of adequate research based on appropriate questionnaires, will have to be based on those pronouncements of Baptists about matters of life and death, my experiences of teaching Baptist ministers, and my experiences with laypersons in dozens of churches I have served as interim minister. The following conclusions are purely my own and I will take responsibility for them even while insisting that they are broadly based in experience, if not scientifically verifiable by the research instruments of the social sciences.

DEATH, SIN AND REDEMPTION

Baptists have a theoretical bifocal view of death: death as a curse due to sin and death as a redemptive possibility because of Christ's vicarious death. In my opinion, they raise one focus of this bifocal view much more than the other. The less-used focus is the death-as-curse-of-sin view. This is particularly true in instances of infant mortality. In this century one never hears about why, theologically, infants die. The death is attributed, when possible, to social or biological reasons. If not, generally divine mystery and other principles of theodicy are invoked. But in all instances the mercy of God and the loving redemption of Christ are held forth as resolutions to the grieving as the simple focus of theological counsel. And, in my opinion, this is all to the good.[9]

The doctrine of the priesthood of all believers teaches Baptists that they are individually competent and responsible before God for their own spiritual well-being. The logical extension of this doctrine is that God cares for those who are, for whatever reason, incompetent to exercise that responsibility. Applying this to infants creates the one-focus view of death. Further, the priesthood of all believers declares that we are to exercise a priestly concern for the incompetent, the uninformed and the powerless. When this aspect of the priesthood of all believers is applied, the roots of Baptist evangelistic impulses are seen. One further step grows from this caring concern of the priesthood on behalf of the hapless. It is the affirmation that life is the gift of God and must be nurtured, particularly for those who cannot help themselves. This is the positive basis for Baptists' objection to abortions in most instances.[10] When extended to the disadvantaged, this regard for the life of others and the guardianship under God for the disabled has provided the impetus for the enviable record Baptists have had in work with the handicapped, the homeless and others in need of Christian social ministries.[11] This affirmation of life as God's gift and the acceptance of the guardian, priestly concern for the hapless are also the basis for a denial of euthanasia.

Returning from the social concerns to the responsible individual, I suspect that most Baptists would not intrinsically relate their own individual biological death to any form of guilt or ancestral sin. Inveterate individualism would tend to see death more as a mark of finitude than a sign of culpability. Whatever Scripture says about the corporate involvements of the individual or the relationships between all men and Adam is left to be worked out by the theologians and the clergy. Baptist lay persons tend toward responsible individualism, even in matters of their own deaths.

The practical stress of Baptists about death is largely, if not exclusively, the positive expression that Christ's death has made our death more bearable, for by His death and resurrection He has overcome eternal death. Likewise, in His death He has identified with mankind in such a way that He is with us in our death. The music Baptists sing is almost entirely on this positive focus. Whether it be the spirited chorus, taught to children, "I've Got a Home in Gloryland that Outshines the Sun" or the more sonorous "O Love That Will Not Let Me Go," the emphasis is on deliverance from death. What is in theory a double view of death becomes, in practice, more of a single focus. The dictum "as in Adam all die, even so in Christ shall all be made alive" is taken seriously by Baptists. But they assume that the individual has a responsibility in both parts of that dictum.

DEATH AS CONCEPT

It is my opinion that by an extensive metaphorical use of death, Baptists find it easier and more comforting to face biological death. The autonomy and hegemony of biological death has created an absolute with attendant fear and dread. If death is more than biology, if in a variety of guises and on a number of levels, one has already experienced death or met it and survived, then the grim reaper is not so grim. Albeit unconscious and unreflective, and I feel it is both, this flattening of death into process serves a good purpose and may actually assist believers in the process of dying.

By the belief that all persons actively rebel against God, place themselves as aliens to him and actualize the destructive possibilities of existence by calling this condition spiritual death, Baptists add a dimension to the concept of death. This dimension of being lost, unsaved, "dead in sins and trespasses" is overcome by being born again, by exercising the gift of faith, by an experience that transforms by its promise of hope and by its promise of a restored wholeness with God, the ground of one's being. Conversion is an emergence from spiritual death. Therefore, death in some of its expanded dimensions can be overcome. The liturgical experience of baptism is a visible sign of this renewal. Baptism is a rite of passage, which among Baptists (who adhere to believer's baptism) is performed upon those who are surrounded by relatives and an affirming community who see one "buried with Christ in baptism and rise to walk in newness of life." This transformation, renewal and harbinger of ultimate resurrection is a powerful spiritual and psychological assurance of the overcoming of death.

Furthermore, the Christian pilgrimage is a constant struggle to overcome the lesser self. This "putting to death the old man" is a way of defeating death in life. The ethical actions of Christian conduct should be, in my opinion and often are according to my observation, placed against ultimate values. Why should one give up "enjoyable" habits and actions here and now even if they contradict Christian mores? Because ultimately they shape one who is an essential person and if one's way of life and tastes are contrary to the exclusively life-affirming and positive conditions of the eternal order, there will be a radical adjustment necessary to enter God's world. This daily dying is conducive to ethical and life-affirming actions now. It is also preparatory for the eternal dimension. Among Baptists a common way of expressing this notion is "don't be so worldly that you won't enjoy God's world."

Thus, by way of extension, Baptists have met and fought death many times. To geriatric persons who have used these metaphors, there is bound to be some surplus of comfort when they apply this same principle to biological death, which by relativization has become one form, but not the only form, of death.

THE TWO OPTIONS

A theological, metaphorical use of death provides a broadening of the idea of death. The rigorous and rigid notion of two options following death — heaven or hell — promotes the narrowing of death as the passage to ultimate destiny, felicitous or fatal.

It is obvious how the doctrine of heaven would comfort and sustain believers. It is no less obvious that the doctrine of hell would pose many difficulties for its adherents. The first dilemma for one who believes in hell is the obvious pain of eternal separation from loved ones who are not believers. This is handled in the following ways. Funeral services for unbelievers, those who have consciously rejected Christ, are usually as comforting as possible for those who attend. The funeral service is, after all, for the living. The goodness and mercy of God are spoken of as well as any and all humanly desirable characteristics of the deceased. The general attitude is one of emphasizing the positive and providing bases for future ministry to the mourners. Ministers, when queried, will add some extenuating theological affirmations. These are: (1) God only is judge of all persons, (2) people are judged according "to the light" (awareness or opportunities they have; cf. Romans 1), and (3) there are degrees of rewards and punishments (cf. Jesus' parables in Luke: 7:41-43, 12:47-48 and 19:12-27). There may be those who mourn morbidly or in a sustained traumatic fashion for dead loved ones who were not believers, but I have not known of any personally. I have "heard the confession" of a few older Baptists who acknowledged (despite the formal theology and the general Baptist view of biblical teachings on the subject) beliefs in universalism (all mankind will be saved), annihilationism (the unbelieving do not go into eternal life but pass out of existence), that there is no life after this life and even one hesitant affirmation of reincarnation. Whereas these individual expressions are not numerous, they are an outgrowth of the individualism of Baptists who sometimes extend the "priesthood of all believers" to mean that they may tailor doctrine and biblical teachings to suit their preferences.

The positive use made of the doctrine of hell is a rationale for a militant evangelism. In other words, the best way to avoid the consequences of hell is to accept the offer of heaven and consequently to "seek the salvation of our kindred and acquaintances"[12] so that they too will share the comfort of the promise of being with God in fellowship eternally. It is this positive provision that will be explored in the following section.

WHAT ACTUALLY HAPPENS

People ask more questions and desire more specific details than the biblical materials answer. Based on the sources above, a brief résumé of what happens to the believer at death and beyond would be: individuals undergo the transition of death (i.e., a loss of consciousness); one "wakes up," to use an extension of the New Testament analogy of death as sleep, in the presence of God; one remains with God in a conscious state and in an intermediate form until the final, general resurrection, at which point one is given a final resurrection form and dwells eternally as a recognizable being embodying essential continuity with one's historical identity. Loved ones are known and reunited. Whereas marriage in heaven is not a physical exercise of sexuality (cf. Matthew 22:30), there is no reason to exclude sexual identity as male or female or partnerships from the eternal dimension. The above is based on a logical extension of the biblical theophanies (resurrection appearances) of Jesus and the return to the historical dimension of dead persons (e.g., Moses and Elijah at the transfiguration).

Unanswered or more tenuous are the specific questions people want to know. Will infants grow? Will we live as families? Are physical abnormalities corrected? Presumably so since it is a perfect world. Can a suicide go to heaven? Yes, if one has established a relationship of forgiveness with God in this life, it may be assumed one can ask forgiveness of a final sin in the world to come. What age will we be in heaven? Some incautious ministers have suggested 21, others 33, Jesus' historical age. By and large pastors and professors acknowledge that such specific information is beyond our resources and leave matters in the hands of God. The phrase the *Baptist Faith and Message* uses about the state of the dead would be the phrase most repeated and held by Baptists. The dead are "with the Lord."

DEATH AND APOCALYPSE

What of the escape clause? Will those who are living at Christ's return die? No. But two observations should be noted: (1) it is not known whether "translation," the going into the eternal dimension directly without undergoing physical death (e.g., Elijah), is intrinsically any different from death — the transition is analogous to sleep with its next moment of conscious waking; and

(2) one must reckon that, according to biblical materials (Matthew 25:13; Mark 13:32), one cannot know the specific time of the end of the age. Many people and their elaborate systems of the end times have lived and died. The only specific apocalyptist one should take seriously is the sign-carrying recluse who has left all to proclaim the end. And what one should take seriously about such an apocalyptist is his zeal, not his knowledge.

It is my experience that geriatric persons do not take too seriously the apocalyptic escape clause. Aging persons, by and large, are not planning on getting out of life alive. Via the routes of pain and problems, many have come with firm faith to look upon death as a friend and even a welcome relief. It is often the young and the over-achieving middle-aged who, in the blush of vigor and strength and in the period of acquisition of things (all of which are heavily insured), desire the insurance of getting out without death. And one suspects that if it were put to a vote, most people who are agitating academically for an immediate closure of the age would vote for a delay. Most senior citizens have lived long enough to take life and death as it comes. The promise of grace, the prospect of heaven, these are the mainstays of our faith. As to our fate and that of those we love, we are able to say — and most often do reply — that they and we through Jesus Christ are "with the Lord."

Notes

1. William Richardson White, *Baptist Distinctives* (Nashville: Sunday School Board of the Southern Baptist Convention, 1946), pp. 12-20. Harold L. Fickett, *Baptist Beliefs — A Series of Seven Studies in Distinctive Doctrines* (Nashville: Broadman Press, 1945), pp. 2-8. Herschel H. Hobbs, *The Baptist Faith and Message* (Nashville: Convention Press, 1971), pp. 18-30.
2. William Latane Lumpkin, *Baptist Confessions of Faith,* rev. ed. (Valley Forge: Judson Press, 1969). W.J. McGlothlin, *Baptist Confessions of Faith* (Philadelphia: American Baptist Publication Society, 1911), pp. ix-xii.
3. The following is a list of general works by representative Baptist theologians:
   James Petigru Boyce, *Abstracts of Systematic Theology* (Baltimore: H.M. Wharton, 1887).
   Walter Thomas Conner, *Christian Doctrine* (Nashville: Broadman Press, 1937).
   Langdon Brown Gilkey, *Message and Existence* (New York: Seabury Press, 1979).
   William L. Hendricks, *A Theology for Children* (Nashville: Broadman Press, 1980).
   Dale Moody, *The World of Truth* (Grand Rapids: W.B. Eerdmans, 1981).
   Edgar Young Mullins, *The Christian Religion in Its Doctrinal Expression* (Nashville: Sunday School Board of the Southern Baptist Convention).
   Augustus Hopkins Strong, *Systematic Theology* (Philadelphia: Judson Press, 1907).
4. Many Baptists are oblivious to Heidegger's definition that "life is unto death," and many Baptist ministers have railed against what they hear of existentialism. Nevertheless, the strong experiential and implicit common sense realism of Baptists would bear a parallel translation of theological pietism to many existen-

tialist insights.

5. *The Baptist Faith and Message* (Nashville: The Sunday School Board of the Southern Baptist Convention, 1963), p. 10.
6. See above in note 3.
7. *Baptist Faith and Message,*" p. 15.
8. For an explanation of this view see Ray Summers, *The Life Beyond* (Nashville: Broadman Press, 1959). For an explanation of this exclusion of Christians from suffering see Dwight Pentecost's *Things to Come: A Study in Biblical Eschatology* (Grand Rapids: Zondervan, 1972).
9. See William Hendricks, *Theology for Children* (Nashville: Broadman Press, 1980).
10. It is my opinion that it is a stronger position to stress this positive aspect than it is to belabor exclusively the prescriptions of the divine commands against killing, which serve as the necessary negative base for these positions.
11. Marv Know and Dan Martin, *Challenge of the Cities* (Atlanta: Home Mission Board of the Southern Baptist Convention, 1981). Arthur B. Rutledge, *Mission to America: A Century and a Quarter of Southern Baptist Home Missions,* rev. ed. (Nashville: Broadman Press, 1976), pp. 172-183. "Program Report of the Home Mission Board," in *Annual of the Southern Baptist Convention* (Nashville: Executive Committee, Southern Baptist Convention).
12. A phrase taken from a church covenant widely used in Southern Baptist churches, found in Walter Hines Sims, *Baptist Hymnal* (Nashville: Convention Press, 1956), p. 476.

Buddhism

Anne C. Klein, PhD

BACKGROUND OF THE FAITH

Discussions of impermanence and death are at the heart of Buddhism's understanding of the human situation and recommendations for its transformation. These views derive from the historical Buddha, known as Gautama or Shakyamuni. He is revered as an extraordinary teacher who, in the 5th century B.C., demonstrated how enlightenment is attained. He is neither the first nor the only enlightened Buddha to appear, but what sets Gautama apart is that he revealed his attainment when the teachings of the previous Buddha, Kashyapa, who lived prior to historical time, had disappeared. Having manifested enlightenment at age 35, he spent the remaining 45 years of his life teaching others how to attain it.[1] All the many schools of Buddhism throughout Asia trace their origins to the discourses known as *sutras,* that were believed to be spoken by Gautama during this period. Moreover, it is commonly understood that Gautama's observation of human disease and death provided a major impetus for his spiritual quest.

According to Buddhist legends, Gautama was born a prince in the Shakya clan of northern India. At his birth, a seer predicted he would excel as either a worldly monarch or spiritual leader. His father, wishing to ensure the former, ordered all persons whose ugly, decrepit or unwholesome appearance might inspire other-worldly interests to be barred from the royal compound and did not allow the young prince beyond its confines. In time, Gautama married and became a father; he reached the age of 29 having known only the luxurious life of his father's contrivance. Certain Hindu gods intervened at this juncture to alter the young man's goals forever.[2] On three different occasions, they caused sick man, than a very old man and finally a corpse to appear along the prince's chariot route. Stunned at what he had never seen before, the sheltered prince demanded an explanation. Each incident was more disturbing than the previous one. The following explains what happens after the third experience, the encounter with death:

> Courageous though he was, the king's son was suddenly filled with dismay. Leaning his shoulder against the top of the chariot rail, he spoke these words in a forceful voice: This is the end which has been fixed for all, and yet the world forgets its fears and takes no heed! Turn back the chariot! This is not time...for pleasure excursions. How could an intelligent person pay no heed at a time of disaster, when he was aware of his impending destruction?[3]

Returning home, the prince began to meditate on birth and death. Soon his mind was concentrated and blissful. At this juncture, a religious mendicant approached and revealed that "terrified by birth and death, [I] have adopted a homeless life to win salvation. Since all that lives is doomed to extinction...I search for that most blessed state in which extinction is unknown."[4] His sense of urgency aroused by this confrontation with death, Gautama left home to seek the "blessed state of freedom."[5] Specifically, he sought liberation from the endless round of birth and death known by Hindus and Buddhists as *samsara.* He began seven years of severe ascetic practices, according to the custom of his day. When these practices brought him to the brink of death rather than to liberation, he became determined to forge his own path.

The culmination of this endeavor occurred under a pipal tree in Bodhgaya, in northeast India, about 531 B.C. Buddhist tradition holds that Gautama took his seat there in the evening, vowing not to arise until he achieved enlightenment. He meditated throughout the night and attained his goal at dawn. In doing so, he became the fourth Buddha of the present aeon, during which 1000 persons will openly reveal themselves as Buddhas in our world. This world, most Buddhists believe, is one of the billion worlds that make up a world system. All of these billion world systems in the cosmos go through cyclical periods of production, abiding, destruction and disappearance.[6] There is no time envisioned when all billion world systems — which include heavens and hells into which one can be reborn for long periods of time — will be destroyed simultaneously so that continued rebirth is impossible.

According to the older traditions of Buddhism, especially Theravada, "the way of the Elders," Gautama is the only person in the present aeon who will attain Buddhahood.[7] Thus, practitioners in this tradition do not seek Buddhahood but liberation from cyclic existence as an *Arhat*. This term is variously translated as "Worthy One" or "Foe Destroyer," one's own afflictions and limitations being the foe that prevents liberation. After an Arhat attains liberation, he spends the remainder of his life in beneficial activities, especially teaching. At his death, his continuum is extinguished in a state known as parinirvana and he never again takes rebirth.

Mahayana Buddhists, whose traditions emerged in force in India 400 years after Buddha's death, consider the nature of the mind to be such that its utter cessation is impossible. Thus, they find Hinayana mistaken regarding the final destiny of its Arhats.[8] According to Mahayana, Arhats eventually encounter compassionate Buddhas who teach them to attain full enlightenment. In the Indo-Tibetan Mahayana tradition, both male and female practitioners are exhorted to seek the complete enlightenment of Buddhahood in order to fulfill their ultimate religious goal of offering maximum help to humanity. As a Buddha, one does not disappear at death but has full control over the process of death and rebirth, conjoined with an omniscient understanding of where and how one can be of most help. Buddhas continuously take birth or manifest in ways and in places that provide greatest help to others. Virtually all Mahayana schools believe that every living being can attain Buddhahood.[9] Moreover, countless persons have already attained this station, though they do not necessarily reveal themselves as enlightened but take on any appropriate or useful role.

Buddhism flourished in India until the 11th century B.C. when a combination of internal political and economic changes, especially repeated Muslim invasions from the northwest, virtually destroyed it, leaving only small pockets in the northeasternmost regions of India to continue. By that time, Buddhism had spread to much of Asia. Buddhist emissaries became established in Central Asia by the 1st century B.C.; from there Buddhism made its entry into the Han Dynasty of China.[10] Monks sent by the Indian King Ashoka in the 3rd century B.C. brought Buddhism to Sri Lanka and Burma. In the 7th century A.D., Indian Buddhist scholars and adepts visiting Tibet initiated an extensive period of contact with Indian Buddhist thought. From these areas — Sri Lanka and Burma, China and Tibet — Buddhism gradually spread yet further abroad.

China, where Mahayana Buddhism predominated, was a major force in the first millennium of Buddhist history. From there, Buddhism traveled via Korea to Japan in the 6th century. Chan or Zen first surfaced in 7th-century China, later taking hold in Korea and Japan. Since the 1950s, Soto and Rinzai Zen have been popular in the United States; these date back to 13th-century Japanese developments in the Zen tradition.

The Theravada Buddhism initially fostered by Ashoka's emissaries in Sri Lanka and Burma took hold in the 12th century in Cambodia and later in the 13th century in Thailand.[11] Since the mid-1970s, Theravada insight meditation teachers have established centers and conducted meditation retreats in the United States and other Western countries.

Another major sphere of Buddhist influence developed north of India. In the 7th century teams of Indian and Tibetan translators began a 400-year-long collaboration for the purpose of translating Indian sutras and commentaries into Tibetan. Mahayana held sway in Tibet and in the countries that identified with its religious traditions: Sikkhim, Ladakh (both now part of India), Bhutan, Mongolia and the Sherpa peoples of Nepal.[12] In the last 15 years, teachers from all four orders of Tibetan Buddhism — Nyingma, Geluk, Kagyu and Sakya — have established centers in the West. Thus, the present century has been paradoxically significant for Buddhist history. Ravages of war and revolution have virtually destroyed it along with other great cultural achievements of Cambodia, China, Laos, Tibet and Vietnam. At the same time, and to a significant degree aided by the dispersal of Asian refugees, Buddhist influence has been increasingly felt in the U.S., Canada, Western Europe and areas of Australia, New Zealand and South America.

MAJOR PRINCIPLES OF BUDDHIST PRACTICE

On the eve of his enlightenment, Gautama saw the cyclical birth, death and rebirth of all living beings everywhere. He recalled innumerable past lives, both others' and his own, linking this knowledge with a direct understanding of the process of karma, the cause and effect of actions.

> With the purified divine eye surpassing that of (ordinary) human beings, I see people as they move on or come to be; I comprehend that beings are mean, excellent, comely, ugly, proceeding well or proceeding badly according to the consequences of their actions....[13]

Buddhas are considered the most exalted type of beings that exist. However, they neither created the world nor arbitrate rewards and punishments after death. This is governed by the process known as the cause and effect of actions, or karma, according to which, just as fire heats and ice chills, good actions lead to happiness and bad ones to suffering. This process has been at work beginninglessly. Unlike the West where, as classically stated by Thomas Aquinas, an infinite regress of cause and effect is widely considered unworkable, Buddhists find this less problematic than explaining how a first cause such as a creator deity could arise. Buddhists therefore find it more logical to propose that the universe has no creator-god and no first moment.[14] Buddhas and other special god-like beings can help one to cultivate the virtues that yield happiness in future lives, but it is one's own behavior that brings this about. Circumstances of life and death therefore result from one's own actions, not from judgment by a superior being. Because even the best rebirth leads to suffering and death and because as long as one lives, one inevitably creates causes for future rebirths, the only way to eliminate suffering is to escape this process entirely. One does this by changing the mind in specified ways. The training involved and the type of mind cultivated bear on Buddhism's discussion of death.

Thus, death and its sister subject, impermanence, are significant in the mythic origins of Buddhism as well as the meditative and philosophical traditions that are an important part of its religious life. Following several strands of Buddhist discourse, we will discuss the fact and nature of death in several contexts. Briefly stated, these have to do with (1) the importance and method of facing one's own mortality, (2) the relevance of this understanding for a classic presentation of the path to enlightenment, (3) the stages of dying and their significance for practitioners of meditation, and (4) descriptions of the period after death and of rebirth. Because Buddhist traditions are far too diverse to accommodate with brevity and because specifics are more informative than generalities, we will focus on the Tibetan Mahayana's particularly rich treatment of these four issues.

FACING MORTALITY: DEATH AS INCENTIVE

For Buddhists, the conviction that birth follows death heightens the imperative to make best use of the present life. Although rebirth is guaranteed, the type of rebirth is not. Because a human life is the result of powerful virtue, it is difficult to attain. Even more difficult is a human life in which one has the physical and mental leisure to give some attention to spiritual development.

The difficulty of gaining a human life in which religious practice is possible is likened to the plight of a blind turtle in a turbulent ocean. At the surface drifts a golden hoop, just large enough for a turtle's head. The likelihood that this blind turtle, who comes up for air once in 100 years, will put his head through the hoop, exemplifies our chances for another leisurely human life. Therefore, one who now has such a circumstance must not waste it. To overcome the universal tendency to do so, Tibetan Mahayana Buddhists, incorporating several elements common to Theravada, use a detailed meditative strategy for dealing with issues such as death's inevitability. This is so simple intellectually and so difficult psychologically that it takes practice to slow the mind down sufficiently for its import to be internalized. For this reason, Buddhism developed ways of deconstructing this simple point into topics for reflection. Paul Ricoeur once said that deconstruction means getting to the questions behind the answers in a text or tradition and emphasized that this is really a religious issue.[15] In the Tibetan tradition, one probes fundamental questions such as "How can I know that my death is definite, its time indefinite, and what will be most helpful to me in that circumstance?" Specific patterns of reflection, grouped into three main segments, are suggested.[16]

First, to internalize the certainty of one's own death, one can reflect that all great persons of the past — saints, heroes and geniuses — have died; that even planets, suns and galaxies are subject to destruction. How then could I escape it?[17] Also, the time remaining to us continually decreases and cannot be extended. Tsong-ka-pa, a 14th-century major religious figure in Tibet, writes:

> When animals such as sheep are led to the slaughter, they move closer to death with every step they take. The water carried by the current of a strong river or the water in a waterfall on a steep mountain quickly disappears. Just so, one's life is quickly spent and gone.[18]

Second, death is inescapable. It cannot be avoided through any of the techniques familiar to us: there is no place we can go to escape it, no amount of money that can ransom or bribe it and no weapons that might counter it. Our own death is definite. Not only this, but the exigencies of life allow very little time for spiritual development. Tsong-ka-pa states that if we subtract time spent in gaining maturity, sleeping, taking care of necessities, illness and old age, a lifespan of 60 years allows five years for religious endeavor. But there is no certainty that we will be allowed 60 years, or any definite period. This compounds the issue. Though we might accept death as inevitable, if we know it will not come round for, say, 20 years, we can plan accordingly. But we do not know when death will visit us. Our lifespans are of uncertain length and our bodies vulnerable. Although causes of life are relatively few, causes of death are many. If misused or polluted, even life-sustaining elements like food and water become causes of death.

Having incorporated the view that one's death is definite and imminent, the third phase is to ask what can help in the face of death. Friends and relatives can neither alter one's fate nor accompany one through death. One must die alone. Possessions too will be useless; they give no enjoyment as one lies dying. One cannot carry even a needle and thread through this transition. Nor is one's body of use; it will not accompany us. The mind, however, *does* continue, so that wholesome capacities developed internally — especially love and compassion, as well as insight into the dependently arisen yet empty nature of things — will help at death. Each of these points is the focus for one or several sessions of meditation. In reflecting thus, one alternates between analytical and stabilizing meditation.[19] To contemplate reasons and examples of death's inevitability and unpredictability is a form of analytical meditation. When some degree of internal experience arises, one leaves aside words and concentrates or stabilizes on that effect.

In this way, Buddhists seek to internalize the reality and unpredictability of death and to engender a sense of urgency regarding spiritual development. This is not meant to exclude other responsibilities but is a call to organize time and choose activities with real concern for their ultimate value. That value derives more from the spirit in which "religious" or "worldly" actions are done than their surface nature. In general, any activity done with good motivation, especially if conjoined with an understanding of the nature of reality or the emptiness to be discussed below, is seen as a Mahayana practice.

What is the net result of such reflection? Tsong-ka-pa says it relieves our fear of death, which he describes as derived from the implicit hope that it can somehow be escaped. Presumption of immortality breeds excessive attachment to one's own physical identity and material possessions, the result of which is that the menace of death looms even larger. In short, these reflections are intended not only to direct increased energy toward goals chosen in recognition of death's inevitability but also to make death itself less fearful.[20] Near-death experiences in our culture typically result in a heightened sense of life's joys, renewed energy and a willingness to overlook lesser annoyances. The purpose of facing death through systematic reflection is to reap the benefits of such an encounter early in life and without the risks of an actual brush with death. For Tsong-ka-pa, contemplating death not only revivifies one's energies but also turns them toward goals that have ultimate value for Buddhist practitioners.

Given the conclusion of these reflections that only religious practice is beneficial at death, the next questions naturally have to do with the nature of religious motivation and practice. Here, too, impermanence and death figure significantly.

IMPERMANENCE AND THE RELIGIOUS PATH

Non-religious and religious motivation are distinguished in the Indo-Tibetan Mahayana tradition. Persons who use worldly or religious activities to pursue happiness in this life with no concern for future lives are not seen as religiously motivated. At the very least, religious motivation is concerned that future lives take place in fortunate circumstances. This, however, is inferior to either non-Mahayana or Mahayana concerns. Non-Mahayanists seek liberation from cyclic existence because they consider that to wander in cyclic existence is to be like a fly trapped inside a jar — one can go higher or lower but always remains trapped. Six realms of rebirth are enumerated; the lowest and most painful being the hot and cold hells. Rebirth as a hungry ghost or animal also involves extreme suffering; relatively happy are births as humans, demi-gods or gods.[21]

Even the best rebirth — that of a god in a heavenly realm — involves suffering when, like a rocket running out of fuel, the virtuous activity that propelled one there is consumed and one must leave that blissful realm for a far inferior rebirth. To seek liberation is thus a more suitable and hence higher goal than merely to seek a good rebirth. The Mahayanist, who shares this perspective, has an additional concern that he or she be able to help others achieve their own highest welfare and for this reason seeks not merely liberation but the full enlightenment of a Buddha so as to be able to lead other beings to their enlightenment.[22] The Indo-Tibetan tradition sees one with such motivation as a person of greatest capacity.

In this way, all levels of religious motivation — to achieve good rebirth, liberation or a Buddha's capacity for helping others — derive from a recognition of the present situation as impermanent. The Mahayanist specifically connects this understanding with a concern for others' welfare. Initially, compassion merely sees beings as suffering and in need of solace; as insight progresses, beings are understood also as impermanent, not only because they are mortal but because they are "evanescent or momentarily disintegrating, like (a reflected) moon in water stirred by a breeze."[23] Building on this, Mahayana compassion becomes akin to wisdom as it becomes a concern for persons seen as characterized by coarse and subtle impermanence. The *most* insightful compassion is that directed at persons seen not only as impermanent, but as empty of inherently existing.[24]

Understanding the instability of life is thus a necessary component of the wish to leave cyclic existence; knowing living beings as impermanent is a necessary aspect of the more profound forms of Mahayana compassion. These, the determination to leave cyclic existence and the compassionate aspiration to enlightenment, are two of the three principal features of the path to enlightenment described in the Indo-Tibetan tradition.[25] The third feature — cultivation of wisdom — is discussed below. In brief, it involves reversal of ordinary assumptions regarding apparently static or solid objects. Such reorientation itself presumes the momentary change and disintegration of all produced things. Thus, whereas reflection on one's own death can provide sustained impetus toward religious practice, the chief elements of that practice — the decision to leave cyclic existence, the gaining of mature compassion and wisdom — come to completion in large measure through reflection on death and other forms of impermanence. In this way, impermanence, whose hallmark is death, has a central role in this form of Buddhist practice.

The motivating potential, compassionate insight and wisdom that deep recognition of impermanence and death can instill is not the only significance this issue has for Buddhist thought. For a fuller perspective we turn now to the Tantric branch of Mahayana, which, originating in India, dominated Tibetan understanding of the process of dying, death and rebirth. Much of what follows is unique to that perspective, being altogether absent in Theravada and differently elaborated in other Mahayana traditions.

DEATH AS RELIGIOUS OPPORTUNITY

Wisdom and skillful methods are both essential for enlightenment. Compassion is the chief skillful method of Mahayana and, at its most profound, wishes others to be free from suffering while seeing them as insubstantial and evanescent. In short, it understands that beings lack or are empty of the type of solid, substantial, inherently independent status that one ordinarily presumes them — and oneself — to possess. Such overly reified or solidified status as the "self" is negated in Buddhist theories of selflessness.

Selflessness, in both sutra and tantra, does not mean persons do not exist at all. "Self" here does not signify the "you" or "me" of ordinary language but refers to an overly concrete and otherwise misconstrued existential status. Nothing — neither persons, places, Buddhas, nor enlightenment itself — exists *inherently*. But they *do* exist. Only the inherently independent existence attributed to them does not. If, as some have misunderstood Buddhism to mean, persons did not exist at all, then the essential Buddhist doctrines of the cause and effect of actions, the process of rebirth and death, would be impossible. The compatibility of cause and effect, of the world of objects, with the principle of emptiness is an essential feature of Indo-Tibetan Mahayana. It means that neither emptiness nor realization of it undermines successful functioning in the world. Rather, when things and, especially, one's own mind are understood as empty, their full potential becomes apparent. It may *seem* easier to live with the concept of a permanent, autonomous self, but this is deceptive.[26] Through holding onto a mistaken concept of self, good and bad actions, causes of future birth and suffering, are undertaken; moreover, to the extent that the present self is over-concretized, one foregoes transformative growth. Still, if what we ordinarily consider self does not exist, what takes rebirth? Clearly, the body does not. In Buddhist countries this is usually burned or, as in Tibet, dismembered and left to feed wild animals. There is no expectation of bodily resurrection. Thus, only some form of mentality or consciousness can take rebirth. This is what is not stopped by death.

In the process of dying, the senses and energies that worked in concert with consciousness deteriorate and so become incapable of supporting the workings of consciousness. Consciousness itself, described as an entity of clarity and knowing, retreats from the sense organs, finally gathering at the center of the heart before departing the body. During this process, the dying person has eight distinct visions, corresponding to the withdrawal of consciousness from specific areas of the body. Meditators study these stages as a traveler might pore over maps of a foreign country. Knowing them serves as a guide. A person familiar with this process is less likely to be frightened by it. Most important, advanced meditators are able to simulate this experience at will, thereby gaining control over this process. Full control is tantamount to Buddhahood and even partial control means one can choose the next rebirth instead of being, as all ordinary persons are, simply blown about by uncontrolled forces unleashed by one's previous activities.

Prior to this, while the dying person can still relate to others, family members and friends are advised to bid the person farewell. Ideally this is done without tears or drama, so as not to cause excessive regret or longing in the dying person. Such states of mind could, in conjunction with tendencies established by non-virtuous activities of this or an earlier life, precipitate an unfortunate rebirth. The state of mind in which one dies is a powerful determinant of the next rebirth. Suicides, therefore, who generally die amid powerful feelings of depression, anger or desperation, are considered at great risk.

These eight stages occur in all living things; in humans they ordinarily span from twelve hours to three days.[27] In more subtle form, the eight transpire each time one goes in or out of sleep or dream, sneezes, faints, or has an orgasm.[28] This is considered a process ingrained in our being, yet we have no awareness or control of it except through considerable training.

The eye organ is the first to be affected; one's eyesight dims and there occurs a mirage-like vision, marking the first of the eight stages. Second, the ear loses its capacity to hear; its humming sound disappears; at this time there is an internal appearance of smoke. Next, the nasal sense is incapacitated; at this third stage one is no longer mindful of the affairs of persons with whom one has been closely involved and one has an internal vision likened to fire-flies in smoke.

During the fourth stage, tongue and body lose their sensory capacities and one ceases to be mindful even of one's own concerns. The internal vision now is of a sputtering candle flame. *Inhalation and exhalation cease.* Nonetheless, four stages remain before the person is considered dead. Usually Buddhists do not disturb the body while the consciousness remains there. To do so makes it even more difficult for the person to accomplish any spiritual purpose during the latter stages. Most accomplished teachers maintain that since ordinary persons cannot remain aware at this time, handling of the body or other disturbances do no harm. Still, out of a sense of respect and, perhaps, an acknowledgment that one cannot know with certainty the capacity of another, peaceful surroundings are preserved. For skilled meditators, an important feature of the fourth stage is that all thought ceases. Because the mind operates without its usual sense of subject and object as distinct, it spontaneously comes to approximate wisdom, the third element of the path. Moreover, being non-dual, clear and steady, it is a powerful consciousness with which to realize emptiness. If one can use this mind to know or merge with emptiness, full enlightenment is at hand.

In the fifth through the eighth stages, one has successive visions likened to the suffusing light of (5) white moonlight, (6) red sunlight, (7) black darkness and (8) white dawn pervading a clear, expansive sky. It is as if one's mind is wholly fused with the clear sky pervaded by such light. During the period of darkness, the seventh stage, one swoons as in a faint and then awakens into what is called the *clear light of death,* the eighth stage. At this time consciousness exists as a very subtle mind sustained by a subtle form of energy that, having withdrawn from the extremities, abides at the heart center. The more one can remain aware during these eight stages, the more likely it is one will remember this life after rebirth. For, according to the present Dalai Lama,

> This is like the fact that if at night before going to sleep we strongly determine with clear awareness what time we want to rise in the morning and what we are going to do after rising, then even if while asleep we are not remembering this, due to the previous intentionality we rise right at that time and immediately remember what we are to do.[29]

Witnesses report some persons have remained in the clear light as if asleep for weeks without any odor coming from the body, even in the heat of India.[30] The consciousness has not yet left the body; it is radiantly non-dualistic, thus enhancing one's possibility of deepening realization of selflessness such that one can complete the causes of enlightenment. If successful, the consciousness can proceed at will to its next manifestation.

During these stages the dying person's religious teacher, a knowledgeable friend or relative, may recite instructions, reminding one to remain calm and aware of the clear light of death. Prayers, mantra recitation, incense or other offerings may also be made for the person's benefit. The subtle consciousness has innumerable predispositions for happy and unhappy rebirth; dying with a virtuous mind such as a wish for others' happiness, in a peaceful meditative state, or in reflection on impermanence or emptiness, can cause virtuous predispositions to take precedence over non-virtuous ones, thus sending one to a good situation. The prayers and blessings of friends and teachers may also have this effect. The essential presumption is that one's existence continues; thus, there is a saying in Tibetan that although there are persons who have died, there are no dead persons.[31]

Once the consciousness leaves the body, an occurrence augured by excretions from nose, genitals, or both, relatives may dispose of the corpse. The body of a highly regarded meditator is often displayed for a time so that disciples and others may pay respects by circumambulating and bowing down to it. In any case, disposal of the body, though usually presided over by a religious figure who leads recitation of appropriate prayers, is not the central concern of Buddhist ritual at this time. Focus is on the consciousness that is now in a particularly precarious situation.

For an indeterminate time, the mind of clear light remains utterly still. Then the merest quiver of movement occurs within it and the eight visions commence in reverse order, beginning with the all-pervasive blackness. From this moment one is in the intermediate state. The all-pervasive red and white appearances then arise in sequence, through to the mirage-like vision. Having departed the body, the unit of subtle energy and consciousness that had gathered at the heart is in a state between death and rebirth. One may not realize immediately that one has died, but try to converse with friends and relatives. Their lack of response is puzzling until one understands what has happened. During this period one can travel anywhere instantaneously; although without a material physical body, one has the capacities of all five senses. One's mental body is indestructible; also, it is not obstructed by walls, mountains or anything except its future place of rebirth. The intermediate state is traditionally said to last no more than 49 days. Like tumbling into a dream, delightful and terrifying images can occur. An extensive literature, of which the *Tibetan Book of the Dead* is but one example, describes experiences that may occur at this time. If while alive one trained in visualization and other meditative techniques to become familiar with them, peaceful and wrathful deities famous in Tantric iconography can appear. If one is deluded as to their nature, one cannot avoid being plunged into rebirth at the mercy of one's own past actions. However, if on the basis of previous practice one recognizes the nature of these and moves toward them, instead of toward less frightening apparitions of light, which treacherously lead to rebirth and suffering, one can gain the enlightenment one failed to achieve during the clear light of death.[32] Persons able to recognize when they are dreaming and who can control dream events are in a good position to remain aware in the intermediate state. By realizing the true status of intermediate state visions, one can be freed from uncontrolled rebirth.

Prayers for the well-being of a person in the intermediate state are recited daily or weekly for 49 days. These prayers, conducted by monks or teachers and usually attended by the family can involve considerable ritual, but the purpose is simple: to remind the departed that she or he is in the intermediate state, that the manifold appearances cannot harm unless one is deceived by them and that one has an opportunity for liberation. Prayers are also made to increase the potency of the person's good actions or karma, so that these, rather than any unwholesome ones, propel the next rebirth.

Until rebirth occurs, one whirls unimpeded over vast distances, until finally, impelled by one's own previous actions, one is driven to the womb, egg or other environment from where one will be reborn. In the case of humans, the consciousness is attracted by its vision of a copulating couple and enters into the midst of the drop of sperm and blood in the mother's womb. If one is to be born as a female, one rushes there due to an overwhelming attraction to the father, and if as a male, out of attraction to the mother.[33]

This drop containing the subtle consciousness is the core around which the body forms and the receptacle into which the consciousness later dissolves at death. Thus, everything included in the name "person" folds and unfolds from the mind of clear light. The sequential visions culminating with clear light mark one's death from the intermediate state; a continuation of such clear light enters the center of the semen and blood of father and mother, making the connection to the new life. Then the other visions arise and with them associated factors such as dualistic thought and the capacity to function in concert with sense and mental consciousness.[34] This emergence from and dissolution into the mind of clear light can be likened to the workings of a kaleidoscope. Rich designs spiral out of its empty white space, then dissolve back again, only to emerge in an altogether different configuration. Complexity and brilliance of design in no way undermines the essential clarity that is the design's source and foundation. However, whereas everything arises from within the kaleidoscope, Buddhists believe that the new individual's consciousness, unlike the body, does not result from the union of father and mother.

Why presume that the consciousness originates elsewhere than in the new mother's womb? Buddhists in general agree that although form and consciousness function in close alignment, one cannot cause the other. Only form can act as a cause of material form and only a consciousness as a cause of consciousness. For, all impermanent things must have a cause similar in substance to themselves. The substantial cause of a clay pot, for example, is clay; of a table, wood, and so forth. Consciousness cannot arise solely from material causes. Thus, the mind — like cyclic existence — is beginningless. It always arises as the effect of a former moment of mind. Mother and father provide the physical bases in connection with which a mind can function, but the material substances of sperm and egg cannot themselves produce consciousness.

Just as issues associated with impermanence and death are woven throughout the fabric of the Buddhist path, so it is with rebirth. We have seen that the prospect of endless rebirths is an incentive to leave cyclic existence and that this motivation is the first of three classic elements of religious practice in the Indo-Tibetan tradition. Moreover, given that everyone has experienced countless rebirths, we have all been in every possible relationship to one another — most importantly, mother, father and best friend. In short, we have a long and intimate history with others during which we have received much kindness for which we can be grateful and which it is appropriate to repay. On this basis, and recognizing that, like oneself, everyone must face death and uncertain rebirth, one cultivates concern for others' well-being.[35] Thus, discussion of rebirth reinforces the second element required for highest enlightenment — the chief Mahayana method of compassion.

Perception of life as a kaleidoscopic continuum of change can counter an overly solidified identification of oneself and others as limited to the present condition. It denies an inherent identification with one's present mind and body and in this way loosens the misconceived sense of self. Indeed, the premise of rebirth is used to aid development of the third essential element of religious practice, wisdom. Such wisdom transforms the mind, vanquishing the misunderstanding that is an essential component of the cyclic existence. When the mistaken conception of inherent existence is overcome, the otherwise intractable cycle of actions and their effects — the workings of karma — is broken. Thus, although no beginning can be assigned to the process of wandering among the regions of rebirth, enlightenment brings one's own wandering to an end. Anyone who achieves the compassion and insight necessary for this state attains it, whether Buddhist or not; the advantage Buddhism sees for itself is its rich textual and oral traditions that detail the theoretical principles and methods most efficacious for accomplishing this goal.

Finally, descriptions of dying, death, the intermediate state and rebirth bespeak a profound optimism regarding human potential. The mind is deeper than its ordinary uses lead us to suspect; it is capable of sustained, conscious activity even when dualistic conceptions like subject and object, on which all ordinary experience is based, vanish. When its capacity is realized, mind is transformed. In this way, descriptions of death and rebirth are meant to reveal the processes by which ordinary persons achieve full enlightenment. Analysis of these processes provides a basis for understanding the enlightened state, with its capacity for consciously choosing future births, as a style of endless activity on behalf of all other, closely related, living beings. Underscoring this is the possibility that one can entirely overcome rigid, obscuring conceptions while still retaining vibrance and clarity of mind. Finally, for Buddhists, the profound harmony of variegated appearances with such clarity points to the possibility of enlightened, compassionate engagement with the world.

EDITOR'S NOTES

The goal of Buddhism is to achieve enlightenment and thereby be set free of the cycle of death and rebirth (in other words, to gain acceptance into heaven and avoid hell). Buddha taught that whenever the world is in decline another Buddha will come to renew it. Therefore, he taught that God does not leave humanity alone and will send "Manifestations of Himself" at different stages throughout history. Scholars disagree on whether Buddhism is a deistic religion. Although traditionally God was rarely discussed in Buddhist scripture, modern scholars have emphasized how Buddha referred to God as the "Eternal," the "Unoriginated" or the "Causeless Cause." Jameshed K. Fozdar's book, *The God of Buddha*, is one of the first real efforts to eliminate centuries of erroneous non-deistic representations of Buddha's message.

Notes

1. Chronology here follows A.K. Warder, *Indian Buddhism* (Delhi: Motilal Banarsidas, 1970), p. 44.
2. Hindu gods were occasionally appropriated into Buddhist stories, probably to impress their Hindu audiences. The deities here are the Shuddhadhivasa — pure-dwelling or perfumed gods — mentioned by Ashvagosha in the *Deeds of the Buddhas* (Buddha carita). See deBary, ed., *The Buddhist Tradition* (New York: Modern Library, 1969), p. 61.
3. "Deeds of the Buddha," translated by Edward Conze in *Buddhist Scriptures* (Middlesex, England: Penguin Books, 1968), p. 40; see also *The Buddhist Tradition*, p. 64.
4. *Buddhist Scriptures*, p. 43; see also *The Buddhist Tradition*, p. 65.
5. This is how the future Buddha justifies leaving home when urged by his father to remain a householder: "O King, if I were given a guarantee on four matters.... That my life would not be committed to death; that my health would not be overcome by disease; that my youth would not be marred by old age; and that prosperity would not be taken away by disaster" (*The Buddhist Tradition*, p. 66).
6. A traditional Tibetan interpretation. See Jeffrey Hopkins, *Meditation on Emptiness* (London: Wisdom Publications, 1983), pp. 353-355; see also Khetsun Sangpo, *Tantric Practice in Nyingma* (Ithaca: Snow Lion, 1982), pp. 57-58.
7. *Meditation on Emptiness*, p. 392.
8. See *Compassion in Tibetan Buddhism* (Ithaca: Snow Lion, 1980), pp. 170-171, for Tsong-ka-pa's views on the meaning of cessation; this is a translation of *dbU ma dgongs ba rab gsal (Illumination of the Thought)* (Dharamsala: Tibetan Cultural Printing Press, n.d.), p. 34.22.
9. The Cittamatra (Mind-Only) school of Asanga is the major exception.
10. Kenneth Ch'en, *Buddhism in China* (Princeton: Princeton University Press, 1964), pp. 20-21.
11. Major sources for historical overview here, in addition to Ch'en, are: Richard Robinson and Willard Johnson, assisted by Kathryn Tsai and Shinzen Young, *The Buddhist Religion* (Belmont, CA: Wadsworth, 3rd ed., 1982), and H. Byron Earhart, *Japanese Religion* (Belmont, CA: Wadsworth, 3rd ed., 1982).

12. Two excellent sources for the history of Tibet are: Snellgrove and Richardson, *A Cultural History of Tibet* (Boulder: Prajna Press, 1980), and R.A. Stein, *Tibetan Civilization* (Stanford: Stanford University Press, 1983).
13. *Bhayabherasutta (Discourse on Fear and Trembling)* from *Majjhima-Nikaya* (London: Pali Text Society), I:22, translated by I.B. Horner as *Middle Length Sayings*, Vol. I (London: Pali Text Society, 1976), p. 29.
14. For a discussion of theological and philosophical implications of a creatorless religious paradigm, see A. Klein, "Non-Dualism and the Great Bliss Queen," in the *Journal of Feminist Studies in Religion*, Vol. I, Spring 1985.
15. In a faculty colloquium at Harvard Divinity School, Spring 1983.
16. This discussion is largely from Tsong-ka-pa, *Great Exposition of the Stages of the Path (Lam rim chen mo)* (Dharamsala: Shes rig par Khang, 1964), p. 65b.1ff. My presentation is also based on lectures delivered by Ven. Lati Rinbochc, abbot emeritus of Ganden Shardzay Monastic College in Mundgod, India, while Visiting Professor at the University of Virginia in 1977. He synopsized the three main headings into nine segments:

    I. Death is definite.
      a. Death will come and we will not be able to escape it.
      b. Life diminishes uninterruptedly; we cannot augment it.
      c. A normal life leaves little time for religious practice — one is too young, too busy with family, or too old.

    II. Death's coming is unpredictable.
      a. Life in general is short; moreover, the young and healthy may die before the old and infirm.
      b. There are many causes of life, few of death and the former can easily turn into the latter.
      c. The body is weak and susceptible.

    III. Only religious practice is of help at death.
      a. Wealth is no help.
      b. Friends and relatives cannot help.
      c. The body cannot help at that time.

    Similar themes are discussed by Gam-po-pa in *The Jewel Ornament of Liberation*, translated by Herbert Guenther (Boulder: Prajna Press, 1981), pp. 41-54. For a Theravada meditation on death, see Buddhaghosa, *The Path of Purification (Visuddhimagga)*, translated by Bhikhu Nyanamoli (Boulder: Shambala, 1976), pp. 248-259.
17. A strikingly similar theme appears in the *Path of Purification*, (p. 251) where, as part of the meditation on death, one compares oneself to a famous person of great merit, strength or power.
18. Translated by Donald S. Lopez, Jr., unpublished ms., 1984. Tsong-ka-pa here appears to echo a motif of the Samyutta Nikaya (i. 109), quoted in the *Path of Purification*, p. 249:

    The nights and days go slipping by
    As life keeps dwindling steadily
    Till mortals' spans, like water pools
    In falling rills, is all used up.
19. *dpyad sgom* and *'jog sgom*. These Tibetan terms appear to have no Sanskrit equivalents. They are analogues, but not equivalents, of the more well-known terms

"insight" (Skt. *vipasyana,* Tib. *hlag mthong)* and "calm abiding" (Skt. *samatha,* Tib. *gzhi gnas*).

20. A similar perspective emerges in, for example, existential psychotherapy. Irvin D. Yalom, a major proponent, finds failure to come to terms with death to be an eminent source of psychological dysfunction. An unrecognized fear of annihilation can vent itself in symptoms such as fear of becoming a true adult, reluctance to complete relationships or projects lest one be "finished," or an exaggerated sense of specialness. See Irvin D. Yalom, *Existential Psychotherapy* (New York: Basic Books, 1980), especially pp. 27-49 and 117ff.
21. Sufferings of the six realms of rebirth are detailed in numerous texts; see, for example, *Tantric Practice in Nyingma,* pp. 64-72.
22. Classification of motivation is from *Compassion in Tibetan Buddhism,* pp. 17-21. The first section of this book is an excellent introduction to Tibetan Buddhism, especially the conjunction of its ethical perspective — exemplified by the altruistic intention to attain enlightenment — with the transcendent wisdom which such empowers.
23. See *Compassion in Tibetan Buddhism*, p. 120ff, for a translation of p. 65. 22ff in Tsong-ka-pa's *Illumination of the Thought,* commenting on v.4 abc of Chandrakirti's *Entry to the Middle Way (Madhyamakavatara).*
24. Ibid.
25. See Tsong-ka-pa's *Three Principal Aspects of the Path (Lam gyi 'dzo bo 'rnam gsum),* translated by Geshe Sopa and Jeffrey Hopkins, in *Practice and Theory in Tibetan Buddhism* (London: Rider, 1976), and by Geshe Wangyal, in *The Door of Liberation* (New York: Girodias, 1973).
26. See Yalom's discussion of this, p. 117ff.
27. For a full description of these, see Rinboche and Hopkins, *Death, the Intermediate State and Rebirth* (Ithaca: Snow Lion, 1979). The present discussion of these stages is taken from the text, a translation by the 18th-century scholar A-skya Yongs'dzin of *Lamp Thoroughly Illuminating the Three Basic Bodies*, in *The Collected Works of A-skya Yongs'dzin,* Vol. I (New Delhi: Lama Guru Deva, 1971).
28. Ibid., p. 20
29. His Holiness Tenzin Gyatso, 14th Dalai Lama, in *Kindness, Clarity, and Insight* (Ithaca: Snow Lion, 1984), p. 177.
30. Ibid., p. 178. The Dalai Lama states that since 1959, when Tibetan refugees began arriving in India, approximately ten instances of incorruption have occurred. The scholar-meditator Denma Locho Rinboche reports that Para Rinboche, a high-ranking monk of Ganden Monastic University, remained for seven days in Buxador, India: "His body did not decay despite the fact that it was subjected to the heat of many butter lamps left as offerings in addition to the great heat of the area itself" (unpublished University of Virginia transcript, p. 71).
31. Ven. Denma Locho Rinboche, University of Virgina seminar, 1979.
32. *Kindness, Clarity and Insight*, p. 180. Texts such as the one by A-skya Yongs'dzin, our main source here on stages of death, describe the intermediate state solely in terms of the powers one possesses there and how one enters and leaves it. There is no reference to the appearance of deities, something that is so stressed in works such as *The Tibetan Book of the Dead* which have dominated western understanding of Tibetan views of the intermediate state. The latter text is not explic-

it about whether such appearances are "automatic" or not; the implication seems to be that they are. For a clear description of the series of intermediate state visions, see Freemantle and Trungpa, *The Tibetan Book of the Dead* (Boulder: Shambala, 1975).

33. *Jewel Ornament of Liberation* (Boulder: Prajna Press, 1981), p. 63.
34. See *Death, the Intermediate State and Rebirth*, p. 58ff.
35. For a seven-fold meditation developing love and compassion based on this principle, see *Compassion in Tibetan Buddhism,* pp. 1-50.

Christian Science

Elaine R. Follis, PhD

HISTORY AND ORGANIZATION

Apart from issues of theology, two facts about Christian Science are noteworthy — it is a religion that was founded by a woman and it is a religion native to the United States. The Church of Christ, Scientist was established by Mary Baker Eddy in Boston, Massachusetts. Today, somewhat more than 100 years later, its Christian ministry of spiritual healing has adherents around the globe.

Christian Science is firmly established on the Bible. The Bible brought direction, inspiration and healing to the life of the woman who discovered Christian Science and opened the door to her extraordinary healing ministry. Mary Morse Baker was born in Bow, New Hampshire in 1821. The youngest of six children, she grew up in a family environment characterized by responsible citizenship, hard work, devout Calvinism and the idealism and independence of spirit typical of 19th-century New England. In her autobiography, *Retrospection and Introspection*, she describes how she regarded her gentle mother as a mentor in matters spiritual, how scriptural tradition and idiom formed the centerpiece of her culture and how openness to direct revelation from God early became a part of her nature.[1]

As a young woman, Mary Baker learned firsthand the devastating effect death can have on a family. The demise in 1841 of her beloved older brother, Dartmouth-educated attorney Albert Baker, cut short a promising political career and profoundly affected Mary. Then, seven months after a happy marriage to George Glover, he suddenly fell ill and died. Five years later her beloved mother, too, passed away. In the wake of these tragedies, she sought a home for herself and her young son, born three months after Glover's death. A second marriage, to Daniel Patterson, whose promise to reunite her with her son proved as empty as his promise to be faithful, ended in divorce. Mary Baker moved from boarding house to boarding house, eking out a living and finding no lasting comfort. Although she investigated various health care methods of the day, including conventional medicine and homeopathy, her health and hope were failing. Throughout this time, she remained a faithful student of the Bible. Then a dramatic event took place in which she herself came "near the confines of mortal existence, standing already within the shadow of the death-valley."[2]

The year was 1866. One wintry day in February, Mary Baker fell on an icy patch of sidewalk and sustained serious internal injuries that were expected to be fatal. She called for her Bible and turned to an account of Christ Jesus' healing. Years of familiarity with and love for the Scriptures suddenly culminated in a moment of profound insight and she was healed. She later described this event as "the falling apple that led me to the discovery how to be well myself and how to make others so."[3]

Although she welcomed the physical relief after years of suffering, Mary Baker set out to learn what power had brought about her cure. She now dug even deeper into the Bible, convinced that Scripture contained the answer she sought. The second half of her life was filled with the task of establishing what she had discovered, which she later called Christian Science, so that others might benefit from it as she had. Convinced she had found the Christianity that Christ Jesus taught — the spiritual laws by which he had healed both sickness and sin — she began to tell others about them and proved their validity by healing. In 1875, nine years after her healing, she published the first edition of the Christian Science textbook, initially titled *Science and Health*; the words *with Key to the Scriptures* were added later. She spent the remainder of her life clarifying the language and expression of this, her principal work. The book first appeared under the name Mary Baker Glover; when she married Asa Gilbert Eddy in 1877, she adopted the name Mary Baker Eddy, by which she is best known.

In addition to *Science and Health*, Mrs. Eddy authored a number of books and sermons that have been published collectively under the title *Prose Works*.[4] She also wrote *The Manual of The Mother Church*, a slim volume that continues to govern the church and its branches. She established five Christian Science periodicals, the best known of which is *The Christian Science Monitor*, an international newspaper that continues to be a vital feature of the church.

The Church of Christ, Scientist was first organized in 1879 and 13 years later was reorganized to its present arrangement. Guided by the *Manual*, a self-perpetuating group of five members known as The Christian Science Board of Directors oversees all church activities. The Board elects church officers, appoints Christian Science lecturers, approves teachers of Christian Science and maintains publishing activities.

Branch churches as well as Christian Science Organizations for faculty and students at colleges and universities have spread to nearly 70 countries. The government of these churches and organizations is local and democratic. Also, The Mother Church and its branches have no clergy. Although Mrs.

Eddy and some of her students preached sermons until 1895, she later ordained the Bible and *Science and Health* as pastor of The Mother Church and all of its branches worldwide. At each Christian Science church service, elected lay members read from the Bible and *Science and Health.* In addition to a Sunday service, which features a Bible lesson studied throughout the preceding week by Christian Scientists everywhere, Christian Science churches hold Wednesday meetings where testimonies of healing are given by those attending. Christian Science churches conduct Sunday school exercises for those under 20 years of age, maintain Christian Science Reading Rooms where the public is invited to read or purchase Christian Science literature and sponsor public lectures on Christian Science. Local Committees on Publication serve as spokespersons for the church to officials in local government and the media.

Christian Science practitioners are experienced church members who have received instruction from a teacher of Christian Science and whose spiritual growth and Christian discipleship have prepared them for the full-time healing ministry. Christian Science nurses give practical, non-medical care to those relying on Christian Science treatment.

ASPECTS OF PRACTICE

To a Christian Scientist, theology is the understanding of God which, applied in daily experience, glorifies Him by revealing the health and harmony that characterize His creation. Christian Scientists see their theology as a statement of the universal principles that underlie Jesus' Christianity and are at the heart of its healing practice. Christ Jesus, the Master Christian, explained his practical theology:

> the works that I do in my Father's name, they bear witness of me.... If I do not the works of my Father, believe me not. But if I do, though ye believe not me, believe the works: that ye may know and believe that the Father is in me and I in him.[5]

He also promised:

> He that believeth on me, the works that I do shall he do also; and greater works than these shall he do; because I go unto my Father. And whatsoever ye shall ask in my name, that will I do, that the Father may be glorified in the Son.[6]

Christian Scientists maintain that the essence of Christian theology is found in its practice. This is how Christ Jesus showed his divine authority; and this is an essential way in which Christianity shows its spiritual origin and nature.

A set of six tenets articulates significant aspects of Christian Science theology. Responding to the question, "Have Christian Scientists any religious creed?" *Science and Health* states:

> They have not, if by that term is meant doctrinal beliefs. The following is a brief exposition of the important points or religious tenets, of Christian Science:
>
> 1. As adherents of Truth, we take the inspired Word of the Bible as our sufficient guide to eternal Life.
> 2. We acknowledge and adore one supreme and infinite God. We acknowledge His Son, one Christ; the Holy Ghost or divine Comforter; and man in God's image and likeness.
> 3. We acknowledge God's forgiveness of sin in the destruction of sin and the spiritual understanding that casts out evil as unreal. But the belief in sin is punished so long as the belief lasts.
> 4. We acknowledge Jesus' atonement as the evidence of divine, efficacious Love, unfolding man's unity with God through Christ Jesus the Way-shower; and we acknowledge that man is saved through Christ, through Truth, Life and Love as demonstrated by the Galilean Prophet in healing the sick and overcoming sin and death.
> 5. We acknowledge that the crucifixion of Jesus and his resurrection served to uplift faith to understand eternal Life, even the allness of Soul, Spirit and the nothingness of matter.
> 6. And we solemnly promise to watch and pray for that Mind to be in us which was also in Christ Jesus; to do unto others as we would have them do unto us; and to be merciful, just and pure.[7]

Every member of The Mother Church, The First Church of Christ, Scientist, subscribes to these tenets, which provide a brief but comprehensive overview of ideas basic to the teachings of Christian Science. Some elements are quite typical of mainstream Christianity, such as the central authority of Scripture, the saving grace of God and the Lordship of Christ Jesus. One important difference, however, concerns the concept taught by Christian Science that reality is spiritual, not material. Scriptural authority for this assertion is found in the first chapter of Genesis, which characterizes creation as the expression of God and as "very good," like God Himself. It teaches that man — generic term for His children, male and female — made in the image and likeness of God as part of a divinely created universe that is complete and harmonious. Christian Science describes God, not simply as the creator or sustainer of life, but as Life itself, expressed throughout all creation. All being exists in God, the divine Mind. This spiritual universe, Christian Science maintains, is reality and it is to be progressively shown forth in how one lives, works, speaks and thinks. Thus to a Christian Scientist the term "spirituality" points to the basic nature of man's eternal relationship with God.

According to Christian Science, the material world of good and evil that is described in the second and third chapters of Genesis is a counterfeit, a waking dream, a distorted view of reality. Matter, the objectification of this view, has no actual substance, but is a kind of illusion, a distorted image in thought. To the physical senses, matter appears solid and real and has influence and power to the degree that people believe it. Thought and behavior based on this mortal, material sense of life is what Christian Scientists mean by sin. As such, sin is not an inevitable condition into which each human being is born, but is, rather, the initial error or mistaken view that God and His creation are material, not spiritual; that there are many mortal minds, not just one divine Mind, God; that life naturally includes disease and moral discord; and that life inevitably ends in death.

The mission of Christ Jesus was to destroy sin, sickness and death by awakening human consciousness from these illusions and showing — by way of his own example — man's essential identity as the idea, the image, of God. This was the deep significance of his healing ministry: not only to bring relief from pain or to wield miraculous power in people's lives, but to show them how to be what God made man to be — the wholly pure and perfect expression of His being. Christ Jesus taught his followers, in antiquity and today, that they have divine authority to banish pain, sickness and disease. These are contrary to God's will and have no place in His spiritual and wholly good creation. Death is the ultimate illegitimate assertion that matter, not Spirit, is real and that man, the expression of God, can be destroyed. Christian Scientists view the crucifixion, death and resurrection of Christ Jesus as actual fact and consider the resurrection as evidence of the victory over the "last enemy" called death. Death did not destroy Christ Jesus and death cannot destroy any of God's children.

When discord of whatever sort appears, healing is the natural outcome of rejecting the distorted and erroneous testimony of the physical senses and knowing the powerful truth that God and His creation always have been and now are spiritual and perfect. Even a modest healing in Christian Science affirms, through faith and in experience, God's perpetual, universal, loving care and man's present perfection. Also, the individual healed, more often than not, experiences moral and spiritual regeneration in Christian character. The following "scientific statement of being," together with I John 3:1-3 as correlative Scripture, is read in Christian Science churches at the conclusion of each Sunday service.

> There is no life, truth, intelligence, nor substance in matter. All is infinite Mind and its infinite manifestation, for God is All-in-all. Spirit is immortal Truth; matter is mortal error. Spirit is the real and eternal; matter is the unreal and temporal. Spirit is God and man is His image and likeness. Therefore man is not material; he is spiritual.[8]

More than a century of Christian Science practice shows that the understanding of the reality and allness of Spirit and the corresponding unreality and nothingness of matter changes human experience for the better and reveals God's loving, healing presence under the direst of human circumstances.

Because sin, disease and death are regarded, not as solid reality, but as consequences of a mistaken view of creation, Christian Science treatment or prayer addresses, not discordant matter, but *thought*, presenting to it the spiritual facts that establish God's absolute goodness and power until the testimony of the physical senses yields to the truth of being. Christian Science teaches that body is not matter, but thought externalized. When thought changes, its object — body — changes also. When thought is spiritualized, the natural harmony that characterizes all creation appears. Mrs. Eddy explains: "The effect of this Science is to stir the human mind to a change of base, on which it may yield to the harmony of the divine Mind."[9] The words "divine Mind" are supremely important in this statement. Christian Science is not "mind over matter" or the effect of human will governing the body. Christian Science practice is the operation of the laws of God, the one divine Mind. Healing takes place as individuals relinquish the belief of a mind separate from God and realize God as their very Life and Mind. Christian Scientists strive to know themselves and others only as God knows them: as His wholly good and perfect offspring. To a Christian Scientist this is what is meant by the biblical exhortation, "Let this mind be in you, which was also in Christ Jesus."[10]

The consistent practice of Christian Science involves dedication to the spirit of Christian discipleship — especially its ethical principles, based on unconditional love. The development of such dedication calls for repentance, humility and patience — learning to let each thought, word and act flow forth from God as the expression of His nature rather than as some personal accomplishment. In line with this, Christian Scientists abstain from practices and activities that would impede their ability to pray and think clearly, including the use of tobacco, alcohol and drugs.

God is always the power in the healing work. This fact and its results in experiences both small and great, gives Christian Scientists the confidence to rely on God to meet their every need, as Christ Jesus did. Experience, not blind faith, lends conviction to their practice. Some families can point to four generations of evidence that Christian Science practice promotes consistent health in body, in mind and in spirit. More than 50,000 verified accounts published in the Christian Science periodicals over the past 115 years represent only a small sampling of the experiences that constitute the active healing ministry of Christian Science in this age.

CONCEPTS AND PRACTICES RELATING TO DEATH

The approach that Christian Scientists take to death and the afterlife is summed up in this basic conviction: that Life is God — eternal and spiritual, present here and now, the only reality. Mary Baker Eddy's article, "Is There No Death?" includes the words, "as there is but one God, there can be but one Life."[11] Christian Scientists endeavor to live out the implications of this conviction on the basis of the following concepts and practices.

Concepts

Christian Science teaches that death results from the persistent, universal, but mistaken belief that Life — God — enters into matter and later departs from matter. In Christian Science, Life is understood to be eternal, changeless and entirely spiritual. Life is God, perpetually expressed throughout His creation. Life never ends; therefore death, because it is not of God, must be fundamentally unreal and untrue.

The assertion that there is no death, like the assertion that sin and disease are unreal, seems at first foolish and illogical. But Christian Scientists, along with the rest of Christendom, look to a higher sense of life than the physical. Many faiths see life as having a spiritual dimension; Christian Scientists find that life is *wholly* spiritual. The qualities commonly associated with heaven — like purity, harmony and perfection — are seen as already fully present, though perceived only indistinctly. Yet their presence is known; most people have experienced glorious moments of awe and beauty in their lives. Such moments provide a "peek" at reality. The study of Christian Science helps to waken consciousness to recognize more and more of this spiritual reality, to understand it and to experience it. To a Christian Scientist, then, heaven is not a place, but a state of thought attuned to God. Hell, conversely, describes a state of thought that is indifferent to or alienated from God — thought impressed by the mistaken belief that life is material and so subject to evil, sin, disease and death.

Christian Science holds that death is never God's will. God's will and His essential nature is always Life. Christ Jesus' ascension illustrates the overcoming and outgrowing of all limitation, of mortality itself. Christian Science teaches that everyone will eventually demonstrate this final freedom from a material sense of life, as sin is fully destroyed and the distortions of physical sense cease to deceive. This is the Christian Scientist's concept of salvation, won individually but available and applicable universally. Christ Jesus' ascension is a giant step beyond death. For now, at least, members of the human family take smaller steps in progressively overcoming mortality, shown in longer, more productive lives and in the healing of grief.

Mary Baker Eddy realized that students of Christian Science would face this greatest human challenge, even as she eventually did. Still, it is worth noting that she healed many, through spiritual means alone, who were very near death, whom doctors had given up or who had apparently died. Also, she herself lived to an advanced age and was unusually active and productive until a short time before her death. She urged patience and practicality in undertaking the task of challenging death, writing:

> During the sensual ages, absolute Christian Science may not be achieved prior to the change called death, for we have not the power to demonstrate what we do not understand. But the human self must be evangelized. This task God demands us to accept lovingly today, and to abandon so fast as practical the material, and to work out the spiritual which determines the outward and actual.[12]

Death is a transition. Christian Science maintains that this transition does not automatically dispel the illusions of physical sense, including sin and disease. Only progress in an accurate understanding of God does that. Christ Jesus proved in his crucifixion and resurrection that death changes nothing. He still bore the wounds inflicted before his death and so convinced his disciples that he was the same individual who had been crucified three days before. A temporary return to a human physical condition after death was part of Christ Jesus' very distinct ministry for the salvation of mankind as a means of proving the ultimate unreality of death. Our progress begins now, in "earth's preparatory school."[13] It continues beyond death until sin is completely abandoned and the individual realizes life as it truly is and knows himself or herself as the wholly spiritual expression of God.

There is no escaping the spiritual lessons demanded of us in this process of salvation. So there is no advantage in suicide or euthanasia as means of "wiping the slate clean." Looking to death as a help or an escape is a mistake. Evil acts bring inevitable distress and must be repented of and repudiated, either before or after death. Yet Christian Science also teaches that every right thought and act during one's human existence manifests spiritual understanding that stays with the individual and is a foundation on which future progress may be built.

It is normal for Christian Scientists to look for evidence of spiritual reality in themselves, in others and in the world around them. They also strive to challenge the "little deaths" that seem so typical of human experience: the death of innocence, of trust, of inspiration or of hope; and the subtle death implied in attitudes of failure, defeat, indifference or apathy. In their dealings with others, they look constantly beyond the body to the qualities of thought and character that constitute true and lasting individuality. And so they find they can heal their grief and learn to know their loved ones who have gone through the experience of death as God knows them: as His pure, spiritual likeness, without the limitations of matter.

Those who have experienced the transition of death continue on in a new state of consciousness and do not communicate further with those who have not died. Spiritualism, therefore, is no part of Christian Science, nor does Christian Science teach reincarnation. And, although Christian Science affirms that life is not material but spiritual, psychic phenomena such as out-of-body experiences and telekinesis are not included in Christian Science practice.

Practices

When Christian Scientists experience the death of a relative or friend, they confront the same sense of grief and loss that anyone else would feel. Sometimes the experience can be very difficult. But they know that the loved one continues as God's image and likeness and is embraced in His Love. This often brings comfort. Another helpful insight, pointing to each individual's true incorporeal existence, is expressed in these words of St. Paul:

> Wherefore henceforth know we no man after the flesh: yea, though we have known Christ after the flesh, yet now henceforth know we him no more.[14]

Mary Baker Eddy well understood the hardships that the experience of death can present. She cherished memories of her mother, of her brother Albert, of George Glover and Asa Gilbert Eddy. When asked, "After the change called death takes place, do we meet those gone before — or does life continue in thought only as in a dream?" she replied:

> Man is not annihilated, nor does he lose his identity, by passing through the belief called death. After the momentary belief of dying passes from mortal mind, this mind is still in a conscious state of existence; and the individual has but passed through a moment of extreme mortal fear, to awaken with thoughts and being, as material as before. *Science and Health* clearly states that spiritualization of thought is not attained by the death of the body, but by a conscious union with God. When we shall have passed the ordeal called death or destroyed this last enemy and shall have come upon the same plane of conscious existence with those gone before, then we shall be able to communicate with and to recognize them.
>
> If, before the change whereby we meet the dear departed, our life-work proves to have been well done, we shall not have to repeat it; but our joys and means of advancing will be proportionately increased.[15]

Because death is never seen in Christian Science as an element of the divine will to which people are to give their assent, martyrdom is inconsistent with the teachings of Christian Science. Death is a lie about God and His creation, and as such, death is to be opposed vigorously and persistently through prayer. Death, the Bible says, is an enemy to be overcome.[16] Even when, despite someone's best efforts, death occurs, Christian Scientists maintain that death is still a lie about Life and man, still a mistaken view of reality. Death changes nothing of God's goodness, His constant care for His creation and the essential spiritual nature of everyone. While Christian Science practice does not seek simply to prolong human life but to awaken individuals from the basic misperception that life is mortal, Christian Scientists certainly expect to enjoy normal, healthy lives. There is no easy explanation to be offered when this does not occur, and death — especially that of a child or young person — is always a human tragedy.

When a Christian Scientist dies, families may choose not to hold observances at all, to have a private service or to have a ceremony at a funeral home, at the graveside or elsewhere. Generally if a casket is present, it is closed and many Christian Scientists choose cremation. A typical memorial service includes readings from the Bible and Mrs. Eddy's writings along with music and prayer. A church reader or a family member or friend may officiate. Obituary notices appear at the family's discretion; it is not unusual for them to encourage donations to a church or favorite charity. Christian Scientists obey pertinent laws and cooperate fully with local coroners and medical examiners and church members lend support in whatever practical ways are needed.

Death touches individuals and families, but on occasion death has gained far greater scope in human affairs. The bitter facts of genocide, for instance, present lessons to the world from which no one can turn away; they demand, more compellingly than ever before, that a deeper spirituality be expressed in daily deeds. The horrors of holocausts, honestly faced, strip away hypocrisy's mask and compel every individual to look deeply into the mirror of self examination, confronting and destroying whatever is unlike God. It urges the practice of a love that expresses the divine nature and that bears within it grace to transform and redeem the world. It reminds us, after all, of the need to know what Life truly is. *Science and Health* states:

> We all must learn that Life is God. Ask yourself: Am I living the life that approaches the supreme good? Am I demonstrating the healing power of Truth and Love? If so, then the way will grow brighter 'unto the perfect day.' Your fruits will prove what the understanding of God brings to man. Hold perpetually this thought — that it is the spiritual idea, the Holy Ghost and Christ, which enables you to demonstrate, with scientific certainty, the rule of healing, based upon its divine Principle, Love, underlying, overlying and encompassing all true being.[17]

An Exemplary Experience

The best way to understand Christian Science is to study its textbook, to apply its teachings oneself or to see those teachings through the eyes of someone who has experienced healing. Christian Science teaches that eternal life is a present fact and many can cite instances when Christian Science treatment saved someone at the very brink of death. Ruth Elizabeth Jenks of Chicago, Illinois, describes such an experience.

> A few years ago I was very actively engaged in work that required total focus and dedication. A physical condition developed that made it impossible to continue.... The constant pain, coupled with a total inability to care for myself, was fertile ground for the subtle claim of death to whisper its tempting tune 'Why hang on?' In my case, the question was provoked not by fear or a feeling of hopelessness but by what appeared to be the logic of the argument that I had already had a wonderful life, satisfying in every aspect, with marriage, children, career, friends, purpose. Also it occurred to me that the world would probably catalog me as an 'old lady'.... Then there was the suggestion that death would be a relief to me from the suffering. I hadn't thought that accepting that suggestion would be a form of suicide. But looking back, I realize that that is exactly what it would have been. Such reasoning was totally inconsistent with what I had been taught [as a Christian Scientist]. It was totally inconsistent with the fact that I had been able to prove the illusive nature of harmful conditions many times throughout my life, as a child and later on as a mother with my own children. And now I was seeing my children proving it with their children. Sin, sickness and death were to be challenged, not accepted as God's will or as inescapable.... I realized that Christianity as taught by Jesus shows man's complete freedom from every material concept or so-called law, including death. I reread the four Gospels in the New Testament, paying special attention to five specific instances in which Jesus challenged death.... I soon discovered the answer to 'why hang on?' In fact, it ceased to be a question in my thought. I was too busy expressing life more fully — first by turning away from the questioning to spiritual reasoning and then by moving beyond simply expecting a change of evidence to accepting that change as my natural state of being. I had needed to persevere, to hang on! As a result, not only was the healing complete but all suggestions that the problem had been a wearisome ordeal vanished in the joy of discovery — discovery that the mythological, theological and philosophical misconceptions of life as in or of matter and subject to death have no actual power over any of us. Once the illusion was exposed, I found myself experiencing greater mental, spiritual and physical activity than ever before, and all of it with real purpose.[18]

Experiences like this one are inspiring and illustrate the healing works of which Christian Science is capable. Christian Science proclaims Life.

Notes

1. Mary Baker Eddy, *Retrospection and Introspection* (Boston: The Christian Science Publishing Society, 1891); hereafter *Ret.* In addition to Mrs. Eddy's own account of events in her life, numerous books have been written about her by both supporters and detractors. The most comprehensive scholarly biography to date is a three-volume set by Robert Peel, a Christian Scientist, published from 1966 through 1977.
2. Mary Baker Eddy, *Science and Health with Key to the Scriptures* (Boston: The Christian Science Publishing Society, 1875), p. 10; hereafter *S&H.*
3. *Ret.*, p. 24.
4. *Prose Works* include *Miscellaneous Writings* (1896); *Retrospection and Introspection* (1891); *Unity of Good* (1887); *Pulpit and Press* (1895); *Rudimental Divine Science* (1891); *No and Yes* (1891); *Christian Science versus Pantheism* (1898); three *Messages to The Mother Church* (1900, 1901, 1902); *Christian Healing* (1886); *The People's Idea of God* (1886); and *The First Church of Christ, Scientist and Miscellany* (1913).
5. John 10:25, 37, 38. All biblical quotations are from the King James Version.
6. John 14:12, 13.
7. *S&H*, pp. 496-497.
8. *S&H,* p. 468.
9. *S&H,* p. 162.
10. Philippians 2:5.
11. *Unity of Good,* p. 37.
12. *S&H,* p 254.
13. *S&H*, p. 486.
14. II Corinthians 5:16.
15. Mary Baker Eddy, *Miscellaneous Writings* (Boston: The Christian Science Publishing Society, 1896), p. 42.
16. I Corinthians 15:26.
17. *S&H,* p. 496.
18. This experience was published in an article entitled "Death: A Mythological Misconception," in *The Christian Science Journal* (Vol. 115, No. 4, April 1997), pp. 4-6.

The Churches of Christ

Thomas H. Olbricht, PhD

BACKGROUND OF THE FAITH

The Churches of Christ in America result from an indigenous American movement seeking to restore the church of the New Testament. For this reason, the term "Restoration Movement" has been employed as a self-designation, though this particular phraseology is not widely employed to identify these churches by outsiders. Three sizable constituencies jelled from the early beginnings. The names of these groups are more widely recognized: (1) The Disciples of Christ, (2) The Christian Churches and (3) The Churches of Christ.[1] The Churches of Christ tend to be the most theologically conservative of the three. They are the conservative wing of the first major split in the movement identified independently by the federal Census Bureau in 1906. Today, the Churches of Christ have more than 2 million members throughout the world, most of whom live in the United States.[2] The majority in the United States are located in the region running from Pittsburgh to El Paso, with the northern border extending from Pittsburgh through Indianapolis, St. Louis, Wichita and Albuquerque and the southern through Atlanta, Montgomery, Baton Rouge, Houston and San Antonio.

HISTORICAL ROOTS

The roots of the Restoration Movement extend backward to the period after the Revolutionary War in which several Americans with religious interests grew restless over autocratic structure, confessional boundaries and European control and theology. These pressures revamped the mainline churches, but also resulted in independent constituencies springing up in various regions. Four such groups of independent churches played a role in the crystallization of the Restoration Movement in the 1830s. Two of these groups were in New

England and Virginia. Their roles were contributory rather than direct. In Virginia, in the 1780s, a group of Methodist ministers led by James O'Kelley sought freedom from supervision so that Methodist circuit riders could determine their own itineraries. For a time it seemed they would win out, but the result was that preaching assignments were placed in the hands of the bishop. Those who favored self determination broke away, founding the Republican Methodist Church. In 1794 they changed the name of the body to the Christian Church.[3] In New England, especially in the newly developing regions, persons of Baptist heritage, chiefly Abner Jones and Elias Smith, formed new believing bodies. They went by the name Christian Church or Christian Connexion. They championed defeat of tax support for establishment ministers and rejected the Calvinistic features of Puritan theology. In both cases the Bible was heralded, especially the New Testament, as the only source of authority and faith. In their opinion, Christians should cut adrift from the historical encrustations so as to create the New Testament church in its 1st-century purity.[4]

The two most important tributaries for the larger movement resulted from the work of Barton W. Stone and of Thomas and Alexander Campbell. At the turn of the century, the second Great Awakening titillated the Kentucky and Ohio frontiers. Camp meetings sprang up throughout the region, the largest being the 1801 extravaganza at Cane Ridge, Kentucky, northeast of Lexington. Denominational barriers crumbled away and the call to struggle and conversion diluted traditional election theology. As the months wore on, some of the preachers, especially among the Presbyterians, favored the ecumenical flavor of the awakening. They therefore formed the Springfield Presbytery, the members of which held these sentiments. Not long after, carrying their interests to their logical conclusions, they dissolved the presbytery in order to "sink into union with the body of Christ at large."[5] These leaders found many frontiersmen ready to embrace this view and rapid growth ensued. Barton W. Stone eventually emerged as the chief spokesman.

In 1807, Thomas Campbell (of Scottish descent) arrived in Pennsylvania from Northern Ireland, settling in Washington. A long-time Presbyterian minister, he exerted considerable energy in the land of his nativity, struggling to bring together dissident Presbyterian groups. His efforts at similar rapprochement in Pennsylvania resulted in litigation to oust him from the presbytery in which he was licensed. Seeing the handwriting on the wall, he resigned and with others of like mind, formed the Christian Association of Washington. In 1809, his gifted son Alexander arrived from a stint at the University of Glasgow in Scotland. From these men's efforts, and those allied with them, churches were formed in the region around Pittsburgh. After 1816, the Campbells associated with Baptist ministers, winning several Ohio and Kentucky Baptist churches to their views.[6] The Campbells envisioned a mass exodus of believers from sectarian Protestantism who would become one body, one New Testament church as set forth in the pages of the New

Testament. Early in the 1830s, the churches from the Stone and Campbell groups commenced merging. By 1850, Alexander Campbell, because of his journal editing, book publishing, debating and lecturing, became the best known leader of the movement. His ideas left a permanent stamp on all of his descendants. His views definitely influenced the Churches of Christ even though the leadership of David Lipscomb in the latter part of the 19th century modified some of them.[7]

By the 1830s, immigration patterns brought persons from these four groups together in the border states east of the Mississippi. What occurred was the emergence of a mainstream with all four groups contributing. The Campbell and Stone forces provided the core for the growing constituency. Some churches, however, from the three groups other than the Campbell movement, remained independent even in Ohio and Indiana and in the 1890s formed a coalition of their own.[8]

CENTRAL AFFIRMATIONS

Because of these concerns in their early history, the Churches of Christ have grounded their theology and world views in biblical perspectives as they have ascertained them. Because they placed their emphasis on restoring the New Testament church, they focused on practical aspects of church order and worship. Beliefs about life after death developed out of traditional Protestant conservative views, but always in the light of the scriptures, especially the New Testament.[9]

THE MEANING OF LIFE AND DEATH

By consensus, persons in the Churches of Christ see life on earth as a period in which an individual, living in the face of God's call and command, makes decisions that determine where he will spend eternity. The basic decisions he faces are whether to obey God and thereby become a Christian, and having made that decision, whether to live as a Christian in a style of life consistent with the commands of God.[10]

The sequence of these decisions is as follows: The basic first step should be made when a child reaches a level of maturation at which he can understand commitments and their ramifications. This crucial step is called the age of accountability and is normally thought to be about 12 years old.[11] Children who seem mature and understand that Christ died for their sins may, on occasion, be baptized as young as 8 or 9. In this period, when the child learns of God's action in Christ, he is expected to make a decision whether or not to accept God's gracious gift of salvation. If he decides to respond to the call, he believes that Jesus is the Christ, the Son of God, repents of his sins, confesses his faith "with his lips," and is "buried with his Lord in baptism."[12] He is not considered a Christian until all these stages have been completed, including baptism. Once the decision has been made and acted upon, the crucial matter of where one will spend eternity, that is, heaven, has been settled.

The act of becoming a Christian does not alone, however, settle the matter of eternal destiny. Even a Christian can disobey God and be rejected on the day of judgment. To live eternally with God one must be scrupulous in keeping his commands as found in the New Testament.[13] The one who is faithful until death is permitted beyond the grave to live with God forever in eternal peace and rest. The person who fails to measure up is doomed to eternal punishment, along with all those who failed to become a Christian for whatever reason.

In the conviction of most members of the Churches of Christ, God is one, Jesus is his son, but a different person, and the Holy Spirit is a person, and in the opinion of some, only acts through the influence of the scripture when it is read.[14] In any case, the Holy Spirit does not now convert or teach the ways of God. The scripture and its proclamation is the channel through which God now does his work among men. God is obviously different from man. Not much more can be said except that he is spirit and for that reason other than flesh and blood.

The universe was made by God *ex nihilo,* that is, from nothing through words spoken by God. "And God said, 'Let there be lights in the expanse of the sky to separate the day from the night, and let them serve as signs to mark seasons and days and years, and let them be lights in the expanse of the sky to give light on the earth'" (Genesis 1:14-15). Once created, the universe functions through the natural laws which God set in place. Since the days of creation, any time God has acted in the world it has been necessary that even He suspend the natural laws. Any time God does so a miracle occurs. It is the majority conviction among the members of the Churches of Christ that while God pushed the button to stop the laws several times from Adam to John the Apostle, since the 1st century he has left the universe to pursue its own course consonant with the natural laws. Miracles therefore ceased when the New Testament was completed.[15] Man was created by God in the same manner as the universe. In the case of the first man, Adam, God provided a biological body but a non-organic soul. God creates the soul of each human sometime in or after human conception. The typical view is that God creates the soul at the time of conception and, if not then, at least before birth. A consensus position has not as yet emerged. The soul, once created, is indestructible.[16]

Death is the separation of the soul from the body. The body of flesh and blood remains in the visible human universe. The indissoluble aspect of man, the soul, goes to the place of the dead awaiting the end of history. The soul retains consciousness even after death and is transported to Hades, the place of the dead. Hades is divided into Paradise, where the righteous are settled in and Tartarus, the location for the wicked.[17] At the end of history Jesus will return and the dead will be raised for judgment. Those who have accepted Christ and have lived faithfully according to God's way will enter the heavenly realm of God. Those who have not accepted Christ along with those who failed to live according to their Christian commitment will be punished in Gehenna (Hell) forever. Many church members may not be able to reiterate accurately these details and Bible scholars who work in the Churches of Christ may question whether the New Testament use of these words warrants the traditional delineation; nevertheless these divisions of the place where the dead reside until judgment are perpetuated.[18]

Among members of the Churches of Christ the long-held rule of thumb for interpreting the scripture is that all statements are literal unless the context makes explicit a figurative interpretation. It is therefore the universal conclusion that the devil is a literal person in scripture and must be so construed in conviction.[19] The devil is believed to influence human behavior through working on the emotions and especially during the excitement of extreme passions. Exactly how he accomplishes this feat is not spelled out. It is commonly held that the devil no longer appears to people, talks with them or inhabits their innermost being through demonic possession, though he did so in Biblical times.[20] Satan is always at work distracting and luring the unwary away from the safe fold of God. He rules and controls the lives of those who spurn the salvation offered by God through his Son. One ramification of salvation is that through appropriating it by obedience to Jesus Christ one is saved from the wiles of the devil.

Life is a testing ground. It is a boot camp for soul-making. God is the friend and champion of those who seek what is good. Satan is the great enemy, tempting, distracting and deceiving. The believer is ultimately victorious only if he accepts God's salvific offer and responds openly to the continual presence and assistance of the Son and the Holy Spirit. Death is a traumatic prospect because the merit of the life of most believers is touch and go. The unknown is always a cause for fear and anxiety. The experience of death brings much anxiety, because it is the great unknown. The parameters of the experience of death are unexplored and the prospect that one will have to face up to life's miscues is unnerving. One is continually confronted by the possibility that, even as a believer, at any point he may be weighed in the balance and found wanting.[21] An increasing conviction, however, affirms that if one truly believes in the glorious hope held out by God, fear of death and judgment will abate. With such deep trust one can face death in peace, anticipation and hope.[22]

The prevailing view among members of the Churches of Christ is that suffering and death is caused by sin in certain obvious situations, for example, when a person becomes intoxicated, hits a bridge abutment and dies. It is agreed, however, that on occasion some persons suffer without obvious cause and that death may be inopportune because of both age and situation. In the first six decades of this century, most people held that God in his wisdom has reasons for these inexplicable turns of events.[23] Man, however, has no channel for inside information and cannot ascertain most of the reasons, nor is it proper for him to speculate on them. What we cannot learn now, God will disclose in the end time. The words of an old hymn express well the common sentiment, "We'll understand it better by and by."[24]

The last few years have brought increasing conviction that, in fact, man is not without powers of discernment. If he puts his mind to it and seeks understanding through prayer, he may well be able to ascertain why hardships and catastrophies occur. Suffering may be for the purpose of strengthening faith and conviction, for enabling onlookers to share empathy and goods and for disturbing the complacency of friends and relatives who are unbelievers.[25] If one is open to the ways of God, it may be possible to discern what he is out to accomplish in a series of events. To do so, however, requires a person who is into the Word and prayer.

The common belief among members of the Churches of Christ is that life is a time of sifting and weighing to determine whether, in the life beyond, one will reside in heaven or hell. One is assisted by God or distracted by the devil, but in the final analysis, the decision about whom to follow belongs to the individual. Death is cataclysmic for the unbeliever and the believer who doesn't have his house in order. For the person who has been faithful to the demands of God, however, death is a welcome relief and the passageway to eternal rest in the presence of God and his Son. If one is obedient and follows the path of servanthood, death is not a threat. It is not improper, however, for friends and relatives to mourn and express sorrow. Sorrow on the part of believers is not for the fate of the loved one, but rather for themselves because they can no longer share moments of rejoicing over favorable developments or ponder ominous ones.

FUNERALS

Funeral practices in Churches of Christ vary according to local customs. Most funerals were held in church buildings prior to World War II. Since that time, with the advent of chapels in mortuaries, the majority of funerals are arranged there and not in church buildings. Respected public figures and church leaders, as well as persons known and loved throughout the community, often warrant services in church buildings because mortuary chapels are too small to seat all those who wish to attend. To some extent this development represents a secularizing of the funeral.[26]

The funeral attains only a quasi-religious status as far as most members of the Churches of Christ are concerned. In that regard, it belongs in the same category as the marriage ceremony. That which has official status in the church is identical with that which has scriptural warrant. Scriptural authority prevails for gatherings in which the central focus is the teaching of God's word. That which has the highest priority is the Sunday service or services, normally held in the morning and the evening. These services attain their status by the fact that the five acts of worship authorized by God take place there: singing, praying, preaching, giving and the celebrating of the Lord's supper.[27] A meeting of believers on another day of the week, for example, Wednesday night, contains all these acts, especially teaching (preaching), except for the Lord's supper and the contribution. The funeral, as well as the wedding, however, are not settings in which these worship acts occur. Rather they are extraordinary. Because they do not fall into the regular routine, they are at best quasi-religious. It is proper, however, for the focus to be religious even though the religious overtones are optional. Most members of Churches of Christ would not object to a funeral or a wedding conducted by military regulations, if appropriate and therefore mostly civil in orientation. Funerals probably have become more secular in the last 50 years while weddings have become more religious. Weddings are much more likely to be held in church buildings these days than in former times. While a nonmember civic figure or churchman from another religious group would be prohibited from conducting a worship service, it is acceptable for such persons to conduct or assist with a funeral.[28]

Ministers achieve their status in Churches of Christ as the result of an individual congregation permitting them to function as a minister. For that reason ministers are not ordained as a religious action; such, it is argued, is not in keeping with the scriptures. Any person is qualified to render service to God. In states, however, in which ordination is required for performing marriage ceremonies, the eldership of a church will attest to a minister's ordination without holding a formal ordination ceremony. Because of these convictions any male member is considered qualified to conduct or participate in a funeral. Normally, however, funerals are conducted by the minister or one of the ministers in a multi-staff church or by an elder who may have served as a minister previously.[29]

Fifty years ago most funerals were held in church buildings. The family made most of the arrangements except for the service itself. The preacher was approached about a funeral sermon and that was the extent of his involvement. The service consisted of singing without accompaniment (because musical instruments are prohibited in church buildings), reading the obituary, prayer and extended remarks, usually designated a funeral sermon.[30] The singing was typically congregational, though on occasion a small group or mixed quartet was employed. Comments were made for the benefit of the auditors. They were the ones to contemplate the seriousness and consequences of death and the call of God to a righteous life. It was also considered improper to judge the whereabouts of the deceased, whether in paradise or torment, unless their life and works clearly indicated their destination and even then perilous, because the final decision is up to God. The appropriate course of action in the sermon was to bring the audience to serious confrontation with their own eternal destiny. The occasion of the funeral was thought to be particularly appropriate for observations of this sort because a person's status beyond death is foremost in his mind as he faces the death of an acquaintance, friend or relative. It was therefore the duty of the preacher to set forth the precise ways of God for his church, the plan of salvation and the call for sinners to repent.[31] For believers who had become negligent or dropped out, the sermon was a call to take up former ways and live for God. The sermons therefore tended to be judgmental and were so construed by those directly affected. The service throughout was a strong demand to get one's life in order so as to be prepared to meet God.

Funeral services have changed over the years even though the basic structure remains much the same. These days the minister, especially if well known by the family, is looked to for all sorts of advice and comfort and the normal expectation is that the one called on to do the service will spend considerable time with the family during these trying days. He also visits regularly during the illness if it lasts for an extended period. One reason for these new expectations is that in the 1930s most preachers were evangelists traveling about the country. It was thought they should be out preaching the gospel rather than taking care of individual needs. The singing at the service is now much more likely to be a mixed group of six to twenty. In mortuary chapels, organ music is permissible before and after the service, but is rarely employed in the service proper. The sermon normally focuses on the personal qualities of the deceased and then words of comfort and hope pertaining to the resurrection.[32]

Most of the activities at the time of the death of the church member occur on the day of burial, except that frequently a viewing of the body is arranged the night before at the mortuary. The visiting time extends from one to three hours. Usually several of the relatives are present to greet the visitors.[33] No refreshments are served. If the funeral is in the afternoon, the family gathers at the residence of a relative to eat a light lunch. The food is normally supplied by women from the congregation. When the funeral is over the family will likely eat together again, sometimes in facilities of the church if the group is large. These meals exhibit a serious mood, but not one of mourning. They are convenient occasions for members of the family to catch up on what the children and grandchildren are doing because at least some are likely to live a considerable distance away.[34] During conversations on this occasion, family members are likely to remember some kindness or anecdote about the deceased. A second meal will involve more friendly banter, but also the sadness of saying goodbye to persons with whom little future time together is possible.

A funeral service is always projected as the norm whether in a church building or in a chapel and that is followed by a graveside service. If it is anticipated that only a few persons will be present, graveside rites alone are acceptable. Because worship patterns are never written in books of prayer, no standard liturgy exists for funerals in regard to songs, prayers or sermonic materials.[35] In fact, in recent years, the preferences of the family are consulted and most ministers tailor the prayers, remarks and songs to take into account the deceased, the situation and the preferences of the relatives. Reading scriptures that offer assurance and hope for life beyond the grave is characteristic of most services. Funeral times follow local customs, sometimes in the morning, more frequently in the afternoons in small towns and usually not on Sunday because it is the day of worship. A Sunday afternoon funeral may occur, however, and is acceptable if it is the most convenient time for everyone involved.

The approaches to burial essentially follow the local customs. Normally a funeral plot and casket is purchased and arrangements are made for embalming. The grave is later marked by a standard granite marker, though some cemeteries now prohibit markers. No theological reasons influence the decision whether or not to embalm, whether an autopsy should be performed or whether it is acceptable to donate organs or the body to science.[36] The first two occur according to the laws of the state, local customs and secular needs. The donation of organs and the body now occurs more frequently. Fifty years ago most members of the Churches of Christ lived in rural areas. In that setting the donating of a body to science would be unusual and therefore questionable. Religious scruples might be raised, but no consensus resulted. Cremation is viewed from the same perspective. Those in the churches who argue for a resurrection of the physical body either see cremation as exceedingly objectionable or feel extremely uneasy about it. An age-old Christian tradition prohibits cremation because it destroys the physical body which is later to be raised.[37] The matter is little discussed in the churches, but may be more in the future as the incidence of cremation increases.

It is the standard practice for the casket to remain closed during the funeral but opened for viewing following the service. Funeral directors arrange for persons to walk one at a time past the open casket. In case of accidents and disfiguration, the casket remains closed. The family may exercise its preferences, for example, keeping the casket closed only to be viewed by the immediate family or only open before the service to be viewed by those who wish to walk by at their own discretion.[38]

The manner in which church members assist the bereaved is not well defined. There are no mourning rituals. Standard approaches are to call at the house where the family gathers or at the mortuary. There friends and fellow church members visit, express sympathy and pay their respects. In addition, fellow believers often send sympathy cards and attend the funeral. Following the funeral, arrangements are often made to supply food for the immediate family for three or four days. It is commonly assumed that what is needed most is support and friendship, not so much the right set of words. It is always appropriate to recall kind deeds and favorite expressions of the deceased, but inappropriate to bring up the matter of the eternal destiny of the one who has passed on. A century ago much conversation may have ensued on the future prospects of the deceased.[39]

THE AFTERLIFE

Although details about the afterlife have been set out, it may serve a useful purpose to reiterate them in schematic fashion. Members of the Churches of Christ believe that we only have one lifetime and that the decisions made in that lifetime determine our future. Life beyond the grave will not be upon the earth because the earth will be destroyed. Immediately upon death the soul resides in an intermediate place awaiting final judgment. When Christ returns to earth (the second coming) all the dead will be resurrected, both good and evil. The judgment will then occur after which each individual will dwell in hell or heaven forever.[40]

Because of these convictions, reincarnation is rejected as entirely foreign to the Biblical faith. Reincarnation suggests that more than one chance to prepare for heaven is possible and because the scripture tells of only one life, reincarnation must be rejected. For the same reason purgatory is unacceptable because the doctrine implies that souls may be rescued from this realm with certain actions on earth.[41] Limbo is rejected on the ground that it is not mentioned in scripture; furthermore, there can be no future place for those who are neither good nor bad, that is, in limbo, because there is only a place for the good, at first paradise, then heaven, or the bad, Tartarus, then hell.

No precise information has been advanced about the location of the dead in the in-between time. A hundred years ago most members probably believed that the intermediate place of the dead is somewhere in the interior of the earth and hell is located deep in the center. Heaven then was located somewhere up in the sky.[42] But now most members accept modern cosmology. Where souls exist in the in-between time is not clear. The souls of the dead are neither in the earth nor anywhere in space in an identifiable location. Perhaps sophisticated minds will conclude that they are in another dimension, but few members of the Churches of Christ would suggest that they depart through black holes.[43]

The person who makes it to heaven must hear the gospel, believe that Jesus is the Christ, the son of God, repent of his sins, confess faith in Christ and be immersed. Everyone who does this is a member of the Church of Christ whether or not he worships in a building with a sign proclaiming Church of Christ above the door. The early proponents of the Restoration Movement saw it as their task to encourage Christians to exit from the denominations in order to be just Christians. They claimed not to be the only Christians, but Christians only. At the time when the division formed two wings, the Disciples of Christ and the Churches of Christ, the members of the Churches of Christ thought in exclusive terms, considering themselves to be the only Christians. The majority of members still identify the church of Christ with the Churches of Christ, but such exclusivism has been attenuated in some quarters.[44]

Most members of the Churches of Christ now believe that, because we will have a spiritual body in heaven, we will know each other there because the spiritual body has continuity with the physical body. Fifty years ago the view prevailed that we will not know each other in heaven, for if we were to know each other, once in heaven we could ascertain whether our mother, father, sister, brother, wife or husband made it.[45] If our loved ones fail to make it, we can only be miserable for eternity, so heaven will not be heaven after all; that is, a place of peace and contentment. Heaven is best realized if we are without that information and resultant misery.[46]

CONCLUSION

The message for life and death proclaimed in the Churches of Christ is that life is the singular opportunity to declare for God through believing in his son Jesus Christ. The person who accepts Christ lives a full, fruitful, rewarding life here and now and at death goes to be with God for eternity. This is a message of great hope, comfort and joy. The person who refuses to accept Christ or who never hears the gospel proclaimed or who accepts, but is unfaithful, lives a shallow, confused and troubled life here and now and on the other side of death is punished for eternity. Even though the joys and rewards of eternal life are known, the majority succumb to the temptations of Satan and in the end are consigned to eternal punishment. Death therefore is an anxious moment because in it one faces the unknown. For the one who believes he has been faithful to his trust, it is a time of peace, a passageway to the joys of eternal life. The one, however, who rejects the gracious salvation offered by God should of necessity greatly fear death. For him it is a passageway to separation, torture and eternal destruction.

Notes

1. The standard histories are: about the Disciples of Christ, William E. Tucker and Lester G. McAllister, *Journey in Faith* (St. Louis: Bethany Press, 1975); the Christian Churches (NACC), James DeForest Murch, *Christians Only* (Cincinnati: Standard Publishing Co., 1962); Churches of Christ, Earl West, *Search for the Ancient Order* (Vol. 1, Nashville: The Gospel Advocate Co., 1949; Vol. II, Indianapolis: Religious Book Service, 1950; Vol. III, Indianapolis: Religious Book Service, 1979) and Leroy Garrett, The *Stone-Campbell Movement: An Anecdotal History of Three Churches* (Joplin, MO: College Press Publishing Co., 1981). For a survey of recent studies, see Richard T. Hughes, "Twenty-Five Years of Restoration Scholarship: The Churches of Christ," *Restoration Quarterly* (Part I, 25: 4, 1982, pp. 233-256; Part II, 26:1, 1984, pp. 39-64).
2. For a historical overview of membership in the Churches of Christ, see Mac Lynn, ed., *Where the Saints Meet* (Austin, TX: Firm Foundation Publishing House, 1983), pp. v-ix.
3. Winfred Ernest Garrison and Alfred T. DeGroot, *The Disciples of Christ: A History* (St. Louis: The Bethany Press, 1948), pp. 82-87.
4. Thomas H. Olbricht, "Christian Connexion and Unitarian Relations: 1800-1844," *Restoration Quarterly* 9:3, 1966, pp. 160-186.
5. "The Last Will and Testament of the Springfield Presbytery," in Charles

Alexander Young, *Historical Documents Advocating Christian Union* (Chicago: The Century Company, 1904), pp. 19-26.

6. Garrison and DeGroot, pp. 123-179.
7. Robert Hooper, *Crying in the Wilderness: A Biography of David Lipscomb* (Nashville: David Lipscomb College, 1979).
8. Milo True Morrill, *A History of the Christian Denomination in America* (Dayton: The Christian Publishing Association, 1912).
9. Though sometimes spelled out more specifically, the views stated in The Westminster Confession of Faith (1646), chapters XXXII and XXXIII, are acceptable to most persons in the Churches of Christ. See *Creeds of the Churches,* John H. Leith, ed. (Atlanta: John Knox Press, 1977), pp. 228-234.
10. These views, though not always explicitly stated, are nevertheless implicit from Alexander Campbell on. See *Compend of Alexander Campbell's Theology,* Royal Humbert, ed. (St. Louis: The Bethany Press, 1961), pp. 202-234. See also J.J. Turner, *Life, Death, and Beyond* (Shreveport: Lambert Book House, 1975), pp. 20-22.
11. This is expressed in a book of sermons mined by preachers in the 1940s and 1950s as a treasury of model discourses. Leroy Brownlow, *Why I am a Member of the Church of Christ* (Fort Worth: Leroy Brownlow Publisher, 1945), pp. 154-167.
12. This formulation of the steps of salvation is obvious in speeches made at lectureships sponsored annually at Abilene Christian University. These lectureships are representative of mainline Churches of Christ theology. William S. Banowsky, *The Mirror of a Movement* (Dallas: Christian Publishing Company, 1965), pp. 186-189.
13. Brownlow, "Because It Teaches That a Child of God Can So Sin As To Be Eternally Lost," pp. 143-153.
14. Banowsky, pp. 146-164.
15. Brownlow, "Because It Teaches That the Miraculous Manifestations of the Spirit Have Ceased," pp. 159-167.
16. Ross W. Dye, "We Shall See the Dead Again," in *Sorrow and Joy,* J.D. Thomas, ed. (Abilene: Biblical Research Press, 1963), pp. 22-25. The Platonic view of the soul is that it is immortal, by which is meant that the individual soul has always existed. It is infinite in time. The standard Christian position is that the soul comes into existence at the moment God creates it, but once created exists without gap from that point on.
17. A classical graphic illustration of this position, which has wide circulation in traditional churches, may be found in Dickie Hill, *Death and Dying* (Abilene: Quality Publications, 1982), p. 85.
18. Turner, pp. 47-52, does not fine tune "Tartarus" and "Gehenna" inasmuch as they are not used in a precise manner in the New Testament. He calls the intermediate place of the dead "Hades," the realm for the righteous "Paradise," and that of the wicked "Hell," and separates these two regions of "Hades" with a "Great Gulf."
19. John Allen Hudson, *How to Read the Bible: Historic Interpretation* (Fort Worth: The Mauney Company, 1958), pp. 121-133. On Satan, *Compend,* R. Humbert, ed., p. 221. *The Devil You Say? Perspectives on Demons and the Occult,* John Allen Chalk, et al. (Austin: R.B. Sweet Co., 1947), pp. 19-23.
20. Ibid., p. 28.

21. The designation for sin after conversion is popularly "backsliding." The sermon "Backsliding Preventatives," from a book of sermons popular in the 1950s, makes this point. Fred E. Dennis, *Fifty Short Sermons* (Grand Rapids: W.B. Eerdmans, 1944), pp. 100-102.
22. K.C. Mosier was a precursor for this view. K.C. Mosier, *Galatians* (Austin: R.B. Sweet Co., 1965), p. 66.
23. This is demonstrated by Rex Kyker's refusal to speculate on why people die young other than in cases where they brought about their own death. The section "Services for Those Young in Years" is especially pertinent. Rex Kyker, *God's Man in Time of Death: A Ministry of Comfort* (Abilene Christian Bookstore, 1982), pp. 23-36. Also Turner, *Life, Death,* pp. 25-29.
24. A hymn by Charles Albert Tindley written about 1905. The first line is "Trials dark on every hand." The title is sometimes listed as "By and By."
25. John T. Willis, "Suffering: A Universal Human Experience," in *God and Man: Then and Now* (Austin: R.B. Sweet Co., 1974), pp. 19-24.
26. Kyker, *God's Man,* p. 80, expressed a preference for the funeral chapel unless other factors prevail.
27. This standard formulation is set out by Leslie G. Thomas in *What the Bible Teaches* (Austin: Firm Foundation, 1962), Vol. II, p. 208.
28. Kyker mentions military or masonic rites without impugning them. Kyker, *God's Man,* p. 87.
29. Leslie G. Thomas, *What the Bible Teaches,* Vol. II, p. 69ff.
30. The reading of the obituary contained almost all the personal references about the deceased. The sermon contained much of the exhortatory remarks from regular sermons designed to impress the auditors with the need to get right with God, because one can never predict the time of death.
31. I heard funeral sermons of this sort in the 1930s. In unusual circumstances Rex Kyker makes remarks which imply that the deceased has not accepted the Gospel. His approach, however, is non-judgmental and indirect. *God's Man,* pp. 28-31.
32. These emphases are obvious in Kyker's funeral remarks. See especially *God's Man,* pp. 37-69. See also the suggestions in *Sorrow and Joy,* J.D. Thomas, ed. (Abilene: Biblical Research Press, 1963), pp. 1-18.
33. Whether a visitation is arranged depends on how many friends or relatives of the deceased remain. Kyker, in *God's Man,* does not discuss the matter.
34. Kyker mentions the changing custom of taking food to the fellowship room of the church rather than to the home. He makes a case for this development. Kyker, *God's Man,* p. 75ff.
35. Kyker, in *God's Man*, mentions repeatedly the need to respond to the wishes of the family and to tailor the remarks to the circumstances and the situation of the deceased.
36. J.J. Turner argues for a resurrection of the physical body, but does not discuss the implications for such a resurrection as it respects embalming, autopsies, etc.
37. I have heard the matter of cremation discussed very little in church situations. Perhaps one reason is that few members of the Churches of Christ go that route. I have never been involved in or attended a funeral of a member of the Churches of Christ in which cremation was involved. I have heard of a few. Kyker, in *God's Man,* p. 16, rejects cremation, but respects the wishes of those who prefer it.

38. Kyker, in *God's Man,* p. 80, recommends abiding by the wishes of the family.
39. The changes in matters appropriate for discussion are vivid to me from having contrasted conversations I heard in my childhood with those in the 1980s. Kyker tells of his conversations with the bereaved and always highlights words of comfort. Hill, in *Death and Dying,* offers suggestions about how those in sorrow may be assisted, as does Turner in *Life, Death,* pp. 87-91. Turner especially stresses the importance of not being judgmental.
40. Leslie G. Thomas, *What the Bible Teaches,* Vol. II, p. 19. "The judgment at the last day...will be the time for meting out rewards and punishments, upon both the righteous and unrighteous." Guy N. Woods, *The Second Coming and Other Sermons* (Memphis: Guy N. Woods, 1948), p. 15.
41. John David Stewart, A *Study of Major Religious Beliefs in America* (Austin: R.B. Sweet Co., 1964), p. 17ff. See also J.J. Turner, *Life, Death,* p. 7ff.
42. G.E. Woods, *Sermons in Outline* (Union City, TN., 1949), p. 142.
43. Proposed by W.G. Pollard, "Science and the Bible," *The Interpreter's Dictionary of the Bible,* Supplementary Vol., Keith Crim, ed. (Nashville: Abingdon, 1976), pp. 289-294. Pollard is an Episcopalian.
44. A clarion call for every baptized believer to be included under the rubric "churches of Christ" was issued by Rubel Shelly, *I Just Want To Be a Christian* (Nashville: 20th Century Christian, 1984). Shelly presents the other view and quotes several historical documents.
45. Leslie G. Thomas, *What the Bible Teaches,* Vol. II, 1961. See also Hill, *Death and Dying,* p. 99ff, who raises the problem, and Turner, *Life, Death,* pp. 61-65.
46. Turner, *Life, Death,* has a chapter, "Heaven: The Eternal Home," pp. 79-84.

The Church of Jesus Christ of Latter-day Saints

Richard M. Eyre

BACKGROUND OF THE FAITH

While they are often called "Mormons," members of The Church of Jesus Christ of Latter-day Saints know that the full name of the church is both more accurate and more descriptive of the distinctive claim made by the faith. That claim is that there are three organizational categories of Christian churches in the world: (1) Catholic, (2) Protestant (which came about as a result of a reformation) and (3) The Church of Jesus Christ of Latter-day Saints, which, as the name suggests, is the original Church of Jesus Christ, lost from the earth during the Dark Ages and now restored by God in modern or "latter" times.

Mormons then agree with Protestants that there was a great apostasy through which many of the "plain and precious" parts of Christ's gospel, along with His authority or priesthood, were lost. However, unlike Protestants, Mormons believe that more than a reformation by men was required to reconstitute Christ's church once it was lost. They believe it required an actual restoration by God.

In this context, Joseph Smith was not a reformer or even the Church's founder. Rather, he was a messenger or a prophet called by God to be a vehicle or conduit through which things that were lost could be restored. The process of truth being lost from the world and then being returned by God has occurred frequently in scripture. Enoch, Noah, Abraham and Moses — each was a prophet to whom a separate dispensation or restoration of truth was given. While He lived on the earth, Christ himself again restored truth after it was lost. A great apostasy followed the death of Christ and His apostles. Rome first persecuted Christianity, then adopted it, making it a religion of politics and pageantry. In the process, doctrines were changed and compromised and the true authority of God was taken from the earth. The Dark Ages that followed are aptly named. The Renaissance and Reformation then opened men's minds and prepared the world for the restoration that God brought about through His prophet Joseph Smith beginning in the year 1820.

Mormons believe in living prophets and think that it is illogical and inconsistent to believe that a just and loving God called prophets anciently but does not do so today when our need for truth and guidance is as great as it has ever been. When Joseph Smith was killed by a mob, Brigham Young, leader of the Church's 12 apostles, became the second prophet-president of the Church. Mormons believe that this chain was continued and that there is a living prophet on the earth today.

Thus the restoration that occurred through Joseph Smith is consistent both with sacred history and with the world's ongoing need for living prophets. Many of the great reformers who preceded Joseph Smith recognized this need. Calvin, Wesley, Luther and Roger Williams, among others, indicated that they, while doing all they could to reform Christianity, were awaiting a more complete restoration by God himself. Mormons simply believe that this awaited restoration did occur and that it occurred through the prophet Joseph Smith, beginning in 1820 when he prayed for guidance and received a vision of God the Father and Jesus Christ, who told him that the original Church of Jesus Christ would be reconstituted in these latter times. The things that were restored might be put into three categories: (1) accurate doctrine or information about the nature of God and man and about where we came from, why we are here and where we are going after death; (2) the priesthood or true authority of God; and (3) additional scripture and ancient records which support and enhance the Holy Bible and lend further clarification to our knowledge of Christ and His gospel.

Let us deal with these three categories in reverse order so we can end with the main subject matter of this chapter — the Mormon belief in eternity and in life after death.

Additional Scripture

Joseph Smith was directed by God, through an angel, to a set of ancient records, inscribed in a form of hieroglyphics on thin sheets of gold, which contained the religious and secular history of earlier inhabitants of the American continents. This record was called the Book of Mormon, named after a man who collected and abridged the 1000-year history of his people. The record, which Joseph Smith was empowered to translate, tells of a man named Lehi, who left Jerusalem about 600 B.C. and came with his family by boat to Central America. A long succession of different generations of writers then give their accounts of their period of history. The people of the Book of Mormon, who are some of the ancestors of the modern American Indians, passed through many cycles of righteousness and wickedness. They had among them, at times, prophets of the Lord who taught God's commandments and who prophesied the coming of Christ. In perhaps the most important and fascinating part of the book, an account is given of the coming of Jesus Christ to the Americas. Immediately following His crucifixion and resurrection, He descended from Heaven to the people of this hemisphere, taught them His gospel, called apostles and established His church and told them that they were the "other sheep" whom he had told His followers in Palestine he must also visit (as recorded in John's Gospel).[1]

The teachings of the Book of Mormon complement and, in some cases, clarify those of the Bible. Mormons view the Book of Mormon as a "fifth gospel" — as a further witness of Christ and of His divinity. The subtitle of the book is "Another Testament of Jesus Christ." They use the book hand-in-hand with the Bible and believe that it is, in fact, the "stick of Joseph" that Ezekiel spoke of and prophesied would become "one in thine hand" with the stick of Judah (the Bible).[2] Mormons believe that Christ was and is the Savior of the entire world and that it is therefore logical that He visited more than one small part of the earth. He said that He had come to the whole House of Israel. The people in the Americas, having come originally from Jerusalem, were of the House of Israel. The nickname "Mormon," of course, comes from the belief of The Church of Jesus Christ of Latter-day Saints in the Book of Mormon. Additionally, Mormons use two smaller books of scripture called *The Doctrine and Covenants* and *The Pearl of Great Price.* These books contain additional revelations received by Joseph Smith.

Priesthood or Authority

Mormons believe that ordinances like baptism for the remission of sins and the laying on of hands for the gift of the Holy Ghost must be done with the true priesthood or power of God to be effectual. Part of the restoration was the returning of this priesthood to the earth. God sent Peter, James and John, Christ's three chief apostles, back to the earth as angelic messengers. They laid their hands on the head of Joseph Smith and an associate, Oliver Cowdery, and gave them the authority by which they could perform God's ordinances and once again organize His church. This organization consisted of 12 apostles, of bishops, elders, teachers, deacons, pastors and evangelists — indeed, of the exact organization that Christ established for His original church (see Ephesians 4:11-13).

The Church of Jesus Christ of Latter-day Saints was officially organized in 1830. Since then it has become one of the fastest growing Christian churches in the world and today includes some 10 million members. When 19 years of age, most young men in the Church elect to serve a voluntary, unpaid "mission" for the Church. They are called to go somewhere in the world (very often where they must learn a foreign language) for two years and preach the

Gospel of Jesus Christ to whomever will listen. Young women in the church also often serve missions. Mormons believe that the "fruits" of the Church of Jesus Christ (fast growth, low divorce rate, longer life expectancy, high level of education, efficient worldwide welfare system, etc.) are testaments of the truth of the restored gospel (see Matthew 7:16).

DOCTRINE AND INFORMATION ABOUT THE NATURE OF GOD AND MAN

In his first vision, Joseph Smith relearned much of what man had forgotten about God. He learned that God the Father and Jesus Christ, His son, are separate and distinct individuals. He learned that they both have bodies of flesh and bone and that man is literally created in their image. He learned that they are one in purpose, in spirit and in testimony and witness. They are one in the same way that they desire us to be one with them (see John 17:11, 21).

Some time after the organization of the Church of Jesus Christ of Latter-day Saints, Joseph Smith was asked to summarize the fundamental beliefs of the Church. He did so in what is called the "Articles of Faith"[3]:

> *Article 1:* We believe in God, the Eternal Father, and in His Son, Jesus Christ and in the Holy Ghost.
>
> *Article 2:* We believe that men will be punished for their own sins and not for Adam's transgression.
>
> *Article 3:* We believe that through the Atonement of Christ, all mankind may be saved, by obedience to the laws and ordinances of the Gospel.
>
> *Article 4:* We believe that the first principles and ordinances of the Gospel are: first, faith in the Lord Jesus Christ; second, repentance; third, baptism by immersion for the remission of sins; and fourth, laying on of hands for the gift of the Holy Ghost.
>
> *Article 5:* We believe that a man must be called of God, by prophecy, and by the laying on of hands by those who are in authority to preach the Gospel and administer in the ordinances thereof.
>
> *Article 6:* We believe in the same organization that existed in the Primitive Church, namely, apostles, prophets, pastors, teachers, evangelists and so forth.
>
> *Article 7:* We believe in the gift of tongues, prophecy, revelation visions, healing, interpretation of tongues and so forth.
>
> *Article 8:* We believe the Bible to be the word of God as far as it is translated correctly; we also believe the Book of Mormon to be the word of God.
>
> *Article 9:* We believe all that God has revealed, all that He does now

reveal, and we believe that He will yet reveal many great and important things pertaining to the Kingdom of God.

Article 10: We believe in the literal gathering of Israel and in the restoration of the Ten Tribes; that Zion (the New Jerusalem) will be built upon the American continent; that Christ will reign personally upon the earth and that the earth will be renewed and receive its paradisiacal glory.

Article 11: We claim the privilege of worshiping Almighty God according to the dictates of our own conscience, and allow all men the same privilege, let them worship how, where, or what they may.

Article 12: We believe in being subject to kings, presidents, rulers and magistrates, in obeying, honoring and sustaining the law.

Article 13: We believe in being honest, true, chaste, benevolent, virtuous, and in doing good to all men; indeed, we may say that we follow the admonition of Paul — we believe all things, we hope all things, we have endured many things and hope to be able to endure all things. If there is anything virtuous, lovely, or of good report or praiseworthy, we seek after these things.

Through the process of the restoration, both in his translation of the Book of Mormon and through other visions and revelations he received, Joseph Smith learned more of the nature of God and man and of the answers to the three key questions of the ages: Where did we come from? Why are we here? And where are we going? Perhaps we can briefly summarize the answers to these three questions by quoting from a Church film called "Man's Search for Happiness." Following the quote we will present more detail:

Sometimes, in your search for happiness, you ponder the meaning of your life.

You sift your memory for beginnings; you send your mind ahead for directions, but all you really know is now. And you are lost in the present.

Who am I? How did I come to be? Time — where does it take me? Toward death? And then what? Who am I? Where did I come from?

To understand why you are here, you must first understand your beginnings. At birth you did not suddenly flare into existence out of nowhere. You have always lived.

In pre-earth life you were with your Heavenly Father. There, as his spirit sons and daughters, you lived until you were ready to come to earth.

As the poet Wordsworth said:

Our birth is but a sleep and a forgetting;

The soul that rises with us, our life's star,
Hath had elsewhere its setting,
And cometh from afar;
Not in entire forgetfulness,
And not in utter nakedness,
But trailing clouds of glory, do we come
From God, who is our home.

Upon entering mortal life, the memory of your life before birth was blotted out that you might live by faith and further prepare for the everlastingness of life.

This mortal body in which your spirit now dwells is subject to pain, to difficulties, to death. For it is through opposition that you grow in strength of character. You must know pain to appreciate well-being, difficulties to develop courage, death to understand eternal life.

You then, whoever you are, are related not only to every person upon this earth who lives, who has lived, who will yet live, but to God, the Father of us all, and to his son, our Savior.

With your acceptance of the responsibility of earth life, you were given a wondrous mortal body in the likeness of God.

"So God created man in his own image; in the image of God created He him, male and female created He them."[4]

"And the spirit and the body are the soul of man."[5]

As sons and daughters of God, is it any wonder that you are an eternal part of his plan and purpose? And coming from such a noble heritage, that you have possibilities far beyond your greatest dreams?

Be assured that your personal search for happiness has real purpose. Be assured that your life is worth living.

Life offers you two precious gifts — one is time, the other freedom of choice, the freedom to buy with your time what you will. You are free to exchange your allotment of time for thrills...

You may trade it for base desires…

You may invest it in greed…

You may purchase with it vanity…

You may spend your time in pursuit of material things…

Yours is the freedom to choose. But these are no bargains, for in them you find no lasting satisfaction.

Every day, every hour, every minute of your span of mortal years must sometime be accounted for. And it is in *this* life that you walk by faith and prove yourself able to choose good over evil, right over wrong, enduring happiness over mere amusement. And your eternal reward will be according to your choosing.

A prophet of God has said: "Men are that they might have joy"[6] — a joy that includes a fullness of life, a life dedicated to service, to love and harmony in the home, and the fruits of honest toil — an acceptance of the Gospel of Jesus Christ — of its requirements and commandments.

Only in these will you find true happiness, the happiness which doesn't fade with the lights and the music and the crowds.

God has placed you on earth without memory of your premortal past, but he hasn't left you without hope or without faith in life after death.

This he has promised you: "I am the resurrection and the life; he that believeth in me, though he were dead, yet shall he live."[7]

One of the best attested facts of sacred history is the resurrection of the Lord Jesus Christ. Three days following his crucifixion the disciples were gathered together as recorded in scripture:

"Then the same day at evening, being the first day of the week, when the doors were shut where the disciples were assembled...came Jesus and stood in the midst, and saith unto them, 'Peace be unto you.'"

"And when he had so said, he showed unto them his hands and his side. Then were the disciples glad, when they saw the Lord."[8]

Just as you lived before mortal birth, just as you now live in this life, so through the love and sacrifice of your Savior do you continue to live after death.

Like every member of the human race, you were born and you must die. Your birth is a matter of record — you take it for granted. But death, that uncertain door that leads ahead, has been for man an awesome mystery.

Life's greatest test comes with the death of a loved one, and without faith in the immortality of the soul, the separation of death looms forever comfortless.

After death, though your mortal body lies in the earth, you — your spirit self being eternal — continue to live. Your memory of this life will remain with you, and the knowledge of your life before birth will be restored.

Like coming out of a darkened room into the light, through death you will emerge into a place of reawakening and find loved ones waiting to welcome you.

There with your loved ones you will await the resurrection, which is the reuniting of your spirit and your body. There you will continue toward the limitless opportunities of everlasting life.

So here you are on earth, with no memory of what went before and only faith to whisper what comes after...

Be assured that you are here, not by accident or chance, but as part of a glorious everlasting plan.

By a still, small voice within you and through revelation to his appointed prophets, God our eternal Father guides the affairs of his children.... Today as in the past.

In 1830, God re-established his Church and restored the fullness of his Gospel once more among men through a modern prophet...Joseph Smith.

By revelation our Savior made known again the plan of salvation and exaltation.

Salvation comes as a gift to every man through Jesus the Christ, but *exaltation,* which is the highest of eternal opportunities, you must earn.

It is not enough just to believe in Jesus Christ. You must work and learn, search and pray, repent and improve, know his laws and live them.

This is the way to peace and happiness and the fullness of everlasting life. It is your Heavenly Father's way.

LIFE BEFORE BIRTH

Mormons do not believe in a "one-way eternity." They believe that there is a "forever backward" as well as a "forever forward." This belief, however, should not be confused with reincarnation. We believe that we have always lived, but always as *ourselves,* never as someone else or in another life-form. We do not pass from one identity to another. Rather, we remain ourselves and pass through one place and phase of existence after another. We lived with our Heavenly Father who, as part of His plan for our growth and happiness, created this earth for us and, much as a wise father who sends his children to a fine school, allowed us to come here and become more like Him through the process of being tested, gaining physical bodies and becoming parents and having families of our own.

In the pre-mortal existence before any of God's children had come to live on this earth, God's plan for our growth through agency and self-choice was presented to us all by the Firstborn Spirit of our Heavenly Father who was Jesus. The plan, which allowed mortal mistakes, was made workable by Jesus' willingness to perform His atoning sacrifice. Lucifer, another spirit-leader, presented an amendment to this plan which offered man coercion rather than freedom and which conferred upon Lucifer the glory and power. One-third of the hosts of heaven followed Lucifer, who became Satan and who tempts man today and tries to lead him away from God.

The understanding of our life before birth is a good example of a doctrine that was taught by earlier prophets, but which was distorted and lost during the apostasy. The Bible contains many references to our earlier spiritual life (see Jeremiah 1:5, John 17:3, John 3:13, Job 38:7, Ephesians 1:4, Ecclesiastes 12:7), but the references are vague and oblique enough that they have been ignored or misinterpreted. It is points like this that were clarified by the additional scripture and revelation given through Joseph Smith.

Belief in a pre-mortal existence is important for many reasons. It helps explain the feelings of *deja vu* that all experience — and the longings we feel and our sensation that there is more "in us" than just the results of this one short mortal life. It helps us believe in the fairness and justice of God over the course of eternity, even though we see great inequality here and now on this earth. But most importantly, our belief in a pre-mortal existence helps us better understand why we are here and how this life ties in with God's eternal plan for His children.

PLAN OF SALVATION

This mortal life is a portion of God's plan for the salvation and exaltation of His children. The experiences and choices we face here present us with opportunities for growth and learning that make us more like God. When this life ends, our spirits leave our physical bodies and we go to a post-earthly spirit world where we continue to grow and progress and where we await the resurrection and judgment. In this spirit world, all people who have not had an opportunity to hear the full Gospel of Christ receive that chance. As recorded by Peter, this is the place that Christ went to preach to those who had lived during the wicked time of Noah and therefore had no opportunity to know of the true God and His laws.[9]

Those spirits who accept Christ and His Gospel in the spirit world can receive the same blessings, even the blessing of baptism, as those who accept the Gospel in mortality. Since baptism is an earthly ordinance involving water, it is done by proxy by someone on this earth for and in behalf of one who has died and is in the spirit world. This "baptism for the dead" is referred to in the New Testament[10] and is God's way of "linking" people, particularly families, with each other by allowing the living to perform works of love for their ancestors and others who died without knowing of the full Gospel of Christ. This proxy baptism would not be effective for a spirit who did not accept the Gospel in the spirit world. These vicarious works are performed in the temples of the church and are one reason for Mormons' intense interest in genealogy. Spirits who accept the full Gospel in the spirit world but do not have a descendant on earth who is baptized for them will have this work done during the millennium, the 1000-year period in which Christ will reign personally on earth after His second coming.

The resurrection (a literal physical resurrection of all men) will continue with the Lord's second coming in connection with the judgment. This will be essentially a self judgment, with each person going to dwell with those who are most like him or to where he is most comfortable. Those who have been obedient to God and valiant in their belief in Christ will be comfortable in living with God and will dwell with Him in the Celestial Kingdom.

Mormons believe in the three general divisions of heaven that Paul describes in Corinthians. The highest "degree of glory" (the Celestial) is compared with the sun. The second degree (Terrestrial) is compared to the moon and the third level (Telestial) is compared to the stars.[11] All three are kingdoms of glory and the principal punishment of those in the lower degree will be the regret and realization of what they could have done. The only persons who will not participate in any of the three degrees of heaven will be those who received a sure knowledge and then willfully sinned against the Holy Ghost by rejecting it. This relatively small number will be in outer darkness, becoming numbered among Satan's followers.

Within the highest or "Celestial" degree of glory there will be a "highest level" where families will continue. Thus, in Mormon temples, marriages are performed not "till death do you part" but "for time and all eternity." The eternal nature of marriage and the family is a fundamental belief among Mormons and is partly responsible for the strong family orientation of the church. Civil marriage (or "till death do you part" marriages) are recognized as legal by the church, but "celestial marriage" performed in the Temple is seen as preferable because it binds families together beyond the grave. The continuation of marriage and family relationships after death is seen as important, not only because of the happiness and joy it will bring to individuals but because it allows people to be more like God himself who is our *Father* in Heaven and thus continues to be surrounded by His family.

In connection with their belief in "eternal progression," Mormons believe that, as they progress, they become gradually more and more like God...like their Heavenly Father. This belief (in a loving and personal Father God who wants his children to progress toward what He is) is not unique to Mormons. Dr. Scott Peck, in his bestselling book *The Road Less Traveled*, concludes that "all of us who postulate a loving God, come to a single terrifying idea — God wants us to become Himself. We are growing toward Godhood."[12] While many individuals share this view, the Church of Jesus Christ of Latter-day Saints may be the only church that carries an official doctrinal belief in a God who desires that we become as He is. Mormons view God as a loving Heavenly Father who wants His children, in the distant eternities, to become gods themselves.

Funerals, in the context of eternal families' eternal progression, are sad in the sense that a loved one has departed, but *happy* in the sense that that person is with God and that those left behind can someday join him there. Funeral services usually dwell on the comforting and reassuring of those left behind with the conviction that it is we on the earth who suffer the most grief, not the departed spirit who is now continuing on his or her journey of eternal progression.

To further clarify and elaborate the Mormon belief in life after death, for the balance of this chapter, I will quote selectively from a book I co-authored called *The Birth That We Call Death.*[13] In it I quote extensively from priesthood authorities in the Mormon Church.

> When a loved one has passed on, two kinds of comfort are available. One comes with condolence and love of friends, the soothing words of poet and philosopher and the comforting presence of the Holy Spirit. The other lies in knowledge and insight — knowledge of where the loved one is and insight into what he is doing. Through revelation to his appointed prophets, our Heavenly Father has given us this knowledge. Because of his love for us and his understanding of our need for comfort, he has told us with positive clarity and strong assurance where our loved ones go. By studying his revealed word, we can be sure of six things:
>
> 1. That the spirits of all men, immediately upon death, go to the spirit world to await the resurrection.
> 2. That, for the righteous, the spirit world is a place of joy and peace.
> 3. That it is also a place of continued progress and a place of missionary work, where those who have received the gospel can teach it to those who have not.
> 4. That our departed loved ones are changed only in that they are temporarily separated from their physical bodies; that in personality, character and characteristics they remain the same; that the spirit does not change.
> 5. That the spirit world is not far removed from us but close by, though invisible to our mortal eyes.
> 6. That some departed spirits know and understand our thoughts and feelings; that they are aware of us and retain their love for us.

The following statements of prophets give us this knowledge and assurance. Note how positive and precise they are, how specific and complete they are.

> Behold, it has been made known unto me by an angel, that the spirits of all men, as soon as they are departed from this mortal body, yea, the spirits of all men, whether they be good or evil, are taken home to that

> God who gave them life. And then shall it come to pass, that the spirits of those who are righteous are received into a state of happiness, which is called paradise, a state of rest, a state of peace, where they shall rest from all their troubles and from all care and sorrow.[14]

> When the spirits leave their bodies they are in the presence of our Father and God; they are prepared then to see, hear and understand spiritual things. But where is the spirit world? It is incorporated within this celestial system. Can you see it with your natural eyes? No. Can you see spirits in this room? No. Suppose the Lord should touch your eyes that you might see, could you then see the spirits? Yes, as plainly as you now see bodies, as did the servant of Elijah. If the Lord would permit it, and it was his will that it should be done, you could see the spirits that have departed from this world, as plainly as you now see bodies with your natural eyes.[15] — Brigham Young

> The spirits of the just are exalted to a greater and more glorious work; hence they are blessed in their departure to the world of spirits. Enveloped in flaming fire, they are not far from us, and know and understand our thoughts, feelings and motions, and are often pained therewith.[16] — Joseph Smith

> When a person who has always been good and faithful to his God lays down his body in the dust, his spirit will remain the same in the spirit world. It is not the body that has control over the spirit, as to its disposition, but it is the spirit that controls the body. When the spirit leaves the body, the body becomes lifeless. The spirit has not changed one single particle of itself by leaving the body.[17] — Heber C. Kimball

Imagine for a moment that you are about to cross the country on a train. You get on board and as the train starts you find yourself sitting next to a fine person who is making the same journey that you are. Because the trip usually takes almost four days, you begin a serious attempt to get to know him. You find that you have much in common and by the time the train steams into the darkness at the end of the first day, you feel a remarkable closeness and begin to feel that the relationship you are forming may be the most important part of your journey.

After a sound night's sleep in the Pullman car, you rejoin your friend and the two of you spend another day relating to each other and experiencing the journey together. Your rapport grows still stronger and you find yourself feeling a little sorry that the day passes so fast. By the second night your train is deep into the flat middle plains and as you fall asleep you think about the things you want to talk about with your friend the next day.

In the morning you return to your seat and find, to your dismay, that your friend is gone. When you inquire, someone tells you that he got off during the night.

Got off during the night? But he had a destination very near your own and you had planned on having the next two days with him. There was so much left to say! Suddenly you realize that you never found out where he came from or who he was and that you never learned why he was on the train or exactly where he was going. Worst of all, you realize that you don't know whether you'll see him again — that you don't know how to find him or contact him.

The feeling is a mixture of sadness and frustration which together produce something in between bitterness and anger. Why did he have to leave? Did someone or something make him leave? Should you be upset at him for leaving or at someone else who made him go against his will? It's not so much that he's gone, it's that you don't know *where* he's gone and you want so much to see him again.

At that point the porter comes down the aisle to your seat. The message he leaves is very simple, but it changes night into day and bitterness into joy. He tells you that your friend was indeed going to the same place as you — that he was going there to see his father. During the night your friend received an emergency message that his father needed him right away and that he should get off the train at the next stop and catch a plane to get home more quickly. The porter leaves you a phone number so that you can contact your friend as soon as you arrive.

The porter's simple message turns your frustration into peace. You are still sorry to miss the two days of discussion that you had anticipated you would have with your friend, but your sorrow is no longer bitter or blind; rather, it is sweet with the knowledge that you know where he is and the assurance that you will see him again.

The sorrow we taste with the loss of a loved one can be bitter or sweet, depending on one ingredient — the ingredient of knowledge — the simple, pure knowledge of our origin, our purpose and our destination. The restored gospel gives us this knowledge. It tells us our origin; it reveals our purposes on earth; and it teaches us of the life hereafter, assuring us that loved ones will meet us there and that death is a temporary separation and not an utter loss.

As in the imaginary journey on the train, the sense of temporary separation that comes to one who knows the plan of salvation does not carry the sting and panic of permanent loss. Benjamin Franklin once said:

> Our friend and we were invited abroad.... His chair was ready first, and he is gone before us. We could not all conveniently start together; and why should you and I be grieved at this, since we are soon to follow, and know where to find him.[18]

Any dear possession, if separated from us for good purpose and if returned in even better condition, produces joy rather than agony and peace rather than frustration. One man loses his billfold containing a large sum of money.

Another man who has the same amount of money sets goals and makes a planned investment. Both are now separated from their money, but one feels the bite and bitterness of permanent loss, while the other anticipates the day when he will retrieve his investment and enjoys the knowledge that it will probably grow in the meantime.

A loss we cannot comprehend or accept (and a loss that is considered permanent) is bleak and stark and comfortless; but a temporary separation as a part of a goal and plan is acceptable and, in a way, even joyful. The loss of a loved one — the parting of the spirit from the physical body — is not a permanent loss, neither is it a separation we cannot accept or comprehend. Rather it is indeed an indispensable part of the goal and plan of God. In the comprehension of the goal and plan of God lies true and lasting comfort and the ability to view death as the Book of Mormon Prophet Jacob did: "Death hath passed upon all men, to fulfill the merciful plan of that great creator...."[19] God is the literal father of our spirits and Christ the Firstborn, is our eldest spirit brother. We stood with them in the pre-earthly existence and may have heard our Father state his goal: "For behold, this is my work and my glory, to bring to pass the immortality and eternal life of man."[20]

God the Father had achieved immortality and eternal life in a perfected, resurrected body. His goal was that we should become like him. As an infinitely wise father he had achieved ultimate joy and as an infinitely good father he wanted us to become like him and thus to share that joy.

In that pre-earthly existence there were three broad differences between ourselves and our spirit Father, differences that had to be overcome if his plan were to be fulfilled and we were to become like him. First, God had a body, a glorified, perfected physical body that gave him certain capacities that we did not have. Second, he had power and intelligence and knowledge far beyond ours. Third, he was perfect and had great characteristics that we had not. We realized, as he did, that we could begin to overcome these differences only through the experience of a mortal existence on a physical earth. This realization and the prospect of gaining physical bodies and experiencing earth life, aroused within us such gratitude and elation that, according to the Old Testament, we and all the hosts of heaven "shouted for joy."[21] There in the pre-earthly existence we must have had certain insights that we lack now, insights into the great value of earth experience and into the importance of that experience in God's plan of eternal progress. We anticipated the joy of being able to relate to both spiritual and material things. We knew we needed physical bodies to feel with, to learn with, to react with. Having defined both his goal (that we should become like him) and the vehicle for that goal (a physical earth), God ordained a plan, a plan that would bring about his goal, a plan for the salvation of his children.

Another direction was presented — by Lucifer, sometimes called a son of the morning. It must have had the appealing, safe sound of a guarantee, for Lucifer's promise was that he would redeem all mankind, that not one soul could be lost. Apparently he would do this through coercion, making sure we all did what was necessary for salvation. Hence his plan contained no opportunity for failure or for growth and development. And all he asked for himself was everything — the full credit, the whole glory.

While Lucifer's power-play was rejected, the Father's plan was wholeheartedly accepted by Jehovah (Jesus Christ), the Firstborn. It called for agency and initiative. It included free choice and the opportunity for both success and failure. Because of its freedom, the plan offered the possibility of pleasure but also of pain, of virtue but also vice. Because it was realistic, it anticipated sin and error which, unatoned for, would permanently separate men from God. Thus Jehovah offered to be that atoner, to come to earth himself, to gain a physical body and, as Jesus Christ the Only Begotten Son of the Father, to willingly sacrifice his life for the redemption of the world. As spirits we realized that through the operation of this great plan of salvation Adam would fall, bringing spiritual death and physical death (mortality) upon mankind. Jesus Christ would atone for Adam's transgression so that, in Paul's terminology, just as all men would die, all would subsequently be made alive,[22] and thus physical death and physical resurrection would become two automatic transitions in eternity. Christ's atonement would also be, in John's words, the propitiation[23] or payment for everyone's sins so that, as we would repent, those sins could be removed, thus allowing us to overcome spiritual death as well as physical death.

There is as much comfort in the knowledge of a "forever backward" as there is in a "forever forward." Knowing where a loved one came from, why he was here and that he achieved the basic purpose of his earth life, turns death from "the terrible unknown" to a necessary step in the attainment of an immortal body and in the achievement of our eternal goal. If, in the pre-mortal existence, we looked forward to birth, which was the leaving of our Father and our eternal family, how much more we must have looked forward to death, which would be a later and essential step in the coming home!

Mortality is the prerequisite to immortality; it is by passing the tests and gaining the progress of this world that men obtain eternal life. Thus death (passing from time into eternity) is as important and as wonderful as birth (passing from eternity into time) and both are among the essential transitions in the Father's plan for our salvation. President Brigham Young said:

> There is no period known to them [the dead] in which they experience so much joy as when they pass through the portals of death and enter upon the glorious change of the spirit world.[24]

On this earth we view death from the perspective of one who stays behind, much as a man views a long journey when he is sending someone else off rather than going himself. He puts his friend on the train or plane and waves goodbye, only able to imagine what the trip is like and what the friend will find when he gets where he is going. If we could glimpse, for even a moment, the glory and excitement that a departed one faces when his eyes close on time and open on eternity — if only we could glimpse this, perhaps there would be more understanding in our sorrow and more joy in our grief.

We know almost enough, through scripture and revelation, to imagine what death's awakening may be like. Lift yourself for a moment from your own shoes and into the role of one who is departing from this earth. You close your eyes for the last time on the sights of this world and become aware that you are being pulled and lifted up and out and away from your physical body. You feel somehow lighter, perhaps both in weight and in illumination. Your eyes, this time spiritual eyes, now become open and you are aware that you see and hear and feel and sense things that were closed to you while on earth.

Because you somehow have powers you lacked before, you can see the realm of spirits which you now enter. You recognize some of those you see. There is great rejoicing as they reach out and you embrace in the light of love and peace. You already miss your physical body and somehow you now understand its importance, but you know it will be returned to you in the resurrection; and so you go forth meeting and remembering those you knew before. President Joseph F. Smith said:

> Those from whom we have to part here, we will meet again and see as they are. We will meet the same identical being that we associated with here in the flesh.... Deformity will be removed; defects will be eliminated, and men and women shall attain to the perfection of their spirits, to the perfection that God designed in the beginning.[25]

President Brigham Young said:

> We cling to our Mother Earth and dislike to have any of her children leave us....But could we have knowledge and see into eternity, if we were perfectly free from weakness, blindness and lethargy with which we are clothed in the flesh, we should have no disposition to weep or mourn....It is true it is grievous to part with our friends. We are creatures of passion, of sympathy, of love....Should we not...rejoice at the departure of those whose lives have been devoted to doing good...?[26]

Thus, we know that the spirits of all men, as soon as death occurs, go directly to the spirit world where they await the resurrection, the final redemption and the judgment. As the Book of Mormon Prophet Alma says, "There must needs be a space betwixt the time of death and the time of the resurrection."[27]

In general terms, the spirit world, to which all spirits go at death, is divided into the abode of the righteous (paradise) and that of the wicked.[28] After his death, the Savior bridged the gulf between them by bringing the gospel to the spirits in prison.[29] Since that time, righteous spirits have been called to minister and teach the gospel to those who did not have it on this earth. Thus the spirit world is a place where those who had no opportunity to hear and accept the gospel on earth will have that opportunity, so that they can "be judged according to men in the flesh, but live according to God in the spirit."[30]

It has been said that all truly deep and meaningful happiness stems from one of two sources: (1) service, helping and giving to others; and (2) anticipation, looking forward to and waiting for something important or fine. If indeed these are the two key sources of joy, the spirit world must offer great potential happiness, because it contains the greatest conceivable opportunity for service and holds in its future the event most worthy of eternal anticipation. A righteous spirit in paradise can teach other spirits the most important and indispensable knowledge in the universe and anticipate the greatest event: the glorious resurrection which makes possible the continuing eternal progression of the righteous. Speaking of the great service and mission being performed by the righteous in the spirit world, President Brigham Young said:

> Compare those inhabitants on the earth who have heard the gospel in our day, with the millions who have never heard it, or had the keys of salvation presented to them, and you will conclude at once as I do, that there is a mighty work to perform in the spirit world.[31]

If you can imagine the happy anticipation of a boy who has been away at a severe and demanding boarding school and who now returns to the beautiful home of his father whom he loved dearly — if you can imagine that happiness and then magnify it a million times, then perhaps you can glimpse the joy of a righteous spirit awaiting his glorious resurrection. The joy we anticipate in the spirit world will come into full fruition in the resurrection, when our spirits will reunite with perfected resurrected bodies, our own physical bodies, which we will rejoice in finding again and which will be immortal and incorruptible.

No two facts are more clearly and explicitly stated in sacred scripture than these — the reality of Christ's resurrection and the certainty of ours. The apostles witnessed the wound in Christ's resurrected body and watched him eat the fish and the honeycomb. They went forth testifying, as he had, that just as all men would die because of Adam, so also all men would live because of Christ. President David O. McKay said:

> If Christ lived after death, so shall men, each one taking the place in the next world for which he is best fitted. Since love is as eternal as life, the message of the resurrection is the most comforting, the most glorifying ever given to man; for when death takes a loved one from us, we can look with assurance into the open grave and say, "He is not here," and "He will rise again."[32]

In the resurrection the spirit will reenter its physical body, which initially will be in exactly the same state as when the spirit left it. Bodies that were sick, infirm or deformed will then be restored to health and perfection, apparently almost instantly — as Amulek says, to a "proper and perfect frame" (Alma 1:43, in the Book of Mormon). Nor will he at time of death determine a resurrected being's appearance. President Joseph Fielding Smith said:

> Old people will not look old when they come forth from the grave. Scars will be removed. No one will be bent or wrinkled.... Of course, children who die do not grow in the grave. They will come forth with their bodies as they were laid down and then they will grow to the full stature of manhood or womanhood after the resurrection, but all will have their bodies fully restored. [33]

In his supreme wisdom and in his sublime love, God has laid out before us a plan of such excitement and such beauty that it is difficult, while in the flesh, to fully comprehend it. As we learn it, though (by outward study of the word and inward study of our souls), we are lifted to higher realms, we face more easily the trials of our lives and we feel the joy that can go with the sorrow of bereavement.

The Lord said to the Prophet Joseph Smith, "Wherefore, fear not even unto death; for in this world your joy is not full, but in me your joy is full."[34]

EDITOR'S NOTES

An interesting LDS belief not covered in the chapter lies in the area of marriage. LDS marriages take place as either "church weddings" or the ultimate "temple marriage." In a temple marriage, the couple is "sealed" to each other "by time and all eternity." An annulment of this eternal contract can only be granted by the Church President (as in the recent case of Marie Osmond). In cases where a spouse dies, the husband can remarry in the temple and be "sealed" to a second wife, but the wife can only remarry in a lesser church wedding and would remain "sealed" to her first husband.

Notes

1. John 10:16.
2. Ezekiel 37:15-17.
3. *The Pearl of Great Price.*
4. Genesis 1:27.
5. *Doctrine and Covenants* 88:15.
6. 2 Nephi 2:25, *The Book of Mormon.*
7. John 11:25.
8. John 21:19.
9. 1 Peter 3:18-19, 4:6

10. 1 Corinthians 15:29.
11. Ibid., pp. 40-42.
12. M. Scott Peck, *The Road Less Traveled* (New York: Simon and Schuster, 1978), p. 269.
13. Richard M. Eyre and Paul H. Dunn, *The Birth That We Call Death* (Salt Lake City: Bookcraft, 1976).
14. Alma 40:11-12, *The Book of Mormon.*
15. Eyre and Dunn, op. cit., p. 27.
16. Ibid., p. 27.
17. Ibid.
18. Ibid., p. 33.
19. 2 Nephi 9:6, *The Book of Mormon.*
20. Moses 1:39, *The Pearl of Great Price.*
21. Job 38:7.
22. 1 Corinthians 15:22.
23. 1 John 2:2.
24. Eyre and Dunn, op. cit., p. 53.
25. Ibid., p. 54.
26. Ibid., p. 55.
27. Alma 40:6, *The Book of Mormon.*
28. Alma 40:11-14, *The Book of Mormon.*
29. See 1 Peter 3:18-21; Moses 7:39, *The Pearl of Great Price; The Doctrine and Covenants,* Section 138.
30. 1 Peter 4:6.
31. Eyre and Dunn, op. cit., p. 56.
32. Ibid., p. 57.
33. Ibid., pp. 57-58.
34. *Doctrine and Covenants* 101:36.

Hinduism

Anne Mackenzie Pearson, PhD

As a mirror covered with dust shines brightly when it has been cleaned, even so the embodied self when it has seen the true nature of the Soul, becomes united, attains its end, and is freed from sorrow.
Svetashvatara Upanishad 2.14

From the unreal lead me to the real!
From darkness lead me to the light!
From death lead me to immortality!
Brihadaranyaka Upanishad 1.3.28

BACKGROUND OF THE FAITH

Hinduism is one of the oldest living religions, with its earliest extant sacred texts (the Vedas) dating back at least 3000 years. In numbers of adherents, it ranks third, behind Christianity and Islam, with close to 750 million followers resident in 94 countries. Over the past century or so, about 1,300,000 Hindus have emigrated to North America. The vast majority of Hindus, however, continue to reside in India, the place of this religion's birth.

The word "Hindu" derives both from the Sanskrit word *Sindhu*, referring to the river that flows in northwestern India into the Arabian Sea, and from the Arabic word *Hind*, the general name the Arabs gave to the South Asian subcontinent. Following an earlier Persian usage, the Greeks, when they entered India on a military campaign in 326 B.C.E., described the river Sindhu as "Indos," which was sometime later changed to "Indus." Since then, the country east of the river Indus came to be known as India, its people as

Hindus or Indians and their religion as "Hinduism," a word first coined by the British in the 19th century. Historically, people of India referred to their land as "Bharata" and to their faith as *Vaidika Dharma* (the religion of the Vedas) or *Sanatana Dharma* (the eternal religion), suggesting that religion itself knows no age.

Unlike many other religions, Hinduism has no historical prophet-founder or precise founding dates, nor does it identify with a single holy book. All aspects of knowledge, either religious or what is today thought of as secular, were considered sacred in ancient India. Thus, over the centuries, Hindus have inherited an enormous body of sacred literature, the most ancient and revered of which are the Vedas (books of "knowledge"), whose eternal truths are said to have been "heard" by (or revealed to) meditating sages millennia ago. The Vedas are referred to as *shruti*, "that which is heard." A second order of scripture in Hinduism is called *smriti*, "that which is remembered," and these texts are considered authoritative accounts of those learned Hindus who faithfully interpreted the teachings of the Vedas and who compiled, organized and analyzed the traditions of the community. The well-known text, the *Bhagavad Gita*, belongs to this second category of scripture.

A characteristic feature of Hinduism, and one that renders the task of accurately generalizing about the tradition so difficult, is that it has tended toward inclusiveness and pluralism. That is, ancient ideas and ritual practices often survived alongside new ideas and practices, and new ideas (such as those deriving from the Buddhist or Jain traditions, or from reformist movements) were seldom entirely rejected, but instead were synthesized with the older views. The Hindu funeral ceremonies, described later, are a good example of the longevity of ancient ritual practices on the one hand and the expansiveness and adaptability of the tradition on the other. In many ways, the term Hinduism best describes an umbrella under which one may find a great diversity of philosophies, beliefs and practices; a diversity which, over the course of its long history, has not, however, generally led to persecution or to antagonistic sectarian tension.

Speaking about Hinduism's large body of sacred literature, one Hindu scholar has noted, "Being a religion that promotes freedom of choice, its adherents are free to accept them all or reject some and accept others."[1] This freedom of choice for Hindus also extends to beliefs, rituals and other practices. Indeed, Hinduism has no single creedal statement nor a set of beliefs that all those who describe themselves as Hindu would accept. There is therefore no single institutional arbiter of orthodoxy ("correct belief") or even orthopraxy ("correct practice") though ritual is tremendously significant in Hinduism. Nevertheless, there are a set of basic beliefs and practices to which a majority of Hindus adhere in some form or other and it is to a description of some of these basic beliefs and their relationship to Hindu views of death and the afterlife that we now turn.

MAJOR BELIEFS

Creation and Cosmology

Nearly all Indian philosophies have accepted the ideas that the universe has no beginning and no final end, that the world was not created out of nothing, that the universe (and thus our world) undergoes vast cycles of creation, dissolution and recreation and that there is a divine intelligence behind it all. Life and death on both a microcosmic and a macrocosmic scale are viewed as interdependent phases of the natural rhythm of the universe.

The Vedas contain a number of different creation stories to explain how the world and its creatures came to exist. One hymn (*Rig Veda* 10.190) suggests that Cosmic Order and Truth were the first things to be created by "the Arranger." Another hymn from the *Rig Veda* (10.90) describes the creation of the world through the sacrificial dismemberment of the body of the primeval man. Out of each part of his body came some aspect of the natural world, including the Vedic gods and the four classes of human beings. Sacrifice (*yajna*), understood to produce energizing, creative and transformative power, was the central ritual practice of Vedic religion. While initially using animals, the sacrifice came to use, more often, plants and clarified butter. Much of Vedic literature is concerned with the description and explanation of the rituals of sacrifice and the relationship of these rituals to human and cosmic realities. On one level, the sacrifice reduplicated the periodic deterioration and rejuvenation of the entire cosmos. The myths and rituals addressed to the Vedic god Prajapati, the "lord of creatures" usually invoked as the creator, but also as the divine personification of time or death, celebrated "the inescapable fact that the procreation of new beings depends upon the provision of the necessary life-forces and living space by removing a certain number of creatures from the world."[2]

God or Ultimate Reality

At first glance, Hindus appear to believe in many gods. Certainly a visit to a Hindu temple may give this impression and a cursory reading of the great Hindu epic, the *Mahabharata*, or of a compilation of Hindu sacred stories will acquaint one with a wide variety of names, iconographies and stories of various deities. Most Hindus, however, will affirm that God is one and that the many forms and names of the gods are "aspects," emanations or symbols of the one formless, eternal God.

There have been essentially two major views of the nature of the divine in Hindu religious history. The first view, expressed in many of the metaphysical or speculative texts that constitute the Upanishads (texts composed between about the 8th and the 1st centuries B.C.E. and considered the end or culmination of the Vedas) and articulated systematically in Vedantic philosophy, conceives of God or the "Absolute" as an abstract, impersonal principle, or simply as "Absolute Reality," the ground or basis for all that is. The most common designation for this attributeless, genderless Reality is "Brahman." The second major view of the divine is a theistic view; God is both the Supreme Being, responsible for the creation, preservation and dissolution of the universe and is personal and in active relationship with His creation. The theists' view of God has two major subdivisions: one group of theists understand God to be without form or characteristics. They often prefer to worship God without reference to a physical iconography or image. Other theists prefer to conceive of God through attributes and to worship God in a particular form or image. The most prominent names or forms of the theists' God today are Vishnu, Krishna, Rama, Shiva, Murugan, and the Devi (or goddess, known by many names, such as Sri or Durga).

The term "Brahman" first appears in the sense of the one unchanging reality behind the changing visible world in the Upanishads. However, even earlier, though the Vedic hymns are directed to numerous gods, there were hints of the One, "who created the many gods" (*Rig Veda* 10.121) and "that which is One the sages speak of in various terms." A dialogue between a sage and his student in an early Upanishad reduces the number of gods from 3, 306 down to 33, then to six, three, two, one and a half, and finally to one. "Who is the one god?" the student asks. "Breath. He is called 'Brahman,'" the sage replies (*Brihadaranyaka Upanishad* 3.9.1-9[3]; "breath" refers to "life-force"). While there are different understandings about the nature of Brahman in the Upanishads, Brahman is not generally presented as an object of worship, but of knowledge and meditation.[4] Brahman is often described in this literature by the use of negatives: Brahman is "not this and not that." While usually presented as an impersonal principle, however, Brahman is not considered an unconscious one; rather Brahman is the supreme conscious reality. Later Vedantic philosophy speaks of the essence of Brahman as "Being-Consciousness-Joy" (*sat-cit-ananda*).

While most of the Upanishads tend to describe a monistic perspective (where Brahman, pervading all that exists, is the only reality), other Upanishads reveal a theistic perspective, where God is to be adored as the Lord. According to the *Svestashvatara Upanishad*, for example, God is "That which appears to possess the powers of all the senses but is devoid of every sense, which is the Lord, the ruler of the whole world, the vast refuge of the whole world" (3.17); and, in another passage: "After we have first venerated that adorable God displaying every form, the source of all beings, as residing within one's heart, and then recognized him as the one who bestows righteousness and removes evil, as the Lord of prosperity, as abiding within ourselves (*atman*), as the Immortal residing in all beings — we will find this highest God among gods, the highest master among masters, the God beyond the highest as the adorable Lord of the universe" (6.6-7).

The theistic perspective finds one of its earliest and most profound expositions in the short text of 18 chapters called the *Bhagavad Gita*, "The Song of the Lord," composed in the form of a dialogue between the warrior Arjuna and his friend and teacher, Krishna. The entire 10th and 11th chapters eloquently describe the power, glory, mercy and fearfulness of God, here identified with Krishna. For example, "of utterances, I am the single syllable aum; of offerings I am the offering of silent meditation.... Of trees I am the tree of life.... Of weapons I am the thunderbolt.... Among creators I am the creator of love.... I am the beginning, the middle and the end of all that is. Of all knowledge I am the knowledge of the Self [*atma*].... I am death that carries off all things, and I am the source of all things to come.... Know thou that whatever is beautiful and good, whatever has glory and power is only a portion of my own radiance" (10.25-42).[5]

Other texts praise Shiva or Vishnu or Devi, the great goddess, as the one God who is the supreme creator and ruler of the universe. While many Hindus develop a special relationship with one particular deity with its own particular characteristics, bodies of myths, prayers, songs and rites of worship, they readily recognize that other deities may serve the same role as "faces" of the one God or reality whose true essence is beyond all human comprehension.

The concept of *avatara*, or the "descent" of God in human form, articulated in Vishnuite theology, allowed for the possibility of divine intervention in human history, an intervention whose purpose is to restore religious or spiritual order (that is, *dharma*). As Krishna says in the *Bhagavad Gita* (4.7-8): "Whenever there is a decline of *dharma* (righteousness) and a rise of *adharma* (unrighteousness), O Bharata [Arjuna], then I send forth Myself. For the protection of the good, for the destruction of the wicked and for the establishment of righteousness, I come into being from age to age." Thus, in the Hindu tradition, one of the important ways to know God, to understand the will and teachings of God, is through these divine-human teachers.

Human Beings and Their True Essence

As an omniscient, omnipotent being, God cannot be fully comprehended by our finite, embodied selves, yet, as has just been mentioned, real knowledge about God is possible. The ancient Hindu tradition recognized that this knowledge was obtainable through study of the sacred texts, meditation, and above all, through knowledge of the self. The Upanishads are sometimes described as records of the search for truth. In particular, the Vedic and Upanishadic thinkers focused on the hidden interconnection between three aspects of life: the ritual (chants, prayers and ceremonies of the sacrifice), the cosmic realities (the gods, heavenly bodies and natural forces) and the human person (the construction of the body, its vital powers and faculties, the cognitive processes and the essential core of a human being).[6] The seat of the vital powers (of which "breath" was the most important) was understood to be located in the cavity of the heart. More significantly, the Upanishads reveal that the essence of each human being is the imperishable Self or soul, which does not die with the body and which may be identified with Brahman, the "Cosmic Soul." The human "soul" (or *atman*) is described as intangible, indestructible and unbound (*Brihadaranyaka Upanishad* 3.9.26). In other Upanishads it is described as the size of a thumb and as residing in the hearts of people (*Svetashvatara Upanishad* 3.13; 5.9; *Katha Upanishad* 2.12). "Finer than the finest, larger than the largest, is the self [*atman*] that lies here hidden in the heart of a living being. Without desires and free from sorrow, a man perceives by the creator's grace the grandeur of the self" (*Katha Upanishad* 2.6.20). The "body and the heart are called the 'city of Brahman,' which contains everything, yet when old age overtakes it, the soul remains free from evil, age, death, sorrow, hunger and thirst, for it seeks only Reality."[7] From at least the time of the Upanishads, then, Hindus have accepted the belief in the existence of the human soul, which is the "true (divine) nature" of the person and which persists after the death of the body.

Rebirth (Reincarnation) and the Law of Karma

The majority of Hindus also accept the belief that when human beings die, their soul is reborn into another physical body in this world. This doctrine of transmigration not only affirms life after death in a physical rebirth, but also life before death, a pre-existence. The seemingly endless cycle of birth, death and rebirth, to which, in the Hindu view, we are all subject, is known as the wheel of *samsara* ("going-through") — the wheel of rebirth. The doctrine of rebirth as it is now accepted was only hinted at in the Vedas. It was not fully articulated until the Upanishads, when simultaneously the notion of an imperishable soul was developed. The *Bhagavad Gita* compares the rebirth of the soul after death to its continuity through the changing phases of our bodies during our lifetimes: "As the Spirit of our mortal body wanders on in childhood and youth and old age, the Spirit wanders on to a new body" (2.13). In another passage, it compares the process of rebirth to the putting on of new clothes: "As a man leaves an old garment and puts on one that is new, the Spirit leaves his mortal body and puts on one that is new" (2.22).

The wheel of rebirth is both fueled and directed by the law of karma, or the law of cause and effect, another key Hindu doctrine developed in the Upanishads. The term *karma* means deeds or actions. In the Vedas, the term karma applied principally to sacrifices and sacred actions and then it was enlarged to include works or actions in general. It then came to have a moral connotation and to be tied to the notion of rebirth. The doctrine of the law of karma is encapsulated in the statement from the *Brihadaranyaka Upanishad* (3.2.13): "Verily, one becomes good through good deeds and evil through evil deeds." In other words, as a person thinks and acts, so he or she becomes; and further, the sum total of a person's desires or volitions and deeds in the present life determines his or her predispositions, character and social status in the next life. Thus each person is responsible for his own rise or fall in the round of existence. While the law of karma came to be seen as the all-sufficient reason to explain the different conditions of human beings, the varying degrees of suffering and good fortune each person is allotted in life, karma is not the same as unalterable fate determining an unalterable future. On the one hand, belief in rebirth and the law of karma is a stimulus to action, because by good action now one might rise to a better condition in the next life and conversely, by bad actions one will find oneself in a worse condition if not in this life, then certainly in the next. On the other hand, the theistic traditions in Hinduism allowed for the possibility of God's grace intervening to "save" a devotee from rebirth. For example, the *Bhagavad Gita* (12.6-7) says: "But they for whom I am the End Supreme, who surrender all their works to me, and who with pure love meditate on me and adore me — these I very soon deliver from the ocean of death and life-in-death, because they have set their heart on me."

Social and Ethical Teachings

Hindu teachings concerning how one should live, or human values, goals and social organization are found systematically described in a group of texts called Dharmashastras, or "teachings on *dharma*." The concept of *dharma*, loosely translated as "religion," "law" or "righteousness," has three applications: the first relates to natural law or the laws governing the spiritual-physical universe; the second relates to the laws governing society; and the third relates to the laws governing the individual. The Dharmashastras are concerned primarily with the latter two applications.

The codifiers of the Dharmashastras, beginning from just prior to the turn of the Common Era, singled out four human aspirations or values around which social and moral duties were grouped. These are called the *purushartha*s, or "goals of man." The first value is *dharma* itself, here meaning virtue, duty and the practice of religion in its individual context, including daily rituals, prayers, meditation, practice of virtues and avoidance of prohibited acts or things. The second value is economic or material well being (*artha*), by which is meant gainful employment, the acquisition of material goods and the appropriate disbursement of monies and goods to the family and to the needy. The third value is pleasure or aesthetics (*kama*), which includes the enjoyment and/or the learning of the arts (from music, theater and dance to the arts of love). The fourth value is salvation (*moksha*), which involves the study or pursuit and achievement of divine knowledge that leads to "self-realization" and "liberation" from the wheel of *samsara*. This last value was sometimes viewed as being in tension with the previous three, because many held that the pursuit of *moksha* could only successfully be undertaken away from society and its focus on the attainment of well-being in this world. To accommodate this aspiration and its otherworldly focus, the Hindu law codifiers assigned its proper place to the fourth and last stage of a person's life.

The Dharmashastras articulate an ideal scheme of social organization in which every member of society at every major period in his or her life has certain duties and responsibilities which, if faithfully executed, will lead to personal and societal harmony, order and righteousness.[8] Hinduism has recognized four major hereditary and endogamous social divisions, probably based initially on occupation. These are: the Brahmins (or priestly class; those whose primary function it was to study, preserve and transmit the Vedas and other collections of sacred knowledge); the Kshatriyas (or military and governing class); the Vaishyas (or mercantile class) and the Shudras (or the laborer class).[9]

In addition to the four castes, the law codifiers identified four stages in life. The first is the student stage (the first 15 to 25 years of one's life, depending on one's caste and sex). The second is the householder stage, comprising the major portion of one's life, when one marries, works at a profession and raises children (*artha* and *kama* are preeminent concerns at this stage, as regulated by *dharma*). The third stage is that of the recluse (*vanaprastha* — the stage of retirement to the forest). This stage is understood to be the period in one's life when the children have grown up and married and one can now simplify one's life and concentrate on explicitly spiritual (*moksha*-oriented) concerns. The last stage in this ideal scheme is that of the ascetic (*sannyasa*) — an option taken by relatively few Hindus. Though supposedly the last stage in life, the option of "renouncing the world" (that is, one's family, profession and social position) in order to focus exclusively on spiritual pursuits, in fact, has been taken up by individuals at any age who felt drawn to this way of life. Becoming an ascetic usually requires one to ritually conduct one's own funeral, so that one "dies" to one's former socially constructed identity. As a *sannyasin*, one is assured *moksha* or liberation from physical rebirth at one's bodily death.

In general, the Dharmashastras consider the householder stage as the most important one because on this stage depend all the others. As the *Manusmriti* (3.77-8) says: "Just as all living creatures depend on air in order to live, so do members of the other stages of life subsist by depending on householders. Because people in the other three stages of life are supported every day by the knowledge and the food of the householder, therefore the householder stage of life is best."[10]

The *Yogasutras,* Dharmashastras and other religious texts of the Hindu tradition describe a number of attitudes and behaviors that are required to live a moral or virtuous life, a life in conformity with *dharma*. Several texts summarized these behaviors into 10 practices or observances (*niyamas*). The *Agnipurana* (175.10-11), for example, gives the following list of observances: forgiveness or patience (*kshma*), truthfulness (*satya*), compassion (*daya*), charity (*dana*), purity *(sauca)*, control of the sense-organs (*indriyanigraha*), worship of God *(deva-puja)*, fire sacrifice (*homa* or *agni havan*), contentment (*santosha*) and not-stealing (*asteya*). Together with the practice of vows and fasts, the ultimate purpose of these *niyamas* was the cultivation of inward and outward purity and physical and spiritual discipline required to take a person closer to God.

While the Dharmashastras are the most explicit and systematic religio-juridical manuals for right conduct, other texts, such as the *Bhagavad Gita*, provide the undergirding philosophical framework for living a spiritual life in relationship with God. The *Bhagavad Gita* describes three discrete but interrelated "paths" that take one toward the goal of life, articulated variously in different Hindu philosophies as spiritual freedom, self-knowledge, liberation from the wheel of rebirth, union with Brahman or eternal life with God (*ishvara*). One path is the path of action (*karma yoga*). Even God, unaffected by the law of karma or by the actions of His creatures, is constantly acting, constantly at work in the world, for if He was not, the universe would fall apart (*Bhagavad Gita* 3.22-24). The path of action requires that one focus on service in a spirit of faith and detachment. Without detachment, action can bind one further to the world. However, the teachings of the *Bhagavad Gita* reject the idea that one can ever withdraw from action by withdrawing from society. According to the *Bhagavad Gita*, the path of action must be informed by right (or pure) intentions, sound judgment and knowledge.

The second path is that of knowledge or wisdom (*jnana yoga*). Here the focus is on the study of scripture, on the practice of meditation and on the acquisition of insight and understanding, "for wisdom is in truth the end of all holy work" (*Bhagavad Gita* 4.33). "A constant yearning to know the inner Spirit, and a vision of Truth which gives liberation: this is true wisdom and all else is ignorance" (*Bhagavad Gita* 13.11).

The third path is that of devotion (*bhakti yoga*). This path involves developing the love of God; letting God's love inform and direct one's actions, speech and thought; and surrendering one's self to God. This path is considered by the *Bhagavad Gita* to be the supreme path: "The greatest of all Yogis [spiritual aspirants] is he who with all his soul has faith, and he who with all his soul loves Me [God]" (6.47).

The key to each of these paths, to living the good (spiritual) life, is to cultivate an attitude of detachment or disinterestedness ("non-attachment" or negative attachment to the fruits of one's actions); to act, that is, to perform one's responsibilities out of love of God, rather than out of ego or concern for one's own well-being. In short, according to the *Bhagavad Gita*, the goal in this life is to cultivate a positive attachment to the love of God; to dedicate oneself wholly to God while living in the world and to achieve inner wisdom, equanimity and peace.

VIEWS OF DEATH AND LIFE BEYOND DEATH

The poets of the early Vedas, such as the *Rig Veda*, appear to have been concerned principally with well-being in this world, that is, with the acquisition of material prosperity and children, with the achievement of good health and a long life and generally with the maintenance of order through the rituals of sacrifice in which gods and humans work together, each assigned certain duties and functions. Death was viewed with sadness as an inevitable, though unwelcome, event; an event that marked a transition from one state of existence to another. The "person" separates from the body at death, as it does when one dreams, but now the separation is permanent. Various images of an afterlife are offered — images suggesting that the dead assumed a new "body" and went to rejoin their ancestors in a pleasant place somewhat similar to life on earth. One funeral hymn addressing the dead man tells him not to linger but to "Go forth...on those ancient paths on which our ancient fathers passed beyond.... Unite with the fathers, with Yama [lord of the dead], with the rewards of your sacrifices and good deeds, in the highest heaven...merge with a glorious body" (*Rig Veda* 10.14.7-8).[11] Another hymn (*Rig Veda* 10.16) alternately addresses Agni, the god of fire, and the dead man. It tells the god not to burn the corpse entirely, but to "cook" him perfectly, so that the body will be purified and accepted by the ancestors, just as the sacrifice was understood not to be destroyed by the fire but to be purified and thus made perfect by the heat so that it was accepted by the gods. Then it addresses the dead man and speaks of the ultimate dispersal of the old body to the elements: "May your eye go to the sun, your life's breath to the wind. Go to the sky or to the earth, as is your nature; or go to the water, if that is your fate. Take root in the plants with your limbs" (*Rig Veda* 10.16.3). The hymn addresses Agni again, asking him to lead the dead man (with his new body) to heaven, to Yama, and to the fathers, where he may take his place as one of the honored ancestors. Another hymn describes different levels of spiritual attainment and after each description requests that the dead man go to join with these distinguished individuals (*Rig Veda* 10.154). Articles of food and other necessities were provided for the three-day journey to the ancestors (offered in the fire), so that the person would not suffer hunger and thirst.

Finally, one hymn suggests that the dead person may be buried, rather than cremated (the usual practice today). The priest addresses the body lying in the burial ground: "Open up, earth; do not crush him. Be easy for him to enter and to burrow in. Earth, wrap him up as a mother wraps a son in the edge of her skirt.... I shore up the earth around you; let me not injure you as I lay down this clod of earth. Let the fathers hold up this pillar for you; let Yama build a house for you here" (*Rig Veda* 10.18.11 and 13). It is possible that this hymn is a remnant of a former custom of burial and that as the cult of the sacrifice became more established, cremation, itself regarded as a sacrifice, became the most prevalent way of disposing of the body.[12]

In sum, the early Vedas offer several views of the disposal of the dead and the fate of humans after death: the dead person merges with a glorious body in some sort of "heaven"; his mortal body is purified and renewed or perfected by the fire and united with his ancestors; the parts of his old body are dispersed to the elements of the cosmos; or, he may return to the welcoming womb of mother earth.

In the Brahmanas, texts that are part of the Vedic corpus, composed around 900 B.C.E., and that consist of ritual descriptions and analyses or glosses on the *Rig Veda*, death appears to be more feared than it was in the Vedas. It is also associated with evil. One scholar has argued that the central concern of the Brahmanas is the fear of death and the obsessive search for rituals that can overcome it.[13] In particular, the object of fear seems to be the idea of recurrent death (*punar mrtyu*), which may include a form of "deathliness" brought on by old age; death in the world of the ancestors; a series of ritual deaths within an average life-span or rebirth (and so redeath) in the physical world. A recurrent idea in the Brahmanas is that death may be "conquered" through ritual or esoteric knowledge[14]; that is, correct ritual knowledge has the power to extend life here (and beyond death).

In one vivid passage, Death, personified, is described as the "Ender"; the one who goes to the end of a life-span "by means of day and night" (i.e., through the passage of time) and conquers or "eats" the person. As well, though the doctrine of physical rebirth in this world is not yet fully articulated, there is the suggestion of rebirth for the ignorant:

> The gods were afraid of this Ender, Death; they thought, 'Let him not go to the end of our life-spans by means of day and night.' They performed the sacrificial rituals and became immortal. Death said to the gods, 'All men will become immortal in precisely this way, and then what share will be mine?' They said, 'From now on, no one else will become immortal together with the body. But as soon as you have taken [the body as] your share, then, after separating from his body, he will become immortal — if he is someone who has achieved immortality through knowledge or through action [*karma*].' And those who have this knowledge, or who do this ritual, they come to life again when they have died, and as soon as they come to life again they come to immortal life. But those who do not have this knowledge or who do not do this ritual, when they die they come to life again, but they become the food of this [Death] again and again (*Satapatha Brahmana* 10.4.3.1-10).[15]

Initially the gods are subject to death, but then they perform the rituals and become immortal. Death is worried that he will have nothing to sustain him. The gods allow that Death may consume the bodies of men (as before), but those who had the sacred knowledge and performed the correct rituals will "live" forever, as do the gods, while those who are ignorant will repeatedly experience redeath (either in the "other" world or in this world).

The Upanishads elaborate more specifically the two paths that the dead may take: the path to the ancestors and the path to the gods. As has been noted, the Upanishads developed the concept of an imperishable Self or soul, and with it, the notions of the law of karma and rebirth. The authors of the Upanishads had come to view life in this world negatively, as a place of suffering and unhappiness caused, essentially, by ignorance. Thus, escape or liberation from this undesirable cycle of rebirth, from redeath, became the goal. The state of *moksha* is the ultimate defeat of death. The usefulness of the old forms of ritual practices, centered as they were on attaining a long life and well-being in this world, to help one to achieve the new goal of attaining liberating spiritual knowledge, were called into question. The techniques of meditation, asceticism and vigorous analysis and inquiry into the true nature of reality were seen as more efficacious or salvific than sacrificial rituals. Nevertheless, not all could or should engage in asceticism and meditation. Thus, in the description of the two paths, allowance is made for those who may choose to be reborn after death, but reborn in a better condition. According to the *Brihadaranyaka Upanishad* (6.2.15ff.) and the *Chandogya Upanishad* (10.1-6), those who do auspicious deeds, live a good life and correctly perform the rites of sacrifice, after they are cremated, go up to the moon in the form of smoke, pass into the world of the fathers and eventually through various other transformations they return to the earth as food where they are consumed, turned into semen and are reborn in a better condition. Those who have not led good lives are reborn in a worse condition (in an "inferior womb"). But those who purify their minds and bodies through asceticism and meditation and who achieve liberating knowledge (wisdom and insight), go the way of the gods after death, to the world of Brahman, never to return.

The *Bhagavad Gita* (composed after the Upanishads), urges us not to fear death, nor to grieve the deaths of our loved ones, for although our bodies perish, the embodied self (or soul) is "enduring, indestructible and immeasurable" (2.18). The "Eternal in man cannot die" (2.19), Krishna assures Arjuna; "Weapons cannot hurt the Spirit and fire can never burn him. Untouched is he by drenching waters, untouched is he by parching winds" (2.23); "Invisible is he to mortal eyes, beyond thought and beyond change. Know that he is, and cease from sorrow. For all things born in truth must die, and out of death in truth comes life. Face to face with what must be, cease thou from sorrow" (2.25-26). Those who can free themselves from attachment to the transient world of the senses, who act without egotism, who fix their minds and hearts firmly on God, find wisdom and peace (2.55-71). "This is the Eternal in man. Reaching him all delusion is gone. Even in the last hour of his life upon earth, man can reach the Nirvana of Brahman [the bliss of God] — man can find peace in the peace of God" (2.72).

Several verses in a later section of the *Bhagavad Gita* refer to the idea that "the knowers of the three Vedas" who perform the prescribed rituals and pray to go to heaven will indeed reach Indra's heaven and enjoy the pleasures of the gods, but when the merit of their good deeds is exhausted, they will return to the world of mortals; they obtain "what comes and goes," what is subject to birth and death (9.20-21). That is, their desires for rewards, their attachment to their good deeds, no matter how well performed, will lead back to this fleeting and changing world. But to those who worship God "with a pure oneness of soul, to those who are ever in harmony," God increases what they have, and gives them what they have not (9.22); that is, he increases faith and gives "true" immortality (knowledge of God, dwelling with God). Harkening back to the Upanishadic description of the two paths that the spirit of the dead may take (to the gods and to the ancestors), Krishna in the *Bhagavad Gita* suggests that one will go to or become whatever one worships or identifies with: "Those who worship the gods, go to the gods, and those who worship the fathers go to the fathers. Those who worship the lower spirits go to the lower spirits; but those who worship me come unto me" (9.25).

In sum, the existence of death as a natural and inevitable process is recognized by Hindu theists and non-theists alike. The Vedic peoples were intent on promoting human longevity as much as possible, but the few hymns in the *Rig Veda* that focus on death and the afterlife suggest that death itself was not particularly feared, being viewed as a passage to a new life in the world of the ancestors. The composers of the Brahmanas and Upanishads, in linking death with rebirth (and redeath), were far more preoccupied than their Vedic predecessors with "conquering death," that is, with learning the secret or hidden truths which, once understood, would lead to a final release from the wheel of rebirth, even from the world of the ancestors, to blissful and eternal union with Brahman. The *Bhagavad Gita* turns our attention back to how we live our lives in this world even as it tells us not to be anxious about death, for our spirits are immortal. Nor, however, should rebirth be feared, for our destiny is not determined solely by an impervious law of karma, but it lies with an omniscient and gracious God and the response of devotees to Krishna's guidance.

In the compendia of religious and philosophical lore found within the grand Hindu epic, the *Mahabharata* and within the medieval texts of the Puranas, numerous reflections on death and the afterlife are offered. The arrival of death itself is associated with the whims of the divine personification of Death (Yama), the will of God, the unpredictable machinations of time (*kala*) or destiny (*daivam*), a person's deeds in his or her previous life or some combination of these factors. Even premature or accidental death never occurs without some reason beyond the immediate cause (such as a fatal illness or drowning), though we may not ever know the full picture. The epics and Puranas contain many stories that illustrate these hidden causes, but that often also offer hope that God may intervene on behalf of his devotees to forestall fate, time or karma. There are tales of those who have managed to outwit Death (for example, the stories of Savitri, Naciketas, Sudarshana and Oghavati) and those who postponed or escaped their preordained appointment with Death, usually by exhibiting unswerving devotion to Vishnu or Shiva (for example, the story of Prahlada).

HEAVEN AND HELL

Heaven

"Heaven" (*svarga*) is often mentioned in Hindu texts of the early and classical period as the promised reward for the practice of good deeds, for the observance of *dharma*. Heaven is simply and vaguely described as a desirable place to go after death. It is the "place" where the gods reside. In the Upanishads, the attainment of heaven is especially associated with the acquisition of spiritual knowledge. The heavenly world is "endless and invincible" (*Kena Upanishad* 4.9); it is the place of the "immortal gods," and "upon reaching there a man who knows this [sacred knowledge] becomes immortal" (*Kausitaki Upanishad* 2.13). But for persons who have not achieved the ultimate liberating knowledge, heaven is a temporary sojourn, according to the Upanishads. "Wallowing in ignorance time and again, the fools imagine, 'We have reached our aim!' Because of their passion, they do not understand, these people who are given to rites [the sacrificial rituals]. Therefore, they fall, wretched and forlorn, when their heavenly stay comes to a close.... When they have enjoyed their good work [the fruits of their positive *karma*], atop the firmament, they return again to this abject world" (*Mundaka Upanishad* 1.2.9-10).

In later texts, such as the *Manusmrti* (or "code of Manu"), attaining heaven is often mentioned as one of several rewards accruing to the person who acts according to *dharma* (who does good deeds and avoids vice). For example, one passage states: "The revering of guests wins wealth, a good reputation, long life and heaven" (3.106). In the Puranas, each of the major gods has his or her own heaven (*loka*s) where their respective devotees will repair after death. But again, these heavens are all temporary places for the soul that has not yet achieved liberation (*moksha*). When a person's merit is used up, his desires and attachments will drag him down to earth and to rebirth (in some life form, human or animal) once again. "When their merits are exhausted, the virtuous souls fall from heaven and are born in the house of kings or nobles of illustrious character, where they enjoy various pleasures. Thus men go up and down the ladder" (*Garuda Purana* 2.3.89-90).

Hell

Vedic literature does not describe a "place" of punishment and suffering. In the early Vedas, the abode of the ancestors is the only "place" to which the departed go. In the Upanishads, "hell," so to speak, is the cycle of rebirth itself. This fleeting and often painful world in which we live is sometimes depicted as "hellish." The *Bhagavad Gita* also does not describe hell as such, but rather the text focuses on the conditions that lead to *adharma* (that is, lawlessness and social disorder), for example, the marital mingling of castes and the destruction of family laws. It also says that the three cardinal vices of desire, anger and greed are "the three gates of hell" (1.42-44; 16.21).

However, the Dharmashastras and the Puranic literature, composed centuries later, vividly describe various terrible hells *(naraka)* to which those who have committed wrongs go for punishment and atonement.[16] There are said to be numerous hells, below the surface of the earth, full of fire and instruments of torture, with which Yama, the god of this underworld, has sinners punished.[17] The *Manusmrti* describes what happens to the person who has committed sins after death:

> After the death of men who have done bad deeds, another solid body, designed to be tortured, is born out of the five elements. When [the living souls] here have suffered with that body the tortures given by Yama, [the bodies] dissolve, each part distributed into its own basic element. And after he has suffered for faults that are born of attachment to sensory objects and that result in unhappiness, his stains are erased.... If he mostly does right and only a little wrong, he is enveloped in those very elements [acquires a "heavenly body"] and experiences happiness in heaven.... Seeing with his very own intellect these levels of existence of the living soul that result from right and wrong, a man should always set his mind and heart on what is right (12.16-23).

The *Garuda Purana* (2.3.3) states that there are thousands of hells "where the evil-doers are thrown mercilessly." The text goes on to describe at length the principal hells and the various misdeeds that direct the dead person to one or the other of the hells for periods of time. The sins or violations of *dharma* enumerated include: hoarding wealth, giving false testimony, stealing, murder, sexual misconduct and selling liquor. Sinners may be boiled, torn apart by vultures, crushed, burned, exposed to extremes of cold and heat and so forth. The text suggests that those in heaven and those in hell are aware of the conditions of either state: "The gods look down and see the fierce hells. The sinners of hell also look up and see the gods above" (2.3.77).

FUNERAL RITES

For more than two millennia, many traditional Hindus, especially those of the Brahmin, Kshatriya and Vaishya classes, have marked stages of development and transition over the course of their lives with rites called *samskaras*, a Sanskrit word often translated as "sacraments." Essentially, the *samskaras* are ceremonies intended to purify, refine and sanctify the body and mind of an individual so that he or she may progressively become a full-fledged ("cultured") member of the community. These sacraments are grouped into five major divisions: the prenatal rites, the rites of childhood, the educational rites, the marriage rite and the funeral ceremonies. It is said that through the *samskaras* performed when one is alive one conquers this earth and through those performed by one's relatives after death one conquers heaven.[18]

The Hindu funeral ceremonies are called the *antyeshti samskara*. There are also a series of rites for the departed, performed at the time of death, in the days immediately following and at regular intervals (usually annually) thereafter, called *sraddha*. The *sraddha* rituals, consisting essentially of prescribed food offerings, are intended to nourish and promote the well-being of the deceased ancestors, as well as to commemorate their memory. Altogether, the *antyeshti* and initial *sraddha* ceremonies are intended to prepare and effect a smooth transition for the deceased from the world of the living to the world of the dead and from "ghosthood" to the realm of the ancestors and thence rebirth. In their full form these rites are lengthy and complicated, requiring the assistance of a number of specialists (funeral priests). Like the Hindu marriage rituals, the funeral rites are based on an archaic Vedic model that continued to be elaborated over a 2000-year period. Thus the rites incorporate both Vedic and post-Vedic rituals and world views: the importance of sacrifice and the ancestors, along with beliefs in reincarnation and God's grace. Testifying to the antiquity of these rites, verses from the *Rig Veda* and the *Atharva Veda* accompany the main body of funeral ceremonies, but at the beginning or end verses from the *Bhagavad Gita* or more recent devotional literature may be recited. In general, the Vedic verses are concerned with the ease and enjoyment of the dead; they are not concerned with salvation or with release from the cycle of rebirth.

Few Hindus today undertake the entire sequence of rituals for the dead (which may take a full year), as they are both time-consuming and costly. However, the Hindu tradition has always made allowances for shortened and simplified ritual procedures, taking into account individuals' capacities and circumstances. Thus, for example, instead of performing daily rituals for the first 10 days after death (the normal requirement), some Hindus may do all the rituals on the 10th day only.

A fully detailed description of all of the Hindu rites for the dead, even without including the historical and geographical variations, and the different rites accorded to children, ascetics and other special cases is well beyond the scope of this chapter.[19] Instead, a brief survey of the main sequence of events as observed in India, along with a selection of verses or mantras from the Vedas that accompany each action, is presented below. Variations in practice among Hindus in North America will also be noted.[20]

Approach of Death

When death is thought to be near, the friends and relatives will gather around the dying man or woman to hear the final wishes. It is customary for the Hindu who is dying to give gifts to Brahmins and to the needy. Traditionally, the gift of a cow was held to be most meritorious and valuable. She is called "Vaitarani" and was held to be the dead person's guide over the river that separates Yama's kingdom. The dying person may be laid out on a couch with feet facing south near the domestic hearth. The *Gita Mahatmya* or verses from the *Bhagavad Gita,* the *Ramayana* or some other holy text are read out so that he or she may die hearing the name of God. A lamp should be lit near the dying person as a sign to the soul that it should go straight up.

Predisposal Rites

Vedic customs, such as the rite of *homa* (offerings to the deceased's domestic fires), have generally been replaced with simplified Puranic practices. "When it is ascertained that life has gone out of the body, the son should bathe and wash the corpse with pure water without delay" (*Garuda Purana* 2.4.41). Hair and nails may be clipped. Drops of sacred water from the Ganges River and a few *tulasi* (basil) leaves may be placed in the mouth of the dead person as well as special mixtures (*pancagavyam*) and small pieces of gold or precious stones (*pancaratna*), related to the five elements of the body. Sandalwood paste may be applied and blades of *kusa* grass may be placed in the hands. Sesame seeds, barley and clay from the Ganges may also be used in the predisposal rites. All of these substances serve to purify and protect the corpse from evil spirits. Married women should have a piece of gold on their persons. Only close relatives of the deceased are allowed to touch the body.

Next, the body is wrapped in a white, unbleached cotton cloth. In North America, many Hindus have adopted the practice of dressing the body in a suit or sari. Because cremation normally took place within a day or two of death, embalming the body has not been a practice in India. However, some Hindus in North America have preferred to send the body back to India for full funeral rites and therefore, means to preserve the body are necessary in these circumstances. Lamenting and weeping for the deceased is conducted by the female relatives.

The Funeral Procession

The body is placed on a bier made of bamboo and often covered with flowers. The funeral procession is headed by the chief mourner, usually the eldest son, who may carry a torch kindled by the domestic fire. If possible, the bier is carried to the cremation ground by the deceased's male relatives, who are to walk barefooted. Other mourners follow behind. While processing, mourners repeat the name of God (e.g., "Ram, Ram"). Traditionally, there are six stops along the way where *sraddha* rituals are performed and mantras recited. At the first stop, the following verse from the *Atharva Veda* may be recited: "O Lord! May this soul traveling by the devayan or pitriyan path to the sphere of our forefathers accompanied by Lord Yama be happy, satiated and well protected by Yama's two emissaries" (18.2.11). In North America, the body is usually placed in a coffin and the procession takes place in cars.

The Cremation

In the Hindu tradition cremation of the body is regarded as an offering into the sacred fire, which transforms the corpse and takes it to heaven as a sacrifice. It is because it is a sacrifice that purificatory rituals must be performed. The ancient manuals specify the details regarding the length and depth of the trench for the cremation, the kind of wood (often sandalwood) to be used, and the size and orientation of the pyre, the manner in which it is to be purified and the hymns and verses to be chanted at each stage of the preparations. A formula is chanted to scare away demons and ghosts, while sprinkling water around the pyre. The bier is placed on the pyre and water and clarified butter (*ghi*) are sprinkled on it, accompanied by the recitation of Vedic verses.

Food offerings of sweetened rice and milk may be offered to Brahmins who are understood to receive it on behalf of the souls of the departed for their appeasement and pleasure. Water is also offered to Brahmins for the satisfaction of the ancestors. Then the pyre is lit by the eldest son (or youngest son, or brother's son or wife or grandson, or member of the same lineage [*gotra*], or, if there are no relatives, by the priest). A father may not light the pyre or perform other funeral ceremonies for a son. While lighting the pyre, prayers from the *Rig Veda* (10.16) and *Atharva Veda* (18.1.56 and 18.3.71) are recited.

The *Garuda Purana* (2.4.66-68) stipulates that when "the body is half burnt, a quantity of *ghi* should be poured over it with the [prayer]: 'You are born from it, you be born again. Let this be for heaven, Svaha.' He should recite this [prayer] announcing the name of the deceased and pour forth butter along with gingelly seeds while the relatives weep loudly. This gives comfort to the departed soul (still wandering in the air)." Finally, the pyre is circumambulated by the mourners before they depart.

Where electric crematoria are used in India and in North America, some of the traditional rituals are not possible. The body is kept in the coffin, its lid is closed and a small oil lamp (*dip*) is placed on top. The eldest son (or relative) will light the lamp and later turn the crematorium switch. Later, some of the ashes of the cremated body are collected and are immersed in a river, as rivers are held to be sacred and purifying. North American Hindus often will either send the ashes back to India to be deposited in a river (especially in the Ganges) or they will take the ashes back to India themselves when there is an opportunity to fulfill this sacred duty.

Bathing and Water Offering

If possible, mourners are to bathe in a stream or river before they return home. Facing south (the direction of death) water is offered again in the rite of *udakakarma* or *jal anjali* for the welfare of the deceased. This rite may be repeated 365 times at once or, ideally, performed daily by the eldest son for a year.

Mourning and Reflection on Death

Mourners gather to share praises of the deceased and to hear consoling stories from the sacred texts. The *Garuda Purana* (2.4.82-85) suggests that "a learned person well-versed in the Purana should alleviate their [the mourners'] sorrow discoursing on the...unsubstantial nature of the universe," and on the transience of life.

Period of Impurity

A death within the family creates ritual defilement or impurity for family members for a period of time ranging from two days to one month, depending on the age and sex of the deceased (the death of a young child, for example, creates only one or two days of ritual impurity for the parents), the relationship of mourners to the deceased and caste rules. During this period of mourning relatives are to forego pleasures and comforts and are to restrict their diets. Men are to remain unshaved. Activity outside the home is curtailed. On the 10th day after death (the most common period of time for mourning and the observance of ritual defilement rules), a rite called the *Santi-karma* may be performed by male family members. Four oblations are offered to the hearth fire with mantras. The old hearth fire of the deceased, which was extinguished upon his death, is replaced by a new hearth fire. A feast takes place and survivors may return to normal life.

Offerings to the Dead

When a person dies, his "soul" is believed to hover around first his body and then the family for a period of time. Deriving from the time of the Vedas, the rites of *sraddha* and *pindadan* which are performed by the deceased's relatives in the days immediately following death and which culminate in the rite of *sapindikarana* (on the 12th day or at the close of one year), are intended to provide the spirit of the dead with a "body" so that it may successfully traverse the world of the living to the abode of the dead ancestors. Each day, balls of rice (*pinda*) and water are offered by the eldest son (or other suitable relative) to Brahmin funeral priests who receive it on behalf of the departed. Day by day, the soul's "body" is gradually ritually constructed and nourished. On the 11th day the spirit of the dead person has attained its full ancestral body and is thus released from the liminal state of ghosthood, enabling him or her to cross the ocean of mortality and to arrive at the abode of Yama. The 11th day ceremonies end with a feast and gifts given to 11 Brahmins who represent the company of the ancestors. "Of all the complex stages in the Hindu rites of death and dying," one author has noted, "the most arresting moment comes at the *sapindikarana*, the time-filled action of blending the deceased with his forefathers, of transforming the vulnerable, disembodied spirit (*preta*) of this world into the secure *pitr* [ancestor] of that other world. The *sapindikarana*...is a 'creating of the *sapinda*' relationship, that is, an establishing of the ritual bond between generations of those (living) who *offer* and those (deceased) who *receive* the *pinda*, a symbolic meal of food pressed into a ball."[21] Thus, in these ancient rites, the living relatives are viewed as responsible for securing the transfer of the dead to their proper place in the cosmic order and for ensuring the continued well-being of their ancestors in the world beyond.

Additional *sraddha* rites for one's ancestors (specifically, the immediate four generations) may be offered at monthly, semi-annual or annual intervals. For the recent deceased, the annual rites are observed on the death anniversary. There is also a fortnight period in the Hindu calendar called *pitr-paksa* when Hindus may offer *sraddha* rites for the continued well-being and satisfaction of one's ancestors and as an occasion for memorial observances. In recommending the faithful performance of rites for the ancestors, the *Garuda Purana* states: "Age, sons, fame, heaven, glory, health, strength, splendour, cattle, happiness, wealth and grain — all these can be procured by worshipping the manes [souls of the departed]. The rites performed in favor of the manes are more beneficial than the rites performed for the deities" (2.9.56-58). This text also suggests that all worship, whether directed to the ancestors, the deities, the Brahmins or the Vedic fire, is ultimately the worship of God, "the soul of all beings" (2.9.60).

CONCLUSION

In sum, Hindus understand all individuals to be constituted by a material body as well as an "essence" — a spirit or soul (*atman, jiva* or *purusha*). The longevity of the physical body may be prolonged by certain practices (for example, ascetic exercises), but death is finally inescapable. Upon physical death, and after cremation, a new subtle body may be reconstituted through *sraddha* rites and the spirit secured in the abode of the ancestors. However, "The fire consumes his body but the merit and demerit accompany him. The body is burnt by the fire but the actions perpetrated by him keep him company" (*Garuda Purana* 2.12.26-27). Thus the spirit may be punished in "hell" or rewarded in "heaven" depending upon the choices made during a person's life. Eventually, according to the laws of karma, the spirit is reborn in a new physical body. Thus the "real" self, the inner soul or spirit (called by the *Bhagavad Gita* the "witness," "isolated," "neutral" and "seer") never dies. It "cannot be killed," as the *Bhagavad Gita* and Upanishads affirm. When the effects of karma are finally burned up through asceticism, self-knowledge, self-less action, devotion and/or the grace of God, the imperishable soul or spirit is released to commune or unite eternally with God.

By taking shelter in Vasudeva [God], possessing pure intellect, controlling the self with fortitude, discarding the objects of enjoyment and leaving attachment and envy, serving without expecting a reward, controlling speech, body and mind, practicing meditation and Yoga, taking recourse to detachment, leaving pride, force, desire, anger, thus calm and serene, he attains brahma (*Garuda Purana* 2.10.93-96).

Notes

1. Ajit Adhopia, *The Hindus of Canada: A Perspective on Hindu Canadians' Cultural Heritage* (Mississauga: Inderlekh Publications, 1993), p. 91.
2. J. Bruce Long, "Death as a Necessity and a Gift in Hindu Mythology," in Frank Reynolds and Earle Waugh, eds., *Religious Encounters with Death: Insights from the History and Anthropology of Religions* (University Park: The Pennsylvania State University Press, 1977), p. 76.
3. Passages quoted from the Upanishads are from Patrick Olivelle, (trans.), *Upanisads* (Oxford: Oxford University Press, 1996).
4. Geoffrey Parrinder, *The Indestructible Soul: The Nature of Man and Life After Death in Indian Thought* (London: George Allen & Unwin, 1973), p. 41.
5. Passages quoted from the *Bhagavad Gita* are adapted from the translations by Juan Mascaro (London: Penguin Books, 1962) and S. Radhakrishnan (London: George Allen & Unwin, 1948).
6. See Olivelle's introduction to the *Upanisads*, pp. xlix-liii.
7. Parrinder, *The Indestructible Soul*, p. 42.
8. The word "caste" more appropriately translates the Sanskrit word *jati*, which refers to the many dozens of occupation-based social groupings usually assigned to one or other of the four larger "classes." There can be social mobility among the castes, but not among the classes as a whole. The origin of the "four castes," the English word that used to translate the Sanskrit word *varna*, but which recently has been replaced by the term "class" and its various ramifications in Hindu social and religious history, is a complicated subject.
9. Some recent Hindu thinkers, reexamining the ancient texts, have argued that these four divisions are best understood not as hereditary occupations, but rather as human dispositions or religious types. That is, some individuals are disposed to scholarly or intellectual pursuits, others to active engagement or service, others to professions or activities where "feelings" are important, and so forth. See S. Radhakrishnan, *The Hindu View of Life* (New York: Macmillan, 1927); and Arvind Sharma, *Hinduism for Our Times* (Delhi: Oxford University Press, 1996).
10. Quoted in *The Laws of Manu*, translated by Wendy Doniger with Brian K. Smith (London: Penguin Books, 1991).
11. Passages from the *Rig Veda* are from the translation by Wendy Doniger O'Flaherty (*The Rig Veda: An Anthology*, New York: Penguin Books, 1981). Some of the material for this discussion of views of death and the afterlife in the Vedas and Brahmanas is derived from the essay, "Reincarnation in Hinduism," by Wendy Doniger (in *Reincarnation or Resurrection?* edited by H. Haring and J.B. Metz (Concilium 5, 1993, London: SCM Press), pp. 3-15.
12. This position is argued by Rajbali Pandey in his *Hindu Samskaras: Socio-Religious Study of the Hindu Sacraments* (Delhi: Motilal Banarsidass, 1969), pp. 239-241.

13. Doniger, "Reincarnation in Hinduism," p. 5.
14. See *Satapatha Brahmana* 2.2.2.14.
15. Passage translated and condensed by Doniger, "Reincarnation in Hinduism," pp. 5-6.
16. "Whatever sin a man commits consciously or unconsciously stands in need of purification and atonement" (*Garuda Purana*, 2.4.1; translations from this Purana are from the Ancient Indian Tradition and Mythology Series (Delhi: Motilal Banarsidass, 1979). The Dharmashastras and Puranas offer numerous ways to atone for various specific sins while one is still living.
17. The *Manusmrti* (4.88-91) lists 21 hells, each with its own name, such as "Darkness," the "Thread of Time," "Burning" and "Stinking Earth."
18. The *Baudhayana Pitrmedhasutras*, 3.1.4, translated in Pandey, *Hindu Samskaras*, p. 234.
19. It may be noted that traditionally, young children and ascetics were not cremated but were buried or placed in rivers. Readers interested in more detail regarding funerary rites and beliefs about death and the afterlife may wish to consult the following primary sources: the 10th *mandala* or chapter of the *Rig Veda*; the 18th chapter of the *Atharva Veda*; the *Baudhayana Pitrmedhasutra*; the *Garuda Purana*, part II — Dharma (Preta) Kanda; and the following secondary sources: Rajbali Pandey's *Hindu Samskaras*; Kane's *History of Dharmasastra*, vol. 4, pp. 179-333 (Poona: Bandharkar Oriental Research Institute, 1962); Jonathan Parry's *Death in Banaras* (Cambridge: Cambridge University Press, 1994); and David Knipe's article, "*Sapindikarana*: The Hindu Rite of Entry into Heaven," in F. Reynolds and E. Waugh (eds.), *Religious Encounters with Death* (University Park: The Pennsylvania State University Press, 1977), pp.111-124.
20. The material for this description is drawn primarily from Pandey's *Hindu Samskaras*, the *Garudapurana*, *The Hindu Antyeshti Sanskar Paddhati*, compiled and abridged from the Vedas with Hindi and English translation by Mahshai Deonarine (Calcutta: the Banaras Mercantile Co., n.d.), and interviews with the temple priest, Pandit Sharma and functionaries from the Hindu Samaj Mandir, Hamilton, Canada.
21. David Knipe, "*Sapindikarana*: The Hindu Rite of Entry into Heaven," p. 111. In this same article Knipe poses the logical question: If "transmigration of the imperishable self is...assured, why is a great company of deceased ancestors still existent in some extraterrestrial world? Further, if the inescapable laws of *karma* stand effective, how can it be that these ancestors subsist in continued dependence on the ritual activities of their descendants?" (p. 112). He offers one answer by suggesting that the ritual world view of early Vedic religion was able to survive the challenge of the new doctrines and theologies that eroded the institutional structure of Vedic religion in the individual funeral and ancestral rites, for, "Although the concern shifted away from the early Vedic desire for a state of perpetual non-death or immortality to the dilemma of *samsara* and the ideal of *moksa*, the *intention* of the *sraddhas* survived, and the understanding of the passage of the deceased as a cosmogonic progression, with an individual's salvation dependent on the correct ritual activity of his descendants, permitted these archaic ceremonies for the dead to continue to the present day" (p. 121, emphasis added). The *Garuda Purana* amalgamates the various views in saying that when, after a year (or 10 days), the soul's new "body" is complete, "He has

assumed...a body composed of the essence of his merit accruing from the gift of riceballs." He has been enabled to make the difficult journey to Yama's kingdom, whence he meets fierce Yama who metes out his fate, to a "good or bad state" (2.5.143). The dead, however, who do not receive the *sraddha*s remain as ghosts who then may torment and bring misfortune to the living. Thus these ceremonies must be performed.

Islam

Jane Idleman Smith, PhD

BACKGROUND OF THE FAITH

Islamic faith in the life after death is based directly on the twin messages of the Qur'an, which were the earliest revelations to the Prophet Muhammad: the oneness of God and the inevitability of the day of resurrection and judgment. Because God is one, human beings are enjoined to live lives of integrity (integratedness), of ethical and moral responsibility and it is on the quality of that ethical and moral life that final judgment is rendered by God. Thus, those who have earned a place of reward in the Garden of Paradise are called *ahl al-tawhid* — people who affirm God's unity.

Islam itself signifies both the vertical dimension of personal response to God and the horizontal dimension by which the community of believers is designated. Thus, it is at once the act of submission to the divine and the recognition that all those who so submit are joined in community (*ummah).* Insofar as it refers to the basic human impulse toward the divine, Islam is understood by Muslims to be primordial, natural and innate in all humans. As the conscious adoption of divine revelation from God through the Prophet Muhammad, forming the basis for a universal community of believers, Islam officially "began" as a religion in 622 C.E. in the heart of Arabia.

The Prophet Muhammad, himself unlettered and as the last in a succession of prophets and messengers, received and preached God's message to a then polytheistic society. This final revelation was recorded by the believers as the Prophet recited it and after his death in 632 it was collected into a book entitled the Qur'an (Koran). Its literal meaning, "The Recitation," suggests its dynamic and oral character. The Qur'an, along with the message of divine oneness and the reality of human responsibility and judgment, also contains clear guidelines for individual and communal behavior. Thus from the dictates of the Qur'an, supplemented by reports from and about the Prophet himself, developed the *Shari'ah,* or law that governs both the personal and the social life of the ideal theocratic Islamic society.

During Muhammad's lifetime, the new religion spread throughout Arabia and within a century of his death, it moved northeast into Iraq, Persia and adjacent areas and then south and west across North Africa and Spain into southern France. Today it is a worldwide faith shared by more than 800,000,000 adherents. Despite pervasive elements of commonality, there exists today, and have always existed, a wide variety of practices, beliefs and interpretations. And, as is inevitably the case with such a cultural and demographic spread, there are various identifiable sects and groupings, as there have been from the earliest days.

The major sectarian distinction in Islam is between the Sunnis, comprising some four-fifths of the Muslims and the Shi'ites, who are located primarily in Iran and parts of Iraq. The split began originally over the issue of community leadership after the Prophet died without leaving a designated successor. Those who considered themselves as followers of the way (*sunnah*) of the Prophet, the so-called Sunnis, thought that the leader should be elected by the consensus of the community on the basis of appropriate moral and leadership qualities. Such a leader was called the Caliph, literally meaning the one who comes after the Prophet himself. The task of interpreting religious law was assigned to the *ulama*, persons learned in questions of theology and jurisprudence. The Sunni world was technically headed by a Caliph until the office was abolished by Kemal Ataturk in Turkey in 1924.

Others in the young Muslim community felt that leadership should come not by election but through membership in the family of the Prophet. Such a leader they designated the Imam. The Imam is understood to have innate knowledge by virtue of his bloodline and thus to be able to give both political leadership and authoritative interpretations of the Qur'an and traditions. The cousin and son-in-law of the Prophet, Ali bin Abi Talib, was recognized as the first Imam by a group who broke away from the main body of believers. They were known as the Shi'a or Shi'ites, partisans of Ali. The succession of Imams is believed by the Shi'ites to have continued through seven Imams — as believed by those known as Ismailis, followers of the Aga Khan — or through twelve Imams — as held by the Ithna Ash'ari or Twelver Shi'ites. For the Twelvers, the group dominant in Iran, the twelfth Imam is believed to have gone into occultation or hiding, to emerge at a penultimate time to lead his community again to a state of perfection. (It should be noted that Imam has also been used by both Sunnis and Shi'ites to refer more generally to a learned leader.)

This specific eschatological expectation in Shi'ite Islam suggests that a fuller treatment is needed to do justice to the Shi'ite understanding of time and history than is possible in this brief chapter. For the most part, the following discussion will center on those elements of the afterlife beliefs shared by all Muslims. Another significant movement in Islam that has been an identifiable phenomenon since the very early centuries is that of the Sufis or mystics. This movement began with individuals who, influenced by Christian and Jewish communities in the area, desired an intense personal relationship with God through means of asceticism and devotion. By the 12th century, Sufism, a path to the divine adopted by certain individuals of both the Sunni and Shi'ite communities, had become a very significant phenomenon and was organized into major paths or *tariqas,* many of which are still active today. For some Sufis, the eschatological impulse is translated from a historical context that sees judgment and consignment to the Garden or the Fire as a future event to include an understanding that the merging of divine and human as the ultimate eschatology is potentially realizable at any moment. Again, as with the particulars of Shi'ite eschatology, the complexity of the Sufi interpretation deserves greater attention than is possible here.

THE MAIN TENETS

For all Muslims, men and women, certain duties and responsibilities are clearly set forth. It is primarily on the basis of these responsibilities that one's life will be assessed in the final reckoning when judgment will be rendered. These are generally understood to be five in number: (1) Giving verbal testimony based on assent of the heart that there is no God but God (acknowledging divinity in any being or reality outside the one God is the greatest sin in Islam and leads with certainty to damnation) and that Muhammad is the Prophet of God. This is the *shahadah*, the basic testimony of faith. (2) Participating in the public prayer (*salat*) at five regularly scheduled times during the day. (3) Participating in the fast (*saum*) observed during one month of the year (Ramadan). (4) Sharing one's material goods with the needy of the community through paying the alms-tax (*zakat*). (5) Joining with other members of the community at least once in a lifetime in the great pilgrimage *(hajj)* to the holy cities of Mecca and Medina.

There is a very clear and direct connection in Islam between this world (*al-dunya*) and the next world (*al-akhirah).* Muslim children are taught from an early age that life on this earth has no purpose if it is not to prepare oneself specifically for life in the next and that to live ethically in recognition of God's oneness is virtually to assure a felicitous hereafter in the gardens of paradise. In this sense, there is no distinction in Islam between faith and works (although, as in Christianity, scholastic theologians have disputed the relative merits of each). One of the main concerns of contemporary Muslim theological writing about the afterlife is to underline its intellectual plausibility. "Thus the Qur'an has explained the life hereafter in a manner acceptable to the intellect and has called for faith in it," says Muhammad al-Mubarak of the University of Mecca.[1]

Aside from unity or oneness, the central characteristic of the divine, God is understood in Islam to have an infinite number of attributes, often described as 99 in number to signify infinity. Of these, the most often cited are omnipotence, omniscience, justice and mercy. Because of the great emphasis that is put on judgment at the last day and the just dispensation of souls, justice has often been seen as overriding in the Islamic conception of the divine. In fact, all but one of the 114 chapters of the Qur'an begin with the invocation "In the name of God, the merciful, the compassionate." With the requirement to live lives of ethical obligation is also the Qur'anic understanding that as humans we will err and that the mercy of God is abundant.

As part of God's creation, humans can be assured of two things: first, that there is a virtually limitless distinction between humanity as created and God as creator and that our best efforts succeed only insofar as God wills it; second, that behind all events is a divine plan and order. Humans are created from clay and put on the earth for a specific time (*ajal*) known beforehand only by God. But despite our lowly origins, we have, because of our intellect, potential to be vice-regents on earth.[2] Humans are not described in Islam as inherently evil or misguided, although Adam and his wife did foolishly succumb to the temptations of the serpent in primordial time. We are often subject to error, but always have the potential to recognize the truth and to act accordingly. The only real "fallen" creature is Iblis, an archangel ejected from paradise by God for insubordination and residing eternally as the chief denizen of the underworld. Iblis is occasionally portrayed as a temptor, but does not attain the proportions of a full-blown devil as in Christian thought. He is accompanied by numerous other demons and tempting spirits who contribute to the tortures of the damned in the fires of punishment.

Essential to an understanding of the Islamic view of the afterlife is a consideration of the flow of time and history. Time in the overall perspective has a beginning and an end. All of human history moves from the creation to the eschaton. Looking structurally at the overall conception of time in the Islamic understanding, one sees the pattern of collective time, that lasting from creation to eschaton, juxtaposed over that of individual time, the specific events of each individual existence. For the individual, the sequence runs inevitably from birth to death, followed by the existence of the soul in the grave (or elsewhere) awaiting the resurrection, to participation in a series of eschatological events experienced by everyone together. Collective time encompasses everything from the creation of the world through the passing of history to the warning of the impending judgment, the events of the day of resurrection, the final consignment and passing into eternity. Let us turn to the particulars of these individual and collective events.

DEATH AND BURIAL PRACTICES

Because Muslims participate in such a variety of cultures, it is inevitable that funeral and burial practices will differ somewhat. On the whole, however, a general pattern can be identified that is based on a common understanding of the meaning of death and on the advice given by the Prophet as to what is fit and proper.

When it appears to those accompanying a dying person that death is near and certain, someone is called to read verses of the Qur'an. Normally this is a person who is specifically trained in that function. Among the traditions of Islam is one describing the visit of Iblis to the one who is dying, tempting him or her to deny faith in God and adherence to Islam by offering water to the parched victim. To help in the struggle against such temptation, drops of water (or, as in India, honey) are placed in the mouth of the dying. At the moment of death, the eyes are closed and the jaw is bound up and the body is carefully arranged while waiting for a physician's examination.

One of the most important components of the funerary process is the washing of the body. Cleanliness and ritual purification are essential in Islam; prayer is always preceded by ablutions. Embalming is not practiced, as it is believed that the body should be allowed to quickly return to the earth whence it came.[3] The washing is done by a professional washer at home, at a hospital, or in a special place outside the mosque. All items involved in the ablution must be newly purchased and the water, thought to be polluted after use, must be disposed of carefully. During the washing ceremony, verses from the Qur'an are usually recited. After the body is dried, cotton plugs are placed in body orifices and the body is carefully wrapped in a shroud. Normally it is put into a simple wooden coffin, narrow at the feet and wider at the shoulders and then borne to a mosque.

Attending a funeral and, in particular, helping to carry the dead in the funeral procession, is considered an act of piety. The coffin is usually carried by relays of male relatives and friends. In some places, such as Lebanon, the coffin precedes the mourners, while in other places, such as Egypt, it comes after them. Also, local custom dictates whether or not women participate in the procession. At the mosque, a funeral service is held and even those who did not know the deceased often attend. On completion of the service, the body is either carried or taken by hearse to the graveyard. Burial takes place within 24 hours of death.

To speed decomposition, the body is usually taken out of the coffin before it is buried. The shroud is loosened and the corpse is put into the grave with its face toward Mecca. The body is always handled with extreme care because it is believed that it is still able to experience pain. Because of this belief and because Muslims understand that the agonies of the fire are for God alone to prepare for the sinful, cremation is not practiced. While the body is being buried, until the grave is filled with earth, prayers are continually recited. In some cases, a brief sermon is preached. Usually plants rather than cut flowers are placed on the grave, which is marked by flat or sometimes rounded markers of wood or stone. In some instances, domelike structures are erected over the grave.

The question of mourning for the deceased is an interesting one in Islam and it is clear from the traditions that the Prophet forbade it. Nonetheless, grieving normally takes the form of clear and outward lamenting and sometimes loud and prolonged wailing. Traditionally, this has been a role played by women. On certain occasions, professional mourners are engaged. Generally, it is understood that while mourning should not be taken as a sign of lack of faith in God's goodness or in a felicitous hereafter for the righteous, communal grieving is an important sign of support and caring for the loved ones of the deceased. Differing according to locale, certain rites and ceremonies, grave visitations and communal meals are held at specified times after the burial.

There are opportunities for intercessory prayers for the dead. Repeating the Fatihah (the brief opening chapter of the Qur'an) when visiting or passing a grave, for example, is considered efficacious. In general, however, the community must take solace in the knowledge that the departed one is in God's charge and that in the fullness of time, justice and mercy will assure an appropriate station.

BETWEEN DEATH AND RESURRECTION

Chapter 23, verse 100 of the Qur'an describes a partition (*barzakh)* or barrier separating the land of the living from those who have died.[4] The interpretation of this has been that the deceased will in no way be able to return to the earth. There is nothing in the Qur'an to support the idea of reincarnation or multiple births; its message is clearly that we have one life on earth and our future existence will be determined on the basis of the quality of that life. With rare exceptions in some splinter sectarian groups, Islam has consistently rejected the notion that human souls could or would be reincarnated in different bodies for the purpose of working off past debts or accumulating further merit.

If we return again to the time outline discussed above, we see that the expectation of a day of resurrection and judgment of necessity means that there is a kind of waiting period of individuals between death and that day when resurrected bodies will be joined with souls to pass through detailed eschatological events. The term *barzakh* has also come to be applied to the place/time in which the dead wait for the day of resurrection in a variety of conditions. Precisely what happens to souls during this period of waiting is not discussed at all in the Qur'an and consequently has been a subject of great speculation. Islamic tradition has willingly filled in a great many of the details, with varying degrees of authenticity and reliability.[5]

Contemporary Muslim writers vary in the degree to which they accept much of this traditional material as descriptive of what will actually happen, but it is certainly the case that many if not most, Muslims accept that certain events are inevitable.[6] The theme of prefiguration of joys and torments to be experienced at the time of final judgment by the righteous and the faithless respectively is repeated in a variety of ways as one follows the sequence of death and afterdeath events. Often, there is a welcome given by the grave to the one who has just died and it is obvious that the form of this greeting is determined by the relative virtue of the deceased. In some instances, the grave greets the faithful by promising an expansion of vision and a continuing look at the gates of the Garden of Paradise. Many more narratives, however, describe the agony to be endured by the faithless. The grave is said to warn such persons that it is a place of darkness, isolation and loneliness.

One of the most commonly accepted narratives is one that describes immediate events after the death of an individual. The soul, now separated from the body, embarks on a journey. Apparently it is modeled on the mystical journey (*mi'raj*) undertaken by the Prophet Muhammad in which he ascended to the heavens and was able to look down into the layers of hells. A good soul is said to slip easily and painlessly from the body and wrapped in perfumed coverings, it is led by the angel Gabriel through the seven layers of heaven to see what will eventually be its abode. The end of the journey is a vision of God, after which the soul returns to the grave.[7] Wicked souls, or those of persons who have not followed God's command in life, leave the body painfully and wrenchingly. They are foul smelling and they are rejected from even the lowest levels of the heavens. Given a vision of what awaits them at the day of judgment (glimpses into the fires of punishment), they also return to the grave.

One very commonly accepted event is the visit of questioning angels.[8] Sometimes they are identified by the names of Munkar and Nakir, appellations that are non-Qur'anic and appear rarely in the canonical traditions. Their descriptions vary slightly from one account to another, but in general they are understood to be fearsome to behold, black in appearance with green eyes, with voices like thunder and eyes like lightning. Their long fangs rend the ground. They ask the deceased about his or her knowledge of God, the Prophet Muhammad and Islam. One's ability to answer these questions, easy for the righteous and impossible for the faithless, determines the quality of one's stay awaiting the day of judgment.

Sometimes it is said that, for the good soul, windows will be opened in the top of the tomb so that one can feel the sweet breezes from the Garden and that for the evil soul a similar opening on the bottom will allow the hot stench of hell to penetrate. Or, graves will either be expanded for greater comfort or contracted so that the suffering soul will shriek in agony. Muslim folklore has it that animals passing through graveyards can sometimes hear the piercing cries of the tormented damned. Suicide is one of the particular sins for which punishment in the grave is said to occur. The giving and taking of life in the Islamic understanding is for God alone.

While the blissful rewards are sometimes mentioned, punishment in the grave has received far more attention in theological writings and in folk traditions. It is interesting to note that while no Muslim would doubt the reality of the disintegration of the body in the earth (with the exception of saints, whose bodies remain intact), it is also the case that the punishments and pleasures of the grave are understood in a very physical way. Along with the narratives suggesting that the soul is experiencing joy or pain in the grave are those that indicate that the soul is in fact apart from the tomb and going through appropriate pleasure or purgation elsewhere. Souls of the damned, for example, are sometimes said to already be in the fire, or suffering somewhere in pits of snakes and other loathsome creatures. Souls of the righteous, on the other hand, are sometimes said to be free to wander through the spheres at will, or to be at the right hand of Adam, or to be waiting at the gates of the Garden of Paradise. Some traditions suggest that the righteous are very much aware of life on earth while waiting for the resurrection; sometimes they are described as praying for the living or even attempting to greet us.

THE COMING OF THE DAY OF RESURRECTION

As we move through the time sequence of after-death events, we come to that period dramatically portrayed in the Qur'an in which the natural order will be disrupted and cataclysmic events will occur, signaling the resurrection of the bodies (*ba'th*). The first warning of the impending cosmic upheaval in traditional and in many contemporary accounts is actually a disruption of the ethical/moral order. Some of the signs of this are that liars and traitors will be trusted and the righteous belied; usury will be acceptable; a man will disobey his parents and obey his wife (thereby upsetting the family structure); wine-drinking will be commonplace and the like. Many accounts say that this time of moral chaos will conclude with the arrival of a guide *(madhi)* who will then reign over a millennial period of justice and peace. This figure is sometimes identified in Sunni Islam with the person of Jesus and is understood to be more of a leader than a savior.

The actual arrival of the day of resurrection is made known to all upon earth and in the heavens through a series of events that are clearly cosmic in nature. According to the understanding of the Qur'an, this is a day when the heavens are split apart, when the earth will be rent asunder, when the mountains will be set moving, when heaven will be rolled up like a scroll and many other specific signs will be given indicating the reversal of the natural order and a disintegration of the structure of the universe.[9] The drama of the Qur'anic description is captured in this excerpt from al-Ghazali's famous medieval treatise on eschatology, *al-Durrah al-Fakhlrah,* describing the events after the angel Israfil sounds the trumpet heralding the imminent end of the world:

> Then the mountains will be scattered and will move like the clouds; the seas will gush forth one into the other and the sun will be rolled up and will return to ashes; the oceans will overflow until the atmosphere is filled up with water. The worlds will pass into each other, the stars will fall like a broken string of pearls and the sky will become like a rose

> balm, rotating like a turning millstone. The earth will shake with a tremendous shaking...until God orders the stripping off of the spheres. In all of the seven earths and the seven heavens, as well as the vicinity of the Throne, no living being will remain.[10]

After the final cosmic disintegration we then have a dramatic description of what Islamic tradition has seen as God's absolute oneness in the universe. Here God is not only the sole God, he is all that remains in the universe. An ethical disintegration, a cosmic disintegration and finally the stunning vision of God's absolute aloneness. Were this the end of the story, we would have to conclude that human claims on immortality are temporary at best, confined to a reflection of divine oneness through the expression of faith and works. But as the drama unfolds, we see that after the manifestation of absolute aloneness comes the return to a focus on human accountability. God brings all humanity back to life in the resurrection of bodies, the ingathering and infusing of new life as the first step in the process of calling human beings to an accounting for their earthly deeds.

RESURRECTION AND JUDGMENT

The fact of the resurrection of the body has been of continuing importance to Muslims. It was not really a point of issue for early Islam, but came to be hotly debated among theologians and philosophers. Contemporary Muslims are firmly convinced that bodily resurrection is basic to the Qur'anic message. The first mortal to be raised is generally said to be the Prophet Muhammad. The stress on the importance of Muhammad's resurrection before the other believers is related not only to his recognized status as the seal of the prophets, but also to the general understanding of his role as the intercessor for his community.

The Qur'an, along with later eschatological writings, describes in great detail the day of judgment as one in which even the most pious will be afraid. The resurrection itself is scarcely pictured as a time of joy or gratitude on the parts of those to whom life is given again. Medieval manuals delight in elaborate portrayals of individuals awaiting in terror the actual judgment, standing in sweat up to their ankles, their waists, their shoulders. It is at this time that souls experience most graphically the results of their deeds and misdeeds on earth.

The Qur'an makes it clear that each individual alone is responsible for his or her past deeds and that one will have to encounter those deeds and their consequences in very graphic form on the day of judgment. On that day the record will be revealed to each person individually, the result of the reckoning obviously predetermined by one's being ordered to take the book in either the right or the left hand. For the heedless, this revealing of the record will come as a tremendous shock.[11]

References in the Qur'an and the elaborations of tradition have added several other events to the picture of the last day. The Qur'an mentions the *mizan* or balance, which in the singular means the principle of justice. The plural has the clearer eschatological reference of the scales by which deeds are weighed. The image of a specific weighing has thus been adopted as one of the modalities of judgment. Another such modality is the bridge (*sirat*), adopted into Islamic tradition to signify the span over Gehenna, the top layer of the Fire. It is said that both the saved and the condemned must pass over the bridge, although the judgment process actually has been completed at the point at which the bridge is mentioned in most narratives. Those judged guilty of sin but still considered to be believers fall from the bridge into the Fire, but only for a limited period of purgation. Those who have neither faith nor good deeds to their credit, however, find that the *sirat* has become sharper than a sword and thinner than a hair and that their fall into the Fire of everlasting punishment is inescapable. The faithful, on the contrary, move easily and swiftly across a broad bridge, led by the Prophet himself.

INTERCESSION

This raises the issue of intercession and whether or not it is recognized in Islam. Technically the Qur'an says that there is no possibility of intercession, although some verses lend themselves to more flexible interpretation. No intercession would be in keeping with the dominant conception of a God of absolute justice. As mercy has been understood to be one of God's primary characteristics, however, so the possibility of an intervening being has come into the Islamic picture of eschatological realities. Aside from some possibility of intercession by saints, the main figure credited with the intercessory function is the Prophet Muhammad. Sometimes intercession is said to take place at the bridge; more often it occurs at the basin or pond *(hawd)* at which Muhammad will meet the members of his community. Its general location is somewhere near the balance and the bridge. The Qur'an leaves no question whatsoever that divine justice will prevail on the day of judgment and that no one can bear the burden of anyone else's actions. With the possibility of intercession, however, one sees a softening of the formula of unrelenting retribution; sometimes it is said that even the smallest deed registered to one's credit may in the long run be sufficient to bring one to salvation.

THE GARDEN OR THE FIRE?

The Qur'an leaves no doubt that the alternatives for each individual at the day of judgment are two: the bliss of the Garden or the torment of the Fire. One reference in the Qur'an to what is called "the heights" (*al-ac raf)* in verse 7:46 has led to the development of what some have called the "limbo" theory of Islam, or the supposition that there is a place for an intermediate class of people who do not automatically enter the Garden or the Fire. While there are a variety of interpretations of this verse, most exegetes have said those on the heights are persons whose good deeds keep them from the Fire and whose evil deeds keep them from the Garden — in other words, those whose actions balance in terms of merit and demerit and who are therefore the last to enter the Garden.

Because of the full and graphic descriptions of the Garden and the Fire in the Qur'an, Islam has often been accused of a very materialistic conception of the afterlife. As with the modalities at the hour of judgment, the Muslim community has expressed a variety of interpretations about whether or not the rewards and punishments of the life to come are to be understood in their most literal sense. While the dominant understanding has been an affirmation of the reality of physical torment and pleasure, proponents of this view generally have not insisted that the realities of the next world will be identical with those of this world. While clearly physical, recompense in the ultimate sense is generally understood to have a reality beyond what we are able to comprehend.

The Qur'an itself does not offer a detailed plan of the realms of the Fire or the Garden. The term *Gehenna* is sometimes used to refer to the totality of the Fire and sometimes only to the top-most circle. In the Qur'an (15:43-44), Gehenna is described as having seven gates; this led to the popular notion that the Fire consists of seven descending layers of increasing torment. An elaborate structure of relative punishments came to be worked out around the seven layers of Fire and later tradition supplied each of the gates with guardians who torture the damned. At the bottom of the lowest level grows the dreaded tree Zaqqum (37:62-68) with the heads of demons for flowers. The Qur'an offers a number of specific indications of the tortures of the Fire: its flames crackle and roar; it has fierce boiling waters, scorching wind and black smoke; the people of the Fire are sighing, wailing and wretched.

In some ways the divisions of the Fire directly parallel those of the Garden, although the Garden is sometimes said to have eight rather than seven layers (and at other times is described as being of four portions). The opposite of the tree Zaqqum is the lote tree at the top of paradise. Garden (*jannah*) is the general name for paradise, although the Qur'anic descriptions are of gardens in the plural. The most spacious and highest part of the Garden is directly under the throne of God, from which the four rivers of paradise flow. Qur'anic references to the joys awaiting the dwellers in the Garden are sufficiently rich that tradition has done little but amplify and elaborate on them. The faithful are content, peaceful and secure; they enjoy gentle speech, pleasant shade and fruits neither forbidden nor out of reach, as well as cool drink and meat as they desire; they sit on couches facing each other, wearing green and gold robes of finest silk. One of the joys afforded to the inhabitants of the Garden is the companionship of beautiful young virgins (*houris*) with dark eyes like gazelles. Some traditions suggest that families will be reunited in the Garden, but this is not discussed in the Qur'an. While the Qur'anic descriptions do not mention God, the clear understanding of Muslims is that the faithful will gaze upon his face, a joy that the inhabitants of the Fire are denied.

For the most part, Islamic theology has not concerned itself with questions about the location and structure of the Garden and the Fire, on the understanding that only God knows these particulars. Theologians have, however, speculated at great length on the question of whether or not they are already in existence. Orthodoxy has concluded that they are created and do exist, awaiting their inhabitants on the last day.

On the basis of the Qur'anic assurances in descriptions of the Gardens as well as a firm faith in God's justice in addition to his mercy, neither the theologians nor the traditionalists have questioned the eternal nature of the Garden and the residence of the faithful in it. The question becomes more problematic in relation to the Fire, however. The majority have held to the view that despite the Qur'anic indication that sinners will stay eternally in the fire, it is not only possible but even likely that at some future time all sinners will be pardoned and the Fires of judgment will be extinguished forever. Equally complex has been the issue of whether or not non-Muslims will be able eventually to enjoy the Garden. The general conclusion is that they will, but only after a period of purgation.

It is clear, then, that afterlife beliefs in Islam are a blend of Qur'anic description, traditional elaboration, theological speculation and popular belief. There is much in the general Islamic understanding that is intended to comfort the bereaved as well as to reassure and challenge the community as a whole. Many contemporary Muslim writers do not deal directly with issues of life after death because they see the basic affirmation of the Qur'an as so natural and reasonable as to require no defense or elaboration. To the extent they do, it is generally to affirm to the Muslim community and the world at large that the strength of Islam lies in the faith that the fruits of today's labor will be reaped in the hereafter and that God will reward all in justice and mercy in the world to come.

EDITOR'S NOTES

Islam has a world following of nearly one billion devotees, approximately 20 percent of whom are in the Middle East, with the largest concentration in Indonesia. There are over 4 million Muslims living in the United States. There has been an active Muslim contingent in North America for over 300 years, since the time the religion arrived with West African slaves.

When studying the Qur'an, it is important to remember that no council of scholars has ever translated it into vernacular languages, as was done with the Bible. The original translation of the Qur'an, by George Sale, is based on Maracci's Latin version, and was made for the purpose of discrediting Islam.

The Qur'an initiated huge social change by forbidding drinking, gambling, usury and all forms of vice. The Qur'an was the first of the sacred books to put a restriction on polygamy, reducing the number of wives a believer could have from hundreds to no more than four. Muhammad forbade the vengeance of blood and all blood feuds and he taught Muslims to love all Christians. Muhammad has been called one of the greatest champions of women's rights the world has ever seen. Islam gives women the same property rights as men, allowing them to inherit and dispose of property. They also have the right to alimony and they must be treated with respect. There is no color or race prejudice in Islam — color is a "sign of God" (Surahs 30:21 and 35:25). Islam teaches love of country and the unity of its different peoples and this is one of its greatest contributions.

Notes

1. Muhammad al-Mubarak, *Nizam al-Islam* (Beirut: Daral-Fikr, 1970), p. 148.
2. Qur'an 2:29-30.
3 "He has made all that he has created good. And He began the creation of man from clay...." (Qur'an 32:7).
4. "...behind them is a barrier (*barzakh*) until the day when they are resurrected."
5. Much of this material is contained in eschatological manuals that ordered the many traditions that came into circulation in the Muslim community concerning life after death. While descriptive in effect, the function of these manuals as a whole is didactic and homiletic, intended to encourage the hearer to redouble efforts to live ethically and justly.
6. See Sayyid Uways, *al-Khulud fi hayat al-Misriyin al-muasirin* (Cairo: al-Hay'at al-Misriat al-Aam lil-Kitab, 1972).
7. This vision of God is often described in extremely vivid terms, as in this passage from the *Durra al-fakhira* of the medieval theologian and mystic, al-Ghazzali: "Then they penetrate the coverings affixed to the Throne of Mercy. There are 80,000 pavilions of the Throne, each pavilion having 80,000 believers and each balcony having a moon radiant upon God, glorifying Him and venerating Him" (Scholars Press, 1979, p. 14).
8. See contemporary writers such as Ahmad Fa'iz, *al-Yawm al-akhir fi zilal al-Qur'an* (Beirut: Dar Maktabat al-Hayat, 1975); Ibrahim al-Bayjuri, *Sharh al-Bayjuri ala'l-jawhara* (Cairo: Matbaa al-Taqadam al-Alamiya, 1964).
9. See especially Qur'an 81:1-4.
10. Op. cit., pp. 38-39.
11. "As for the one who is given his book in his right hand, he will say: Take and read my book. I knew that I would be called to account. And he will be in a blissful condition.... But as for him who is given his book in his left hand, he will say: Would that my book had not been given to me and that I did not know my reckoning!...and it will be said: Seize him and bind him and expose him to the burning Fire!...." (Qur'an 9:19-31).

Judaism

Rabbi Alan L. Ponn

BACKGROUND OF THE FAITH

The Jewish faith can be described as the first noticeable step away from paganism. The ancient peoples feared the powers in the universe, but speculated widely about the location and the nature of those powers. Groping for answers, the pagans drew initial conclusions about the supernatural that were based on primitive assumptions, superstition and magical explanations. The pagans assumed that a world of spirits, both good and bad, were constantly permeating their living space. They worshipped every natural object that seemed impressive to them — the sun, moon, stars, high trees, imposing animals such as lions and bulls — and they constructed great idols and symbolic poles of their own, which they worshipped in the sacrificial ways of animal and food offerings. Nowhere did they see a oneness in God, a unity of the various deities, or a kindly personal god who cared for humankind.

According to tradition, more than 57 centuries ago Judaism made a breakthrough in experiencing a revelation of God's oneness and of God's personality as a divine parent, both loving and just, a creative presence both inside and outside the inhabited world. Although the Bible begins with the appearance of Adam and Eve, it is Abraham who is known as the first Jew, for the great revelation of God's oneness first appeared to him. Jewish tradition emphasizes that Abraham broke the idols and false gods of his father's household by smashing them to pieces. Little by little, Abraham began to receive words and promises from God that formed the basis of a mutual agreement called a covenant. Religious scholars assume that God was seeking out Abraham who was able to use his reason and intuition to search for God. The covenant that was concluded promised God's blessings and concern for all people in return for their acceptance, faith and belief.

The original Jews consisted of the close-knit patriarchal families of

Abraham, Isaac and Jacob. Each was motivated and transformed by this covenant with God. Judaism was begun, maintained and transmitted by families — and, today, family unity and closeness is still one of the most important Jewish tenets. In his early covenantal promises, God said that Abraham's progeny would be numerous like the stars in heaven, that Abraham would be the father of a multitude of nations and that his seed would someday possess the land of Canaan.

In times of famine in their often parched land, the Hebrews were accustomed to going to Egypt in search of food. From Abraham's time on, this practice led to a considerable population of Jews establishing residence there. Ultimately feared and envied by Pharaoh Rameses II, the Jewish people were then subjugated into degrading slavery. They endured many hardships and they may have been assigned to build monuments and pyramids for the Pharaoh.

This episode of slavery, the rise of Moses, and God's redemption of the enslaved Hebrews led to the most monumental change in this emerging civilization. No longer a small group of patriarchal families, the Hebrews were transformed into a national and spiritual entity. Like the proverbial clay in the hands of the sculptor, they stood ready to be trained, organized and galvanized for the spiritual odyssey that lay ahead.

Into the pagan world of religious anarchy came God's authoritative words of instruction — His law and rules of proper living. The Ten Commandments were only the starting point of elaborate law and ritual that was meant to define explicit religious practice and moral conduct that would assure the people's salvation and preservation. Assurances of God's love were also contrasted with stern warnings about the punishments for misbehavior and disloyalty to the covenant. From Moses' day on, the Hebrews traveled along this pathway from paganism to religious civilization and moral idealism. Many were their failures and backslidings, but guided by efforts of strong kings and eloquent prophets, Judaism became an enduring entity.

Judaism's essential doctrine is simply this: following God's suggested way of life can bring a deepening joy and fulfillment. Judaism does not stress belief in God as much as acceptance of God and the way of life that God has set forth for the adherent. Therefore, there is no emphasis on doctrinal formulations. God is understood as a divine parent who has personal care and concern for humankind. God gave the world law first because the pagan world was in a state of anarchy and needed the direction and discipline that only law could bring. The law was of two kinds. Ritual law and moral law are distributed throughout both the Torah and the rest of the Old Testament. God also expressed his love and compassion for his creatures in the Torah, and God's emotional words of love and attachment to his creation are alternated with legal expression. Therein, these ritual and ethical laws form the basis of the pathway to salvation. Worship of God, good deeds and charitable acts are thought to be the main vehicles of religious expression. Judaism retains the

Hebrew language and the ancient scrolls as a mark of identity to these ancient Jewish roots. Prayer and songs in the synagogue retain these features. Jews believe that the purpose of life is to glorify God on earth by expressing their higher selves or spiritual selves. They consider that they have been made in God's image; yet they are also half animal and they are mortal. The religious challenge is, therefore, to direct personal efforts to the good or higher inclinations and away from the bad or evil inclinations.

God's destiny and that of humans are intertwined. Jews define the partnership as one that requires our ultimate loyalty and dedication as human beings. God, the divine parent, is the epitome of justice and compassion, the source of both good and evil, creation and destruction, knowledge and ignorance. God's purposes are unfathomable, but Jews are loyal to God through intuitive trust such as that given to a human parent.

THIS WORLD AND THE NEXT WORLD

Although the hope for the fulfillment and redemption of the adherent's life is intended to apply to the span of earthly existence, there is ample recognition in Judaism that life does not abruptly cease when the body has died. Something precious remains at the time of earthly demise and these doctrines of immortality and resurrection, heaven and hell, accountability and judgment, are found in Jewish teachings and in the prayer books of the Jewish people. But the first and primary responsibility of the Jew is this life and not the world to come.

The fulfillment of laws and commandments are meant to improve one's life on earth. Devotion to prayer, study and charity are expected to lead to a meaningful way of life as the life cycle progresses from birth to death. This is clearly a recommendation to each Jew to concentrate on his or her responsibilities on earth and not to speculate or postpone life's opportunities while he or she lives. The idea of subordinating life's opportunities, responsibilities or challenges to some greater possibilities in the world to come is alien to Judaism. Judaism can thus be characterized as a religion of this world and it is no accident that the pendant often chosen to be worn as a necklace contains the Hebrew inscription *Chai* which means *life*. *Chai* is characterized as the supreme religious value.

LIFE AFTER DEATH

The belief in life after death, probably the most universal of all of humanity's religious doctrines, grew rather gradually in Jewish thought. During biblical times, only the kernels of the beliefs in an afterworld are to be found. The post-biblical writings, especially the Talmud, put a firm foundation and a complete structure on that slight and tenuous emphasis in the Old Testament concerning the future world. During Talmudic times, Jewish doctrine became more and more specific about resurrection, immortality, heaven, hell and God's judgment. Accordingly, Jewish ritual kept apace. The pattern of the modern Jewish funeral service and the laws of death and burial in the Jewish religion are an elaborate expression of proper preparation for an assured afterworld.

Immortality is a belief that comes naturally with the conviction that God is a divine parent. To be reunited with the divine source of one's being is the hoped-for ending to a pious and dedicated religious life. That God would gather the righteous and sincerely repentant souls around the shelter of his wings is a most yearned for expectation of the Jews.[1] At such time it is hoped that the inconsistencies, mysteries and uncertainties of life will somehow be resolved and reconciled. The deep longing to be reunited with dearly departed relatives will be fulfilled. A peacefulness and tranquility will replace the frustrations and challenges of our earthly existence. For the traditional Jew, immortality will bring resurrection of the soul and the body. For the Reform Jew it will bring a resurrection of the soul only.

JUDGMENT

Jewish tradition emphasizes that God is the true and righteous judge. Each human soul is held accountable before God for the use made of the life given. Thus, our lives cannot be wasted or taken lightly. During the Jewish High Holiday season (the New Year and the Day of Atonement), a chance is given anew each year to redirect the serious goals of one's life. The prayers say: "God records our deeds in a book." This ledger, attributed to God, is called the "Book of Life." In the "Book of Life," God is said to make continual entries concerning the merits of our deeds and the worthiness of each individual to merit continued existence. It is in this context that we read during Yom Kippur, "Choose good and not evil, that ye may live."[2]

The Jewish religious regimen of the New Year, with its emphasis on the purification and cleansing of the soul, paves the way for the sublimity of character that allows entry into the world to come. The theme of the High Holiday season is that change and growth of character are possible through concentrated effort. Yet, even the stubborn and rebellious worshipper can sometimes attain this change and growth through repentance during the latter stages of life. Even at this 11th hour, such sincere repentance is considered acceptable for entry to the world beyond this one.

THE GOOD LIFE

Reincarnation is a popular belief that never settled in the Jewish sphere. Yet the Jewish masses were attracted to it from time to time. With origins in the primitive religions of northern Europe, the reincarnation doctrine spread mostly into the non-Jewish Asiatic centers of population.[3]

The prayer book of Reform Jews, *Gates of Prayer,* states explicitly that "mortality is the tax we pay for the privilege of love, thought, creative work.... Just because we are human, we are prisoners of the years. Yet that very prison is the room of discipline in which we, driven by the urgency of time, create."[4] Such a prayer reconciles the worshipper to his apportioned span of life. One lifetime, according to Jewish thought, is sufficient to make good account of ourselves, if we earnestly try. Fragility and mortality become spurs to accomplishment and creative endeavor. Reincarnation is very much a permanent part of a caste system and of fatalism. Such conditions Jews do not espouse.

First of all, each adherent of the Jewish faith is bidden to develop all parts of himself or herself in one lifetime. If one's occupation is mechanical, one's avocation should be scholarly and intellectual. If one's occupation is scholarly, then one's avocation should stress non-scholarly characteristics. The ideal of the whole person is to be achieved. Such versatility and variety of individual activity is most notably found today in the land of Israel where leaders of high political stature are known to pursue challenging avocations of a contrasting nature.[5] Secondly, fatalism occupies a position of little importance in Judaism. The individual is bidden through prayer and doctrine to accept the active role in God's creative process, to improve God's world and to make it a better place in which to live.

Satisfaction and fulfillment can come only to those adherents who do their share of good deeds *(Mitzvot).* Fulfillment comes especially to those believers who have fully transmitted the heritage to a future generation. Seeing the young imbued with high ideals for the future brings the deepest satisfaction humanly possible. After a lifetime of such effort, death should not bring discontent. Heaven is reality to the adherent, but he is bidden not to be preoccupied with it while he lives. Fulfilling God's precepts and developing a praiseworthy life take first preference on the human agenda of the believer. Few Jewish sermons entice the worshipper to the glories of heaven or threaten the evils of hell. Although Jewish literature is filled with lavish heavenly pictures and lurid thoughts of the underworld, such descriptions never predominate in Jewish pulpit or pew.

HEAVEN AND HELL

There are some assumptions, however, about the nature of these important future repositories of our souls. Primarily, heaven is pictured as a place where the passions no longer frustrate, conflicts no longer cause suffering and anxiety and travail are ended. There is a predominance of imagery in Jewish literature of quiet, peaceful, intellectual activity, with perusal of religious texts.[6] Another popular conception is that of family reunion and devotion among those who had been separated by death. There is also a hope for the resolution of the mysteries of life and an aspiration to draw nearer to God's sheltering protection and love.

Although sadistic descriptions of hell do occur in Jewish literature, Jewish worshippers have long assumed that God's real caring nature could rule out an almighty God practicing sadism for any purpose. Firm is the conviction that God's judgment is real and accountability is as certain as the fingerprints on our hands. Yet the nature of hell is one of the mysteries of Jewish doctrine and the modern worshipper seems content to let it remain a mystery.

Because Judaism is not a creedal religion, adherence to each doctrine, such as heaven and hell, is not entirely obligatory for the worshipper. It would not be surprising, therefore, to encounter a few Jews who still believe the early biblical view that there is no afterworld, because such a view would not be considered heretical in this non-creedal religious approach. The mainstream of Judaism does, by a huge majority, accept the reality of the afterworld as described herein.

How does one gain admittance into the heavenly portals and who of humankind's creatures qualifies? Entrance is gained by righteous deeds and an ethical living pattern. Behavioral performance and helpfulness to others are regarded as the true test of character. Yet people who lack these qualifications can make a special appeal to God's mercy through sincere repentance even a short time before death itself. If the repentance is sincere enough, it is considered highly likely that God will grant pardon even at that late moment. What if the sinner is unrepentant even at the end of life? If the person led a life devoid of good deeds, he or she would really face the stern test of God's tribunal. He or she would expect to be held to account and punished, for wasting his or her life, hurting others and being so callous as to show indifference instead of conscience at the close of his or her mortal days.

What if the person was unaffiliated, an agnostic or an atheist? What if the person was a non-Jew? Anyone who fulfills the basic commandments of proper relationships with others is still regarded as worthy of salvation, although he or she may not have chosen the Jewish pathway. Fervent Jews deplore atheists and agnostics especially, but none would disagree that proper conduct and behavior is the one standard that can be applied to all humankind, Jews and Gentiles, believers and unbelievers, alike. From this it can be stated that Jews do not feel that their religion is the only pathway to God. It is only the one most suitable for the Jews themselves.[7] This tolerant pattern was set in the days of Noah and the biblical characters who preceded Abraham, the first Jew. God's relationship with them was very much an ethical test, too, based on the Noachian laws prohibiting murder, incest and adultery. The deeds of men, regardless of their religious beliefs, are the most important admission tickets to the world to come.

THE END OF THE WORLD AND THE MESSIAH

How long will the world itself last? Can we ever expect an end to the existing world as we know it? The Jews have a distinct interpretation of the scriptural account of the covenant given to Noah directly following the great flood. The Rainbow Covenant, as it is called today, was meant literally as a sign that God will never destroy the world again. This is fervently accepted in all Jewish denominations. Consequently, there is no place among the descendants of Noah for those who carry placards asserting that the end of the world is coming soon.

If Jews believe that God will never destroy the world again, what of messianic belief that is still current in Jewish hearts? The pulse of long-suffering Jewish hearts and souls beats rapidly at the daily services in synagogues everywhere in the hope that a Messiah might yet bring peace. Such a projected messianic intervention will not bring an end to the existing world, according to Jewish thought. Rather it will herald a peaceful age the likes of which the world has never known. Living, breathing, pulsating life will continue indefinitely. Life in its existing form is still considered the supreme value in itself. Its promises and joyful moments are not to be displaced by the messianic intervention, although some very early Jewish literature suggested that they might be.[8]

There is a sifting tendency in Judaism that is very poorly understood outside the fold of Jews. In the thousands of years of evolving tradition, many ideas were placed in Jewish literature, tried, tested and ultimately rejected. Among these were thoughts of Satan, evil spirits (*dybbuks*), original sin and many other doctrines. It is for this reason that doctrines of the imminent end of the world, which had a place in Jewish literature once, became rejected and disregarded by the Jewish mainstream. This change, and all the others mentioned, took place because the post-biblical holy books authorized changes that formed amendments to the biblical authority. The Old Testament formed the constitution to which amendments were permitted in later ages leading to the present time.

THE RESURRECTION

It seems only natural that the Jews' love of life on this earth would overflow into a very strong aspiration for an individual's continued existence in the world to come. Early Jewish teachings virtually ignored the subject. By the time that the Jews and Christians were beginning to separate into two religions, the doctrine of resurrection had permeated Judaism very much indeed. Jesus' ascent to heaven as a resurrected body and soul was in Jesus' day not a new doctrine in the Jewish milieu. Resurrection had become an acceptable amendment to the biblical teachings although the Bible had made little reference to it. Today it is accepted in all Jewish denominations, except that the Reform Jews assert that there will only be a resurrection of the soul.

How did this belief in resurrection become so popular among the Jews? Rabbi Morris Kertzer related it to the time when the Persians dominated Israel. The teachings of Zoroaster were influential among the Jews.[9] Although no specific references in the Bible postulated a definite resurrection, certain biblical characters made indirect references of considerable importance. For instance, Daniel 12:2 asserts, "Many of them that sleep in the dust shall awake, some to everlasting life and some to reproaches and everlasting abhorrence." It was the Pharisees, the progenitors of post-biblical literature, who promoted the doctrine and the Sadducees, the strict biblical constructionists, who opposed it. The Pharisees, who were the more popular party, sought to prove that the body and the soul really belonged together and so they needed to be judged together.

The specifics of resurrection are defined in writing. The Talmud declares that those who rise "will be appareled in their own clothes."[10] The decomposition of the body did not present any difficulty to the sages of the Talmud and the Midrash because resurrection was to be a purely miraculous act of God. The resurrection will take place in the days of the Messiah.[11] Jewish expectations concerning the Messiah differ from the Christian ones. A Jewish precondition for the coming Messiah exists. The Jewish concept of Messiah requires that the world will be brought to a peaceful state as a result of his coming. Until such world peace is demonstrated by the Messiah, complete resurrection must wait.

PURGATORY

Purgatory, or limbo, has deep origins in Jewish literature. Although its doctrinal influence declined and mellowed over the years, it was thoroughly described in the texts that also described hell. Then, like many doctrines before it, the idea became generally unacceptable to the populace. Its unacceptability was based on the growing maturity of the Jewish doctrine of the nature of God and God's likely utilization of intelligent rather than barbaric punishment. Nevertheless, the earlier Jewish descriptions of purgatory were very graphic. The scholarly school of Shammai assigned purgatory to those whose virtues and sins counterbalance one another. The scholars predicted that "they shall go down to Gehenna and float up and down until they rise purified."[12] The Shammaites assumed that the wholly righteous would go directly to heaven and the wholly wicked directly to hell. How long would souls remain in purgatory? The greatest sages, such as Rabbi Akiba, seemed to agree on twelve months. Those souls whose judgment is still not sealed are required to look upon the carcasses of the wicked, the raging fires of hell and the tortures of the netherworld. Although the belief in purgatory apparently became fundamental in the Roman Catholic Church, it never became an influential Jewish doctrine.

SALVATION

Salvation is the dearest goal of any religious devotee. It is the entrance to the gateway of God's sheltering arms. The Jewish pathway to salvation is clearly spelled out in the scriptures and the Talmud. Salvation can be obtained only by active response to the commandments of God. Righteous deeds, charitable acts, service to others and ethical obedience are all primary vehicles for reaching the destination of heavenly redemption. The Ten Commandments serve as the foundation of the many other laws and there are 613 major laws in the Bible and Talmud to which the seeker must show obedience. Because the pathway is primarily the ethical deed, salvation is not, by its standard, open only to Jews, but to any human who truly leads a righteous life. In Old Testament times, sacrificial worship was included in the necessary acts of piety prescribed by law. But since the destruction of the temple, animal sacrifice no longer seemed an appropriate expression of religiosity in the more civilized world of cities and towns.

The struggle to achieve salvation required a suppression of the evil inclination *(Yetzer Ha Ra)* and the concentration on the good inclination *(Yetzer Hatov)*. It means that we must win the struggle over our animal natures and channel human energy into a spiritual and ethical plane of activity. Although it rejects original sin, Jewish doctrine recognizes the evil inclination that wars with humans' higher nature. This internal struggle can be aided by proper habits of prayer, the observance of regular rituals, the practice of good, unrewarded deeds *(Mitzvot)* and the diligent habit of study. The last element, study, is compulsory for Jews of all ages. Study fosters respect for the law. It defines and explains the ethical requirements and the pathways that have civilized humankind in the past. Study should motivate the Jew to active ethical response and true salvation.

DEATH RITUALS

The Jewish faith provides a firm foundation for death rituals as well as the rituals for life. The rituals and ceremonies surrounding the funeral service are very elaborate. The ritual guidelines represent the outlook of the faith and facilitate salvation for the dead and healing for the bereaved. Early burial has always been Jewish practice and it must be accomplished as quickly as possible. There are several historical reasons for burying the dead quickly: it was the only sensible thing to do in a hot climate; it prevented dishonor to the dead;[13] and it seemed to alleviate the grief of mourners. Exceptions to early burial are allowed when relatives must travel a great distance to the gravesite or when burial clothes or a coffin are not immediately obtainable.

The overall guideline for funeral arrangements is simplicity and modesty of materials and cost in order to avoid embarrassing the poor. In death, everyone is to be regarded as equal and it is certainly not a time for economic competition. Traditional Jews insist that each person be buried in a simple standard wooden box casket. They allow no lavish fixtures to adorn the casket or to be used as decoration. The funeral clothes are to be plain white shrouds —

religious garments that represent penitence and piety. These shrouds are placed on the body after a ritual cleansing called *Tahara*, a process that is usually performed by dedicated synagogue functionaries (*Chevra Kadisha*). The use of flowers and expensive decorations is greatly discouraged by orthodox authorities. The reason for this, according to Rabbi H. Rabinowicz, is because long ago these decorations were so commonplace in the idolatrous rites of ancient peoples. Non-traditional Jews make some compromises with these customs and although their approach is more individualistic, the principles remain the same. Non-traditional Jews who choose lavish, expensive caskets have fallen prey, perhaps unwittingly, to the modern American funeral that is so costly. The funeral service itself is a composite of psalms and prayers of comfort, an appropriate eulogy, the solemn *El Moley Rachamim* (God, Full of Compassion) prayer and the well-known Kaddish prayer at the conclusion. Recited in ancient Aramaic dialect, the Kaddish prayer is really an affirmation of praise and faith in God and does not mention the dead at all. The Kaddish is effective in lifting up the spirit of the mourner.

The funeral service is usually divided into two parts. The first is held at the funeral home or synagogue. The second, or interment service, is usually held at the gravesite. At the conclusion of the prayers, traditional Jews shovel some dirt from the ground nearby into the grave. This allows the mourner to participate in the actual fulfillment of the returning of the body to the earth whence it came (dust returning to dust). In the Jewish service, the casket is closed and viewing of the body prior to burial is against the custom of the faith. The service is supposed to be a catalyst and a facilitator for the outpouring of natural grief. The atmosphere is arranged to be as realistic as possible without being maudlin or frightening. Vast displays of flowers or elaborate instrumental music are not present even in liberal congregations.

The Jewish funeral is in no sense a happy occasion. The prayers and the eulogy evoke the natural feelings of sadness at the loss, and words and prayers of courage and inspiration are said. The occasion allows for public expression of the sense of deprivation that mourners are experiencing. For this reason, the bereaved almost always enter the funeral service having torn a portion of the outer garment that they are wearing in symbolic expression of frustrating grief, or they have pinned a mourning black ribbon on themselves that is symbolically torn to express grief. To show respect and understanding to the mourners, others refrain from making light-hearted conversation and discussing casual subjects in their presence or near them.

The care of the dead in the Jewish religion really begins at the stage when the person is about to die, if such determination can be made beforehand. A person who is dying must be constantly attended to and never left alone. Small details relating to the comfort of the dying person must be scrupulously attended to. Relieving a dying person's thirst or hearing a last will and confession are true services that must be provided. Close members of the family circle bear the most important responsibility for such blessed tasks and traditional Jews assign dedicated people to help with this care.

Once the person has died, there are important rituals to be performed and those in attendance are expected to perform such tasks right away. The eyes and mouth are to be closed by the son or nearest relative. "The arms and the hands are extended at the sides of the body and the lower jaw is bound up before rigor mortis sets in. The body is then placed on the floor with the feet toward the door and is covered with a sheet, while a lighted candle is placed close to the head."[14] Prior to burial, the body must undergo a ritual washing before it is placed in the shrouds for burial. These rituals are intended to form a continuous procedure of care and attention from the time a person is about to die until burial itself. Non-traditional or liberal Jews eliminate many of these customs in the modern day, but the general principles of care, consideration and constant attention remain as a general rule.

The practice of embalming is against Jewish custom and usage. Occasionally, when transportation rules and state laws require modifications of this procedure, embalming may be permitted. The practice of quick burial and the aversion of Jewish authorities to showing or viewing the body all reinforce the Rabbis' rules against embalming unless it is required by civil authorities.

Even though autopsy was forbidden throughout the centuries, attitudes toward this procedure are becoming more liberal, even among traditional Jews throughout the world. There are two Jewish values that conflict here. The first that Jews value the physical integrity and wholeness and dignity of the body so that it may be prepared for bodily resurrection. The second is the long-term devotion of the Jews to medical research and the advancement of medical techniques. Some of the world's earliest physicians were Jewish and Jewish leadership in medicine has been consistent through the centuries.

Cremation has long been against Jewish custom and practice,[15] primarily because it interferes with all the natural preparations to return the body to its natural state and with efforts to maintain it intact for bodily resurrection. Also, cremation is a destructive process that does not allow the normal degenerative processes to take over, thereby changing the mood of the natural mourning process. A few cremations do take place among liberal Jews, but they are very rare. It is difficult to predict whether Jewish views on cremation will become more liberal because of external conditions such as the growing problems of lack of space in urban areas and immensely crowded cemeteries in certain localities. But at the present time, no such liberalization is in the offing. Cremation will likely remain a rarity among Jews.

Judaism has an exceptionally well developed system of comforting and responding to the bereaved. Right after the funeral, the bereaved are required to rest and reside in a "House of Mourning" designated for their recovery from the loss. (In practice, the House of Mourning is often the bereaved's own house.) The primary mourning period is seven days for traditional Jews and three days for liberal Jews. Under this system, it is entirely improper for the bereaved to forego this ritual and resume normal activities without it. Right after arriving at the House of Mourning, the next of kin and close friends minister to the bereaved by attending to all their personal needs. The meal of condolence is prepared by the family circle and loving friends and is served shortly after the funeral to the bereaved and to the visitors who arrive as comforters. A hard-boiled egg must be served with this meal, for it signifies life's continuation. In traditional Jewish homes, the mourners sit on low stools rather than the usual comfortable living room furniture. It is the custom also for the traditional Jewish mourner to remove his leather shoes and instead wear cloth, felt or rubber slippers. No work is permitted, for it is a time of meditation and introspection. Traditional female mourners are allowed to do domestic work around the house if they so desire. During the first three days of mourning, the traditional mourner does not acknowledge or welcome his or her guests, and remains in virtual silence. This becomes relaxed after the third day. Non-traditional Jews have liberalized many of these rules. They do not sit on low stools, nor do they remove their shoes and they are allowed to greet their guests.[16] It is the usual custom to have religious services in the House of Mourning especially timed for the fulfillment of the daily prayers that are incumbent upon all Jews. When the services are held at the House of Mourning, special mention is made of the individual who has died. Close friends and relatives bring freshly baked breads, prepared dishes of all kinds and offer their services to clean house, run errands and remain during late hours if the mourner is alone in the house and needs moral support.

The mourning period is divided into three parts of special nature. The first week is the most intense part of mourning. This is when the mourner must receive the comforters and remain in a state of deep contemplation. The second period is the 30-day period after the death when the mourner is restricted from attending most entertainment and formal community events. The third is a 12-month period of mourning. Restrictions about the timing of remarriage fall within this period and during this time, or at its close, the tombstone is officially dedicated in solemn ceremony. Many strict customs still apply to the most pious of traditional Jews. For example, during the first 30 days, while one's hair may be combed, it is inappropriate to cut it. Also, during the first 30 days, the wearing of black is a strict rule and it is a general rule to forbid the mourner from taking a wife. A man whose wife has died is not permitted to remarry until three festivals have elapsed (a period of several months), although exceptions are made in the case of a widower with very young children.[17] A widow is forbidden to remarry until 90 days have elapsed after the death of her husband.[18]

After the funeral service, it is customary to light a seven-day *Yartzeit* (memorial) candle in memory of the deceased. *Yartzeit* candles are lit for 24 hours in the mourner's home on the anniversary of the death each year and also candles beside memorial wall tablets are lit in the synagogue on the Day of Atonement, the holiest day of the Jewish holiday cycle. In some modern, non-traditional synagogues, the names of the deceased are read during religious services on the anniversary of the death and in many synagogues of all types, memorial tablets are erected that list the beloved dead of the congregational family. Charitable contributions in honor of the deceased are an important custom to be carried out by the synagogue family and the local Jewish community. These contributions are often listed in the synagogue bulletin.

The saying of the Kaddish prayer is an essential part of the mourning experience. This famous prayer is distinctive because of its rhythmic cadence and its use of Aramaic language instead of the customary Hebrew. It is incumbent upon the mourner to recite the Kaddish prayer with meticulous regularity during the year of mourning. In practice, the prayer amounts to a virtual petition or intercession for the welfare of the deceased. The Kaddish prayer is supposed to be recited by the next-of-kin at every regular service during the year of mourning.[19] In the event of a legitimate inability to fulfill this Kaddish prayer recitation, then a surrogate must be appointed to fulfill this act of prayer. Non-traditional Jews have permitted leniency in this very stringent rule, permitting absences and periods of excused non-compliance. Originally the Kaddish prayer was supposed to be recited by the son only in the situation of the death of a parent. Traditional Judaism entrusts such ritual obligations exclusively to the male. Today the prayer is used for more than parents and most authorities extend its use for all next-of-kin. Many authorities allow the females to recite this prayer.

During festivals and holy seasons, Jews hold memorial services to remember the dead. The memorial services are added to the roster of prayers normally said on those holidays. The three festivals of Passover, Sukot and Shavuot and the Day of Atonement constitute such occasions. Many synagogues also hold memorial services at the congregational cemeteries during the days of repentance, which occur at the time of the holiest seasons of New Year and Day of Atonement.

An important Jewish procedural rule for care and remembrance of the dead is that no funeral rituals can take place on Sabbaths and holidays. There can be no funeral on the Sabbath or on the first day of a Jewish holiday and the mourner refrains from mourning during these periods. It is felt that the celebratory holiday mood and the mourning mood simply cannot be reasonably combined. Public memorial services and the reciting of the Kaddish are permitted, but the major acts of personal mourning and the funeral services are prohibited during these periods. It is especially important to emphasize the need of the mourner to fully express his or her grief by the natural act of weeping and expressing personal sorrow; to hold in or to restrain one's grief would be harmful to the process of full recovery that is the hoped-for result of the year's ritual of mourning. Overall, practices and beliefs surrounding death in the Jewish religion are meant to reflect God's purpose — for his creatures to have a meaningful and righteous existence in this world and in the hereafter. The hallmarks of the funeral service and the burial are simplicity and rapidity. Ostentation and length of the occasion are greatly limited so as not to delay the evolving of the natural expression of grief.

The year of mourning is divided into three parts and surrounded by ritual prescriptions of all kinds. The mourner should be encouraged to let the tears flow and to sit and grieve while others attend to the necessities of his or her life. The mourner is treated like a sick person who cannot resume normal activities until the spiritual and psychological conditions have righted themselves. The process of honoring, loving and remembering the dead starts at the moment the person begins to die. At this time, personal attention is given by care and supervision of the dying so that the mourner's personal love may be demonstrated and human needs of the dying be met. Details of the departed's life are usually presented in the eulogy and are often personal and quite emotional. The most common form of tribute given by friends and associates is a gift to charity befitting the interests and associations of the departed.

Today, Jewish funerals most often take place in funeral homes, with a committal service at the cemetery. But in the case of a great scholar or dignitary, the services can begin in the synagogue, where special prestige is accorded to the event. When burying a very old person who has few friends and relatives to attend the services, the service is often restricted to a short committal service in the cemetery, known as a graveside service. A non-Jewish person may be buried in a Jewish cemetery, but the officiant and the symbols used must be specifically Jewish.[20]

To love, to honor and to remember the dead is the ongoing obligation of the person who has lost a loved one. By saying the Kaddish prayer during the year of mourning, by lighting the remembrance (*Yartzeit*) lights, by fulfilling the rules of the year of mourning, the process of grief gradually ebbs as the year draws to a close. At that point, although the laws permit it earlier, the tombstone is usually marked and dedicated. Unlike the funeral service, the tombstone dedication is attended only by the close family and a few friends and does not contain an emotional eulogy. It is shorter and simpler in every way.

The *Yartzeit* remembrance lights continue to be lit year after year and the deceased is remembered at the various memorial services in the synagogue. Very often, the dead are memorialized on tablets that have been placed on a synagogue wall. In special instances, donations are given to dedicate portions of rooms or libraries in the synagogue in memory of beloved dead. In many synagogues, the names of the deceased are read aloud on the anniversary of the death. Naming children after the departed also serves to memorialize the dead. Praiseworthy ancestors have always been the ones first considered when children's names must be selected.

In many remote areas, Jews share cemetery space with non-Jews. In such instances, the section is ritually separated and marked off. Inscriptions in Jewish cemeteries invariably contain words or passages in the Hebrew language and are sometimes followed by an English translation. One of the most common inscriptions is: "May the soul be bound up in the bonds of eternal life." When a dead person is mentioned at synagogue services, it is usually in this way: "May he (or she) be remembered for blessing" or be "of blessed memory."

It is the fervent hope of the Jewish believer that the good influence of the dead will always remain as an inspiration for the next generations.

Notes

1. *El Moley Rachamim*, "O God, Full of Compassion." This standard funeral prayer petitions God that the soul of the deceased may be brought under the shelter of God's wings.
2. Deuteronomy 30:15.
3. Charles Braden, *The World's Religions* (Nashville: Abingdon: Cokesbury Press, 1939), p. 81.
4. From *Gates of Prayer* (New York: Central Conference of American Rabbis, 1973), p. 625.
5. "What is the Jewish Attitude Toward Manual Labor?" in Rabbi Morris Kertzer, *What is a Jew?* (New York: World Publishing Company, 1953), pp. 34-35.
6. Very Rev. Dr. Joseph H. Hertz (Chief Rabbi of the British Empire), *Sayings of the Fathers* (New York: Behrman House, 1945), p. 119.
7. Milton Miller, *Our Religion and Our Neighbors* (New York: Union of American Hebrew Congregations Press, 1963), p. 259.
8. *Encyclopedia Judaica* (New York: Keter Publishing Co., 1971), Vol. 11, p. 1412
9. *What is a Jew?* p. 13.
10. Rabbi H. Rabinowicz, *A Guide to Life* (Hoboken, NJ: KTAV Publishing House, 1967), p. 130.
11. Ibid.
12. *Encyclopedia Judaica*, Vol. 12, p. 998.
13. *A Guide to Life*, p. 22.
14. Ibid., pp. 18-19.
15. *What is a Jew?* p. 95.
16. Frederic A. Doppelt and David Polish, *A Guide for Reform Jews* (Hoboken, NJ: KTAV Publishing House, 1973), p. 87.
17. *A Guide to Life*, p. 98.
18. Ibid., p. 99.
19. *A Guide for Reform Jews*, p. 89.
20. Walter Jacob, ed., *American Reform Responsa* (New York: Central Conference of American Rabbis, 1983), p. 340.

Lutherans

Daniel E. Lee, PhD

BACKGROUND OF THE FAITH

Lutheranism is most appropriately understood as a particular expression of Christianity and is envisioned as part of one universal church, rather than as a separate church. Throughout the history of Lutheranism, Lutherans have joined in the ancient confession, "We believe in one holy Catholic and apostolic church."

The Lutheran movement began more by circumstance than by design. As the name suggests, a key figure in the historical development of the movement was Martin Luther,[1] an Augustinian monk born in 1483 in the little town of Eisleben, located not far from Berlin. After entering the Augustinian cloister at Erfurt in 1505, Luther spent a good deal of time wrestling with a variety of questions related to salvation. The process continued after his transfer to Wittenberg in 1511, where he joined the faculty of the university established there by Frederick the Wise. In time, he came to question a number of the beliefs and practices of the Roman Catholic Church of his time.

Luther was not at all reluctant to express his views on matters that concerned him. On the eve of All Saints Day in 1517, he posted for debate a list of theses challenging various practices of the church that troubled him. The Ninety-Five Theses were the spark that lit the powder keg that was to become known as the Protestant Reformation. Even though most of the practices challenged in the Ninety-Five Theses were subsequently changed — many of them within Luther's own lifetime — the theses began a chain of historical events from which there was no turning back.

News of the outspoken monk quickly reached Rome. In 1520, Pope Leo X, a member of the influential Medici family, issued a decree giving Luther 60 days to submit to the authority of the church. "Arise, O Lord, and judge thy cause," the preface began. "A wild boar has invaded thy vineyard."[2] But

Luther was not to be quieted. Tossing the papal decree into a fire near one of the gates of the university in Wittenberg, he continued to challenge the beliefs and practices of the church, questioning not only the authority of the pope but sacramental theology as well.

In 1521, in the city of Worms, Luther was asked again to recant, this time by the young Charles V, a member of the Hapsburg family, who had been chosen Emperor of the Holy Roman Empire less than two years earlier. Again Luther refused. Under the circumstances, it is not surprising that he was excommunicated from the church.

The Lutheran movement spread rapidly because of a combination of religious and political reasons. Parishioners were pleased to hear that they could enter heaven without having to comply with the heavy demands that were placed on them by the Roman Catholic Church. The princes of the fragmented territories that comprised the Germany at that time (there was no German nation as such) were quick to exploit the opportunity to assert more independence from the Holy Roman Empire, of which they were nominally a part, as well as from the Roman Catholic Church, with which the empire was so closely allied.

In time, the Lutheran movement spread to the Scandinavian countries, which eventually became predominantly Lutheran (aided, in part, by the fact that Lutheranism became the official state religion). Immigrants from Germany and the Scandinavian countries brought Lutheranism to the American colonies prior to the American Revolution. Because a number of these immigrants sided with the British crown during the war for independence, Lutheranism set roots in Canada in the years following the war. Subsequent waves of immigrants in the late 19th and early 20th centuries added considerably to the number of Lutherans in the United States and Canada. Missionary work, primarily in the last century and a half, has spread Lutheranism to other parts of the world. Among the countries with sizable Lutheran populations today is Namibia in southern Africa.

In the United States, in January 1988, a merger took place of three Lutheran congregations: the Lutheran Church in America (LCA), the American Lutheran Church (ALC) and the American Evangelical Lutheran Church (AELC). The united congregations call themselves the Evangelical Lutheran Church in America and they have some 8 million members. The more conservative Lutheran Church-Missouri Synod, with approximately 3 million members, remained as an independent body.

BELIEFS

A key role in Lutheran doctrine and beliefs is played by the doctrine of justification by faith. The Augsburg Confession, compiled in 1530 as an expression of basic Lutheran beliefs, states the doctrine as follows:

> It is also taught among us that we cannot obtain forgiveness of sin and righteousness before God by our own merits, works, or satisfactions, but that we receive forgiveness of sin and become righteous before God by grace, for Christ's sake, through faith, when we believe that Christ suffered for us and that for His sake our sin is forgiven and righteousness and eternal life are given to us.[3]

Luther tended to view the world as caught in a struggle between the forces of good and the forces of evil — between God and Satan. In his essay "The Bondage of the Will" and elsewhere in his writings, he insisted that apart from God's intervention, human beings, who are born sinful, are totally under the sway of the forces of evil. The will is so vitiated by sin, Luther believed, that it is not possible even to accept the salvation offered by God without divine assistance.[4]

In the Christ of the cross, Luther believed the ultimate price was paid. In the crucifixion and resurrection of Christ, victory over the forces of evil was gained. Thus, Luther believed, as a result of Christ having paid for the sins of all humanity, God extends salvation to the believer (the act of faith itself being a gift from God). Luther put it as follows in his *Small Catechism*:

> I believe that Jesus Christ, true God, begotten of the Father from eternity, and also true man, born of the Virgin Mary, is my Lord, who has redeemed me, a lost and condemned creature, delivered me and freed me from all sins, from death, and from the power of the devil, not with silver and gold but with his holy and precious blood and with his innocent sufferings and death, in order that I may be his, live under him in his kingdom, and serve him in everlasting righteousness, innocence, and blessedness, even as he is risen from the dead and lives and reigns to all eternity. This is most certainly true.[5]

A classical expression of Luther's theology is to be found in the words of the well-known hymn he wrote, "A Mighty Fortress Is Our God." In this hymn, he states that "though hordes of devils fill the land," Christ "holds the field victorious."[6] In the course of the centuries, the apocalyptic nature of Lutheran theology has softened. In the sermons preached in many Lutheran churches today, there is seldom, if ever, any reference to the devil. Yet the basic doctrine of justification by faith remains central, for Lutherans are unanimous in insisting that salvation cannot be earned by good works and can only be received as a gift from God.

FUNERAL PRACTICES AND MINISTRY TO THE DYING AND BEREAVED

The Lutheran Book of Worship, which originated as a cooperative effort of all major Lutheran groups in the United States and Canada, includes a service for the burial of the dead.[7] Intended primarily to be used in a church with the body of the deceased present, the service is structured so that it may easily be modified for use in other settings such as a funeral chapel, private home or crematory and for situations in which the body of the deceased is not present. The liturgy is a service of worship. Ceremonies or tributes of social or fraternal societies are not allowed within the service of worship. The Service for the Burial of the Dead consists of three parts: the Service of the Word, the Commendation and the Committal. The first part of the liturgy, the Service of the Word, typically begins with a procession that forms when the minister or ministers meet the coffin and the pallbearers and the bereaved at the entrance to the church. The order of the procession is as follows: the cross, the paschal candle or torches, the presiding minister, the assisting minister or ministers, the pallbearers with the coffin and the bereaved.[8]

While the coffin often is open for a last viewing in the narthex (entrance) of the church prior to the service, the coffin remains closed throughout the service. When the service is conducted in some other setting such as a funeral home or a private home, the expectation is that the coffin will be closed there as well, though some ministers will accommodate the preferences of the family.[9] When the service is conducted in a church, a white pall (cloth) may be placed on the coffin prior to the procession. The pall is both to symbolize the righteousness of Christ and to assure a measure of equality by preventing the display of a costly coffin or any embarrassment that might be associated with an inexpensive one. The coffin is placed at the front of the church perpendicular to the altar. An old tradition, still practiced in some churches, suggests that if the deceased is a pastor, the coffin should be placed with the head toward the altar, whereas if the deceased is a lay person, the coffin should be placed with the head toward the congregation. This placement has no particular theological significance but is simply intended to reflect the accustomed role of the deceased in the church, with pastors facing the congregation and lay persons facing the altar.[10]

The Service of the Word includes several readings from Scripture and various prayers. Several options are included in the liturgy. Special music often is part of the service. The Apostles' Creed may be said. The Service of Holy Communion may be included. The service usually includes a sermon. While the sermon may include recognition of the life of the deceased, it is not intended to be a eulogy, but rather, a proclamation of hope and comfort in Christ and thanksgiving for the life of the deceased. In some cases, relatives and friends may comment briefly on the meaning of the life of the deceased for the community.[11] When the service is held in a church, it usually concludes with the Commendation, a prayer asking God to receive the deceased in mercy, recalling the last prayer of Jesus on the Cross, "Father, into your hands I commend my spirit." When the body is cremated, the Commendation may be held in the crematory chapel with the Service of the Word being held in the church as a memorial service.[12]

The Committal is a liturgy usually performed at the interment site. If the body has been willed to science, the Committal may, with appropriate modifications, be performed prior to the removal of the body.[13] When all have arrived at the place of burial, additional prayers may be read. When the coffin is lowered into the grave, handfuls of earth may be cast on the coffin by the assisting minister and those who stand nearby as the presiding minister commits the body to its final resting place.[14]

Many Lutheran ministers believe that it is their duty to conduct a funeral whenever asked to do so, whether by the request of the deceased prior to his or her death or by family members at the time of death. When the deceased is not a member of the congregation, it is usual to omit certain portions of the service that pertain more specifically to those who have been practicing members of the congregation.

Cremation is not widely practiced by Lutherans, but is an option encompassed by the liturgy. The same is true with donation of the body to science, a practice given support by the "LCA Social Statement on Death and Dying" (a position paper adopted at the 1982 National LCA Convention).[15]

The Book of Occasional Services, a cooperative effort of the AELC, the LCA, the ALC and The Evangelical Lutheran Church of Canada, includes a service for comforting the bereaved.[16] This service is sometimes used at the funeral home at the close of visitation with only family and close friends present. The church's ministry is understood as including the time prior to death as well as the time after death. The LCA Social Statement on Death and Dying observed:

> In death-and-dying situations, the Church's ministry of Word and Sacrament through its members and ordained ministers is of great significance. Remembrance of Baptism renews the Christian's sense of unity with Christ and the Church, and the Sacrament of Holy Communion serves as a reassurance of Christ's living presence and offers hope for the life to come. Simply to be with those for whom death is approaching — to pray with and for them, to listen and to respond, to comfort and to console — is also an essential ministry.[17]

PERSPECTIVES ON DEATH AND LIFE AFTER DEATH

Among Lutherans there is considerable diversity of opinion as to how death should be interpreted. One view, held by many individuals in all major Lutheran groups, suggests that death is the result of sin and, accordingly, an intrusion into the natural created order. A document prepared by a Lutheran Church-Missouri Synod working group stated this view as follows:

> God created human beings to live and not to die. Death in any form is

> inimical to what God originally had in mind for His creation.... Death is the very negation of what God has given. Had it not been for man's own rebellion against the kind of intended relationship established by having been fashioned in God's image, there would be no death.[18]

A contrasting view, which also has broad support among Lutherans, characterizes death as part of the natural created order. An ALC document stated that "death is a natural event in the course of human life."[19] A similar view was expressed in the LCA Social Statement on Death and Dying that suggests that death is "a natural part of the life cycle."[20] This view is reaffirmed in an ELCA document entitled *A Message on End-of-Life Decisions* which states that "the integrity of the life processes which God has created should be respected; both birth and death are part of these life processes...."[21]

There is also some diversity of opinion about what happens after death. In theological and philosophical thought, there is a distinction to be made between the doctrine of the resurrection of the body and the doctrine of the immortality of the soul. The doctrine of the resurrection of the body, which is firmly rooted in early Christian thought, suggests that after an interim period of time, those who have died will be brought back to life again. The doctrine of the immortality of the soul, which is Greek in origin, suggests that some aspects of human existence — perhaps including some form of consciousness — continue to exist after the death of the body. Like many other Christians, the average Lutheran sitting in a pew on Sunday morning tends to give no distinction to the two doctrines. While comprehensive surveys of the views of parishioners on these matters are not available, it is probably accurate to say that the typical Lutheran is likely to believe that some part of the person continues to exist after death, but that full restoration to life must await resurrection of the body.

The liturgy of the church, as is evidenced by the Service for the Burial of the Dead, places a strong emphasis on the resurrection of the body. References to the doctrine of the immortality of the soul are somewhat more muted. The Commendation, which, as already noted, is a prayer asking God to receive the deceased in mercy, might be interpreted as implying some type of continued existence. So also might the Apostles' Creed, which speaks of Jesus descending into hell prior to being raised from the dead. (An alternate translation, which is also included in the Lutheran Book of Worship, states that Jesus "descended to the dead."[22])

In keeping with the interpretation of the Sacrament of the Altar (Holy Communion) articulated by Luther, it is not the practice of Lutherans to say masses on behalf of the dead.[23] The early leaders of the Lutheran movement, however, did not preclude the possibility of saying prayers for the dead.[24] In a certain sense, both the Commendation and the Committal in the Service for the Burial of the Dead are prayers on behalf of the deceased. A prayer occasionally used as part of the Service for the Burial of the Dead (though not included in the Lutheran Book of Worship) is even more explicit. This prayer reads, in part:

> Lord...
> You raised the dead to life;
> give to our *brother/sister* eternal life.
> Hear us, Lord
> you promised life to those who believe;
> bring our *brother/sister* to the joys of heaven.
> Hear us, Lord[25]

In practice, however, prayers for the deceased are rare among Lutherans, particularly on occasions subsequent to the funeral. When references in prayers are made to the deceased on subsequent occasions, it is almost always a prayer of remembrance that expresses thanksgiving for the life of the deceased. A commonly used prayer is the following:

> We remember with thanksgiving those who have loved and served you in your church on earth, who now rest from their labors (especially those most dear to us, whom we name in our hearts before you). Keep us in fellowship with all your saints and bring us at last to the joy of your heavenly kingdom.[26]

As noted above, the traditional Lutheran view is that of resurrection of the body and of a life to come. The doctrine of reincarnation does not find support among Lutherans.

SALVATION

Traditional Lutheran belief holds that at some unspecified time in the future, Christ will return, the dead will be raised and a day of judgment will be held. The Augsburg Confession puts it as follows:

> It is also taught among us that our Lord Jesus Christ will return on the last day for judgment and will raise up all the dead, to give eternal life and everlasting joy to believers and the elect but to condemn ungodly men and the devil to hell and eternal punishment.[27]

As previously noted, Luther believed that only those to whom God extends grace will receive salvation and thus be spared eternal punishment. In Luther's view, the fact that someone might go to church regularly and profess to be a Christian was by no means a certain indicator that he or she was a recipient of God's grace leading to salvation and eternal life in heaven. Nor did Luther exclude the possibility that God's grace might be extended to someone lacking in the outward signs of being a Christian.

An equally perplexing problem for Luther (as well as for other Christians) was the question of why a God, who is loving, merciful and all-powerful, would allow some people to suffer in the torment of hell for all eternity. Also troublesome was the question of why it is just for God to punish people if they are born under the bondage of sin and are totally unable to do anything other than sin. All that Luther could say was that "the light of glory...will one day reveal God, to whom alone belongs a judgment whose justice is incomprehensible, as a God whose justice is most righteous and evident...."[28]

As with other aspects of Lutheran theology, beliefs pertaining to the question of salvation and the day of judgment have been softened somewhat in the four and a half centuries since the time of Luther. References to hell and eternal damnation are relatively rare in the sermons preached in Lutheran churches today. Rather, the emphasis is on God's love and mercy. There is some tendency to believe that God extends salvation to all who wish to receive it. Some parishioners go one step further and say that the gift of grace encompasses all persons without distinction.

In a widely read book on the Augsburg Confession, George Forell, a contemporary Lutheran scholar, gives a somewhat temporal interpretation to the reference to a day of judgment in the Confession. In an era in which apprehensions about nuclear annihilation and other fears of impending disaster are widespread, the Augsburg Confession, he suggests, serves to remind us "that the symbol which dominates the final scene of human history is not the cloud but the cross." He continues, "The Christian proclamation in our time is a message of hope rather than despair because Christians believe that history is moving toward Jesus Christ."[29]

Lutherans, like most other Christians, have traditionally understood salvation as being saved from the fires of hell. However, there has been some rethinking in this area as well. Some Lutherans, including several involved in various aspects of counseling, are inclined to view salvation as a healing process involving restoration to wholeness. While there is no consensus as to what wholeness of the person encompasses, it is generally understood as spiritual and psychological well-being in some combination, and, in some cases, social well-being as well. For example, some would consider working through unresolved grief as a form of restoration to wholeness. Quite obviously, the time parameters for such a view of salvation are somewhat different, with salvation at least potentially occurring here and now, rather than in a life to come. The two views of salvation, it might be added, are not antithetical and can be held concurrently, with salvation envisioned as a multifaceted process.

In most cases, suicide is viewed as the result of disturbance or illness, rather than as a sin. In the limited number of cases in which suicide *is* viewed as a sin, Lutherans typically believe that God's love and mercy are of sufficient magnitude to extend forgiveness for this sin, as well as for all other sins.

HEAVEN

Lutherans are not given to speculative theology attempting to determine what heaven might be like, where it might be located, etc. To the extent that Lutherans have a belief about heaven, it is usually envisioned as an eternity in the immediate presence of God, joining in unending praise to the Creator and Lord of all that exists. A traditional Norwegian hymn sung by many Lutherans ("Den store hvide Flok" —"Who Is This Host Arrayed in White") paints the following picture of heaven:

> Who is this host arrayed in white
> Like thousand snow-clad mountains bright,
> That stands with palms and sings its praises
> Before the throne of light?
> These are the saints who kept God's Word;
> They are the honored of the Lord.
> He is their prince who drowned their sins,
> So they were cleansed, restored.
> They now serve God both day and night;
> They sing their songs in endless light.
> Their anthems ring when they all sing
> With angels shining bright.[30]

THANKSGIVING

In the life and liturgy of Lutheran churches, there is a strong emphasis on the theme of thankfulness for the gift of life that God has created. It is in keeping with this spirit that the LCA Social Statement on Death and Dying concludes with Psalm 107:1:

> O give thanks to the Lord, for he is good;
> for his steadfast love endures forever! (RSV)

Notes

1. For a highly readable biography of Luther, see Roland H. Bainton, *Here I Stand: A Life of Martin Luther* (New York: Abingdon Press, 1950).
2. Ibid., p. 114.
3. *The Augsburg Confession,* Article IV. Included in *The Book of Concord: The Confessions of the Evangelical Lutheran Church*, translated and edited by Theodore G. Tappert (Philadelphia: Muhlenberg Press, 1959).
4. Martin Luther, "The Bondage of the Will," *passim.* Selections from "The Bondage of the Will" are included in *Martin Luther: Selections from His Writings,* edited by John Dillenberger (Garden City, NY: Anchor Books, 1961), pp. 166-203. The translation of the Dillenberger volume is by J.I. Packer and A.R.

Johnston.

5. Martin Luther, *The Small Catechism,* commentary on the second article of The Apostles' Creed. Included in *The Book of Concord,* p. 345.
6. Martin Luther, "A Mighty Fortress Is Our God." Included in the *Lutheran Book of Worship* (Minneapolis: Augsburg Publishing House, 1978), Hymns 228 and 229.
7. *Lutheran Book of Worship,* pp. 206-214.
8. Philip H. Pfatteicher and Carlos R. Messerli, *Manual on the Liturgy: Lutheran Book of Worship* (Minneapolis: Augsburg Publishing House, 1979), pp. 356-357.
9. Ibid.
10. Ibid., p. 358.
11. Ibid., p. 360.
12. Ibid., pp. 362-363.
13. Ibid.
14. Ibid., pp. 363-365.
15. The Lutheran Church in America, *Social Statement on Death and Dying* (New York: Lutheran Church in America, Division for Mission in North America, 1982), p. 7.
16. *Occasional Services: A Companion to Lutheran Book of Worship* (Minneapolis: Augsburg Publishing House, 1982), pp. 108-112.
17. LCA, *Social Statement on Death and Dying,* p. 6. See also the liturgy for "Commendation of the Dying," *Occasional Services,* pp. 103-107.
18. Commission on Theology and Church Relations of The Lutheran Church-Missouri Synod, *Report on Euthanasia with Guiding Principles* (October 1979), p. 18.
19. Task Force on Ethical Issues in Human Medicine, *Health, Life, and Death: A Christian Perspective* (Minneapolis: The American Lutheran Church, 1977), p. 17.
20. LCA, *Social Statement on Death and Dying,* p. 1. This issue is discussed in greater detail in my book *Death and Dying: Ethical Choices in a Caring Community* (New York: Lutheran Church in America, Division for Mission in North America, 1983), pp. 1-7.
21. The Evangelical Lutheran Church in America, *A Message on End-of-Life Decisions* (Chicago: Evangelical Lutheran Church in America, Division for Church in Society, 1992), p. 2.
22. *Lutheran Book of Worship,* p. 65.
23. See, e.g., *The Babylonian Captivity of the Church* in *Luther's Works,* Vol. 36, p. 55.
24. See, e.g., *The Apology of the Augsburg Confession*, Article XXIV (included in the various editions of the *Book of Concord).*
25. Included in Pfatteicher and Messerli, *Manual on the Liturgy, Lutheran Book of Worship,* p. 361.
26. *Lutheran Book of Worship,* p. 53.
27. *Augsburg Confession,* Article XVII.
28. Luther, "The Bondage of the Will," pp. 200-202.
29. George W. Forell, *The Augsburg Confession: A Contemporary Commentary* (Minneapolis: Augsburg Publishing House, 1968), p. 75.
30. *Lutheran Book of Worship,* Hymn 314.

Presbyterianism

Ben Lacy Rose, PhD

BACKGROUND OF THE FAITH

The faith of the Presbyterian and Reformed churches[1] was brought to fullness during the Protestant Reformation under the leadership of John Calvin in Switzerland where he built on foundations laid by Ulrich Zwingli and others. Feeling that the Roman Catholic Church had distorted the faith of the Bible, Calvin and the other reformers began the task of uncovering and articulating afresh the teachings of the Scriptures of the Old and New Testaments. Calvin's followers, therefore, do not consider Calvin to be the founder of their faith, but instead, that Abraham, Moses, David and Paul were the founders and that Jesus Christ is the pioneer and perfecter.

Calvin did not consider himself against Martin Luther and his work, even though these two theologians differed in many respects. Today, Calvin's theology is called "Reformed" while Luther's is called "Lutheran." John Calvin was born in 1509, in France, of Roman Catholic parents. He was preparing for a career in law when, around 1533, he was converted to the Protestant cause, which at that time was gaining popularity among the French. Shortly thereafter, Calvin left France and settled in Geneva, Switzerland, where he spent most of his life teaching, writing and preaching. The only positions he ever held were preacher, pastor and professor, but through these he influenced the people of Geneva in a profound way. Calvin's ideas, spread primarily by his writings and by his disciples, moved rapidly to Holland, Germany, France, Scotland and to central and eastern Europe. The Huguenots of France, the Puritans of England, and William of Orange and his followers in the Netherlands, were all spiritual children of John Calvin. Under the leadership of John Knox, who spent several years with Calvin in Geneva, the Reformed faith and Presbyterian policy were adopted by the Church of Scotland. The Westminster Confession of Faith and Catechisms, one of the finest statements of Reformed doctrine, was drawn up by an assembly of divines called together by the English Parliament in 1643.

The Presbyterian and Reformed faith was brought to America by immigrants who were primarily from Holland, Scotland, France and Germany. Today, among Protestants, the Presbyterian and Reformed family is the second largest in the world and the Lutheran family is the largest. Presbyterian and Reformed people have been prolific in the production of creeds. Dr. John H. Leith, in *Creeds of the Churches*, declares that "more than 60 creeds would qualify as Reformed."[2] These creeds differ in many details, yet they exhibit a surprising unity regarding the basic elements of the faith.

MAIN BELIEFS

Some of the main beliefs of the Presbyterian and Reformed faith are set forth in the following paragraphs.

God has revealed himself in the Scriptures of the Old and New Testaments, which, being uniquely inspired by him, are our only trustworthy rule for believing and living. While it is impossible to describe fully the nature of God, one Reformed creed puts it thus, "God is a spirit, infinite, eternal and unchangeable in his being, wisdom, power, holiness, justice, goodness and truth."[3] We joyfully declare that "God is love,"[4] yet at the same time we tremble at his wrath, believing that, even in his anger, his love is revealed. God is creator, sustainer and sovereign ruler of all his creatures and all their actions. "From all eternity God did by the most wise and holy counsel of his own will, freely and unchangeably ordain whatsoever comes to pass, yet so as thereby neither is God the author of sin nor is violence offered to the will of the creatures, nor is the liberty or contingency of second causes taken away, but rather established."[5] God is personal and has revealed himself as a trinity of Father, Son and Holy Spirit. We do not affirm three gods but one God who exists in three persons. God created humankind in his own image and for fellowship with himself. He put men and women on the earth that they might "glorify and enjoy him forever."[6] The glory of God is therefore the purpose of human existence.

Humankind, however, refused to walk in fellowship with God and rebelled against him. Thus, they fell from the estate wherein they were created by sinning against God. Possessing now a fallen nature, human beings are basically selfish and prone to sin. Some Presbyterians believe in a literal Devil and some do not, but all recognize the awful power of evil in the world from whatever source it comes.

In order to redeem humankind and bring them back into fellowship with himself, God sent his only begotten Son, the Lord Jesus Christ, who was born of the Virgin Mary, grew up as would any normal boy, preached and taught in the land of Palestine, and was crucified on a Roman cross near Jerusalem during the reign of Pontius Pilate. Jesus Christ was dead and buried, but God raised him from the dead and set him on God's right hand. From there he shall come again at the end of time to judge the living and the dead.

Salvation comes to human beings through faith in the Lord Jesus Christ. The church, which consists of all who believe in Christ and their children, was created by God to carry the message of God's saving love to all the world. Believers are given the task of witnessing to the faith of Christ and of ministering to persons in his name and spirit. "As servants of the sovereign will of God, Christians are under obligation to their fellowmen and to unborn generations to shape and influence institutions and practices so that the world may be brought more nearly into conformity with the purposes of God for his creation. We believe that our destiny and that of the world are not subject to chance or fate, but to the just and loving sovereignty of God. In this assurance, we face the problems of suffering and evil. Faith in the purpose and providence of God assures us of his presence in suffering and of his power to give it meaning. We are confident that no form of evil can separate us from the love of God, that God works in all things for good and that evil will ultimately be overcome. Therefore, while we cannot fully understand the pain and evil of the present world, we can offer ourselves as active instruments of God's will in their conquest."[7] Finally, we believe in "the resurrection of the body and the life everlasting."[8]

Most Presbyterian and Reformed churches have doctrinal standards that set forth their theology and manuals of government that contain guidelines by which church affairs are to be ordered. Members are not required to accept all that is affirmed in the doctrinal standards, but ministers are required to accept the essentials.

THE FUNERAL

The doctrinal standards and manuals of government of Presbyterian and Reformed churches give very few instructions regarding funerals. No inviolable rules are laid down and no rituals or prayers are prescribed. One manual reads, "Christians should make of the occasion of death a time in which the hope of the gospel is reaffirmed by them with solemn joy.... The funeral service, which should be conducted with dignity and simplicity, is a witness to the greatness and goodness of God and to the love he bears all people, a love which strengthens and supports even in the midst of grief."[9] Most funerals are conducted within two to four days after the death and the body of the deceased is present during the service. Services are held in the church sanctuary more often than in a funeral home, but use of the latter is growing. In Presbyterian circles, sometimes a private interment is conducted with only the family present and a memorial service is held later in the church for the public.

Presbyterian and Reformed ministers often conduct funerals for persons who are not of their faith. Whether or not a minister will conduct such a service is for the minister alone to decide. There are few if any requirements placed on our ministers or our members regarding burials.

TREATMENT AND INTERMENT OF THE BODY

Presbyterian and Reformed churches give no authoritative instructions regarding the disposal of the body and members and ministers are free to follow their best judgement in such matters. Embalming is almost universally used. Autopsies and cremation are neither encouraged nor discouraged. The donation of the body to science is advocated by many ministers. One Book of Order says, "The [funeral] service normally should be held in a church and the casket should remain closed,"[10] but this is not mandatory. Sometimes, before the service begins in the church, the casket is opened so that the body may be viewed, but all churches make a practice of closing the casket during the funeral service. Sometimes the family of the deceased will request that the body not be viewed at any time.

RESPONDING TO THE BEREAVED

The role of the concerned member of Presbyterian and Reformed churches in responding to the bereaved is one of a ministry of presence. By a visit, a phone call or a letter, the members assure the bereaved of their sympathy and concern. During a visit to the family of the deceased, concerned members are not required to say anything, but by their presence, a message of love and support is sent. Members simply stand by one another during a time of grief. Our churches prescribe no mourning rituals.

LIFE AFTER DEATH AND REINCARNATION

Most Presbyterians believe that at death, the souls of believers go immediately to be with God. Regarding the souls of the damned, our creeds tend to say little, but most Presbyterians believe that the punishment of unbelievers also begins immediately at death. After death, Presbyterians believe that those who believe in Jesus Christ and love the things of his kingdom will dwell with him forever in blessedness and peace, while those who reject Christ and do not love the things of his kingdom will experience everlasting suffering and misery. While holding firmly to the *fact* of life after death, we have been reluctant to attempt any description of the *nature* of that life. We recognize that when speaking of that other world, even the Bible must use symbols and figures such as "gates of pearl...streets of gold" or "fire and brimstone...with wailing and gnashing of teeth," which cannot approach the reality of either the glory or the agony. We believe, as the Bible says, that "Eye hath not seen nor ear heard, neither have entered into the heart of man the things which God has prepared for them that love him."[11] We believe also that the torments of the damned are equally indescribable.

Presbyterians believe that what happens in this world determines what happens in that other world — that *that* life is an extension of *this* life. We believe that people who have loved God, purity and other people will continue after death to find joy in that and that those who have loved self, sin and evil will continue to be miserable. For this reason, Presbyterian and Reformed creeds give a large place to the duties of persons in this world but say very little about the nature of the world to come. We are willing to leave those details to God, for we have full confidence that life after death will be for God's people a life of blessedness and peace, a life of worship and work, a life of growth and increasing knowledge.

The doctrine of reincarnation (understood as affirming that, after death, a human soul may be reborn in another body or in another form of life), while not discussed in any of the Presbyterian and Reformed creeds, is vigorously denied by Presbyterian and Reformed theologians as contrary to the Christian concept of salvation and of God's deep respect for the individuality of each person.

HEAVEN AND HELL

Heaven is an estate of perfect holiness and joy and hell is an estate of indescribable misery and suffering. Presbyterians have not tried to locate either heaven or hell as though they could be found on some distant star, but have emphasized that heaven is a realm of blessedness and peace, while hell is a realm of remorse and shame. These are realms of the spirit that cannot be localized in the material world.

According to the Presbyterian and Reformed faith, heaven is not a trophy to be attained by human effort but a gift of God to be received by faith and God gives it to all who trust Him enough to accept it. Therefore, heaven is peopled by those who are happy to be in the presence of the God and Father of the Lord Jesus Christ and hell is peopled by persons who would be miserable in the presence of such a God. "Those who have accepted the forgiving love of God in Christ enter into eternal life in fellowship with God and his people.... This new life begins in the present world and continues into the world to come. Those who have rejected the love of God bring upon themselves his judgment and shut themselves outside the fellowship of God and his people."[12]

Presbyterians have never taught that only those of their particular persuasion would be in heaven. Heaven is the home of all who believe in Jesus Christ. But Presbyterians have differed and still do differ regarding the eternal destiny of non-Christians. One Presbyterian statement of faith declares "persons not professing the Christian religion...cannot be saved."[13] Many Presbyterians take literally the Scripture that says "There is salvation in no one else [except Jesus Christ], for there is no other name under heaven given among men by which we must be saved."[14]

On the other hand, many Presbyterians utterly reject the statement that all non-Christians will be consigned to hell forever. These Presbyterians differ widely among themselves regarding the eternal destiny of non-Christians, but most of them simply leave non-Christians in the hands of a loving God, confident that the God and Father of the Lord Jesus Christ will deal fairly with all such persons. It is the confidence of all Presbyterians that when the final judgment is passed, no person will be able to say truthfully "God did not deal justly with me."

THE END OF TIME

On the question of what will happen to the earth at the end of time, most Presbyterians suspend judgment and are perfectly willing to leave that to God. Our doctrinal statements have seldom dealt with the question. A few Presbyterians believe that a renovated earth will be the final abode of the righteous. Here, they say, will be established the New Jerusalem. Others take literally a passage in the Bible that says, "The day of the Lord will come as a thief in the night, in which the heavens shall pass away with a great noise and the elements shall melt with fervent heat; the earth also and the works that are therein shall be burned up."[15] Most Presbyterians see this passage as figurative and acknowledge that they do not know what will happen to the earth at the end of time.

BODILY RESURRECTION

Presbyterians have always been and still are strong in their affirmation of a bodily resurrection. But here is another place where Presbyterians differ among themselves and a place also where many Presbyterians depart from the statements of their creeds. A typical statement from one creed reads: "The souls of believers are at their death made perfect in holiness and do immediately pass into glory, their bodies being still united to Christ, do rest in their graves until the resurrection."[16] In this, as in most of the early Presbyterian and Reformed creeds, it is affirmed that, for a time after death, the souls of believers are disembodied spirits in the presence of Christ waiting for the resurrection of their bodies and, at the end of time, there will be a resurrection when their bodies will be reunited with their souls. Many Presbyterians today find this view unsatisfactory.

Presbyterians differ among themselves regarding the meaning of the term "the resurrection of the body." Very few believe that this term refers to the same physical body that was laid in a grave. Some Presbyterians believe that, at death, believers go immediately into the presence of Christ, who then and there gives them a new body, a spiritual body which is like their old body, but remade in the likeness of Christ's resurrection body. With this new body they begin immediately to enjoy the blessings of heaven. At the final judgment, those already in heaven will be "openly acknowledged and acquitted" and will have confirmed to them the blessings of God for eternity. On the other hand, these Presbyterians affirm that, at death, the wicked enter immediately the torments of hell. About the "resurrection of the unjust,"[17] most Presbyterians are vague. Still other Presbyterians hold that death is real and that body and soul die together — the body returns to the dust and the spirit ceases to be. But, these same persons declare, at the resurrection, which will take place at some future time, God will give to each of his children a new body and a new spirit. Others find biblical support for the view that after death, while the body ceases to be, the soul enters a period of "sleep" from which it is awakened at the resurrection and given a new and spiritual body. Thus, while Presbyterians believe in a bodily resurrection, they differ widely concerning the nature and the time of this event. In this matter of faith, Presbyterians continue to search the Scriptures for enlightenment.

PURGATORY

Presbyterian and Reformed creeds have unanimously rejected the Roman Catholic doctrine of purgatory — a place where souls that are not ready for heaven remain until they have been purged of all imperfections. However, in recent years, some Presbyterians have moved toward the belief that ultimately the love of God will prevail and that somewhere down the corridors of eternity, all persons will come to acknowledge Christ and will enter heaven. This belief requires that there be some kind of an intermediate state where unbelievers will come to know and accept the grace of God in Jesus Christ.

THE CONCEPT OF SAVING FAITH

When a jailer in Philippi asked the Apostle Paul, "What must I do to be saved?" the Apostle replied, "Believe in the Lord Jesus and you will be saved."[18] For Presbyterians, it is as simple and as profound as that. Numerous books have been written on the meaning of "saving faith," but in its essence, the Presbyterian creeds describe it as "receiving and resting upon Christ alone for justification, sanctification and eternal life."[19] Saving faith includes repentance, which means that the believer turns from his sin and strives to do the will of God as that will is made known in Jesus Christ. Without the desire and the effort to do God's will, saving faith is incomplete. Saving faith is shown to be genuine by works of goodness and mercy. But the sinner is not saved by the works but by the faith. Persons are saved by faith in Jesus Christ and not by their good works, but a person who produces no good works cannot be saved. This saving faith is shared by numerous other Christians besides those of the Presbyterian and Reformed family and to them, as to us, it is effective for gaining salvation. We are confident that God will save all who possess this faith. Whether he will save all who do not possess it is for God alone to decide.

RECOGNITION OF FRIENDS AND FAMILY IN THE NEXT WORLD

While our creeds have not dealt with the subject, most Presbyterians believe that persons in heaven will know and recognize friends and relatives. The disciples of Jesus recognized him in his resurrection body and we believe that we shall be raised in his likeness. We shall not in heaven be more ignorant than we are here and we know one another here. We argue that if we do not know loved ones, then we will have been deprived of our memory and without our memories we are not ourselves. In heaven, family relationships will be remembered, but all relationships there will be lifted to a higher level. The redeemed will be in a loving and trusting relationship with all other persons in heaven, so that the importance of and the need for family relationships will be superseded.

THE SECOND COMING

Almost without exception, Presbyterian and Reformed creeds affirm the second coming of Christ, but they give very few details regarding this event. One statement reads, "As Christ came in humility, he will return in glory for the final judgment and for the consummation of his universal kingdom. The work and promises of Jesus Christ give assurance that the age-long struggle between sin and grace will, in God's holy, wise and loving purpose, be accomplished."[20] A few Presbyterians hold the pre-millennarian position that offers a detailed account of what will happen when Christ comes again. Most Presbyterians, however, do not attempt to give a chronology of those events. Acknowledging that before Christ shall accomplish his holy purpose for the world, he will break into human history in some manner as he did before, we are willing to leave the details of that event to the Lord himself. We see it as our duty to be faithfully doing his work now without watching the clock.

PRAYERS FOR THE DYING AND THE DEAD

Presbyterians believe in intercessory prayer for the dying, but none of our creeds has encouraged or approved prayers for the dead. Presbyterian thought has tended to regard the dead as beyond the reach of our prayers. Our doctrinal standards have said nothing at all about whether those in the afterlife are aware of persons who are still in this life or whether they can or do pray for us. Consequently individual Presbyterians are likely to hold differing opinions on those questions.

A FINAL WORD

The primary message of the Presbyterian and Reformed faith regarding the afterlife is this: Trust Christ and be not afraid. The God who raised Jesus from the dead will also raise up those who love him to be with him forever. Strive to do God's will here and now and leave worry about the life beyond to him. *That* life will be indescribably wonderful and full of all blessings, but you can leave the ordering of its affairs to the Lord. Do not get lost in contemplation of that other world or worry about its details lest you fail to deal fully with the tasks God has assigned to you in this world. By worship and prayer and Bible study, renew regularly your faith in Christ so that you will be saved; and then in the light of that faith-commitment, get on with the business of living a life in which God is glorified and enjoyed.

Notes

1. Instead of the term "Presbyterian faith," it is more correct to speak of "the faith of the Presbyterian and Reformed churches," because Presbyterians share a common faith with those denominations that use the title "Reformed," e.g., The Reformed Church in America, The Reformed Church in Hungary, etc. The term "Presbyterian" refers only to a form of church polity, i.e., government by presbyters or elders, while the term "Reformed" refers to a system of doctrines. Most Presbyterian churches are "Reformed" in their doctrine and most Reformed churches are "Presbyterian" in their polity.
2. John H. Leith, *Creeds of the Churches* (Atlanta, 1963), p. 127.
3. The Westminster Shorter Catechism, Question 4.
4. I John 4:8.
5. The Westminster Confession of Faith, Chapter III.
6. The Westminster Shorter Catechism, Question 1.
7. A Brief Statement of Belief, adopted by the General Assembly of the Presbyterian Church U.S.A. in 1962.
8. The Apostles' Creed.
9. The Book of Order of the United Presbyterian Church U.S.A.
10. Ibid.
11. I Corinthians 2:9.
12. A Brief Statement of Belief.
13. The Westminster Confession of Faith, Chapter XXII.
14. Acts 4:12.
15. II Peter 3:10.
16. The Westminster Shorter Catechism, Question 37.
17. Acts 24:15.
18. Acts 16:30-31.
19. The Westminster Confession of Faith, Chapter XVI.
20. A Brief Statement of Belief.

A Quaker Perspective

Arthur O. Roberts, PhD

Quakers (or Friends) are a family within the Christian community of faith. As such they share a common heritage. A historical summary of their faith and practice provides a context for Quaker views about death and the afterlife. These views are shown in early writings, within various documents of faith and practice, and by literature embodying the witness of individual Friends whose leadership has been evident and respected.

HISTORICAL SUMMARY

The "Quaker Awakening" arose within the milieu of 17th-century English Puritanism, which had been variously influenced by Lutheran, Reformed, Anabaptist and Anglican movements. Participants in this awakening referred to themselves as "Children of the Light," or simply as "Friends" (in accordance with John 15:15, "I no longer call you servants, but friends"). They were dubbed "Quakers" because they trembled in awe before the Lord who they believed was present with them in worship, and the appellation remained, along with more formal designations such as "Friends Church" or the "Religious Society of Friends."

Although the Quakers strongly criticized the existing Protestant churches in England and the Roman Catholic Church, they were definitely within the framework of historic Christianity with an emphasis on the atoning death and resurrection of Christ. Quakers believed that the Reformation on the Continent under Luther and Calvin and in Britain under Presbyterian and Puritan leadership had not gone far enough in affirming in practice the priesthood of believers. Like the Anabaptists, they sought to continue the Reformation by breaking away from state control and from non-regenerate membership. They reaffirmed a central Christian teaching that (they concluded) Roman Catholicism had lost within liturgy, Protestantism within the letter of Scripture, and apocalyptic sects by a preoccupation with a future Second Coming. This central teaching is that Christ is actually present in personal experience and group worship. To use an old Quaker phrase, "Christ has come to teach his people himself." To use modern terms, they affirmed "experiential reality," not "virtual reality." For Friends, firsthand experience of the risen Lord constitutes the highest form of Christian discipleship. This emphasis on the "here and now" impacts Quaker thinking about death and the afterlife in several ways that we will summarize after noting some aspects of the Quaker story.

The leader of the Quaker Awakening was George Fox, a prophet of evangelical faith whose *Journal* is one of the devotional classics of Christendom. The son of a weaver of Drayton, Leicestershire, England, George Fox grew to manhood during the time when the Stuarts were dethroned and Parliament was asserting its power. The two decades from the Long Parliament of 1640 until the end of the Commonwealth in 1660 marked the period of initial outreach by the Friends. The spiritual unrest of the times was mirrored in the troubled wanderings of English youth. For when the lid of Elizabethan conformity was blown off by the pressure of Puritan ideas, many were left spiritually dispossessed. Restlessly, religious people sought for the true church, which had, they felt, fled to the wilderness.

Young George Fox sought help from many sources. Appalled by the evil that abounded about him, he longed for the assurance of personal salvation. He had studied the Bible so thoroughly that he had practically memorized it. Despairing to find the "advice" that would bring peace, he used to ponder the Bible alone in the woods. At the age of 22, when he had despaired of human help and of his own efforts, he heard a voice that said, "There is one, even Christ Jesus, that can speak to thy condition."[1] In the seeking Christ, George Fox found the key to unloose his bonds of doubt and despair. To the spiritually dispossessed groups, such as wistful Seekers, anarchistic Ranters and dissatisfied Puritans, Fox proclaimed with confidence the living Christ who would be their teacher and their present guide. His own assurance of salvation and his personal magnetism attracted many followers, beginning in 1647. Young men and women, including disillusioned soldiers from Cromwell's army, were drawn to his dynamic preaching. A group of evangelists called "The Valiant Sixty" demonstrated their fervent faith by street preaching and personal testimony. By 1655, some 50,000 persons considered themselves Friends; by 1700, the number had doubled.

Anglican Churchmen as well as dissenters joined the ranks. William Penn, Isaac Penington and Robert Barclay added strength of leadership to the movement. Persecution arose in that intolerant era because of beliefs and practices that appeared blasphemous or irregular, and because of the tenacity with which the Quakers held to them. These beliefs were: the evils of a state-financed ministry; the abuse of test oaths, which implied suspected disloyalty and impugned the witness of "Christ within"; and the tyranny of attempts at religious uniformity that forbade religious assemblage and evangelism except by the "establishment." Fox once stated that "truth can live in the jails." He spoke from experience, having been imprisoned several times for asserting religious liberty. Between 1650 and 1687, over 13,000 Friends were imprisoned, 198 were transported as slaves and 338 died in penal institutions or of wounds inflicted while attending their own meetings. In the midst of this persecution and their attendant loss of property, Quakers spread their message of simple faith in the present Christ to Ireland, Scotland, Europe and America. Quakers settled throughout New England, and in 1681, William Penn obtained from the Crown the land grant of Pennsylvania, which became a strong Quaker center. For 70 years, and as long as the Friends had authority, there was peace with the Native Americans.

In the 19th century, the Friends pressed on from the Atlantic states to Canada, from the Carolinas westward through Ohio to the midwestern states of Indiana, Illinois, Iowa, Kansas, Nebraska and the Dakotas, and thence to the Pacific Coast and Alaska. The Quaker movement spread to Mexico and the Caribbean, to India and China, to Australia and New Zealand, to the Near East and Scandinavia, and most recently into Russia. During the 20th century, the greatest growth in the Quaker movement occurred in Africa and Latin America. As with other groups in Christendom, the Society of Friends is no longer predominantly Anglo-American.

DOCUMENTS OF FAITH AND PRACTICE

From the citations that follow, one may discern a viewpoint appropriately labeled "realizing eschatology." The Quakers do not hold to an interim eschatology. Christians need not wait around for Jesus — the Lord who will one day reign supreme is with the church now. Accordingly, they reject as unworthy of Christ the ethic of postponing obedience to Jesus' teachings until some propitious future time. Rather they believe that Christ is present with his people and will continue to be so present in the future.

The early Friends, especially, had a dramatic sense of living out the apocalyptic vision of John the Revelator, experiencing both the terror of Babylon and the ecstasy of the conquering Lamb. They believed that the Lord had begun a major spiritual renewal in their times, in which the good would increasingly triumph over evil. Sometimes they referred to this contest of powers as "the Lamb's War," distinguishing it carefully from the world's warfare, in which they refused to have a part. Thus they believed both in the redeemed life now and in a future resurrection from the dead, in the gathering of believers into the Kingdom of God now and in the gathering of the nations to the reign of Christ at the end of the age. In their early fervor they felt themselves in the vanguard of that gathering of peoples to the Kingdom. Jesus, they said, is both "come and coming." This bimodal motif about human redemption may be discerned in the documents cited below.

When Faced with Martyrdom, Quakers Affirm the Afterlife

Quakers consider themselves members of Christ's kingdom set to overcome by truth and love the evil powers of the world. They are confident of both the present and the future reality of the Kingdom of God. This can be said about Quakers martyred in 20th-century Rwanda and those slaughtered for their convictions in 17th-century Massachusetts.

In 1660 to 1661, four Quakers were hanged in Boston by order of Governor Endicott (as a witness to the cost of religious liberty, a statue of Mary Dyer, who was one of the four, now stands on Boston Common). William Robinson used vivid Pauline and apocalyptic language in anticipation of his death by hanging. He wrote:

> Hallelujah unto the Lord, who hath redeemed me by his living power from amongst kindreds, tongues and nations. And now the day of my departure draweth near, I have fought a good fight, I have kept the holy faith, I have near finished my course, my traveling is near at an end, my testimony is near to be finished, and an eternal crown is laid up for me, and all whose feet are shod with righteousness and the preparation of peace, even such whose names are written in the Book of Life, wherein I live and rejoice with all the faithful Seed forevermore.[2]

On the gallows, Friend Marmaduke Stephenson said, "I suffer for Christ in whom I live and for whom I die...this day we shall be at rest in the Lord." A Quaker spared martyrdom by the timely intervention of the British Crown said this about the death of his friends who were not so fortunate:

> Thus the faithful witnesses sealed their testimony for the Lord against the Dragon's power, and blessedly departed with praises in their mouths, entering joyfully with their beloved into Everlasting Rest.[3]

When Defending Their Christian Teachings, Quakers Affirm the Afterlife

Along with other dissenters, early Quakers used print media to defend their Christian faith against attacks from the ranks of established religion. In his often-reprinted *Apology,* Robert Barclay, a leading apologist and well-educated Scot, refutes accusations that their emphasis on the contemporary presence of the Kingdom of God implies no belief in a future life. The Quaker insistence on accepting the judgment of the Light now doesn't imply disbelief in a final judgment, or in heaven or hell. Simply talking about the outward life of Christ, he wrote, won't redeem or justify people — they must know "Christ resurrected in them." If people partake of the first resurrection, in other words, inward redemption from sin, they are better able to judge the second resurrection. We are called, he said, to be the first fruits of those who serve and worship Christ, not "in the oldness of the letter but in the newness of the Spirit," until "all the kingdoms of the earth become the kingdom of Christ Jesus."[4]

George Fox also defended the "come and coming" character of Quaker belief about the Kingdom of God. In a letter to the Governor of Barbados, Fox wrote:

> We own and believe in the only wise, omnipotent, and everlasting God, the Creator of all things both in heaven and earth, and the Preserver of all that He hath made: who is God over all, blessed forever; to whom be all honor, glory, dominion, praise, and thanksgiving, both now and forevermore.... We believe that He alone [Jesus] is our Redeemer and Saviour, the Captain of our salvation, who saves us from sin, as well as from hell and the wrath to come, and destroys the devil and his works; He is the Seed of the woman that bruises the serpent's head, to wit, Christ Jesus, the Alpha and Omega, the First and the Last.[5]

When Writing Their Books of Faith and Practice, Quakers Affirm the Afterlife

At an 1887 conference in Richmond, Indiana, representatives from a large segment of American Quakers adopted the "Richmond Declaration of Faith," which remains a foundation statement for many Friends around the world. The following is an excerpt from that Declaration.

> We sincerely believe, not only a resurrection in Christ from the fallen and sinful state here, but a rising and ascending into glory with Him hereafter; that when He at last appears we may appear with Him in glory. But that all the wicked, who live in rebellion against the light of grace, and die finally impenitent, shall come forth to the resurrection of condemnation. And that the soul of every man and woman shall be reserved, in its own distinct and proper being, and shall have its proper body as God is pleased to give it [Scriptures noted: Corinthians 15:44, 50; Luke 20:36; Philippians 3:20-21].
>
> We believe that the punishment of the wicked and the blessedness of the righteous shall be everlasting; according to the declaration of our compassionate Redeemer, to whom the judgment is committed, 'These shall go away into eternal punishment, but the righteous into eternal life' (Matthew 25:46).[6]

British Friends have included interpretive essays in their book, *Faith and Practice.* These theological statements tend to be couched in less systematic and more experiential modes of thought. The following citation is from

William Penn, the venerable colonist of Pennsylvania, who, although cautious about details of the afterlife, was certain of it. Penn wrote:

> They that love beyond the World, cannot be separated by it.
> Death cannot kill what never dies.
> Nor can Spirit ever be divided that love and live in the same Divine Principle:
> the Root and Record of their Friendship.
> If absence be not Death, neither is theirs.
> Death is but Crossing the World, as Friends do the Seas; they live in one another still.
> For they must needs be present, that love and live in that which is Omnipresent.
> In this Divine Glass, they see Face to Face; and their Converse is Free, as well as pure.
> This is the comfort of Friends, that though they may be said to Die,
> Yet their friendship and Society are, in the best Sense, ever present, because Immortal.[7]

In the following citations one can discern that, for some Friends, a caution about details of the afterlife under the impact of modern thought has resulted in a shift from resurrection of the body to a more generalized concept of impersonal immortality. This trend has continued so that, at the close of the 20th century, the views of theologically very liberal Friends are closer to Unitarian-Universalist ideas than to historic Quaker or traditional Christian beliefs (a change that should be noted when reading the Quaker responses to the questions in the last chapter of this book).

Rufus M. Jones was a major Quaker scholar in the first part of the 20th century. In his writings, he linked Quakerism with classical mysticism. Although he affirmed the historic character of Christianity, Jones sought to locate its dynamic within a more universal and mystical religious context, which modern scientific thought seemed to require. (Subsequent Quaker scholars felt that the link with mysticism was forced, and on the basis of historic studies, they reemphasized the Puritan setting for the Quaker Awakening.) Jones' effort at blending Quaker and mystical thought produced some powerful characterizations about the interplay of the temporal and the eternal. Concerning the afterlife, Jones wrote:

> [Quakerism] has kept pretty close to the central meaning of the Incarnation, the definite breaking in of God into the course of history, the coming of eternity into the midst of time, in the form of a living, visible human-divine Person, through whom all life on its highest levels is to be interpreted. But it discovers no temporal end to that life here in the world. The Christ who was a visible presence in Galilee and Judea

> is just as certainly alive and present now.[8]

In its various versions, the book of *Faith and Practice*, used by British Friends historically, has included statements aimed at articulation of Quaker thought in non-creedal ways. The following passage shows an emphasis on what used to be called "holy dying." Here the focus is on achieving a personal serenity and the continuity of human community in facing one's death. The Quaker belief about the Kingdom now and the Kingdom in an afterworld is bold in affirming the present but cautious about the future. "Eternal" is more readily connoted as quality of life than duration through or beyond time.

> The faith of Christ is one that teaches more than courage in face of death. The very character of death is transformed, replacing a gloomy prospect of loss and dissolution by a sense of liberated life. As we come to a more intimate experience of the reality of God we may enter into the overcoming power and strength of the great words of Christ, "I am the Resurrection and the Life." Death is swallowed up in victory, and, for those we love, is no longer a dark place of shadows, but an entrance into the fuller light of God.[9]

Most Friends today would express confidence in an afterlife using more evangelical language. The following statement is drawn from the *Faith and Practice* of the Northwest Yearly Meeting of Friends.

> We believe the Church is called to demonstrate in this life the righteous character of Christ's present and coming kingdom. The kingdom is present now to the extent that the people of God hear His voice and obey it. The coming kingdom will be initiated by the second appearing of Jesus Christ (as foretold by the prophets) and by the resurrection of the dead. The world will then be judged righteously by Jesus Christ and there will come everlasting punishment for the finally unrepentant wicked and everlasting blessedness for the righteous. At that time the world will be freed from the grip of evil and satanic power, and Christ will reign over a restored universe.[10]

In Their Writing about Spirituality, Quakers Affirm the Afterlife

Because Quakers feel they cannot adequately encapsulate spiritual experience within the compass of theological tenets, they have developed a rich literature of spirituality in which one's relationship to the Divine is narrated rather than argued. We turn now to some of that literature that includes theological insights about dying and practical insights about how the community of faith should respond to death.

One of the classics of Quaker spirituality is Thomas Kelly's book, *A*

Testament of Devotion. This book and its sequel, *The Eternal Promise,* accent the Quaker view that all of life is filled with the promises of God and that the "Eternal Presence" floods personal and corporate life with Divine grace through every opened door. Kelly, a Quaker college professor (Wilmington, Earlham, Haverford), had a short but fruitful life. His spiritual journey illustrated the struggle between faith and reason in the first part of the 20th century. *A Testament of Devotion,* first published in 1941 as war burst upon the world in monumental waves of violence and holocausts, jarred Quakers loose from a too-easy feeling of optimism that assumed that education and technology inevitably produced better people. The book served as a catalyst that forced Quakers to acknowledge the enormity of evil in the world but at the same time reaffirm their Christian wonder at the magnitude of God's grace within it. At the end of a very violent 20th century, Friends acknowledge having had a vivid object lesson about evil and its deadly consequences. Death from old age as a passage to a better world is one thing, but what about civilians and soldiers slaughtered in war? What about people who die of starvation or who die as victims of tribal warfare? What about children murdered by predators? What about victims of rape, drunken driving or random shootings? What about those who die in accidents or plagues? Where is holy dying in all this? Death is indeed the final enemy, and all the more terrible because of suffering and enormous waste.

This terrible parade of death has challenged the faith of Quakers, as it has others. A Job-like anguish at the impenetrable ways of God induced loss of faith for some Quakers, an aggrieved agnosticism for some, but a deeper, more Christian faith for most. Quakers learned again the words of William Penn, that they must bear the cross who would wear the crown. At the mid-point in the century, Thomas Kelly provided insights that helped restore faith in a God who cares. Kelly called Quakers once again to the Cross of Christ. Passionately he called on them to let Christ inflame their hearts and minds — to become Christlike in their love for the world and everyone and everything in it. He also linked such experience of the Eternal Presence with the life to come.

> But I must confess to a passionate devotion to God, as the spiritual reality *par excellence.* If He be real, and if He be concerned for me, I ask no more. I believe He cares, and that He continues our lives after death, in a fellowship of which we have a foretaste here. And I believe that the Eternal Christ, who is this same God, viewed as active and creative, is ever in the world, seeking, knocking, persuading, counseling men to return to their rightful Home.[11]

Much of Quaker devotional literature concerns what it means to affirm the Presence of Christ in this life, not the next. Richard Foster's books illustrate this perspective as he deals with the disciplines of Christian living.[12]

The late D. Elton Trueblood called death one of four "common ventures of life" (marriage, birth, and work being the others). Trueblood shows why death is the major theme in literature. First, "death is a greater leap in the dark than any other," and second, it is universal. Trueblood avers that death should be *celebrated* by the worshipping community. We experience the death of others, and their death leads us to honor the departed. Indeed, his book, written 50 years ago, contributed to a Quaker trend to move away from funeral services toward the now more standard practice of holding a memorial meeting for worship as a way to celebrate those who have passed on to eternal life. Sorrowing loved ones, Trueblood insists, want their loss to be felt and shared. Their sense of loss should not be demeaned by triviality, maudlin sympathy or commercialized ritual. For such memorial worship, he emphasizes the public reading of the great biblical passages that support a steady faith in God, a faith "that all the world is one house, and that, if we move out of the present room of our finite existence, we are not thereby going out from under the loving care of the Father's roof, but only into another and perhaps a more wonderful room."[13]

Pearl Crist Hall, a thoughtful Quaker leader, wrote a book specifically about death.[14] As activist Friends, Crist and her husband disparaged talk about the afterlife as a way of avoiding constructive social tasks in the present. But through observing the simple faith of a Christian woman cleaning rest rooms, she came to realize that without the eternal dimension, efforts at social amelioration lack stability and will fail. To be fruitful, love in action requires awe before the Almighty and the perspective of eternity. So Pearl Hall recovered resurrection hope, and with it, greater insight about serving the present age. Here are some passages from her book:

> At the moment of death if I choose to be forgiven and long to be with God, when my soul is free from this flagon of flesh and bone, I will be unencumbered of all this partial knowledge and halfway capability. Then with clarified vision I will be free to choose love, participate in everlasting creativeness of God, or like Dives, I can choose to stay by myself in hell.... Death has as its culmination a celebration of wholeness attained.... The loveliest story I know that illustrates coming home after death is that of the Prodigal Son. He got up out of the pig pen where he found himself with good and evil and far from home. He began running down the road and ran right into the arms of his father coming to meet him. The Bible has many such passages describing what lies beyond: "being with me in Paradise"; "as a banquet and state of glory"; "inheriting the glory of God"; "unspeakable contentment"; "a house with many rooms." This is resurrection...a continuing event...
>
> The duration of ecstasy is short and the moments are rare. Yet all our lives we will remember how it was when we think of a *something* that is too spiritual and close to speak about. The very limitations and imper-

fections that cut us off from such deep experiences give hope of the nature of our expectations. They bind us, stimulating our seeds of longing for the wholeness of that Other that is still beyond. We are here on earth as hard seeds sprouting before we arise as flawless delicate flowers in God's kingdom. This is the long road to freedom, right now we are traveling through.

In the resurrected Me, my deepest being comes rushing free at last and with it "all my winters turn to spring." There will be no sting in the moments that follow. Anticipated revelation becomes genuine experience. Such awareness is beyond the present and all that has been seen as through a glass darkly, now shines perpetually. And I shall find myself unbelievably alive with the marvel of true life and with whatever splendor, compassion, truth and wisdom God holds for me.[15]

Kenneth Boulding was a Quaker economist of considerable renown, particularly for his creative approach to systems analysis. He never succumbed to economic theories that reduced human commerce to statistical probabilities. But in 1993, at the age of 83, he did succumb to cancer. His was a lingering death. During his dying time, he wrote a book of sonnets. These poems convey a sense that eternity is God's presence now, but also a wondrous future that can be glimpsed enticingly, as though through a curtain. Consider this sonnet, "Outrageous Joy," written shortly before his death:

Joy is outrageous. Here we are on a cliff
In a cloud; and we know there is a brink
That well may be much closer than we think,
We could be over it in just a jiff.
Over all broods the silent sound of "if"
And even when where we stand we sense a stink
Of pain and human misery — we shrink
And then comes, almost like a clown saying "Piff,"
Absurd joy to the world, the Lord is come
Like fresh sap rising in a withered tree
A flame of praise, rising exultantly
Beyond all reason in a world so glum.
There is a vast refreshment in the sky —
What matters cliffs indeed to those who fly?[16]

Another Quaker poet recently offered this prayer sonnet as a gift of words for a dying friend:

TO VERNON

Dark times, Lord, not just at night
but dark by day, outside, inside.

Against death's swelling tide
it's hard to hold in clear sight
that homing beacon of your Light.
There eternal certainties reside —
Barbara standing at my side,
memories in which I delight.
There is the family whom I love,
kinfolk, yes, but also many more
good folk sent from heaven above
to light my path from shore to shore.
Even darkest nights give way
and brighten into Day.[17]

CONCLUSION

This same Quaker poet and author wrote further about death and resurrection. We conclude with his thoughts.[18]

Clock time is tied to the movement of stars and the circadian rhythms of our biological life. Like a pre-set metronome it ticks out the days and years. There is no stopping it. But lived time is different. It can be visualized as dips and spikes and movements perpendicular to the forward line on a graph. We have our ups and downs, we say, and rightly.... Certainly as I have become older the line of time forward is broader, because of multiple experiences, than it was when I was younger. Then I stood on the tip of time's arrow and leaned forward, reaching for an unknown future from the edge of a limited past. Presently, with the forward line in prospect shortened, I must accent the perpendicular, ranging as far as possible along the terrain of the moving present. The hug of a grandchild lasts longer, for example, in this kind of temporal meaning than it used to, even though clock time may be the same duration.... We compensate for diminished length in time by providing more depth and height to our living. Growing older we have more past to cherish than when we were younger. The garden of lived experiences grows more lush with time. We are trying to balance past with future and live, presently, in both. All times are in God's hands, and we are grateful for God sharing these different times with us.

The four dimensions of time-space afford boundaries that lie within a larger world. Each of us lives within a world delineated overtly by articulated clusters of human relationships we call culture or civilization — a fifth dimension. We live, too, in a realm hardly contained in the boundaries of reason but rather hinted at covertly in dreams and longings too intangible for words although strong enough to quicken our yen for the yet-to-be-revealed. Ultimately, however, I find my strongest sense of being in a seventh dimension — the Kingdom of God — which encircles all others and defines their meaning and their limits.

This Kingdom Christ revealed so fully in the heart as well as in history, gives coherence to all circles of relationship. All belonging comes within the judgment of this perimeter, whether ethnic, or political, or social, or family, whether the tight circles of the inward self or the rippling circles of the social self.... Most of all, Jesus Christ, the Risen Lord, is here among us. We are Jesus' disciples. This place, this Kingdom, is not just a spot to visit occasionally, it is not fantasy within a "real world" of stuff and realpolitik.... To put it another way, the Kingdom frames our geographical and ideological places to reveal the artistry of God.

And so within this framework...life sparkles with earthly mysteries we had been too busy since childhood to probe. In due season we will explore life from the resurrection side of the larger cosmos, of which this world is but a part. It is enough now to trace patterns in the sand and listen to songs of the sea. With greater and greater intensity we feel ourselves a part of a vibrant community of creation that rings the world with hope, and beckons the cosmos into a community of life and love. That circle binds into one body all who are guided by the Light. To all who long for God's Kingdom the universal Christ offers witness. I love that community of Christ, the Church, and although I lament its structural weaknesses, I know it to be a circle of ordinary persons who acknowledge themselves to be recipients of God's mercy and grace, and who cling joyously to that vision for themselves and the world that Jesus Christ has revealed.

> And hope does not disappoint us,
> because God has poured out his love
> into our hearts by the Holy Spirit,
> whom he has given us (Romans 5:5).

The Spirit is at work in the world. Hope is more than a verbal construct, more than an emotion, more than an inference. Hope infuses the physical body, its muscles, bones, organs. It flows with the blood and lodges in the brain. At its best, hope is a sensuous longing for holiness, for God. Each sense is a thoroughfare for anticipated encounter with the person of God and the persons of others at the core of their being. In the experience of hope every neuron of the body tingles with Divine fire. In the experience of hope the senses celebrate Sabbath rest. They lay themselves on the altar of reality as living sacrifices to the Creator and hymn praises for the beauty of life.

Hope affirms a bodily resurrection. And why not? However reconstructed, the body arising from the other side of death will be fully cognitive, fully alive. Such is the daring conviction inferred from Jesus' own resurrection. More of personal reality not less, more of life, not less. The Holy Spirit is our pledge of life eternal. The earthly body is seed buried in the ground awaiting the flowering of the heavenly body. In this hope we greet each day as an opening into eternity. The world is going somewhere and we are part of that exciting cosmic journey. Jesus is the pioneer, the first one through the mountain pass, as it were. Knowing this, we are content, however difficult the struggle, however dim the light, however we might blunder. Because Christ lives, we, too, shall live. This is strong hope; the gates of hell will not prevail against people of faith!

It is not death that many older or terminally ill persons fear, but the dying. They need this word of resurrection hope. But they also need comfort in process. They experience pain, sometimes mental diminishment and a loss of physical strength. To use a good old word, they need comfort — one to be strong with them. The call for comfort is expressed in this poem:

> When I am very old and cannot walk,
> come sit with me awhile, and talk
> of paths where we have strolled
> together, or apart.
> When I am very old and cannot see,
> could you read the Bible, maybe,
> or a cherished book
> to give light to my heart?
> When I am very old and cannot hear,
> do not shout, just stand quite near
> and touch me while you speak,
> so I can feel your words.
> When I am very old and out of touch
> with what used to matter much,
> be patient, hold me then,
> as once I held you.
> When I am very old and do not know
> even that you come and go
> about my lonely room
> your love will keep me true.
> When I am very old, your love will guide
> my body and my mind and soul
> across the bridge of years
> to Life, and calm my fears.[19]

Notes

1. *The Journal of George Fox,* edited by Geoffrey F. Nuttall (New York: Cambridge University Press, 1952), p. 11. This is a standard edition, but there are others. Canby Jones, *"The Power of the Lord is Over All": The Pastoral Letters of George Fox* (Richmond IN: Friends United Press, 1989) gives readers a feeling for the rhetorical power of the first Quaker leader.
   Useful introductory books about the Quakers include:
   Elfrida Vipont, *George Fox and the Valiant Sixty* (London: Hamish

Hamilton, 1975)

H. Larry Ingle, *First Among Friends: George Fox and the Creation of Quakerism* (New York: Oxford University Press, 1994)

John Punshon, *Portrait in Grey: A Short History of the Quakers* (London: Quaker Home Service, 1984)

Hugh Barbour, *The Quakers in Puritan England* (New Haven: Yale University Press, 1964)

Jack Willcuts, *Why Friends Are Friends* (Newberg, OR: The Barclay Press, 1997)

Arthur O. Roberts, *The People Called Quakers*, 4th Edition (Newberg, OR: The Barclay Press, 1997)

Early Quaker Writings, edited by Hugh Barbour and Arthur O. Roberts (Grand Rapids: MI, Eerdmans, 1973), is a useful source book.

2. *Early Quaker Writings,* p. 113.
3. Ibid., p. 36.
4. Robert Barclay, *Apology in Modern English,* edited by Dean Freiday (Newberg, OR: The Barclay Press, 1967), p. 439.
5. Cited in Northwest Yearly Meeting, *Faith and Practice* (Newberg, OR: The Barclay Press, 1987), p. 18.
6. Ibid., p. 26.
7. William Penn, *Fruits of Solitude,* cited in *London Faith and Practice,* 1955, p. 125.
8. Rufus Jones, *The Faith and Practice of Quakers* (1927), cited in *London Faith and Practice*, p. 157.
9. *London Faith and Practice,* p. 124.
10. Northwest Yearly Meeting, *Faith and Practice,* p. 11.
11. From a Pendle Hill pamphlet, "Reality of the Spiritual World," cited in *London Faith and Practice,* p. 125.
12. Richard Foster notes as inward disciplines meditation, prayer, fasting and study; as outward disciplines simplicity, solitude, submission and service; as corporate disciplines confession, worship, guidance and celebration. See his *Celebration of Discipline: The Paths to Spiritual Growth* (New York: Harper & Row, 1978).
13. These citations are from Elton Trueblood, *The Common Ventures of Life* (New York: Harper & Brothers, 1949), pp. 104ff.
14. Pearl Crist Hall, *Long Road to Freedom: One Person's Discovery of Death* (Richmond, IN: Friends United Press, 1978).
15. Ibid., pp. 100ff.
16. Kenneth E. Boulding, *Sonnets from Later Life* (Wallingford, PA: Pendle Hill, 1994), p. 177.
17. Arthur O. Roberts, unpublished poem, 1997.
18. These passages are excerpted from Arthur O. Roberts, *Drawn by the Light* (Newberg, OR: The Barclay Press, 1993), and from Arthur O. Roberts, *Messengers of God: The Sensuous Side of Spirituality* (Newberg, OR: The Barclay Press, 1996).
19. "When I am Old," by Arthur O. Roberts, is cited from *Messengers of God*, p. 187.

Roman Catholicism

Rev. Francis X. Cleary, SJ

BACKGROUND OF THE FAITH

Because Christianity has so powerfully influenced western culture, its basic history, beliefs and practices have become common knowledge to most people. With a membership of approximately 900 million, the Roman Catholic Church is the largest and most widespread denomination within the worldwide Christian community of faith. Tradition plays an important role in all religions that preserve fundamental teachings that are central to belief and at the same time, growing and adapting to concrete situations. Roman Christianity traces its roots back to the local Christian church founded in Rome, which, at that time was the capital city and center of the far-flung Roman Empire. This community of believers came into existence only a few years after Jesus' death. It remains the oldest "local church" in continuous existence.

Christianity first appeared nearly 2000 years ago in the Near East, spreading first to Antioch (in modern Syria) from its original centers in Galilee and Jerusalem. The founding members of the Church in Rome, like other very early churches, were Jews. What made the Roman Jewish community different was their unique blend of respect for Jewish tradition and openness to the good points of paganism. They maintained close ties with the Jerusalem "mother" city — religious center of worldwide Judaism. Proud of their heritage, Roman Jews-become-Christians preserved the spirit of those venerable practices that were recorded in the Old Testament and kept alive in Jerusalem Temple worship.

This explains Roman Catholic respect for holy persons, holy places and holy objects. Like the Old Testament priesthood, Catholic priests consciously live as persons set apart, observing distinctive rules governing behavior, dress and function. The same God uniquely present in the Temple Holy of

Holies can be encountered in Catholic shrines and churches. Again under the influence of ancient Jewish Temple practice, Catholics employ a wide variety of religious objects to aid in devotion (e.g., holy water, incense, candles). The use of these sacramentals has been found to date from the first centuries of Christian practice.

A second crucial influence on present-day Roman Catholicism can be traced back to the Jewish-Christian community in ancient Rome. The New Testament Book of Revelation condemned the Roman Empire as an enemy of God, ripe for terrible judgment. Other books, however, took a contrary view. The Gospels, Acts of the Apostles and many Letters (Epistles) view Romans and the Roman Empire very positively. Roman governor Pontius Pilate is presented as only reluctantly sentencing Jesus to death under pressure of Jerusalem's religious leaders. A Roman centurion (military officer) was the first to profess faith in Jesus after his death (Mark); another became the first gentile (non-Jewish) convert (Acts of the Apostles).

Not surprisingly, Roman Jewish-Christians showed pride in their heritage as citizens or inhabitants of the Empire's capital city. They acknowledged its remarkable achievements of peace and prosperity and willingly served in the imperial bureaucracy. They admired the Roman genius with its emphasis on order and clarity and its concern for organizational structure and efficiency. Thanks in part to its own clearly delimited hierarchical system, the Roman Church quickly prospered as leader of all other local churches.

Centralized control allows for remarkable openness to local adaptation without diluting essential traditions. Healthy diversity enhances genuine unity. Across the world, on any given day, identical biblical passages are proclaimed and preached and the same required order of worship is faithfully followed. But overall style differs strikingly. The Church is lived differently in Africa, in the Middle or Far East. Even among Catholic Americans, Native Americans, African Americans and Hispanics maintain their cultural distinctiveness. Parishes reflect local conditions and membership, whether rural or urban, blue-collar or middle-class, German, Italian, Irish, etc. Thus, in spite of potential for abuse, the heritage of appreciation for authority and structure has helped the Roman Catholic Church preserve essential beliefs while adapting to varying conditions.

MAIN BELIEFS

Roman Catholicism's distinctiveness centers on the Bishop of Rome, acknowledged as successor of Saint Peter and leader of the worldwide Church. As for the rest, at least for mainline Christian denominations, there is much that unites and little that divides. Differences mainly concern organizational structure and lines of authority, plus inevitable divergences in prayer and worship customs that shape the concrete practice of a common faith commitment. Modern scholarly studies indicate substantial agreement among most Christian denominations about basic articles of faith. This is often demonstrated concretely in the ecumenical movement, when various denominations come together for prayer and fellowship. The following brief overview of some Catholic teachings basic to issues of death and afterlife would be received with substantial agreement by many other Christian communities, particularly where biblically based.

First, the nature of *God*. Creation proclaims the glory of the Lord, its beauty and marvelous complexity reflecting his own being. But the Bible reveals in a special way God's inmost "personality," what he is really like. An awesome, sovereign Lord shows himself marvelously generous and accepting. He selflessly shares with innumerable creatures the life that is his alone by right. Upholding the moral law yet remarkably non-judgmental, the God of the Old as well as New Testaments returns good for evil, wants to forgive rather than punish, tenderly loves all creatures, earnestly desires their eternal happiness. The Christian doctrine of a three-personed God shows how a selflessly, sharing love lies at the center of divine being: from eternity the Father generating the Son, the Holy Spirit proceeding from both Father and Son.

Second, the nature of *human beings*. Created in God's image, more like him than anything else that exists, we are destined to share his own unlimited life and felicity. But the freedom of self-determination, as well as the accumulating evil in the world, contribute inevitably to universal sinfulness. Apart from special divine help, no one can fully realize the human potential and live as he or she ought. Nevertheless, Roman Catholicism insists on the basic goodness of human nature. Consistent with its openness to the unbelieving world, it acknowledges much that is admirable in paganism, for even there the effect of God's hidden but powerful grace can be discerned.

Third, existence of the *Devil* seems essential to Roman Catholic as well as biblical faith. Such a being represents the only explanation for the pervasive evil that infects our world. As a creature, however, the Devil cannot ultimately compromise or frustrate divine sovereignty. The biblical God reigns, supreme and serene, unthreatened by hostile forces. The story of salvation consists of his progressive triumph over all evil powers, human and superhuman. Dualism (two opposed gods, one evil and one good) has no place in traditional Christian faith.

Fourth, the meaning of *suffering*. Biblically based Christianity acknowledges a God who is all-powerful and all-good. Suffering by contrast is both real and evil, in itself the opposite of fulfilled living. And yet, God remains in charge of his creation. He doesn't directly *cause* suffering, which in a mysterious way results from resistance to his loving purpose. But like loving parent, teacher or friend, he *allows* suffering to exist for its unique potential of furthering human growth. Suffering remains a mystery. People do suffer undeservedly, but the Bible, especially in the example and teaching of Jesus, shows how to deal with it creatively.

What if God sheltered human beings from every encounter with suffering? What would life be like without pain, hurt, loss, failure and frustration? The result would be persons tragically incomplete and unfulfilled, unable to assume personal responsibility, profoundly unhappy. From another point of view, human society would collapse, undermined by monsters of insensitivity and selfish uncaring. But such disciplinary and educational suffering doesn't work automatically. Having taken all prudent means to eliminate pain, humans must creatively cooperate with what can't be changed. Then only can suffering's hidden potential for good be realized; then only can it serve as a unique means of growth toward full humanity.

Often, however, suffering becomes so overwhelming that the individual does not, cannot, grow personally. Pain too easily crushes the spirit, illness diminishes the body. But even here there is potential for meaning, rather than meaninglessness; for hope, not despair. Willing acceptance of handicap, chronic pain and debility can become empowering grace in others' lives, helping them accept what can't be changed. This explains the healing and personal growth many experience in working with retarded or exceptional children and with the terminally ill. Personal problems tend to fall into perspective, complaining yields to fervent gratitude for personal blessings heretofore insufficiently acknowledged and appreciated. Those who accept and live with handicap or imminent death can inspire others to renewed living.

Such suffering becomes redemptive. One person's willing endurance "saves" others, gifting them with fuller measure of life. Redemptive suffering lies at the very heart of Christianity, which proclaims salvation through Jesus' rejection, crucifixion, death and resurrection. Only in the total self-emptying of martyrdom, selfless surrender of his life in the fullest possible expression of love, could Jesus offer life in fullness to a world unable to save itself.

FUNERALS

Because Roman Catholicism is a religion that exists in many parts of the world, funeral practices differ widely and are adapted to local and national customs. Services for the dead celebrate Christian hope in the midst of grieving; sadness at loss is tempered by assurance of "eternal rest" for the deceased. Under the influence of the Second Vatican Council (1962-65), the Church reformed its last rites. "Mass of Resurrection" with white vestments has largely replaced "Mass of the Dead" in which traditional black served as the principal color. Jesus' resurrection is recalled as assurance of future rising for all who have died "in Christ" and are intimately united to his death and resurrection through baptism.

Catholic funeral rituals are structured to acknowledge the loss suffered by those who mourn and to assist them in a healthy grieving process. Friends and acquaintances gather to console with their presence and prayers. In the United States, for example, a waking service, held for one or more evenings prior to burial, includes private prayers and a brief ceremony at the funeral home.

After the funeral Mass, the hearse is followed to the cemetery for final graveside farewell. In some localities mourners gather again after 30 days for a second memorial Mass. Other American Catholics follow their own customs while preserving essentials. Native Americans, for example, may gather in a "sweat lodge" ceremony. The official service book includes a wide range of prayers that encourage adaptation to specific situations. Did the deceased die in old age, in middle years or as a child? If a baby, with or without baptism? Is the gathered community crushed by sudden and unexpected death or resigned and already grieving during long illness? Numerous options allow the officiating priest to respect particular sensibilities.

Catholic funeral services emphasize supportive love for those who grieve from relatives, friends and neighbors. Death moreover is considered a public rather than private event. It serves as solemn opportunity for community reaffirmation of faith in life beyond death. Because believers gather to celebrate God's gracious gift of a life ended on earth yet embarked upon the path to Heaven, eulogies of the deceased are out of place. The words spoken emphasize the good news of what God has done, is doing and will do for us, not the individual's accomplishments during earthly life. Mourning Christians struggle to accept the present while looking back in gratitude and forward in hope.

DISPOSAL OF THE BODY

A corpse may be disposed of in any way that preserves reverence for what it once had been. Burial in the ground acknowledges our humble mortality: bodies made of dust inevitably return to dust. What happens to the corpse in no way affects afterlife or final-day resurrection. Legal, medical, educational and charitable purposes can be served by autopsy, donation of organs or the gift of the body to a medical college. Such options become religiously symbolic, final expressions of loving, self-emptying service to others.

Although it is a practice mostly limited to the United States, embalming can aid the grieving process. On the other hand, attempts at lifelike exhibition that deny the reality of death (for example, a corpse displayed on a couch as though sleeping) are unacceptable. In eighteenth-century Europe, cremation publicly stated disbelief in afterlife. Having lost its anti-religious overtones, cremation once again becomes an approved option for Catholics. It may even be required to hinder the spread of plague, prevent irreverence when a large number have died or preserve valuable land for cultivation of food.

RESPONSE TO THE BEREAVED

Earlier remarks indicated that response to the bereaved represents a principal factor in Roman Catholic funeral practices. Believers are helped to work through their grief, avoiding extremes of death-denial, hopelessness and despair.

REQUIREMENTS FOR BURIAL

Because Christian burial constitutes a religious act and public testimony to the dead person's faith in resurrection, unbelievers would not be granted the regular service. But Catholics, including priests, are free to participate in and even lead memorial services for such persons. Reverent burial of the dead, regardless of religious affiliation or lack thereof, has always constituted an important Christian work of mercy. Local customs and regulations determine the response to lapsed or inactive Catholics and to notorious public sinners. In general, the Church tends to permit rather than refuse Catholic burial in such circumstances, lest she be guilty of harsh judgment. In earlier times, funeral Mass and burial in consecrated ground were routinely denied suicide victims for having deliberately rejected God's gift of life. Today the Church acknowledges that suicides represent a pathetic cry for help or a desperate attempt to flee unbearable psychological or physical pain. One's last conscious act doesn't necessarily determine eternal fate; in death as in life, only God reads hearts. The Catholic Church offers full Christian burial to suicides, peace and hope to their relatives and friends.

LIFE AFTER DEATH

Belief in afterlife constitutes the heart of Christian faith. St. Paul preached resurrection of the body, a concept rejected by Greek philosophers who spoke only of immortality of the soul. In Christian belief death is not something that comes naturally, something already due by reason of creation. Instead, we receive it as the final, quite undeserved and unmerited, gift from God by reason of Jesus' redemptive death and resurrection. The New Testament speaks of rebirth, of entry into a radically new and different form of existence quite beyond present comprehension. The everlasting, glorified existence that Jesus now possesses will one day become the inheritance of all the faithful — those destined to share his triumph over death.

REINCARNATION

Reincarnation implicitly contradicts basic Christian teaching. Biblical texts emphasize the awesome privilege and responsibility of each person to repent and be reconciled with God now rather than tomorrow or in subsequent existences. Neither science nor Christian philosophy can identify any portion of a human being capable of passing over into another earthly life. Moreover, we don't need other lives to work out our salvation through suffering for sins committed in earlier incarnations. Christianity insists that no one earns salvation; it comes only as a free and unmerited divine gift because of what Jesus did.

HEAVEN AND HELL

Heaven designates a condition rather than a place; it is an eternal fullness of life, supreme happiness flowing from intimacy with God. Because glorified bodies exist beyond time and space, heaven is, strictly speaking, nowhere, occupying no location within created reality. The term "heaven" reflects an understandable human tendency to locate the divine realm in the heavens, whence come blessings of sun and rain. The Bible prefers God's "Kingdom" or (more accurately) "Kingship," because life can be fully lived and enjoyed only by doing it his way.

Biblical authors refrain from exact description of afterlife. St. Paul, quoting Isaiah 64:3, insisted that "eye has not seen, ear not heard, nor has it so much as dawned upon humankind what God has prepared for those who love him" (I Corinthians 2:9). But metaphors comparing heaven to present experiences provide some insight. Heaven is something *like* life in a glorious garden where people live in complete harmony with self, others and nature, enjoying privileged intimacy with God (Genesis 1-3). Another and more frequent biblical comparison is the heavenly banquet hosted by God with the saved as honored guests. In the Eucharist (Lord's Supper), Christians sacramentally anticipate this eternal celebration. The image of a banquet acknowledges the bodily component of human existence: we are not spirits temporarily trapped in evil or unworthy matter. The metaphor also stresses our essentially social nature; we are individuals finding fullness not alone but with others.

Christianity insists that humans possess free will, that they are capable of self-determination. God does not compel cooperation with his loving plan for our eternal happiness. The existence of Hell as genuine option guarantees freedom of choice. Like Heaven, it represents a permanent, irreversible state of existence rather than a particular place. Again like Heaven, the Bible can only describe Hell's torments in metaphorical language. Images from our world of experience (fire, the physical and psychological pains associated with burns, despair represented by the gnashing of teeth) cannot be taken literally, any more than Heaven consists in nonstop eating and drinking. Such word-pictures powerfully describe the total frustration creatures experience when definitively separated from the sole source of all blessings.

God doesn't so much condemn to Hell as ratify human self-determination. A God who *is* love can never hate; he who doesn't directly cause suffering on earth cannot directly inflict eternal punishment. Instead he permits humans to accept or reject his offer of eternal happiness. Already in this world, sinful humans prefer doing things their way in spite of painful consequences. The Catholic Church insists on the reality of Hell, but it has never taught that anyone is actually there, for example, Judas Iscariot or Adolf Hitler. Proposed in earlier centuries but soon rejected is the doctrine of *apokatastasis,* eventual salvation for all, including those in Hell. This denies the seriousness of human, final self-determination upon death. If persons have chosen Hell, they want to be and remain there for eternity.

Jesus intended his Church to help rather than hinder worldwide salvation. In an awesome prediction of the Last Judgment (Matthew 25:31-46), he taught that even the unbaptized accept or reject eternal salvation. These, no less than believers, qualify for admission by serving the Lord Jesus. In their case he remained hidden and unrecognized, intimately identified with the world's needy.

> When the Son of Man comes in his glory, escorted by all the angels of heaven, he will sit upon his royal throne and all *the nations* [not just Christians] will be assembled before him. Then he will separate them into two groups.... The King will say to those on his right: "Come. You have my Father's blessing! Inherit the kingdom prepared for you from the creation of the world. For I was hungry and you gave me food, I was thirsty and you gave me drink. I was a stranger and you welcomed me, naked and you clothed me. I was ill and you comforted me in prison and you came to visit me." Then the just will ask him: "Lord, when did we see you hungry and feed you or see you thirsty and give you drink? When did we welcome you away from home or clothe you in your nakedness? When did we visit you when you were ill or in prison?" The King will answer them: "I assure, as often as you did it for one of my least brothers, you did it *for me*" (Matthew 25:31-40).

Jesus will announce to "all nations" (not church members) that by caring or refusing to care for the poor, sick and lonely, each person unknowingly accepts or rejects Jesus himself and his offer of heavenly life. As for God-fearing Christians, Jesus repeatedly warned that "the last shall be first," undermining smug presumption and feelings of superiority.

EVENTUAL FATE OF THE EARTH

Biblical teaching reassures us that the present world, infected with evil and its results (suffering and death), will one day be transformed rather than destroyed. Final-age purification will result in totally renewed creation. Instead of going up into the sky, the saved will enjoy fullness of life on a new earth. Once again, metaphor must not be confused with literal description. However beyond present human understanding, God intends a bright future for the universe he lovingly created and happily pronounced "very good" (Genesis 1). His gift of eternal salvation reaches beyond human beings to include the whole range of existence. More than this cannot be confidently stated. Christian revelation focuses on this-worldly living, resisting the impulse to speculate about future, other worldly conditions. "The world itself will be freed from its slavery to corruption and share in the glorious freedom of the children of God" (Romans 8:21).

BODILY RESURRECTION

Resurrection of the body means eternal life as full and integrated persons, not just as separated souls. It contrasts with resuscitation or return of the dead to this-worldly living. Final-age, perfected existence, already enjoyed by Jesus in resurrected glory, will be shared upon his return, when God's promised Kingdom comes in fullness. Here, too, human concepts and language only approximate reality. Jesus' resurrected "body" exists outside time, occupies no particular space and therefore is nowhere within created reality.

PURGATORY AND LIMBO

Catholic teaching insists on the reality of Purgatory, a condition (rather than a place) of transition and adaptation for those entering heavenly beatitude. Even great saints know sin during earthly life and die affected by selfish self-centeredness incompatible with divine intimacy. Purgatory describes the passage, at once painful and joyful, into purified existence. Then only can persons accept and return God's overwhelming love without hindrance.

Limbo was originally proposed by theologians as a condition (not a place) intermediate between Heaven and Hell for infants dying unbaptized but without personal sin. Never taught as Catholic dogma, Limbo is now generally rejected as an erroneous (but logical) answer to a wrong question. It seems reasonable that an all-good God permits persons never fully developed physically (infants, the severely retarded) the opportunity to attain eternal life.

REQUIREMENTS FOR SALVATION

Christianity firmly insists that no human being, however holy, earns salvation. It comes as a pure gift, graciously bestowed upon the undeserving. God never deviated from his commitment to create a perfect world, but human sinfulness has frustrated this saving purpose. Jesus, sinless Son of God, by giving his life in a selfless act of love effectively neutralized humanity's resistance. Creatures need only accept what Jesus accomplished through intimate union with him in baptism. This sacrament causes what it signifies: death to hopeless existence (going down into baptismal waters), followed by rebirth into newness of life (coming up from the water) as Jesus' follower and sharer in his unique Son-relationship with his Father.

Salvation comes only through Jesus, normally through Baptism and active membership in his Church. The Bible, however, emphasizes God's universal salvific will; and Jesus now reigns as Lord of everyone, not just Roman Catholics. Another biblical theme, election for service rather than merit, reminds Christians that they haven't been chosen because they are better than unbelievers. The Church represents a community called to share with the world God's good news of salvation through Jesus. Because the question wasn't raised or perhaps lest Christians grow negligent in their primary responsibility as apostles, biblical and Church teaching doesn't explain in detail how unbelievers come to salvation. Theologians speculate about "anonymous Christians," unbaptized persons ignorant of Jesus' life and work or scandalized by misleading witness of less than perfect church members. Nonbelievers are open to salvation through Jesus by responding according to their best lights. Everyone can serve the Jesus who is hidden in needy neighbors (Matthew 25:31-46).

SOCIAL RELATIONS IN AFTERLIFE

Christians look forward to a radically transformed existence in the afterlife. It will have a continuity with previous earthly life that nevertheless includes discontinuity. We will be different because perfected, yet will remain ourselves; as much as possible like God himself, while not ceasing to be creatures. Friends and relatives will recognize each other in a situation of changed relationships. The intimacy that close friends and married couples strive with varying degrees of success to attain in this life will be completely realized in Heaven in the union of all persons. "When people rise from the dead, they neither marry nor are given in marriage but live like angels in heaven" (Matthew 22:30). Because the entire community of saved know an intimacy far beyond anything achieved on earth, private groupings in families and friendships have no place.

"PARTICULAR" AND "GENERAL" JUDGMENTS

Death represents the end of human growth. At the same time it's a sort of graduation, when each person finally and fully becomes what he or she tried to be throughout life. Christian theology distinguishes "particular" and "general" judgments. The first takes place immediately at death, when God solemnly ratifies definitive acceptance or rejection of the salvation that has been offered everyone. St. Paul longed "to be freed from this life and to be with Christ, for that is the far better thing" (Philippians 1:23). Catholic teaching affirms what Paul hints at — immediate passage into conscious afterlife rather than a "sleep" until the Last Day. But salvation has a community as well as individual dimension. Those already enjoying fullness of life with God experience a certain incompleteness until the whole of creation has opportunity for radical renewal. The Kingdom comes to individuals at the particular judgment, but God's grand salvific purpose will be realized only at final or general judgment.

JESUS' SECOND COMING

Ancient religions generally looked to the past for a perfect world, an ideal existence long lost and never to return. Judeo-Christianity by contrast looks to the future and anticipates a glorious fullness yet unachieved, a time when creation will be completely perfected. This final age becomes reality with the return of Jesus, cosmic ruler and Lord of History. The Bible's most profound revelation of creation's ultimate destiny is found in I Corinthians 15:20-28. The scenario described there begins with Jesus' present, though hidden, reign as cosmic Lord. But the real hero is God the Father, who is already at work subjecting all evil forces to his son's authority. "Christ must reign until God has put all enemies under his feet and the last enemy to be destroyed is death." This ultimate victory takes place at the Second Coming of Jesus.

Christ's triumph will become occasion for his own selfless self-emptying. "When, finally, all has been subjected to the Son, [the Son] will then subject himself to the One [the Father] who has made all things subject to him." Then follows a statement as profound as it is simple, describing what eternity will be like: "...that God [Father] may be all in all," or "everything to everyone." Here in a few words Paul summarized the purpose and goal of creation and redemption. Universal salvation means God's generous sharing of what is his alone: fullness of life, eternal happiness.

AFTERLIFE: WHAT IT IS NOT

Afterlife in Christian and Catholic understanding isn't something tacked on as a continuation of earthly existence. It's not a reward earned by an elite few who did and said the right things to cajole blessings from a reluctant deity or a gift limited to those lucky to belong to one particular religious group. Far more than something that comes "after," final-age existence represents the culmination, fulfillment and perfection of created being. Life as we now know it serves as an incomplete sign and promise of what could or what will be. Heavenly life corresponds to our deepest longings and reflects God's marvelously selfless love. His firm commitment is to share his being so completely that we become as much like God as possible, while remaining ourselves. It is offered as the purest of gifts: what can't be earned and comes to the undeserving, needs only grateful acceptance.

SOLIDARITY IN PRAYER WITH THE DEAD AND DYING

Human beings from diverse cultures and religions sense a solidarity of the living with deceased ancestors, including relatives and friends. A widow or widower can experience the presence, mysterious but real and intimate, of the lost spouse. Religious persons instinctively pray for the dying that they recover or find easeful death. Also widespread is the feeling that prayers assist the dead in their life beyond this world. Roman Catholics share such sentiments. They appeal for supporting evidence to the Second Book of Maccabees, accepted as part of the Old Testament by Catholics as well as Eastern Orthodox Christians, but not by Protestants or Jews. Second Maccabees was composed 100 or more years before Jesus' birth. It attests to the intercession of saints in heaven for people living on earth (15:11-16) and to the power of the living to offer prayers and sacrifices for the dead ("that they might be freed from sin," 12:39-46).

Prayer for the dying creates no special problem because Christians pray to God for themselves and others in times of need. More complex is prayer that the dead be forgiven their sins and permitted entrance into eternal happiness. God needs no prodding or encouragement, having shown himself eagerly desirous and diligently working to save rather than condemn. Nor can salvation be forced upon anyone, because each individual must personally accept the divine offer. But prayers for the dead fit in with the understanding of Purgatory as described earlier. They serve as expressions of loving support and encouragement during a period of painful but joyful adjustments to heavenly life.

Those now with God in blessedness remain involved and concerned with humans on earth and indeed with the whole of creation. New Testament images such as "body of Christ" and "people of God" apply to both the Church Militant (on earth) and Church Triumphant (in Heaven), so that living and dead form a single fellowship. Those already with the Lord eagerly yearn for the time when everyone and everything can share their fullness. Catholic teaching rejects verbal or other communication with the dead such as seances, ouija boards and ghosts. But the intercession of those now in glory, joined with that of the Lord Jesus, assists the living even more effectively than during their time on earth; they help the living in a mysterious way that respects the world's autonomy and integrity.

Seventh-day Adventist Church

Robert M. Johnston, PhD

BACKGROUND OF THE FAITH

In 1829, during the "Jacksonian" era, the northeastern United States was in a period of ferment, restlessness, experimentation and intense interest in reform of many kinds, but above all, in religion.[1] Old religious groupings and dogmas were breaking down in the cross current of many movements that were sometimes conflicting and sometimes coalescing. There was a pervasive desire to return to primitive Christianity, to rise above denominational differences, to bring everything into harmony with God's will, to throw "the traditions of men" out the window, to shake off a past which was viewed as corrupt or apostate.

It was the genius of Adventism to gather up some of the more helpful of these impulses and reform causes and fuse them into what became a distinctive international religious denomination. The catalytic spark for this was the message that William Miller of Low Hampton, New York began to preach in 1831. After earnestly studying the biblical book of Daniel, Miller concluded that the Second Coming of Jesus would occur in 1843 or 1844. Even though various divines and missionaries of the time in England, Germany, Chile, the Near East and elsewhere also calculated the date of the Second Coming, it was Miller and the associates that came to join him who made the greatest impact. By the time the movement reached its climax, as many as a million people in the United States (out of a total population of 17 million) were caught up in it.

Jesus did not return to earth in 1844 and therefore, for Adventists, this became the time of the "Great Disappointment." But the time of penitent preparation had been a spiritually purifying experience for many and there were those who could not bring themselves to repudiate something that seemed to be from God, even though there was clearly some mistake about it. Hiram Edson of Port Gibson, New York, and some associates concluded that the calculations had been correct but the event was mistaken: the "sanctuary" referred to in Daniel 8:14 was not this earth, as Miller had supposed, but the heavenly temple spoken of in the New Testament epistle to the Hebrews.[2]

In the meantime, other Adventists (as believers in Miller's announcement were called) became convinced that the true Sabbath was Saturday, the seventh day of the week.[3] This view, which can be traced to the Seventh-day Baptists, was energetically promoted among Adventists by Joseph Bates, a retired sea captain who had already had a colorful career as an advocate of temperance and reform of health habits. The keeping of the false Sabbath was identified with the "mark of the beast" which is spoken of in Revelation 14:9. Adventists have come to regard the "Three Angels' Messages" of Revelation 14:6-12 as epitomizing their special mission in the world: the first angel (verses 6-7) proclaims that the hour of judgment has come; the second (verse 8), that the religious world is apostate; and the third (verses 9-12) warns against false worship.

Charles Fitch, a prominent Millerite preacher, had declared that the various denominations, by their rejection of the message of judgment, had become fallen "Babylon." Fitch is also responsible, along with George Storrs, for popularizing in Adventist circles the doctrine that the dead are asleep until the time of the resurrection, when Jesus comes again.

In 1848, in Connecticut, New York, Maine and Massachusetts, a series of meetings were held that gathered into a self-conscious group the scattered Adventists who were sympathetic to all of these ideas. The most prominent leaders who emerged in these meetings were Bates and a newly married young couple, James and Ellen White. James White became the most tireless and dominant personality in the emerging denomination and remained so until his death in 1881. Even before her marriage, his wife Ellen had frequent visionary experiences and she has been regarded by Seventh-day Adventists as a messenger of the Lord, having received the gift of prophecy. Until her death in 1915, she was a strong unifying influence in the denomination and was especially opposed to any manifestations of fanaticism. Her voluminous writings cover a wide range of topics and have been instrumental in institutionalizing various kinds of reforms as part of the denominational program.

In 1849, with his wife's encouragement, James White began to publish a periodical called *The Present Truth*, which in 1850 became *The Advent Review and Sabbath Herald* (now *The Adventist Review)*. In 1863, the church was officially organized, in spite of considerable resistance from those who recalled bitter experiences in their former denominations and were reluctant to see their movement become another denomination; and the name Seventh-day Adventist became official, in spite of the wishes of some who would have preferred the name Church of God. An increasing concern for temperance, health and rational healing led to the establishment of the Western Health Reform Institute in 1866, in Battle Creek, Michigan, which, in 1855, had become the headquarters of Seventh-day Adventist publishing house and eventually of the organization. The Institute grew into the famous Battle Creek Sanitarium, under the vigorous leadership of Dr. J.H. Kellogg, inventor of breakfast foods and meat substitutes.

1874 saw the founding of the first denominational college in Battle Creek and the sending out of the first overseas missionary (to Switzerland), J.N. Andrews, who was also the most able scholar in the early days of the denomination. By that time, the number of members had grown from less than 100 in 1848 to over 6000.

Since that time the membership has grown to more than five million worldwide. What began with a small band of New Englanders has become an international church with four-fifths of its members outside North America, its greatest numerical strength being in the developing nations of Latin America, Africa and Asia.[4] World headquarters are located in Washington, D.C.

BELIEFS

While in order to sustain a recognizably continued existence, Seventh-day Adventists were unable to avoid becoming a denomination, they have resisted the tendency to credalism. They have some definite doctrines and feel that they are important, but they reserve the right to revise them in the light of increasing insight. The first formal list of "Fundamental Principles," promulgated in 1872,[5] was prefaced with a substantial preamble that began as follows:

> In presenting to the public this synopsis of our faith, we wish to have it distinctly understood that we have no articles of faith, creed, or discipline, aside from the Bible. We do not put forth this as having any authority with our people, nor is it designed to secure uniformity among them, as a system of faith, but is a brief statement of what is and has been, with great unanimity, held by them....

The formulation voted at the General Conference session of 1980[6] begins with this preamble:

> Seventh-day Adventists accept the Bible as their only creed and hold certain fundamental beliefs to be the teaching of the Holy Scriptures. These beliefs, as set forth here, constitute the church's understanding and expression of the teaching of Scripture. Revision of these statements may be expected at a General Conference session when the church is led by the Holy Spirit to a fuller understanding of Bible truth or finds better language in which to express the teachings of God's Holy Word.

Changes have demonstrably occurred, but certain convictions have never wavered.

Seventh-day Adventists believe that the final authority in religious matters is the Bible, meaning the 66 canonical books in the Old and New Testaments. They further hold, in common with most conservative Christians, belief in the Trinity, Jesus Christ as the incarnate Son of God and many other central doctrines of Christian consensus. They practice believers' baptism by immersion and the ordinance of the Lord's Supper, preceded by pedilavium.[7] Other doctrines are more distinctive, being shared with only a few other groups, and some may be unique, or may receive a distinctive emphasis. Adventists see themselves, and indeed all humanity, as being caught up in a "great controversy" between Christ and Satan regarding the character of God, His law and His sovereignty over the universe, a controversy in which God will be finally vindicated. Everyone must serve one side or the other. Salvation depends on one's relationship with God in Christ, through whom "we are justified, adopted as God's sons and daughters and delivered from the lordship of sin."[8] This relationship is jeopardized by all deliberate disobedience to truth, which constitutes a denial of faith and an affront to the Holy Spirit, placing the soul in mortal peril. Seventh-day Adventists see themselves as being called to restore a number of biblical truths that have been neglected or subverted and which constitute their special message.

Their denominational name points to two of these doctrines. "Seventh-day" signifies that they keep the seventh day of the week as the Sabbath, in obedience to a literal reading of the Fourth Commandment. For them, the Sabbath begins at sundown on Friday and lasts until sundown Saturday. "The Sabbath is a day of delightful communion with God and one another. It is a symbol of our redemption in Christ, a sign of our sanctification, a token of our allegiance and a foretaste of our eternal future in God's kingdom."[9] "Adventist" refers to the hope and expectation of the imminent second coming of Jesus Christ, according to His promise and the faith of the apostolic church. His advent will be literal, personal, visible and worldwide.[10] When Jesus returns, the righteous dead will be resurrected and together with the righteous living will be glorified and taken to heaven, but the unrighteous will die.[11]

According to Revelation 20, the unrighteous will remain dead for 1000 years, while the righteous reign with Christ in heaven. At the end of this millennium, the unrighteous will rise in the "second resurrection" only to be judged and then destroyed in the "lake of fire," along with Satan and his angels. This fiery destruction, referred to in the gospels as Gehenna, also serves to purify the earth, upon which the Holy City descends. Forever afterward, this earth, made new, becomes the eternal abode of the righteous and indeed (according to Revelation 21) the capital of the universe. This leads to consideration of the nature of man and of death, about which Seventh-day Adventists hold views which were long castigated as peculiar or perverse, but which are now obtaining increasing respect among biblical scholars of many denominations.[12]

THE NATURE OF MAN

Seventh-day Adventists agree with the famous dictum of H. Wheeler Robinson, "The Hebrew idea of personality is an animated body and not an incarnated soul." This conception stands in contrast to the dualistic Platonic view that the body is the prison house of the soul. Though the latter view has been extremely influential, penetrating both Judaism and Christianity, the normative view of the Bible is that which Robinson describes as the Hebraic one. A paradigmatic passage is Genesis 2:7, "The Lord God formed man of dust from the ground and breathed into his nostrils the breath of life and man became a living soul *(nephesh chayyah)*." Adventists are therefore fond of saying, "You don't *have* a soul; you *are* a soul." The soul is a composite of the physical body and the mysterious life force breathed into it by God. Man is thus psychosomatic unity and when God withdraws the life force from the body, the man is no more,[13] except as he remains in the eternal memory of his Creator. Man's spirit is not a conscious individual entity that continues in another mode of life apart from the body. Rather, man is unconscious in death, as described in Ecclesiastes 9:5, "For the living know that they will die, but the dead know nothing, and they have no more reward; for the memory of them is lost." For this reason, and also doubtless because of the appearance of the corpse, both Testaments frequently refer to death as a sleep. The life to come depends on the resurrection of the body.

Viewed as a life-force, the spirit that animates the body and makes man a living soul must be regarded as an impersonal energy, though its source is the Spirit of God. The locus of a man's individuality and personality is nothing less than his total being. In the terminology of Genesis, spirit infused into the body of dust produces the living soul. In more modern language, life joined to body produces the self, the conscious ego. A crude analogy is the electric current (also something of a mystery) that passes through an incandescent bulb and produces a shining light. If the spirit, which at death returns to God, were a conscious entity, then the breath of life, which God breathed into the first man, must have had the same nature, implying some sort of conscious preexistence — something taught nowhere in Scripture. It should be noted that the biblical terms for spirit, *ruach* and *pneuma*, have the primitive meaning of wind or breath, and while they take on a wide spectrum of secondary meanings, none of them contradicts this basic starting point.

From this theological perception, it follows that for Adventists, the body is important and no mere prison house of the soul. Spiritual welfare is bound to bodily conditions and both injurious indulgence and injurious mortification of the flesh can be religiously detrimental. Conversely, both care and discipline of the body are necessary to true spirituality. Deprivation of sleep, drunkenness, extreme hunger, malnutrition, drug abuse and overwork unmistakably illustrate the truth of this perception. The doctrine of man's psychosomatic oneness provides a theoretical reinforcement for the Adventist emphasis on temperance, health reform and healing ministries. In addition to obedience to Christ's example and command to heal,[14] the Adventist doctrine of man provides a motive for making attention to the body a facet of the work of redemption.

LIFE AFTER DEATH

It should be clear from what has been said that death is not ultimately a liberating friend for Adventists, but a denuding enemy, even though it does bring an end of pain to the sufferer.[15] It was to defeat this enemy that Christ died, was buried and rose from the dead.[16] The life to come is not the result of death, but of the resurrection from death which will occur at Christ's second coming. If the real self can live on without a body, Adventists ask, what use is resurrection? Accordingly, death is considered by Adventists as a sleep of total unconsciousness. Therefore, the dead have no awareness of the passing of time. The next thing an individual knows after brain death occurs is the moment of resurrection when "the trumpet shall sound" and he hears the summons of his Lord, the Life-giver. Whether the intervening time is a few moments or thousands of years, it is all the same as it is experienced. This is the Adventist view of the so-called intermediate state, as vigorously set forth by such writers as C.B. Haynes:

> Since Seventh-day Adventists reject the teaching of the natural immortality of all men, their belief regarding man's condition in death does not conform to certain popular views.
>
> They believe that death is not a modification of life, in changed conditions. Death is not a release into a fuller life. Death is not life in misery. Death is not life in happiness. Death is not life at all, in any condition, good or bad. To die is not to live. To die is to stop living. Death is a complete cessation of life.
>
> Death does not mean to go to heaven. Death does not mean to go to hell. Death does not mean to go to purgatory. Death does not mean to go anywhere. Death means the end of life. When a person dies, he does not live somewhere else, in heaven, hell, or purgatory. He does not live at all, in any condition whatsoever. He is dead. And when a person is dead, he is not alive.[17]

The *Sheol* or *Hades* spoken of in Scripture simply signifies the grave.

But there will be a resurrection of the dead, or to be precise, two resurrections (one to life and one to judgment[18]) immediately preceding and immediately following the millennium of the Apocalypse.[19] Immortality is therefore not something innate in man, nor does he have a naturally immortal soul. Rather, immortality is the gracious gift of God through Jesus Christ.[20] Only God is naturally immortal.[21] Because they believe that man is only conditionally immortal and that eternal life is granted on condition of obedient faith, Adventists are rightly called Conditionalists. The resurrection of the righteous will occur on the model of Christ's resurrection. His resurrection body was glorified but not unphysical, a fact vividly portrayed by Luke:

> As they were saying this, Jesus himself stood among them. But they were startled and frightened and supposed that they saw a spirit. And he said to them, "Why are you troubled, and why do questionings rise in your hearts? See my hands and my feet, that it is I myself; handle me, and see; for a spirit has not flesh and bones as you see that I have." And while they still disbelieved for joy, and wondered, he said to them, "Have you anything here to eat?" They gave him a piece of broiled fish, and he took it and ate before them.[22]

The ultimate destiny of the resurrected righteous, after passing the millennium in heaven while the earth lies desolate and sabbatically fallow, will be to dwell forever with their Lord in the purified and renewed earth, free from all weakness, disfigurement, sorrow, grief and pain and to enjoy such satisfaction as this life shall have prepared them for, without sin. The ultimate destiny of the impenitent wicked is to be judged, to suffer punishment and finally, to perish utterly, so that their existence will eternally cease and they shall be as though they had not been. "God so loved the world that He gave His only Son, that whosoever believeth in Him should not perish, but have everlasting life."[23]

It should be clear that Adventists do not believe in the preexistence of ordinary man's spirit or in reincarnation or transmigration of souls. We are given one life now, a time of probation that ends with death, followed by no second chance.

> And just as it is appointed for men to die once, and after that comes the judgment, so Christ, having been offered once to bear the sins of many, will appear a second time, not to deal with sin but to save those who are eagerly waiting for him.[24]

It should be equally clear that Adventists do not pray to the dead or for them. Probation ends at death and there is no purgatory. Adventists pray only for the living.

The resurrection body of the righteous will be a glorified body like that of Christ,[25] delivered from defects, disfigurements and onerous limitations. It will, nevertheless, possess a certain continuity with the present body or else the resurrection self would be a totally other self. Paul compares the relationship between the present body and the resurrection body to the relationship between the seed and the plant that springs from it.[26] In the resurrection we will recognize loved ones and friends. As Ellen White envisioned about this time, "Little children are borne by holy angels to their mothers' arms. Friends long separated by death are united, nevermore to part and with songs of gladness ascend together to the city of God."[27]

POST MORTEM PRACTICES

Death brings separation, loss and grief to survivors, even though by faith they believe the separation is only temporary for believers. Ministers and fellow church members will make their sympathy tangibly felt by their words, presence and loving acts of assistance to the mourners. But it is an observable fact that consolation comes easy to Adventists for they have been taught that death is only an episode. They have often heard and read the words of Paul: "But we would not have you ignorant, brethren, concerning those who are asleep, that you may not grieve as others do who have no hope."[28] Typically, a dying Adventist will admonish his children and spouse to be faithful so that all of them will be reunited in the world to come. The remembrance of such words has often been a strong motivation for perseverance in the faith. Similar exhortations are often included in the funeral service.

Funeral customs do not differ radically from those of the cultures in which the Adventists live, except for modifications when the customs clash with Adventist theology. No candles are burnt for the dead and no offerings are presented to them, but contributions to various good works and causes of the church are commonly made as memorials. In the United States, the funeral service does not greatly differ from other Protestant churches and they are quite commonly conducted in the existing mortuary establishments. There is a tendency to frown upon ostentatious or extravagant funeral arrangements, expensive caskets and monuments, but this is not in any way considered a deficiency of love — it is just that simplicity is more in keeping with the faith and hope of Adventism. But, it is still believed that anything that will both console and edify the mourners is appropriate.

It is understandably an awkward situation when the deceased is known to have lived an impenitently sinful life to the end or to have committed suicide. In such cases, there is a temptation to use the occasion as an object lesson about the deceased as a warning to the living, but most Adventist ministers have the good taste to avoid such crudeness and make the theological point that judgment must be left in the hands of a loving God who can be trusted to do what is best for all. No human being really knows the heart of another at the end of life. Moreover, Adventists do not believe that a momentary aberration just before death is enough to forfeit eternal life. Ellen White wrote: "The character is revealed, not by occasional good deeds and occasional misdeeds, but by the tendency of the habitual words and acts."[29]

As in most cultures, the Adventist funeral service is normally conducted by a minister. In the absence of an ordained minister, a licensed minister (that is, a ministerial intern who has not yet received ordination) may officiate at a funeral. An Adventist minister may conduct a funeral for a nonmember and requests for him to do so are not uncommon. Adventists do not believe that persons who do not belong to their denomination have no chance of salvation. Indeed, even persons who seem to be heathen who have never heard the gospel cannot with certainty be excluded. Ultimately, God will be the judge of such matters, a prerogative no man can usurp.

Even though the dead body is usually buried, Adventists have no objection to cremation or to the donation of the body to a medical or scientific institution. While they base their belief in a future life on their hope of the resurrection of the body, they do not think the resurrection is dependent on preservation of the cadaver. Ellen White wrote:

> Our personal identity is preserved in the resurrection, though not the same particles of matter or material substance as went into the grave. The wondrous works of God are a mystery to man. The spirit, the character of man, is returned to God, there to be preserved. In the resurrection every man will have his own character. God in His own time will call forth the dead, giving again the breath of life and bidding the dry bones live. The same form will come forth, but it will be free from disease and every defect. It lives again bearing the same individuality of features, so that friend will recognize friend. There is no law of God in nature which shows that God gives back the same identical particles of matter which composed the body before death. God shall give the righteous dead a body that will please Him.[30]

The Adventist view is not unlike the metaphor used by Benjamin Franklin in the epitaph which he composed for himself:

> The body of B. Franklin, Printer
> Like the Cover of an old Book,
> Its Contents torn out,
> And stript of its Lettering & Gilding,
> Lies here, Food for Worms.
> But the Work shall not be lost;
> For it will, as he believ'd, appear once more
> In a new and more elegant Edition
> Corrected and Improved
> By the Author.

Notes

1. This general social and religious background is vividly described in the volume edited by Edwin S. Gaustad, *The Rise of Adventism: Religion and Society in Mid-Nineteenth Century America* (New York: Harper and Row, 1974).

2. This and the following matters can be studied in greater detail in the numerous books on Seventh-day Adventist denominational history. Among the more reliable is R.W. Schwarz, *Light Bearers to the Remnant* (Mountain View, CA: Pacific Press, 1979). For the earliest period, see especially P. Gerard Damsteegt, *Foundations of the Seventh-day Adventist Message and Mission* (Grand Rapids, MI: Eerdmans, 1977).
3. Cf. Exodus 20:8-11; Deuteronomy 5:12-15; Genesis 2:1-3.
4. Current statistics can be found in the *Seventh-day Adventist Yearbook* (Washington: Review and Herald, 1997).
5. Reprinted in Appendix II of Damsteegt, op. cit., pp. 301-305.
6. See *Seventh-day Adventist Church Manual*, 1981, pp. 31-46.
7. They find pedilavium, or footwashing, which they refer to as "the ordinance of humility," commanded in John 13:1-17.
8. Article 10 of the "Fundamental Beliefs," printed in *Seventh-day Adventist Church Manual*, 1981.
9. Ibid., Article 19.
10. Ibid., Article 24.
11. Ibid.
12. For a few of many examples, see Oscar Cullmann, *Immortality of the Soul or Resurrection of the Dead? The Witness of the New Testament* (London: The Epworth Press, 1958); H. Wheeler Robinson, *The Christian Doctrine of Man* (Edinburgh: T. & T. Clark, 1958); David G. Myers, *The Human Puzzle: Psychological Research and Christian Belief* (New York: Harper and Row, 1978). The Adventist historian Leroy Froom has compiled a two-volume history of these views, *The Conditionalist Faith of Our Fathers* (Washington: Review and Herald, 1958).
13. Ecclesiastes 12:7 and Psalm 104:29 describe this dissolution which occurs at death.
14. See Matthew 10:8; cf. Luke 10:9.
15. Cf. 1 Corinthians 15:26; 2 Corinthians 5:3.
16. Cf. Revelation 1:17-18.
17. Carlyle B. Haynes, *Seventh-day Adventists: Their Work and Teachings* (Washington: Review and Herald, 1940), pp. 26-27. A thorough medical and theological treatment of near-death, supposed "out-of-body" experiences is provided by Jack Provonsha, *Is Death for Real? An Examination of Reported Near-Death Experiences in the Light of the Resurrection* (Mountain View, CA: Pacific Press, 1981); see also the same author's article "Life after Life?" in *The Ministry* (July 1977), pp. 20-23; cf. David G. Myers, op. cit., pp. 82-86.
18. John 5:28-29.
19. Revelation 20:1-10.
20. Romans 6:23.
21. 1 Timothy 1:17; 6:15-16; cf. John 5:26.
22. Luke 24:36-43. This and most scriptural quotations are from the Revised Standard Version.
23. John 3:16.
24. Hebrews 9:27-28.
25. Philippians 3:20, 21; cf. 1 John 3:2.
26. 1 Corinthians 15:34-44.

27. Ellen G. White, *The Great Controversy* (Mountain View, CA: Pacific Press, 1950), p. 645.
28. 1 Thessalonians 4:13.
29. Ellen G. White, *Steps to Christ* (Mountain View, CA: Pacific Press, 1942), p. 62.
30. Ellen G. White, Manuscript 76, printed in *The Seventh-day Adventist Bible Commentary*, Vol. VI, p. 1093, 1900.

Unitarian Universalism

George N. Marshall, PhD, DD

BACKGROUND OF THE FAITH

In a day when most institutions shy away from using the word "liberal," Unitarian Universalists still find this word to be the most appropriate characterization of their faith. Unitarian Universalism is liberal in that it is a free faith — in the latitude of freedom allowed to its adherents, in the loose construction of its ecclesiastical machinery and in its broad interpretation of Christian doctrine. There have been many outcroppings of liberal religion throughout history, arising for a period and disappearing, to emerge again later. Unitarian Universalism is seen by its adherents as the institutionalization of many of these attitudes.

In a poetic sense, we see this liberal tradition emerging in ancient Egypt under the Pharaoh Akhenaten of the 18th dynasty, who rejected the many gods of Egypt for a concept of one God. We see it in the critical quest of Socrates in ancient Greece and in the reforming movement of Confucius and Buddha on the Asian mainland. It existed in the efforts at reform of the Hebrew prophets. The liberal tradition in Christianity existed in the heresies of early Church Fathers, most notably Origen (185-251 A.D.) and Arius (256-336 A.D.).

Origen, an amazing scholar and prolific writer, set forth both Unitarian and Universalist concepts from his school in Alexandria, including the humanity of Jesus and the universal salvation of souls. At the Council of Nicaea (325 A.D.), Arius argued against the doctrine of the Trinity and was banished by the Emperor Constantine as the Christian Church officially became Trinitarian rather than Unitarian.

During the pivotal era of the Renaissance and Reformation, advanced thinkers such as Erasmus, Servetus, Zwingli and Wycliffe expressed non-Trinitarian views indicating an innate tendency toward Unitarian interpretations of Christianity. However, the real emergence of Unitarianism as a historical movement began with Faustus Socinus (1539-1604), who carried Unitarian teachings from Northern Italy to Poland in 1579. In Racow, he published the first Unitarian catechism in 1585 and this "Racovian Catechism" was soon circulated throughout Europe and arrived in England where it influenced nonconforming churchmen.

In Poland, the Unitarians were known as Socinians, the first popular designation of Unitarians throughout the continent during this era. Persecution of Socinians and their followers in Poland upon restoration of a Jesuit regime led to their flight to Transylvania. In this mountainous region, now divided between Romania and Hungary and for several centuries incorporated into the Austro-Hungarian Empire, Francis David, a remarkable Renaissance intellectual, was a dominant figure. He had been a Roman Catholic bishop until he read the works of Luther and converted to his teachings. Later, the influence of Calvin led to his change to Calvinism. However, in 1566 he began to preach against the doctrine of the Trinity. At that time, he was opposed by Catholics, Lutherans and Calvinists. Upset by his anti-Trinitarian thinking, King John Sigismund summoned representatives of these three churches to appear before him in a debate with Francis David at the Council of Torda in 1568. David's appeal to reason and call to toleration of differing religious views led the youthful king to declare the Unitarian the victor, after which he openly converted to these beliefs. Then the king issued an Edict of Toleration, which became the first legislation for religious freedom in the history of Europe. The Transylvanian Unitarian Church has continued until the present day. However, after the breakup of the Austro-Hungarian Empire following the first World War and the division of Transylvania between Romania and Hungary, it became necessary to establish two separate national churches.

In 18th-century England, the Racovian Catechism influenced such men as Thomas Biddle, Theophilus Lindsey, Joseph Priestley and a host of others. Theophilus Lindsey, an Anglican clergyman, was advised by his bishop to "Stay and do good works, forgetting this nonsense over creeds," but Lindsey's conscience would not allow this. Consequently, he withdrew from Anglican orders and established the first openly proclaimed Unitarian chapel in England on Essex Street in London. In spite of hostile legislation and persecution, a Unitarian movement has continued in England from that day to this. Many of their churches are the old "Dissenting Chapels" in England and the "Non-subscribing Presbyterian Churches" of Northern Ireland (i.e., non-subscribers to the Westminster Confession of Faith).[1]

This faith was brought to American shores by nonconformists and nonsubscribers among the early settlers, including the Pilgrim founders of Plymouth and among the Puritans of Boston. Later, after Joseph Priestley's home, library, laboratory and church were burned in Liverpool, during the frenzy of the reaction against the French Revolution, Benjamin Franklin urged him to come to Philadelphia where Priestley established the first church in America using the name "Unitarian."

In a reaction against "the gloomy theology of Calvin," John Murray (1741-1815) became a follower of the English Universalist leader James Relly. Depressed after the death of his wife and child, Murray came to America, convinced he could never preach again. However, in 1770 he began preaching on these shores and soon many Universalist churches were organized. Whereas Unitarians were primarily concerned with the quality of life in this world and stressed ethical values and rational thinking, Universalists began with a concern over the nature of life after death, which they believed should be a rational extension of this life, based on ethical considerations binding both God and humanity. This led to the famous quip by Thomas Starr King in the last century: "The Universalist thinks God is too good to damn him, while the Unitarian thinks he is too good for God to damn."[2] Thus, these two denominations had long histories going back into colonial days and earlier European history. Through the passing decades they came to work more closely together and in 1961, the American Unitarian Association and the Universalist Church of America merged into the Unitarian Universalist Association. Whether our local churches call themselves Unitarian or Universalist, they are in fact all Unitarian Universalist societies.[3]

Congregational in polity, stressing individual freedom of belief, the Unitarian Universalist Association is managed by a Board of Trustees, which is answerable to and guided by decisions of the annual General Assembly. In the General Assembly, voting delegates of the local societies convene to oversee the health and activities of the movement. Officers are the President, Moderator, Secretary and Financial Officer elected at this Assembly, which represents more than 1000 societies in the United States and Canada. Geographical districts ease administrative communication, but no official of either district or continental organization can interfere in the conduct of the affairs of the local societies that jealously guard their independent congregational status. These local societies may be called churches, parishes, fellowships, congregations or societies according to local decision. A roster of accredited ministers able to serve local societies is maintained by the Association, and other services in education and congregational assistance are provided. Service within the realm of nearly absolute freedom is the distinguishing hallmark of this Association. This distinction differentiates it from nearly all other churches.

PRINCIPLES AND PURPOSES

Non-creedal and non-doctrinal, there is no agreed-upon statement of beliefs; rather a statement of principles and purposes sums up the faith that binds Unitarian Universalists together. Following several years of intense study in many of our congregations and through a study commission, a revised statement was adopted in final form at the 1984 General Assembly. It reads:

We the member congregations of the Unitarian Universalist Association, convenant to affirm and promote:

The inherent worth and dignity of every person
Justice, equity and compassion in human relations
Acceptance of one another and encouragement to spiritual growth in our congregations
A free and responsible search for truth and meaning
The rights of conscience and the use of the democratic process within our congregations and in society at large
The goal of world community with peace, liberty and justice for all
Respect for the interdependent web of all existence of which we are a part.

The living tradition we share draws from many sources:

Direct experience of that transcending mystery and wonder, affirmed in all cultures, which moves us to a renewal of the spirit and an openness to the forces which create and uphold life
Words and deeds of prophetic women and men which challenge us to confront powers and structures of evil with justice, compassion, and the transforming power of love
Wisdom from the world's religions which inspires us in our ethical and spiritual life
Jewish and Christian teachings which call us to respond to God's love by loving our neighbors as ourselves
Humanistic teachings which counsel us to heed the guidance of reason and the results of science, and warn us against idolatries of the mind and spirit.

Grateful for the religious pluralism which enriches and ennobles our faith, we are inspired to deepen our understanding and expand our vision.
As free congregations we enter into this covenant, promising to one another our mutual trust and support.
The Unitarian Universalist Association shall devote its resources and exercise its corporate powers for religious, educational and humanitarian purposes.
The primary purpose of the Association is to serve the needs of its member congregations, organize new congregations, extend and strengthen Unitarian Universalist institutions, and implement its principles.[4]

RESPONSE TO DEATH

In keeping with all other aspects of his religious practice, the Unitarian

Universalist believer is guided by his own sense of what is proper and what makes sense for him or her. However, being a faith that seeks to be in harmony with science and advancing knowledge, he or she tends, in most cases, to prefer a memorial service to a traditional funeral. Major exceptions occur when it would seem to offer more solace to those grieving, such as older family members or others whose suffering should be taken into account. A memorial service for the average member will seek to recall with gladness the life that was lived and shared with us. The service seeks to maintain an integrity with the life remembered and say something to the gathered group about the meaning of his or her life and to enfold us all in the larger community of sharing and caring for one another. When successfully carried out, the service is an uplifting experience that brightens the gloom caused by the death itself. We usually prefer to have a closed coffin both during and after the service. On many occasions, the coffin is already buried or at the crematorium, where a single bouquet may be the center of focus. Memorial services are often held in the church, a place of uplifting and challenging experiences, but they can also be held in the home, or some place associated with the the life that is being commemorated. Only traditional services are held in funeral homes. Because they are not influenced by the problem of body disposal, memorial services can be held at any time that is convenient. Thus, such a service might be scheduled on a weekend, a holiday, in the evening, or any other time that will allow family and friends from distant places to attend. There are no required religious rituals and family and spiritual leaders plan a service that seems to do justice to the life remembered. Cremation is an increasingly favored method of disposal of the body.[5]

Many of the early Memorial Societies were founded as nonsectarian societies by Unitarian Universalists and these societies combined with the Cooperative Funeral Societies to establish the Continental Association of Funeral and Memorial Societies in Washington, D.C.[6] Many memorial societies continue to have their offices in U.U. churches. While such societies are always nonsectarian, reaching out to serve the larger community, there is a view that every U.U. church can serve as a memorial society to its own members, offering guidance to all, assisting in the prearrangement of services and educating families to the value of memorial services.

A growing percentage of our members prefer cremation because it is quick, easy, uncomplicated, less costly than a traditional funeral and it allows a more convenient scheduling of the memorial service. Cremation is also preferred because it advances the cause of science and service to humanity by making the body available for autopsy and for the donation of organs and tissue, both of which are issues that are important to religious liberals.

As religious liberals, we try to form a compassionate, caring community so that in sharing our deepest insights and offering our personal concern, we support and assist one another. Even our ministers, although usually trained in counseling, can do little more. We have no absolutes from On High that give definitive answers, only loving care for each other. Unitarian Universalism is a non-proselytizing faith that offers its services to all people who turn to us in need. It would be demeaning for us to deny comfort and our services at the time of mourning to anyone who asked help. Accordingly, our services are open to all people and no one will fear religious pressures to join. Questions of previous religious affiliations, rites or services are not asked.

Unitarian Universalists accept a scientific view of life and see life as lived in the here and now rather than in the hereafter. Whether or not Unitarian Universalists are agnostic about the existence of God, they tend to be agnostic about the existence of an afterlife. While some may argue with this position, it is common to hear the comment, "No one has ever returned to tell us about the afterlife." We simply do not know and we question scriptural passages that seem to say otherwise. Because Universalism began with an emphasis on universal salvation of all souls with God, it is strange that we have moved entirely away from this concern to a total emphasis on this life. There was an intermediary step in the progression of Universalist thought — the complete denial of the existence of hell and, of course, of purgatory or limbo. From this emerged the doubt of an afterlife, but not a denial of its existence. We simply admit that we do not know whether or not there is an afterlife.

There are undoubtedly some religious liberals who believe that if there is an afterlife, it will be found in some such mechanism as reincarnation, but to my knowledge, there has been no systematic study on the question of reincarnation. I once did hear a learned lecturer say, "The extent to which the 19th-century Unitarian divines believed in reincarnation has never been fully explored." Personally, I have never found any such evidence.

Unitarian Universalists do not associate either heaven or hell with the afterlife or as places located either in the "heavens above" or the places beneath the earth, as these are concepts not in accord with modern astronomical, cosmological or geological findings. Ralph Waldo Emerson, a Unitarian minister, wrote an *Essay on Compensation,* in which he stressed that the good and evil that people do is compensated for in this life. This is the Unitarian Universalist view, to the extent that there is an agreed-upon position. Reward and punishment are in this life, in the here and now. We have no doctrine that distinguishes our members from the rest of humanity.

We accept the view of creation that is offered by the astronomers and astrophysicists who depict an evolutionary view of the universe created according to the "Big Bang Theory" and expanding until the end of time. We have no special doctrines or theories that differ from what we have learned from the scientists. Our religion relies on the scientific disciplines of all other learned professions. Thus we hold no special views of history or medicine other than those offered by historians and the medical profession. We agree with biologists that the body is composed of material that is organized in living cellular fashion, material that will rapidly decay following death so that bodily resurrection is not possible. According to our understanding, the scientific world rejects bodily resurrection as not feasible and it makes such places as purgatory, limbo, heaven and hell improbable.

In the last century, James Freeman Clarke, in a famous statement of Unitarian views, noted that we believe in "salvation by character," and this statement has often been quoted as summing up the view of salvation as something molded by our own character. This does not project salvation to a future life. Unitarian Universalism is not a salvation religion. Rather, it is an ethical religion concerned with how we live. Nevertheless we are concerned with human destiny, which we see as summed up in a poem by the American poet Edwin Markham, who, though he grew up in a church of a different denomination and was a member of it, chose in the final years of his life to attend a Universalist church in Brooklyn and was buried there. He wrote:

> We men of earth have here the stuff of paradise.
> We have enough.
> We need no other stones to build the stairs on to the Unfulfilled,
> No other ivory for the doors, no other marble for the floors,
> No other cedar for the beam and dome of man's immortal dream.
> Here on the common human way is all the stuff to build a heaven.
> Ours the stuff to build eternity in time.

To us, such a view of the place of humanity in the universe is one calling for courage, challenging us to do and dare and to achieve. Just as there is no pot of gold waiting for us at the end of the rainbow, so there is no reward awaiting us after death except that seen by Socrates as he was about to drink the hemlock:

> If we reflect upon it we may well hope that death is a good. For the state of death is one of two things: either the dead wholly cease to be, and lose all sensation; or, according to the common belief, it is a change and a migration of the soul to another place. And if death is the absence of all sensation, and like the sleep of one whose slumbers are unbroken by any dreams, it will be a wonderful gain.... For then it appears that eternity is nothing more than a single night. But if death is a journey to another place, and the common belief is true, that there are all who have died, what good could be greater than this, my judges? What would you not give to converse with Orpheus and Hesiod and Homer? I am willing to die many times if this be true.[7]

The religious liberal is like Socrates, not rejecting life after death, but skeptical and able to relish the final rest as an unspeakable gain. The important point is to make death a passage that is beautiful and fraught with meaning, recalling a life we were privileged to have known and to share our common humanity with one another in a period of deep crisis, when for a moment, the veil between life and death is rent as we behold reality. When we pray, it is for ourselves and for those who mourn with us. It is part of the therapy of consoling one another. In comforting each other, we truly minister. It is the mystic bond of Albert Schweitzer's "fellowship of those who bear the mark of pain" that creates the living church.

Notes

1. Earl Morse Wilbur, *History of Unitarianism*: Vol. 1, European Backgrounds; 1952, Vol. II, English and American Backgrounds (Cambridge, MA: Harvard University Press); reissued by the Meadville/Lombard Theological School, University of Chicago, and available through the Distribution Center, Unitarian Universalist Association, 25 Beacon Street, Boston, MA 02108.
2. George N. Marshall, *Challenge of a Liberal Faith* (New Canaan, CT, 1980): Chapters 5 and 6 for historical backgrounds; Chapters 7 and 8 for review of beliefs in Unitarian Universalism; also available from the Distribution Center.
3. *Unitarian Universalist Association Yearbook,* an annual directory listing all organizations, societies, religious leaders, bylaws and minutes of the last General Assembly (Boston: Unitarian Universalist Association).
4. *Unitarian Universalist World* (The Journal of the Unitarian Universalist Association); see issue of July 15, 1984 for report of the General Assembly with text of the By-law Revision on Principles and Purposes, p. 10.
5. George N. Marshall, *Facing Death and Grief* (Buffalo: Prometheus Books, 1981), Chapter 6: "The Church and the Clergy"; Chapter 7: "The Service: How Traditional?"
6. Publications of the Continental Association of Funeral and Memorial Societies, 1828 L Street, N.W., Washington, DC 20036.
7. Plato, *Apology*. See also David B. Parke, *Epic of Unitarianism* (Boston: Unitarian Universalist Association, 1981). A collection of primary source material from historical documents throughout the ages for the student of this history. Ernest Cassera, ed., *Universalism in America* (Boston: Unitarian Universalist Association, 1984). A collection of primary source materials on American Universalism.

United Methodist Church

James Ivey Warren, Jr., PhD

BACKGROUND OF THE FAITH

Theodore Roosevelt was reported to have said, "I would rather address a Methodist Church in America.... The Methodists represent the great middle class and are, therefore, the most representative church in America."[1] Indeed, the United Methodist Church has shared the history of the United States of America. Its growth periods reflect national growth. Its character reflects a democratic spirit. Its social involvements parallel national issues and crises. Its activist nature agrees with the national taste for adventure, opportunity and accomplishment. The United Methodist Church has a membership of more than 10 million and local churches (congregations or charges) numbering nearly 40,000. The church is at work in more than 50 foreign countries and its publishing house is the oldest and probably the largest religious publishing concern in the world.[2]

The Methodist movement began in the 18th century in England under the influence of John and Charles Wesley. Social, moral and religious conditions in England during the first half of the 18th century were deplorable. Generally, the wealthy upper class was callous and amoral, the middle class was self-satisfied and the lower class neglected and brutalized. For example, penal conditions were shameful and punishments were so severe that even children could be legally hanged for 160 different offenses, including poaching a rabbit on a gentleman's estate. The child death rate was alarming, with three out of four children of all classes in London dying before the age of five. Harlotry and alcoholism were rampant. William Hogarth's famous picture of this period, "Gin Lane," depicts a gin shop with the inscription, "Drunk for a penny. Dead drunk for two pence. Clean straw for nothing."[3]

The religious life of 18th-century England was also at low ebb. Some ecclesiastic appointments paid handsomely (the Bishop of Durham received the equivalent in today's purchasing power of $500,000 per year), while others barely allowed their parsons to eat and be clothed adequately. Generally, the Church of England, the "Established Church," neglected the hordes of poor persons that were being produced by the Industrial Revolution, and the "dissenting" churches, made up of thrifty, middle-class citizens, saw little need to advocate reform. Theologically, deism and predestination pervaded English thought. God was understood in terms of transcendence and viewed as "an intelligence" who, having created the universe with certain natural laws, refrained from interfering in the world's affairs. Predestination, with its accompanying notion of "the elect," resulted in little effort to reach the multitudes outside the care and edification of the church.

Within such conditions, the Methodist Church was born. A few students at Oxford University, including John Wesley, his brother Charles and George Whitefield, founded an association that contrasted markedly with the times. This group had fixed times for Bible study, prayer, corporate worship and acts of love such as visiting those in prison, teaching the poor and caring for the ill. Their fellow students derisively referred to them as "Bible moths," "Enthusiasts" and "Methodists." They were called Bible moths because of their study of scripture, Enthusiasts because of their zeal for worship and service to others, and Methodists because of their methodical and disciplined practices. John Wesley, the leader of the group, accepted the last term and referred to himself and his colleagues as "the people called Methodists." The two Wesleys, Whitefield and others began to preach to the masses of the unchurched people of England. Albert Bailey said of John Wesley: "Until the days of the airplane he traveled more miles, a quarter of a million, mostly on horseback; he preached more sermons, upward of forty thousand; he converted more people, at least one hundred thousand, than any person who ever lived."[4]

As people responded to these "Methodist" ministries, they were organized into bands, classes and societies for study, mutual encouragement and admonition. Wesley did not intend to form a new church, but historical circumstances and the needs of the populace led to the organization of the Methodist Church in England. From England, the Methodist Church spread to Ireland and to the United States, which was still an English colony.

> Methodism was especially adapted to American life...itinerant preachers served the people under conditions where a settled ministry was not feasible. They sought out the scattered homes, followed the tide of migration as it moved West, preached the Gospel, organized societies, established "preaching places," and formed these into "circuits." Thus by the close of the American Revolution the Methodists numbered some 15,000 members and 80 preachers.[5]

Among the German-speaking colonists in America, there were two churches whose theology, zeal and practice were very much akin to those of the

Methodists. One group, led by William Otterbein and Martin Boehm, formed the United Brethren Church in 1800. The second group was led by Jacob Albright, and in 1816, became the Evangelical Association. After a division and a subsequent reunion in 1922, this group became known as the Evangelical Church. In 1946, the two German-speaking bodies merged to become the Church of the United Brethren in Christ. In 1968, the German-speaking Evangelical United Brethren merged with the English-speaking Methodist Church to form the United Methodist Church.[6]

GENERAL BELIEFS AND PRACTICES

Two words may be used to characterize United Methodists' beliefs and practices — mainstream and pluralistic. Their theology traces back to the historic confessions of faith and the United Methodist Church is one of the few major denominations that did not develop a creed of its own. It is probable that most United Methodist congregations use the Apostles' Creed either every Sunday or more times than any other confession of faith. This being true, United Methodists affirm the historic, orthodox elements of belief: God as creator, Christ as Savior and example (true God and true man), the Holy Spirit as guide and source of power, the church as God's agency and as the communion of saints, the resurrection of the body and the life everlasting. Indeed, the Methodist movement began not to establish a new doctrine, but to recover and recall the church to its historic understanding of God as transcendent and imminent, of human beings as free and responsible persons and of the necessity for Christians to pursue lives of holiness.

Within this comprehensive understanding of Christian belief, however, Methodists emphasized certain elements. Arminianism, the belief that people possess free will that allows them to respond to God's grace, was a major Methodist stance. This stance arose largely in opposition to the stern decrees of Calvinistic thought which contended that God preordained some persons to be elect, to be chosen for heaven, and other persons to be consigned to hell. This emphasis of Methodist evangelicalism is most apparent in John Wesley's sermons and in Charles Wesley's hymns. Hymn after hymn concludes with a call or a plea for the sinner to respond. For example, note these lines in Charles Wesley's hymn, "Where Shall My Wandering Soul Begin?"

> Come, my guilty brethren, come,
> Groaning beneath your load of sin!
> His bleeding heart shall make you room;
> His open side shall take you in.
> He calls you now, invites you home:
> Come, O my guilty brethren, come.[7]

A second emphasis of Wesleyan theology is experiential faith. One *knows* one's sins forgiven. One "feels" Christ's blood applied for one's self. Again Charles Wesley gives this emphasis poetic expression:

> How can a sinner know his sins on earth forgiven?
> How can my precious Savior show my name inscribed in heaven?
> What we have felt and seen with confidence we tell;
> And publish to the sons of men the signs infallible.[8]

Not only is this assurance, but it is personal to the point of being overwhelming and mysterious.

> And can it be that I should gain
> An interest in the Savior's blood?
> Died He for me who caused His pain?
> For me who Him to death pursued?
> Amazing love! How can it be
> That Thou, my Lord, shouldst die for me?
>
> 'Tis mystery all! Immortal dies
> Who can explore His strange design?
> In vain the first-born seraph tries
> To sound the depths of love divine.
> 'Tis mercy all! Let earth adore.
> Let angel minds inquire no more.[9]

A third Methodist emphasis relates to the "saved" life. In Wesleyan thought, salvation is being saved from *sin* and from *the power of sin.* Another way of saying this is to speak of the Christian life as the holy or sanctified life. Methodists believe not only in forgiveness of sin but in God's gift to us of power over sin. Charles Wesley's poem stating that Jesus "breaks the power of cancelled sin" refers to Christ's victory over *ingrained* sin. So Methodist belief takes seriously the admonition to "go on to perfection."

Finally, United Methodists emphasize the social dimension of the Christian life. From the Holy Club's involvement with the poor, uneducated and imprisoned to the development of the United Methodist Church's statement of the Social Creed, United Methodists have seen their charge as "to serve the present age, my calling to fulfill; O may it all my powers engage to do my Master's will."[10]

The basic beliefs and emphases of United Methodists are contained in two historical documents: "The Articles of Religion of the Methodist Church" and "The Confession of Faith of the Evangelical United Brethren Church." "The Articles of Religion" number 25 and are an abridgement made by John Wesley of the 39 Articles of Faith of the Anglican Church. "The Confession of Faith" is a similar statement, consisting of 26 articles and is taken from the Discipline of the Evangelical United Brethren Church.

Pluralism is the second major characteristic of United Methodist belief and practice. Within the broad mainstream of faith and life there is ample allowance for diversity and there is wide acceptance of the dictum: "As to all opinions which do not strike at the root of Christianity, we think and let think" (Discipline, paragraph 67, p. 40). Moreover, this "root of Christianity" is determined by a broadly based process that uses four sources: scripture, tradition, experience and reason. "This living core...stands revealed in scripture, illumined by tradition, vivified in personal experience and confirmed by reason."[11]

In regard to ecclesiastical practices, United Methodists form a bridge between "high" church rituals and liturgies and "low" church emphasis on spontaneous, less formal worship services. John Wesley clearly favored "order" and thought highly of the historic forms of worship. He desired that the people called Methodists partake of the sacrament of Holy Communion at least weekly. He stated that when he first began outdoor preaching, he found it abhorrent. However, Wesley's pragmatic nature led him to see the value of departing from and adapting orderly, traditional forms in order to reach unchurched persons. The United Methodist Church today continues this breadth of practice. It not only allows one to think and let think; it allows different local churches to "practice and let practice." Article 22, on "Rites and Ceremonies of Churches, states:

> It is not necessary that rites and ceremonies should in all places be the same, or exactly alike; for they have been always different, and may be changed according to the diversity of countries, times, and men's manners, so that nothing be ordained against God's word.[12]

DEATH AND LIFE AFTER DEATH

Most of the creedal statements used by United Methodists affirm the reality of death and eternal life. The Apostles' Creed states, "I believe in...the resurrection of the body and the life everlasting." The Nicene Creed concludes with, "and I look for the resurrection of the dead and the life of the world to come." The Korean Creed asserts, "we believe in the final triumph of righteousness and in the life everlasting." A modern statement speaks of "our deliverance from sin and death," and of "the Kingdom of God coming upon earth." All of these affirmations attest to the reality of life after death but do not describe it in fine detail.[13]

Two points stand out and call for notice. First the "resurrection" is the resurrection of the *dead*. Christian faith does not deny, avoid or prevent death. Death remains real and inescapable. Rather, the Christian faith proclaims triumph over death. Resurrection is not to be confused with "immortality" (which asserts that we possess some part of us that never dies) or with a "dualism" (that exalts "soul" and denigrates "body"). Instead, resurrection of the dead presupposes the reality of death.

The section on worship developed by the Board of Discipleship of the United Methodist Church has suggested a "service of death and resurrection" with an accompanying theological rationale and commentary. In its commentary it urges its readers to confront bereaved persons with the reality of the body of the deceased, arguing that a "genuinely felt admission of the reality of death, in so far as a bereaved person is capable, best fosters spiritual and emotional health." It points out that the use of euphemisms for death such as "asleep" or "resting" may reflect a tendency to deny the reality of death.[14]

It is even more important, however, to affirm the reality of resurrection. Resurrection is God's action, not ours. It refers to new life and the reorientation of the quality of life. In a sense, the new quality of life begins before death with a spiritual birth, but life after death is "marked by disjunction, renewal, and reorientation of life of a quality incommensurate with what we may know or are able to imagine.[15]

A question frequently asked is, "Will we know each other in the life after death?" The answer most United Methodists give is yes. This is, in part, what is meant by "the resurrection of the body." Consider two expressions. First, the section on worship's report contends that "body" refers to "the total matrix of personality." The second expression comes from the pen of Costen J. Harrel, late bishop of the United Methodist Church:

> Of some things we may be confident. We know that because God loves us as individuals, our personal identity will not be lost in the spirit world. We shall know and be known, we shall love and be loved; we are integral persons whom on earth he called to be his sons and daughters. The New Testament knows no other kind of immortality. And because those with whom we walked on earth shall, like ourselves, continue their personal existence, we know that they will be known by us, and we shall see again "those angel faces smile which we have loved long since and lost a while."[16]

A third expression comes from Bishop Mack B. Stokes, who asserts even more strongly:

> Eternal life is one of peace and joy because it brings together the redeemed souls into a perfect fellowship. Many people ask will we recognize our friends in heaven? The answer is that we shall not only recognize them, we shall see how truly wonderful they are and we shall more perfectly love them.[17]

This position regarding death and life after death is very much in the mainstream of orthodox Christian belief. However, there are three important ideas that should be noted:

1. It is *resurrection, new life* that is offered. "Immortality is a negative assertion that merely claims the soul does not die. Resurrection is a positive assertion: the person is raised to life."[18]
2. It is resurrection of the *person*, body and spirit, the recognizable and lovable person.
3. Resurrection is a present reality (a new life of grace conquering the enemy, sin) *and* a future reality (eternal life conquering the enemy, death).

The genius of United Methodism, as we have noted, is not distinctive faith assertions but the enthusiastic attempt to express its belief in Christian life and worship. Therefore, it is appropriate and important for one to examine the ministries of the United Methodist Church at the time of death and to note how beliefs are expressed in the services of worship of the church.

Four terms can help us understand the ministries of the church at the time of death: death, bereavement, grief and mourning. Death refers to the physical event in someone's personal history. Bereavement is loss experienced by friends of the deceased and grief is the emotion caused by death. "Mourning is the spiritual, psychological, even moral process of coping with and working through grief, of regaining inner wholeness and balance."[19]

Persons' attitudes toward and responses to death vary and call for different kinds of ministries. Different people respond differently to the inevitability of their own death, responding with denial, avoidance, fear and/or superstition. So it is that the church in its ministries must teach the reality of death, refute unfounded notions such as reincarnation, and make clear the Christian hope and its basis.

Similarly, bereavement expresses itself in varying responses. Some bereaved persons feel anger, questioning, bewilderment, guilt and/or relief. For example, in cases of untimely death as might occur in an accident or to a child, bereaved persons may become angry with God or may question God's goodness. A close relative may feel guilt, full of self-blame for not spending more time with or giving more help to the deceased while he or she was alive. Even when responses are not so pronounced, bereaved persons express some degree of grief. Grief may express itself as a sense of loss, in a feeling of emptiness or, as C.S. Lewis observed, in a persistent physical and mental fatigue. In dealing with bereavement and guilt, Christian ministries require sensitivities to human need, awareness of cultural practices and the insights of psychology. Help needs to come not only from the pastoral leadership but from church members and neighbors. Because one's bereavement and grief are occasioned by the loss of a friend and because the felt absence or questioning of God is occasioned by the death of a loved one, it is likely that comfort and renewed faith must be mediated also by a close friend or relative.

Mourning is a necessary process of working through one's grief and may take from six weeks to several months. This process should have several results: (1) a letting go of the dependence that one had on the deceased, (2) an ability to distinguish those concerns that are permanent from those that are transient, (3) an awareness of one's sins of omission and commission, and (4) an awareness of one's love for the deceased and the love of one's friends.[20]

However, Christian mourning is more than simply discovering one's inner strengths and the support of friends. Christian mourning is "an experience of divine grace" and "locates the source of comfort in God." We do not simply comfort ourselves. Nor are we simply comforted by others. We find God's comfort through the efforts of our friends and ourselves. Leslie Weatherhead tells of an occasion when he visited a home where a young person had died. A neighbor was present comforting the mother of the child who was her friend, but the bereaved mother addressed Dr. Weatherhead with anger and questioning. "Padre," she said, "you've often preached about the everlasting arms. Where are those arms now?" Weatherhead pointed to the neighbor whose presence and faith were strengthening the mother and replied, "God's arms are working through her arms."

To summarize, there are several Christian ministries at the occasion of death in which all Christians can participate. First, we can confront the bereaved persons with the reality of death by refusing to use euphemisms that deny it, words like "asleep" or "resting." "A genuinely felt admission of the reality of death, insofar as a bereaved person is capable, best fosters spiritual and emotional health."[21] Second, we can offer supportive presence and action. In many cultural settings persons bring food, send flowers, write messages of sympathy and visit in the homes where death has occurred. These acts are "Christian graces of faith, hope and love...visibly acted out."[22] Third, Christians can affirm their faith and use the occasion of death "to reexamine their life in Christ, to repent, to renew their faith and to rededicate themselves to service in Christ's name."[23]

THE FUNERAL SERVICE

The funeral service is: (1) a corporate act of Christian worship that is (2) comforting and confrontational, (3) that focuses on Christ's victory over sin and death, and (4) that emphasizes committal. As an act of Christian worship, the service should center around Christian themes, use Christian symbols and be a corporate act. Where possible the service should be held in the church building where the deceased worshipped. This setting, itself, expresses Christian themes and points to the continuity between one's participation in Christ's victory over sin and one's participation in Christ's victory over death. It is an ideal setting to recall God's goodness in creation and redemption and to remember the deceased's participation in the Christian faith. If the service takes place in a home or a funeral home, then appropriate Christian symbols should be present, above all the cross to point to God's light and guidance. The funeral service is not a private affair. It is a corporate act of the people of

God, where God is affirmed as worthy of praise and where God is thanked for the life and the witness of the deceased.

The proclamation during the service speaks to the persons assembled in terms of confrontation and comfort. The people are confronted with the reality of their own death, sin and dependence on God. They are challenged to examine their own faith and hope. The people are also comforted and made strong. Christian comfort goes beyond a sentimentally transient level and emphasizes the mercy and power of God's act in Christ as the basis for one's hope and peace. So it is that worshippers are comforted in their grief over the death of a loved one and confronted with their own hope in Christ.

It is appropriate to name the deceased and to praise God for God's love and goodness to him or her and to thank God for that person's life, service and witness. But the central thrust of the proclamation should not be a eulogy to the deceased. Rather, thoughts of and prayers for the deceased should be in the context of Christian worship and his or her death should be viewed as the occasion to affirm one's faith, to recall God's goodness and to express one's gratitude to God for the life and witness of the deceased. "Understood as 'tribute' or 'appreciation,' eulogy is essentially thankfulness, and surely thankfulness to God (even when verbally addressed to people) is not out of place in proclamation."[24]

Finally, the Christian funeral service deals with committal of the physical remains. United Methodists see the importance of committing the deceased's body (or ashes in the case of cremation) to the earth or sea. This part of the service usually takes place at the burial site and recognizes that "the body has been the temple of the Spirit of God. It has been valued and loved. When it no longer serves its purpose in its old form, it is returned to the elements from which it came, with thanksgiving to God for the gift of its wonder."[25]

Second, the service commits the deceased person to God's keeping. Building on the words of Jesus on the cross when he committed His spirit to the Father, United Methodists commit the deceased person to God. Such committal also points to belief in the resurrection of the person. As Bishop Stokes reminded us, eternal life brings the redeemed together in perfect fellowship where we know and love each other even more perfectly. So the funeral service commits the deceased to God and to the "Church triumphant." Further the committal service attests to the truth that "God's love does not cease being the same love after death as it was before."[26] A third sense of committal is present in this service because the service of committal gives one the opportunity to commit oneself to God, to recall that our hope is in God.

SOME SPECIFIC QUESTIONS RELATED TO BELIEF AND PRACTICE

Such then are the United Methodist's general beliefs and practices relating to death and life after death, but there remain some specific questions that deserve to be addressed. Some of these questions concern belief about life after death, while others relate to acceptable practices and ethical stances.

First let us look at some frequently asked questions concerning United Methodist beliefs. Do United Methodists believe in heaven and hell? The pluralism that one finds generally in the United Methodist Church is found specifically in the belief about heaven and hell. The vast majority of United Methodists believe in life after death, that "heaven" is being in the presence of God and that "hell" is separation from God. Within this broad affirmation, beliefs vary among individuals and groups. Some United Methodists interpret some parts of scripture literally and describe heaven as a place where streets are paved with gold and where prosperity abounds as milk and honey. They also view hell in specific, concrete images as a place where torment is present in the form of fire and worms. Other United Methodists understand such language as pictorial and suggestive. They interpret heaven as a place or state of being where fulfillment of persons and communion with God and others are realized. Hell is frequently seen as the absence of such fulfillment and communion. This latter group, while believing in heaven and hell, are not greatly concerned about the specifics, about the "temperature of hell or the furniture of heaven."

Most United Methodists affirm the doctrine of salvation by grace through faith. Persons are "saved" by God's grace through Jesus Christ from sin to holiness and from eternal death to eternal life. This salvation has three tenses. We *have been saved* by God's act in Christ. We *are being saved* by God's continuing grace and our response. We *shall be saved* in the consummation of God's love in the fuller realization of God's kingdom after death. United Methodists affirm quite readily that all who respond in faith and obedience to God's act in love in Jesus Christ are saved, but they are less ready to assert that those who do not respond positively go to hell. Some see this position as a natural corollary to the first position, but others are content to leave the ultimate decision about the unresponsive to God's judgment. However, the missionary and evangelistic fervor typical of United Methodists at least points to the "fear" that the unresponsive may not be saved. What happens to those who have never been confronted with God's grace in Jesus Christ is even less seen from a judgmental position. Generally, United Methodists profess to "know" that God saves through faith in Christ and, therefore, they seek to share this good news. This is the practical result of this belief. The ultimate place of those of other faiths is seen as somewhat speculative and consigned to the area of God's judgment.

Is the body or spirit resurrected after death and will the resurrected know each other? We have already seen that the basic belief in the "resurrection of the body" points to the resurrection of the person in a way that has continuity with earthly life. Moreover, United Methodists believe that we shall not only recognize each other in that fulfillment, but that the communion we partake of on earth shall be complete and full in the "Church triumphant."

All praise to our redeeming Lord who joins us by his grace,
And bids us, each to each restored, together seek his face.

And if our fellowship below in Jesus be so sweet,
What height of rapture shall we know when round his throne we meet?[27]

One further doctrinal area deserves attention. What about the second coming, a final judgment and purgatory? United Methodists strongly affirm the notion of judgment and call (even plead) for persons to respond to God's grace. For some persons, this judgment is coincidental with response, i.e., heaven begins with one's saying yes to God's grace in Jesus Christ and continues after death; hell is separation from God, both presently and eternally. Other persons believe that there will be one specific "day" when Christ will come again, judge all peoples, welcoming some to heaven and assigning others to hell. Generally, United Methodists do not believe in purgatory, because they fear it smacks of "salvation by works" and blunts the importance of decision and response to God's grace in this life. Indeed, Article 13 of The Articles of Religion of the United Methodist Church (which have been seen as theologically binding since 1784) states: "The...doctrine concerning purgatory...is a fond thing, vainly invented, and grounded upon no warrant of Scripture, but repugnant to the Word of God."[28]

Other matters of United Methodist practice that merit specific attention are euthanasia, participation in funeral services of non-Christians or unchurched persons, local/cultural practices regarding death and funerals, and the participation of children in funeral services and related questioning.

United Methodists view life positively. Persons are seen not as a duality of body and spirit, but as a unity. Therefore, Christian responsibility includes care for and service to bodily as well as spiritual aspects of human life. We believe that persons should have all possible opportunity to maximize life and that physical death is a part of life that calls for ministry to persons approaching death and to friends of those who are dying or have died. Euthanasia means "good death" and United Methodists are committed to helping persons have good, positive lives and good, positive deaths. The 1980 United Methodist Discipline addressed the issue of death with dignity and concluded:

> We applaud medical science for efforts to prevent disease and illness and for advances in treatment that extend the meaningful life of human beings. At the same time, in the varying stages of death and life that medical science has occasioned, we recognize the agonizing personal and moral decisions faced by the dying, their physicians, their families, and their friends. Therefore, we assert the right of every person to die in dignity, with loving personal care and without efforts to prolong terminal illnesses merely because the technology is available to do so.[29]

How shall the United Methodist participate in the funeral of someone who was unchurched or was a non-Christian? The task force on worship of the United Methodist Board of Discipleship judges that the Christian position is that one is "free to minister as may be judged appropriate according to circumstances."[30] The task force suggests that such services should be rendered *as a Christian* and that the Gospel should be spoken in ways that respect the integrity of the hearers. Moreover, it is appropriate to share leadership at funeral services with persons of other religious communities so long as each can witness with integrity and so long as each can respect the faith of the others.[31]

How important are local practices in the ministries and worship associated with death and resurrection? Generally, the pluralistic nature and open stance of the United Methodist Church allows and encourages meaningful local practices *when such practices are not incompatible with Christian orthodox beliefs*. Take the example of the viewing of the body before the worship service or before interment. This custom is not prohibited and, indeed, may help persons confront the reality of death. However, neither the body nor the coffin should be the center of the funeral service.

Should the Christian faith concerning death and resurrection be communicated to children and should children be permitted or encouraged to attend Christian funerals? Generally, United Methodists answer these questions affirmatively. Children are greatly affected by the death of a loved one, but they are more likely to be affected negatively by not being allowed to attend funeral services than by being allowed to attend them and to ask questions concerning death and resurrection. Children should be allowed to participate at their own level of understanding and should not be deceived about the reality of death. More important, children should be exposed to the Christian understanding of eternal life. "From the funeral experience, children can learn that their own life is valued and valuable and that it is in the hands of a loving God."[32] May all of us so learn!

Notes

1. J. Paul Williams, *What Americans Believe and How They Worship* (New York: Harper and Brothers, 1952), p. 274.
2. Frank S. Mead, *Handbook of Denominations* (Nashville: Abingdon Press, 1980), pp. 177-180.
3. Albert Edmond Bailey, *The Gospel in Hymns: Background and Interpretations* (New York: Charles Scribner's Sons, 1950), pp. 74-76.
4. Ibid., p. 77
5. *The Book of Discipline of the United Methodist Church* (Nashville: The United Methodist Publishing House, 1980), p. 9.
6. Ibid., pp. 7-18.
7. *The Book of Hymns* (Nashville: The Methodist Publishing House, 1966), Hymn 528.

8. Ibid., Hymn 114.
9. Ibid., Hymn 527.
10. Ibid., Hymn 150.
11. *The Book of Discipline*, paragraph 67, p. 41.
12. Ibid., paragraph 68, p. 61.
13. *The Book of Hymns,* Numbers 738-741.
14. *A Service of Death and Resurrection* (Nashville: Abingdon Press, 1979), p. 22.
15. Ibid., p. 15.
16. Costen J. Harrell, *Christian Affirmations* (Nashville: Abingdon Press, 1961), p. 115.
17. Mack B. Stokes, *Major Methodist Beliefs* (Nashville: Abingdon Press, 1956), p. 86.
18. *A Service of Death and Resurrection*, p. 15.
19. Ibid., p. 17.
20. Ibid., p. 20ff.
21. Ibid., p. 22.
22. Ibid., p. 23.
23. Ibid.
24. Ibid., p. 60.
25. Ibid., p. 27ff.
26. Ibid., p. 29.
27. *The Book of Hymns,* Hymn 301.
28. *The Book of Discipline*, paragraph 68, p. 58.
29. Ibid., paragraph. 71, p. 91.
30. *A Service of Death and Resurrection*, p. 37.
31. Ibid., p. 37ff.
32. Ibid., p. 42.

Unity

Rev. James Gaither, MA

BACKGROUND OF THE FAITH

Unity was one of the religious movements that emerged in 19th-century America in the midst of a new wave of knowledge, optimism and religious experimentation. Western culture became conscious of Asian religion in the 19th century when Max Muller[1] and other Western scholars translated and published texts from Asian scriptures, thereby generating an interest in Eastern ideas among Western intellectuals.[2] A wider religious perspective began to open for some Westerners at this time as they tried to find common ground between East and West.[3] Others began to adopt Eastern perspectives and concepts. Ralph Waldo Emerson and his circle of Transcendentalists used terms and ideas from the East to express their philosophy.[4] Madame Blavatsky adopted Eastern concepts for her Theosophy movement.[5] Westerners began to practice Yoga techniques and explain conditions in terms of "karma" and "reincarnation."

During the 19th century there were exciting advances in science that captured the popular imagination. "Science fiction" became a distinct genre of literature.[6] Controversies about Darwin's theories forced religious leaders to either dig in and resist the march of science or rethink their ways of talking about creation and the nature of humanity.[7] The introduction of hypnosis and the development of modern psychological theories suggested new explanations of human experience in terms of the unconscious or subconscious mind.[8] The development of technology and evolution theory combined in the public mind to create an optimistic expectation of inevitable and perhaps divinely ordained human progress toward an earthly paradise.[9]

Along with Christian Science and New Thought, early proponents of the Unity movement believed in cure of physical illness through mental disciplines and prayer. What in previous centuries had been called "answered prayer" or "faith healing" was now spoken of as a "science of mind," "spiritual science," "divine science," and "practical metaphysics." Some of the early practitioners and writers in this movement adopted not only the language of science, but also language and concepts from Western secular philosophy and Eastern religions.[10] However, the scientific explanations and Eastern ideas were auxiliary to a still predominantly Christian perspective.[11]

Historically, Unity can be seen as part of the broader Protestant tradition that includes the Society of Friends, the Unitarian-Universalists and Christian Science. Those groups are not in the mainstream of Lutheran-Calvinist-Wesleyan theology, yet they clearly emerged from Protestant roots and carry some semblance of the Protestant tradition in their monotheism, ways of worship, moral perspectives and veneration of Jesus. Unity has teachings similar to Christian Science, but with a greater diversity of religious beliefs among its followers. Like the Society of Friends, Unity emphasizes the "inner light" and communing with Spirit in silence. Like the Unitarian-Universalists, Unity believes in rational thinking about religion, but Unity also places emphasis on contemplation of the spiritual meaning of the Bible.

Unity was founded by a married couple, Charles and Myrtle Fillmore, in Kansas City, Missouri. Charles and Myrtle shared a common interest in literature, Transcendentalism and the exploration of spirituality. When Myrtle became seriously ill with tuberculosis, the Fillmores began to investigate Christian Science and New Thought in the hope that spiritual science could produce a cure where medical science had failed. The turning point for Myrtle was a lecture in 1886, at which she was deeply moved by the idea, "I am a child of God and I cannot inherit sickness." Myrtle had been conditioned by her parents and other relatives to believe that she was genetically susceptible to tuberculosis. Adopting the viewpoint that her true inheritance was from God, she rejected the belief that she could inherit illness and began to systematically pray and meditate for healing. She began to focus her attention on different points in her body and affirm the presence of God's life and wholeness. Her health improved significantly and she began to pray for neighbors and acquaintances. As some of these neighbors experienced healing, Myrtle's prayer work and spiritual teachings began to attract more and more attention in the community.

Charles Fillmore had originally been somewhat skeptical about this idea of a spiritual science of healing, but as he saw the results in Myrtle's life and in the lives of others, he began to investigate. His search no doubt was partly motivated by his own ailments which included a hip disease, a shriveled leg and accompanying chronic pain. He studied books on Mind Cure, Christian Science, Theosophy, Spiritualism and related subjects. After attending lectures by prominent metaphysical healers of the time, he found that there were common points among the different teachers, but he also noticed a range of theoretical ideas that was bewildering. He finally decided that if he was spirit and God was spirit, there must be some way to communicate. So in an attempt to receive an experience of God, Charles Fillmore began to practice sitting in the silence, using all the prayer and meditation practices he could find. As a result of his prayer discipline, Charles began to experience greater peace, relief from his chronic pain and a feeling of energy. His leg also began to grow stronger and eventually it filled out and grew and he was able to discard his leg brace. More importantly to him, Charles began to receive spiritual guidance in his dreams and inspiration to teach and preach the Gospel of Jesus Christ from a metaphysical and scientific perspective.

Together the Fillmores began to publish their ideas in a magazine. At various times in the over 100 years since it began, Unity has published magazines on spirituality for business people, children and the general public. The Fillmores started a prayer group that eventually grew into what is now known as Silent Unity. Silent Unity has received thousands, if not millions of letters over the years, testifying to healing, greater prosperity, improved relationships and other answered prayers. The Fillmores started a school to teach the Bible, prayer and metaphysics that eventually became a center of spiritual education for Unity students and for ministerial candidates. The Fillmores also held worship services and their students also started "Unity Centers" for prayer, education, and worship. The centers organized and in 1965 the Association of Unity Churches was formed.[12]

Today, Unity is a global movement of prayer and spiritual education encompassing ministries on every continent. The Unity movement has two guiding institutions: Unity School of Christianity and the Association of Unity Churches. Unity School of Christianity was the original headquarters and it is located in Unity Village, Missouri, near Kansas City. The Association of Unity Churches was formed as an organization to develop and serve Unity ministries. Unity School still has a widespread ministry of prayer, publishing, spiritual retreats and education. The Association and Unity School work together on some projects such as ministerial education and they function separately in other ways.[13]

Unity School's ministries include Silent Unity, a 24-hour-a-day prayer ministry that receives millions of prayer requests from around the world; a daily prayer and devotional magazine, *Daily Word*, which has millions of readers around the world; and other publications for Unity students, including *Unity Magazine*, Unity books and cassettes.[14] Unity has theological teachings, but has found that answered prayer has nothing to do with a person's theology — love and faith in God are the significant factors in prayer. Hence, Unity's prayer ministry and *Daily Word* serve people of all religions as well as those with no current religious affiliation. Adult spiritual education, ministerial education and spiritual retreats are also services provided at Unity Village.

Unity churches and spiritual education centers are organized and served by the Association of Unity Churches in Lee's Summit, Missouri, which is also near Kansas City. The Association is involved in ministerial and adult spiritual education. The Association licenses and ordains ministers and coordinates the placement of ministers in Unity churches and centers. The Association also provides a variety of services to its members, including youth education materials and church management assistance. Unity continues to grow and increase services and ministries around the world.

UNITY TEACHINGS

Unity students refer to our teachings as "Practical Christianity," "spiritual science," "practical metaphysics," and "Truth." There are no official dogmas or creeds to which members of Unity churches are required to subscribe. There are, however, a few basic affirmations that almost all Unity people accept as part of their spiritual beliefs. It is partly these shared beliefs that bind Unity people into the communities known as Unity churches and centers. Listed below are the most basic of these shared beliefs:[15]

There is only one presence and one power in the universe — God the good.
We believe there is ultimately only one Reality — God — and that God is good. The many forms we perceive around us derive their substance, life and intelligence from God, Who is Spirit and Mind. Appearances of separation, lack, limitation or absence of good are illusionary and are based on misperception or false belief. We believe that God has given free will to humanity so that we may learn, grow and fulfill our potential. Nevertheless, although we have freedom, God is ever present within us and around us, as ultimate reality and guiding principle. We believe that our problems are caused by using our freedom in counterproductive ways or that they are challenges that stretch us and help us become the best that we can be.

There is divinity in humanity.
Because we believe God is omnipresent, we believe God is in all human beings. Our main purpose in life is to become more fully aware of the divine within us. God in us is substance, life, intelligence, creativity, love, wisdom, wholeness, peace, joy and other aspects of the one Spirit. As we become conscious of and express the divine attributes within us, we fulfill the truth affirmed by Jesus, "You are the light of the world." We believe that Jesus Christ, in his life and teachings, is the great exemplar of what it means to be a child of God and we seek to follow his example. We also believe that other great spiritual teachers in other cultures and religions are expressions of that same divinity. As we honor those examples of spirituality, we can learn from them as well.

Universal love and forgiveness are essential and great ideals.
As we read of great spiritual teachers such as Jesus, Buddha, Lao-tzu and the saints of all religions, we see that love was their highest ideal. Expressing our divinity means, in part, expressing benevolence and forgiveness to all. We believe that it is more important to love than to convert others to our viewpoint.

There is truth in all religions and in science.
To the extent that any religion teaches love, faith in God or reverence for truth, we believe there is valuable truth in that religion. To the extent that the scientific method reveres and reveals truths about the nature of creation, it reveals something of the nature of the Creator, increases our knowledge and dominion and is of value to us.

We can receive guidance, inspiration, healing, prosperity, harmonious relationships, peace and joy through prayer.
Unity has specific teachings about how to pray effectively, while honoring all spiritual paths that seek God. Unity emphasizes using affirmative statements of the presence, power and goodness of God rather than begging or bargaining with God to do us special favors. Unity emphasizes withdrawing attention and mental energy from apparent problems and following the advice of Jesus to "be not anxious" and "fear not." Unity emphasizes "sitting in the Silence," mental stillness, receptivity and trust in prayer, rather than a constant stream of words. Unity also encourages a positive use of imagination and the development of spiritual qualities such as love, faith, understanding and wisdom. Unity students have found that these approaches to prayer improve the quality of their lives and bring healing to body and soul.

We believe that the mind can change physical conditions.
We believe that God is Spirit, Universal Mind, the source of physical creation. We believe that Universal Mind is the origin of the physical world and that we, as beings with minds, are one with that Universal Mind. Therefore, we believe that we can use our minds, in alignment with Divine Mind, to change physical conditions. We believe that Universal Mind has laws of operation, as when Jesus taught, "whatever you ask for in prayer, believe that you have received it and it will be yours" (Mark 11:24).

We believe in universal salvation.
We believe that God is love, that our Father "makes his sun rise on the evil and on the good and sends rain on the just and on the unjust.... You, therefore, must be perfect, as your heavenly Father is perfect." We believe that a God who is a loving Father would not send any of his beloved children to a place of everlasting torment for the mistakes of one brief lifetime or for not believing in some theological doctrine. We believe that "it is your Father's good pleasure to give you the kingdom" (Luke 12:32). We realize there are passages in the Bible that can be interpreted as indicating everlasting hell for sinners, but we hold that other passages, such as those just mentioned,[16] indicate a God who can find and who wills to find a way to bring all into the kingdom of heaven. Unity people are people whose minds, hearts and spirits tell them that the true doctrine of Christ is universal salvation. We take it that passages indicating otherwise either do not accurately reflect the message of Christ Jesus or were intended to be metaphors for the process of entering the

mystical kingdom of God.[17]

DEATH AND THE AFTERLIFE

If Unity does not believe in a literal hell, how do we interpret the passages in scripture that refer to hell? Since "hell" in the English New Testament is usually a translation of *Gehenna* and because *Gehenna* was a garbage dump outside of Jerusalem, we believe it is appropriate to interpret passages with *Gehenna* allegorically.[18] Some passages that have "hell" in English are translations of the word *Hades*,[19] which is a Greek word for "unseen" and the concept of the realm of souls in the afterlife; it does not inherently indicate a place of torment.

We take it that "hell" is a metaphor for internal torment that occurs when we feel alienated or separated from God. Because we believe that God is omnipresent, we do not believe anyone is ever really separated from God. However, we recognize that people can have the false belief that they are separated from God and we hold it is that belief that makes them feel like they are in hell. So, from Unity's perspective, anyone can be in "hell," but nobody has to stay there![20]

Unity teaches that every day is a "day of judgment" in the sense that every day we experience consequences of our judgments and the actions based on those judgments. We do not teach that there is some final day at the end of time in which all souls who have ever lived are judged for their lives. Many Unity people believe that there is a transition from this world, through death, to another realm. Many Unity people believe part of the transition is a review of one's life, during which the lessons of that life become clear to the soul. The experience, if it occurs, could also be interpreted as a "day of judgment."[21] Unity teachings on universal salvation, judgment, reincarnation and resurrection are best understood when considered as parts of a whole process. At many points, Unity's teachings on these subjects are very similar to those of Origen (185-254 C.E.), the first Christian systematic theologian. Even though Origen was declared to be a heretic by a Church Council in the 6th century,[22] it is well to keep in mind that any Christian denomination today is considered heretical by the standards of some other denomination. What is most important is what is true, which does not necessarily correspond to what a group of church leaders voted or decreed in some particular era of history.

There is a wide range of beliefs about death and the afterlife among Unity people, because Unity has no official dogma or creed on that subject. What follows are the beliefs of the founders of Unity, Charles and Myrtle Fillmore. Their views are not considered binding on Unity people, but are nonetheless regarded with respect.

The Fillmores taught that the divine plan for humanity is to follow Jesus all the way. To them that meant living by his teachings, practicing healing prayer, overcoming death and ascending. The Fillmores believed that at the ascension, Jesus went through a transformation of his physical body into a body of pure spiritual light and energy. They referred to the process and end of that ascension transformation as regeneration.[23]

Regeneration is the final overcoming of death that all souls are to achieve in the divine pattern for salvation. The Fillmores believed that this process requires a physical body and so souls are allowed to reincarnate until they achieve the state that Jesus Christ achieved. Resurrection is understood as the final overcoming of the belief in death, a rising into a higher state of consciousness that transforms the body into an eternal spiritual body.[24] That ultimate state is the ultimate salvation. It is to be achieved by all, according to the teachings of the Fillmores.

Many Unity people believe in reincarnation as a process whereby we ultimately achieve enlightenment, the conscious union of our souls with God. Not all Unity people who believe in reincarnation and union with God believe that the union involves physical ascension. The belief of Unity people in universal salvation naturally means that all people, no matter what their religion, will ultimately enter fully into the kingdom of heaven; but it may take more than one lifetime to achieve that result.[25]

Many Unity people believe in an afterlife either as an ongoing progression into new realms of experience or as a place of rest or learning between reincarnations. Some Unity people believe we will be with those we loved in an afterlife. Others believe that the souls of those we have known in previous lives will be reincarnated with us in new relations. There is no official teaching on these subjects. Unity does not have a teaching on "limbo" or "purgatory." Because many Unity people believe in reincarnation as part of universal salvation, one could say that earth is a kind of "purgatory"; but it is not likely that a Unity person would use that term.

Unity people believe that sins are forgiven, but that we must also learn to have the "Christ mind" which transcends sin. We do not hold that some sins are worse than others. We hold that a sin is any thought or behavior that is rooted in a belief in separation from God or from others. We hold that every thought and action has consequences, according to a divine law of justice, but we do not pretend to know what particular consequences will occur in any particular case. What happens to people who commit suicide? We might speculate that the consequence would be a future life in which a loved one will commit suicide, but we do not know. We do believe in the teaching of Jesus Christ, "forgive and you will be forgiven." Practicing forgiveness results in consequences of forgiveness, according to the divine law of justice. It is not our job to judge others; our job is to do the best we can and, as followers of Jesus, to love and forgive others.

Notes

1. See, for example, *The Upanishads*, translated by Friedrich Max Muller (Oxford:

Clarendon Press, 1879).

2. Catherine L. Albanese, *America: Religions and Religion* (Belmont, CA: Wadsworth, 1992), p. 268.
3. Ibid., p. 267.
4. Cf. Perry Miller, *The American Transcendentalists: Their Prose and Poetry* (Garden City, NY: Doubleday Anchor Books, 1957). Emerson's poem "Brahma" is the classic example of Eastern influence on Western poetry. Its main ideas are drawn from the *Bhagavad Gita:*

   If the red slayer thinks he slays,
   Or if the slain think he is slain,
   They know not well the subtle ways
   I keep, and pass, and turn again.
   Far or forgot to me is near;
   Shadow and sunlight are the same;
   The vanished gods to me appear;
   And one to me are shame and fame.
   They reckon ill who leave me out;
   When me they fly, I am the wings;
   I am the doubter and the doubt,
   And I the hymn the Brahmin sings.
   The strong gods pine for my abode,
   And pine in vain the sacred Seven;
   But thou, meek lover of the good!
   Find me, and turn thy back on heaven.

5. Cf. Sylvia Cranston, *HPB: The Extraordinary Life and Influence of Helena Blavatsky, Founder of the Modern Theosophical Movement* (New York: G.P. Putnam's Sons, 1993).
6. Franz Rottensteiner, *The Science Fiction Book: An Illustrated History* (New York: New American Library, 1975).
7. Andrew D. White, *A History of the Warfare of Science with Theology in Christendom* (New York: D. Appleton & Co., 1910), pp. 70-86.
8. Abraham Aaron Roback, *History of Psychology and Psychiatry* (New York: Philosophical Library, 1961), pp. 296-300.
9. Albanese, op. cit., p. 262.
10. Cf. Charles S. Braden, *Spirits in Rebellion* (Dallas: Southern Methodist University Press, 1987).
11. Note, for example, the prevalence of "Christian" and "Christianity" in the titles of the most influential authors, such as *Esoteric Christianity and Mental Therapeutics* by Warren Felt Evans (Boston: H.H. Carter & Karrick, 1886) and class lectures given in the 1880s by Emma Curtis Hopkins, which she called *Scientific Christian Mental Practice* (Bridge, CT: High Watch Fellowship, 1958).
12. For a detailed history of Unity, see James Dillet Freeman, *The Story of Unity* (Unity Village, MO: Unity Books, 1978) and Neal Vahle, *Torch-Bearer to Light the Way: The Life of Myrtle Fillmore* (Mid Valley, CA: Open View Press, 1996).
13. For more information on the contemporary Unity movement, contact: Unity School of Christianity, 1901 NW Blue Parkway, Unity Village, MO 64065-

0001, and The Association of Unity Churches, P.O. Box 610, Lee's Summit, MO 64063.

14. For a list of Unity publications and cassettes, contact the Sales Department at Unity School of Christianity (address given above).
15. For another statement of Unity's basic beliefs, see the pamphlet "Unity Today" by Connie Fillmore Bazzy, President of Unity School of Christianity.
16. For other examples of Bible passages indicating universal salvation, see Matthew 18:14, Luke 3:6 and Romans 14:10-12.
17. For more detailed explanations of Unity teachings, see *Lessons in Truth* by H. Emilie Cady (Unity Village, MO: Unity Books, 1897), *Christian Healing* by Charles Fillmore (Unity Village, MO: Unity Books, 1909), and *Discover the Power Within You* by Eric Butterworth (New York: Harper & Row, 1968).
18. Frederick Carl Eiselen et al., eds., *The Abingdon Bible Commentary*. (New York: The Abingdon Press, 1929), p. 1012.
19. For example, in the King James Version, Matthew 16:18, Luke 10:15 and Acts 2:27.
20. See the definition of "hell" in *The Revealing Word* by Charles Fillmore (Unity Village, MO: Unity Books, 1959): "Metaphysically, hell represents a corrective state of mind."
21. See "day of judgment" in *The Revealing Word*: "Any day in which we get the result in body and affairs of some thought or word that we have expressed."
22. *Origen*, translated by Owen A. Greer (New York: Paulist Press, 1979).
23. From *The Revealing Word*: regeneration is "A change in which abundant spiritual life, even eternal life, is incorporated into the body...The unification of Spirit, soul, and body in spiritual oneness."
24. From *The Revealing Word*: resurrection is "The restoring of mind and body to their original, undying state."
25. These comments are not based on a formal study of the beliefs of Unity people. Rather, my comments are based on informal discussions with Unity people in classes and churches during my 18 years in Unity ministry, 13 years of which were at Unity School of Christianity in the Continuing Education Program for Unity students and the Ministerial Education Program.

Zoroastrianism

Jamsheed K. Choksy, PhD

BACKGROUND OF THE FAITH

Zoroastrian beliefs about the process of aging, the death of the body, the afterlife of each soul, and a final or universal eschatology for all humanity are based on a dualistic worldview that gradually became fundamental to every aspect of the religion. Zoroastrianism, or Mazdaism, a faith based on the revelations of the prophet Zarathushtra, was a major religion in ancient and medieval Iran. During that period it influenced Hellenistic, Jewish, Christian and Muslim beliefs. After the Arab conquest of Iran in the 7th century A.D., Zoroastrianism gradually lost adherents through conversion to Islam between the 8th and 13th centuries A.D.[1] Yet Zoroastrian or Mazdean communities persevere not only in Iran but also in India, to which small groups of Zoroastrians migrated after the 10th century A.D. and where they are called Parsis or Persians, and more recently in many other countries around the world. While international dispersion occurred during the 1950s through 1990s, many Zoroastrians still dwell within large cities in Iran like Tehran and Yazd, and within most major cities of India, particularly Bombay, Delhi and Calcutta. The Zoroastrian community presently numbers approximately 76,400 in India, 45,000 in Iran, 10,000 in Canada and the United States, 4000 in England, 2800 in Pakistan, and a few thousand in the other countries of Europe and in Australia. Small groups are also present in Hong Kong, Singapore, Sri Lanka and in the countries of Africa. Low birthrate and prohibition of the acceptance of converts has contributed to the decline in numbers. Despite changes in beliefs and practices over time, especially minor deviations in rites between the Iranian and Parsi Zoroastrians and their descendants worldwide, the core of Mazdean or Zoroastrian views on death and afterlife has remained fairly constant even as practices have changed due to global relocation of the community.

The prophet Zarathushtra lived and preached some time between the 17th to 15th centuries B.C. His homeland, it is now believed, was somewhere in the region that stretches from northwestern Afghanistan to the eastern shores of the Caspian Sea, in present-day Central Asia. His name, Zarathushtra, is a compound word probably meaning "possessor of golden camels." The form Zoroaster, by which the prophet is commonly identified in Western literature, derives from an ancient Greek rendering as Zoroastres. According to hagiographic tradition, Zarathushtra left home at the age of 20. After a decade of wandering and contemplation he received a revelation and returned to preach the religion of Ahura Mazda, "the lord of wisdom" who is the supreme deity of Zoroastrianism. Zarathushtra was opposed by the clergy of the older cults in his native land and had to seek refuge at the court of a neighboring ruler, who was named Vishtaspa, who accepted the religion. Here Zarathushtra preached and gained many followers until, at the age of 77, he was reportedly assassinated by a priest of another sect. The basic sketch of Zarathushtra's life that has survived dates back to the 6th century A.D. or later — in fact, very little is actually known about his life and times other than glimpses that are available from his Gathas, or songs to god. As Zoroastrians experienced centuries of contact with Jews, Christians and Muslims, the prophet's hagiography was gradually transformed to fit the established Near Eastern model of the life of a holy man. This revised sacred biography — with signs of auspicious birth, childhood miracles, revelation after years of wandering and contemplation, an initial ministry that met with limited success in his homeland, fleeing to a nearby region, gaining a royal patron, and finally success as a prophet — fits Zarathushtra into the general image also seen in the personages of religious leaders like Moses, Jesus and Muhammad. The notion of death was incorporated into this hagiography as a form of violence — echoing basic Zoroastrian attitudes toward that particular life process.

Herodotus, the Greek historian of the 5th century B.C., noted that no Zoroastrian religious rite could be performed without the presence of a priest — or *magus*. He also listed practices specific to the magi, such as the exposure of corpses to birds of prey. The magi, originally a priestly clan among an Iranian tribe called the Medes, adopted Zoroastrianism after the religion began to spread widely among the ancient Iranians. In time, the magi claimed that the prophet Zoroaster had been a member of their group. Magian claims proved to be highly effective, for by the 4th century B.C., even Plato referred to Zoroaster as "the magus." Through contact with the magi, the Greeks and Romans learned of Zarathushtra. For the Hellenic scholars, particularly the followers of Pythagoras, Zarathushtra became a mystical figure, a magician, which is a word that derives from the Old Iranian word *magu-paiti,* borrowed into Latin as *magus*. The magi themselves were introduced into Christian belief as the wise men from the east who journeyed to Bethlehem. The contemporary priesthood, whose members are called *mobeds*, traces its lineage to the ancient magi of Iran. Passed from father to son, priesthood involves long years of studying the liturgies and rituals of Zoroastrianism, starting during childhood. This is followed by formal initiation, now through two ranks, as a practicing priest via the *navar* and *martab* ceremonies. Despite Herodotus' assertion regarding the role of the magi, there are indeed certain rites that the magi have only limited contact with — those pertaining to funerals. Again, this is in keeping with Zoroastrian views that death is not a natural or divinely decreed event and therefore should be regarded as unnatural and even unclean despite the fact that it occurs within the life cycle of every person.

The Zoroastrian scripture is the Avesta, or "Pure Instruction." The Avesta includes the Gathas ("Songs") believed to have been composed by Zarathusthra himself. The Gathas were transmitted orally by the magi for centuries, with some variations and additions, before they were finally written down. The Yashts ("Hymns to Divine Beings") and the Videvdad ("Code to Ward off Demons") comprise two other major sections of the Avesta. Prayers such as the Ashem Vohu ("righteousness is good"), recited by the laity in daily religious observances, are gathered together in a text known as the Khorde Avesta, or "Shorter Avesta." Next in importance are religious exegeses written in Pahlavi, a Middle Iranian language. Among the fairly vast Pahlavi literature is the Zand ("Theological Exegesis") on the Avesta. Specifically pertaining to tenets on life after death, the Arda Wiraz Namag ("Book of the Righteous Wiraz") preserves a priest's description of a voyage through heaven, limbo and hell during late antiquity. The Arda Wiraz Namag, together with other Zoroastrian accounts of the afterlife such as Middle Iranian inscriptions that describe the spiritual voyages by a 3rd-century high priest named Kirdir or Kartir, probably influenced the Isna-Miraj ("Night Journey-Ascension") traditions attributed to the prophet Muhammad in Muslim tradition. Accounts of Muhammad's journey, elaborated from Zoroastrian precursors, seem to have provided the basis for Dante's Divine Comedy. Indeed, Dante's introduction of limbo and his use of ice as the punishment in deepest hell were at variance with the Christian tradition of his time, but were well known in Zoroastrian afterlife beliefs and are present in some descriptions of the afterlife among Shi'ite Muslims of Iran. The Denkard, or "Acts of the Religion," is another Pahlavi codex dating from the 9th to 11th centuries A.D. Finally, there is more recent Zoroastrian literature in New Persian and Gujarati such as the Persian Rivayats ("Persian Treatises") and the Rehbar-e Din-e Jarthushti ("Guide to the Zoroastrian Religion") respectively. These texts continued to transmit to the general believer, who no longer understood the Avestan or Pahlavi languages, tenets of the faith and the meanings of rituals. Catechisms of the religion are also now written in English for the Parsis. Many of these documents refer, both directly and indirectly, to the processes that cause aging and death, and seek to reassure believers that their souls do not die and that, at the end of time, their souls will be reunited with their bodies and loved ones.[2]

The Main Tenets

Zarathushtra preached an ethical and moral dualism between *asha* ("righteousness") and *druj* ("falsehood"). This dualism was personified by Zarathushtra in a pair of primal spirits: Ahura Mazda, the lord of wisdom or god, and Angra Mainyu, the evil spirit or devil. Subsequent theological modifications by the magi transformed the prophet's ethical dualistic teachings into a universal one by the 6th century A.D. The orthodox version of Zoroastrianism then came to follow a dualism between righteousness and evil on a cosmic scale. According to established Zoroastrian doctrine, Ahura Mazda, who is regarded as the righteous creator, is by definition a perfect, good, rational and omniscient being who creates light, warmth, good health, happiness and life. Ahura Mazda came to be viewed as a deity from whom no evil can proceed because it is believed that a perfect being cannot originate imperfection. As a result, Zoroastrians hold that Ahura Mazda created the spiritual and material worlds completely pure, they worship him as the chief deity, and refer to themselves as *Mazda-yasni* ("Mazda worshippers"). As a direct consequence of these tenets, all that causes darkness, cold, ill health, sorrow, suffering and pain came to be excluded from the domain of Ahura Mazda's actions. Therefore, irreligiosity, disease, decay and death are perceived in the Zoroastrian ethos as vices created by the evil spirit Angra Mainyu and brought by him into the material world to cause suffering, pain, unhappiness and sin. Hence, for Zoroastrians, the process of the body's aging and eventual demise was and still is regarded as an involuntary, yet inevitable, succumbing to a relentless onslaught on the physique by evil forces. Death is, therefore, never welcomed or viewed as martyrdom.[3]

Zoroastrians believe that Ahura Mazda created six Amesha Spentas or beneficent spiritual beings that represented aspects of the material world — Ameretat (plants), Haurvatat (water), Spenta Armaiti (earth), Asha Vahishta (fire), Khshathra Vairya (metal) and Vohu Manah (animals) — plus Yazatas, or minor good spirits, like Anahita (the female divine spirit of fertility) and Mithra (the male divine spirit of covenants), to assist him in protecting the corporeal creations from the effects of evil. In response, Angra Mainyu is supposed to have generated numerous Daevas, or demons and demonesses, including those that cause sickness (Tafnu), pollution and decay (Druj Nasush), and death (Asto Vidhatu), to attack the spiritual and corporeal realms. Without the presence of evil, it is claimed, Ahura Mazda's creations — including humans — would never suffer, grow old or die. So the causes for death, from a theological standpoint, are evil, indeed demonic, forces. Likewise, death is said to result in uncleanness of the corpse. Again a religious rather than a physiological point of view prevails as the result of a belief that the Druj Nasush enters the flesh and causes a pollution capable of spreading to all persons who have contact with the dead body. Thus, Zoroastrian doctrine laid the basis for viewing the processes of growing old and of dying as negative ones.[4]

Zoroastrian sacred history is divided into two periods. The first period, or cosmogony, is said to have existed when Ahura Mazda and Angra Mainyu were separate from each other. This first period is thought to have lasted 6000 years. The first 3000 years of that period were marked by the first encounter between Ahura Mazda and Angra Mainyu — it was the genesis of beneficent and malevolent spiritual beings by the lord of wisdom and the evil spirit respectively, and an offer of peaceful coexistence in purity, righteousness and immortality made by Ahura Mazda, which was rejected by Angra Mainyu. After Angra Mainyu had spurned Ahura Mazda's overture of peace, he was temporarily defeated by the lord of wisdom who chanted the Yatha Ahu Vairyo or Ahuna Vairya ("as is the lord") prayer. On hearing these holy words, the evil spirit is said to have collapsed, stupefied, back into the darkness. The next 3000 years passed while Angra Mainyu lay in a stupor, and Ahura Mazda transformed the spiritual creations into corporeal ones. Zoroastrian theologians asserted that human beings were created by Ahura Mazda as allies in his cosmic struggle against Angra Mainyu, and that humans consented to assume physical form to further this battle. It was written in the creation story, or Bundahishn, that Ahura Mazda deliberated with the immortal souls (*fravashis*) of humanity who realized that the evil spirit would be vanquished forever if they entered the material world. These souls also recognized that their physical bodies would have to suffer from a process of aging, death and decay, as well as periods in heaven, hell or limbo. Ahura Mazda, in turn, promised to resurrect all humans and grant them immortality once Angra Mainyu had been defeated at the end of time. As a result of this covenant, the religious function of each person is to aid the increase of righteousness and combat the forces of evil through every action performed during his or her lifetime. Good actions by people in the material state aid individual and cosmic triumph of righteousness over evil on the spiritual level. In this manner, tenets pertaining to views of aging, death and afterlife could be based on the notion of a primeval covenant between the chief deity and the souls of humans.

According to religious lore, Ahura Mazda then fashioned the earth inside the sphere of the sky. The sphere of the sky was made of stone and enclosed the oceans, seven continents, and the firmament with the sun, moon, planets and stars. Upon the central continent, Ahura Mazda placed the first human being — an androgyne named Gayo-Maretan ("mortal life") — a primordial bull and a first plant. That 6000-year period of creation was followed, according to the Bundahishn ("Book of Primal Creation"), by the current age of mixture between good and evil, which will also last 6000 years. It is held that at the commencement of this second age, Angra Mainyu was aroused from his stupor by the lesser demons, invaded the world, polluted it and slew Gayo-Maretan, the primordial bull and the first plant. The death and decay introduced into the corporeal world by the evil spirit was counteracted by the lord of wisdom who transformed expiration into generation — humanity, in the form of the first couple Mashya and Mashyana (equivalent to Adam and Eve), arose from the semen of the dying androgyne, the animals and cereals from the corpse of the first bull, and all other plants from the seeds of the initial plant. Hence, cosmogonical beliefs involving eternal souls assuming corporeal shape in human bodies, the entry of death into the material world, the regeneration of life and the persistence of creation under adversity, laid the foundation for tenets relating to afterlife and final renovation or salvation.

After the first events on earth, human history is said to have passed in a scheme resembling the biblical list of generations found in the book of Genesis, with the rise and fall of legendary dynasties until the prophet Zarathushtra was born in the religious year 8970. Thirty years later, Zarathushtra received a revelation from Ahura Mazda, and preached the lord of wisdom's faith. According to this sacred history, the era of Zarathushtra was followed by recorded history — the Iranian dynasties of the Achaemenians (550-331 B.C.), Seleucids (312-175 B.C.), Arsacids or Parthians (c. 238 B.C.-A.D. 224) and Sasanians (A.D. 224-651). Zoroastrianism spread through every stratum of Iranian society during those centuries, even reaching the western shores of Anatolia (or modern Turkey) and the deserts of eastern Central Asia, and finally becoming the state religion of Iran under Sasanian rule. Thereafter, the Arab Muslims conquered Iran, and were succeeded by Turkish invaders. These conquests, and the reduction of Zoroastrians to the status of a religious minority, were incorporated into the faith's history and explained in terms of a steady increase in evil that was supposed to herald the advent of the final days of humanity. Thereafter, time progressed to the present when Zoroastrians are a minority around the world still awaiting the final eschaton.

During the early modern period, Zoroastrian beliefs gradually changed from a dualism based on polytheistic pantheons and pandemoniums to a quasi-monotheism in which Ahura Mazda is regarded as god and Angra Mainyu has become the devil. European Christian missionaries played a pivotal role in this transformation of Parsi and, later via the Parsis, of Iranian beliefs. Minor deities of the original pantheon now have been accorded a variety of positions, usually equivalent to angels. Sundry creatures of the original pandemonium have become minor evil spirits and ghouls. Yet most Zoroastrians continue to believe that human beings serve a vital function in the struggle between god and the devil, a conflict during which they might sin, will die, must face judgment and reward or retribution for their earthly actions, and will eventually be reunited with the divine.

In Zoroastrian belief, the material world is not merely the arena in which human beings combat evil. Zoroastrians regard it as the trap into which the evil spirit was lured. Once trapped in matter, Zoroastrian doctrine claims, Angra Mainyu can be gradually vanquished by divine beings and devotees acting in unison. The Shkand Gumanig Wizar ("Doubt Dispelling Exposition"), a 9th-century text written in the Pahlavi language, describes this belief by comparing the lord of wisdom to a wise gardener who protects his garden, which is paradise or heaven, by luring the attacker into a trap. The sphere of the sky serves as the fortification of this cosmic snare in which divine beings and humans battle every form of evil. The rewards of heaven, after death, are offered to the souls of believers who have upheld righteousness and combated evil during their lifetimes.[5]

AGING, DEATH AND FUNERARY PRACTICES

Because Zoroastrians view aging and death as inevitable consequences of the human condition — of being alive and being exposed to evil — the community has generally adhered to the concept of the extended family in which support mechanisms have existed for the elderly. Until recent decades, several generations of a single family often lived together, each age group providing financial, medical, physiological, intellectual and spiritual support for their parents and grandparents. Elderly Zoroastrians who lacked relatives living in close proximity would be cared for by the community at large, using endowments and trust funds established specifically for the purpose of building and staffing hospices (*dharamsalas*) and for feeding and clothing the residents there. Likewise, hospitals were established in both Iran and India, using community funds and individual donations — providing no-cost and low-cost medical services and counseling to the aged and destitute. Many of these trusts continue to function in present-day Iran and India as an important safety net for less well-off and lonely seniors whose own relatives have either predeceased them or have relocated as part of a gradual breakup of the extended family.[6] In other countries, such as Pakistan, Sri Lanka, Australia and New Zealand, England and the United States, care for the elderly has generally remained within the family unit, even in cases where seniors reside in retirement homes or hospice settings. Indeed, supervision of the aged and setting up of facilities for funerary services proved to be a major impetus for the establishment of Zoroastrian associations in each of the above-mentioned countries. In most cases, shortly after an association is established, a building is built, bought or rented to house that association's headquarters, and then land is purchased or arrangements made with an existing funerary site to dispose of the dead — specific examples include the Colombo Parsi Anjuman in Sri Lanka, the London Association and its successor organizations like the Zoroastrian Trust Funds of Europe, and the Federation of Zoroastrian Associations of North America, which serves as a coordinating organization for 21 regional or state associations.[7]

If a Zoroastrian is known to be in the final hours of life, he or she is supposed to recite the Petit Pashemanih or Patet-e Vadardegan, a prayer of repentance for prior evil deeds, followed by several Ashem Vohu prayers. Because light is believed to be a creation of god that dispels evil, a lamp is lit close to the person's head. Haoma or ephedra juice mixed with crushed pomegranate leaves and milk, believed to confer symbolic immortality, is often sipped by the dying person if he or she is a Parsi Zoroastrian. If haoma is unavailable, as is often the case in the United States, pomegranate juice may be drunk — again the doctrinal symbolism is one of immortality for the pomegranate is a fruit that many Near Eastern cultures believe represents fertility and regeneration. If death occurs unexpectedly, the aforementioned prayers may be recited in the deceased's name by a relative or friend upon being notified of the death. The prayer vigil continues after death, in the belief that the deceased's soul will be comforted during its time of transition — including chanting a hymn specific to the period or *gah* of the day, a repetition of the confessional liturgy and an invocation of the messenger divinity Sraosha or Srosh Yasht Vadi. After the deceased's eyes are closed, the corpse is given a ritual cleaning (termed *sachkar* by the Parsis) either by professional corpse bearers (*nasa salars*) and corpse cleaners (*paksus*) or by relatives or friends of the same sex, all of whom should be Zoroastrians, so as to ensure that the deceased's body is ritually pure for the final rites that follow.[8] The cleansing may occur at the place of death, especially if it was in a home, or at a funeral hall. The chest of the deceased is then draped in a *sudra* or sacred undershirt and a sacred cord or *kusti/koshti* is tied around the waist. Thereafter, the deceased is dressed in white clothes, his or her hands are crossed over the chest (the legs are also crossed by Iranian Zoroastrians but not by Parsi Zoroastrians) and the entire body covered with a white shroud. The face remains exposed. Now relatives and friends may bid farewell to the dead person. As part of the attempts to contain the pollution supposedly present in a corpse, the body is then laid upon a row of three stone slabs or a stone floor, oriented facing southward (regarded as the direction of heaven and warmth) or at least away from the north (regarded as the direction of hell and cold). The numeral three is believed to represent the Zoroastrian creed of good thoughts, good words and good deeds that facilitate the vanquishing of evil; the stone is thought to represent a substance unaffected by pollution and thus capable of protecting the earth underneath the body. Three concentric rectangular furrows (*karsha*) are figuratively drawn around the deceased, with recitation of Ahuna Vairya prayers, thereby demarcating a space (*vara*) within which the death and decay associated with that corpse is believed to be confined. Oil lamps burn nearby to dispel evil.

In Iran and India all handling of corpses is left to professional Zoroastrian corpse cleaners and bearers. Elsewhere, co-religionists perform these duties. Such persons, whether professional corpse handlers or simply other Zoroastrians, dress in white (a color associated with the purity and light of Ahura Mazda), work in pairs of two, four or six, and remain in constant contact or *paywand* ("connection") with each other by holding portions of a piece of cloth or a sacred cord or holding hands — resistance to the evil manifesting itself as death is believed to be held at bay from these persons by their numbers and by their interconnection or unity. Likewise, individuals handling the corpse should have taken an added precaution against the power of evil by symbolically shielding themselves through an utterance called the Srosh Baj, for Zoroastrians believe that *manthras* ("sacred words") are the "outermost wall" of the religion. Recitation of the Srosh Baj is begun before touching the dead body and concluded after the tasks have been completed.[9]

Until the funeral service commences, a prayer vigil is maintained to safeguard the deceased's body and soul from demonic forces thought to be lurking in the vicinity. At the commencement of each period of the day, a rite known as *sagdid* ("seen by the dog") is performed. Originating within a pastoral society where canines played important roles in safeguarding persons, Zoroastrianism witnessed the establishment of a theological notion that dogs could sense the presence of evil and drive it away. In the rite of *sagdid,* a dog is led up to the corpse so that it can symbolically disperse any demons who may have approached the deceased. A dog may also be kept nearby to continually perform a protective function toward the dead.

The actual funeral service, termed *geh sarna* ("chanting of the Gathas") by Parsis, occurs within 24 hours, during the daylight hours (the *havan* or morning, *rapithwin* or midday, and *uzerin* or afternoon periods or watches of the day), so that sunlight — another natural feature attributed to god alone — can keep evils like pollution away from persons attending the funeral as well as purify the corpse. At the commencement of the *geh sarna,* pairs of corpse bearers recite the Srosh Baj along with an invocation formula and then enter the room where the corpse lies. These corpse bearers maintain *paywand* at all times. Two magi perform the basic dedicatory rite of the faith (which involves washing of the hands, face and feet and then untying and retying the sacred cord while reciting prayers), recite additional hymns of praise such as the Khurshid Niyayishn to the sun and the Mihr Niyayishn to the beneficial spirit Mithra, enter the funeral hall and face the body. These priests invoke god's protection via the Srosh Baj, then begin chanting the Ahunavaiti Gatha. During this recitation, the priests and assembled laity pause and turn away from the corpse so as not to be exposed to the Druj Nasush while another *sagdid* rite is performed and the body is placed by the corpse bearers on an iron bier (or on any other metal, which, like stone, is believed to withstand pollution). Once the body has been transferred to the bier, the priests and congregation turn back to the deceased and the Gatha is completed as is the Srosh Baj. In orthodox Iranian practice, the deceased's face is then covered with the shroud, and the bier is carried to the funeral site even before the priests finish the service. In orthodox Parsi practice, the funeral service is followed by a paying of last respects (*sezdo*) by Zoroastrians after which the deceased's face is covered with the shroud. The bier is carried by corpse bearers and, among Parsis in India, by pall bearers (*khandias*). Mourners who wish to follow the bier do so after reciting the Srosh Baj and forming gender-specific pairs. Each mourner connects himself or herself to the other member of the pair, establishing *paywand* with a piece of cloth or a *kusti*. The procession of mourners is led by a pair of priests or one priest plus a dog to ward off evil and pollution. The use of such walking funeral processions continued in Iran, India, Pakistan and Sri Lanka into the late 1970s. Today, in most places, including the United States, the corpse is placed in a hearse that is followed to the funerary site by relatives and friends in a motorcade.

In the early history of Zoroastrianism, human corpses would be buried under the floors of disused buildings, following a practice prevalent in Central Asia during the Bronze Age (ca. 1750-1500 B.C.) in which the faith arose. Later, interment took place in cemeteries. Yet, as practices changed by the 6th century B.C., the original Old Iranian (Avestan) term for a grave or tomb, *dakhma*, came to designate another funerary locale — a place for exposure of corpses or a funerary tower, now also called a tower of silence in popular parlance.[10] Zoroastrians are perhaps best known to Americans and Europeans for this practice of exposing the dead to vultures. As alluded to earlier, the practice appears to have been introduced by the ancient magi in order to prevent pollution of the sacred earth, fire and water by corpses. Orthodox Zoroastrian doctrine holds that earth, fire and water will become polluted if a corpse is buried, cremated or placed in water. Consequently, in Iran and India, the corpse bearers usually carry the bier to a funerary tower where a final *sagdid* rite is performed. The body is then taken into the funerary tower and placed facing east (toward the rising sun with its supposed purificatory powers) within this circular enclosure that is open to the sky. The shroud is ripped to expose the flesh to the elements and to birds of prey who are thought capable of digesting the flesh without assimilating the demonic forces believed to dwell in the corpse. After the corpse bearers exit the funerary tower, the assembled mourners say prayers, especially the final portion of the Srosh Baj and the Dakhma No Namaskar. The *nasa salars* also recite the final portion of the Srosh Baj. All Zoroastrians associated with the funeral then perform an ablution called the *padyab*, which involves washing the face, hands and feet with water, and thereafter they untie and retie their *kustis* while chanting appropriate prayers.[11] On returning home, mourners bathe themselves as an added ritual precaution against pollution. Once the corpse has been desiccated, its bones are collected and placed in a pit (often filled with lime to dissolve the bones) at the center of the funerary tower. In ancient and medieval times, the bones were often placed in an ossuary (*astodan*) rather than being stored or dissolved in a pit.[12]

The 19th and 20th centuries have seen considerable variation in Zoroastrian funerary practices. Exposure of corpses was gradually phased out in Iran in the 1970s, and Iranian Zoroastrians now bury the dead in graves walled with cement slabs so as to prevent the corpse from touching the earth and thus polluting it. Parsi Zoroastrians in India and Pakistan, particularly in Bombay and Karachi, continue the tradition of exposing bodies to vultures in funerary towers. However, in the United States, Canada, England, Australia and Sri Lanka, many Zoroastrians follow the Iranian practice of burial within walled or enclosed graveyards known as *aramgahs* ("places of rest"). Certain Zoroastrian communities, particularly those in North America, even perform cremations. Among Zoroastrians in Iran, India, Pakistan and Sri Lanka, however, orthodox priests will not perform the funerary rites and subsequent memorial rituals if a deceased's body has been cremated (even if the cremation was mandated by the state for medical or hygienic reasons), for they regard the burning of a human corpse as an inexcusable polluting of fire. Among all groups it is still a tradition to keep an oil lamp burning for three days and nights in the deceased's bedroom in memory of the departed and to assist his or her soul in the afterlife.

During the period following the funeral, several other rituals are performed for the soul. These include chanting of a Srosh Baj at the commencement of each period or *gah* of the first three days. Specific practices on the third day (termed *sevvom* by Iranians and *uthamna* by Parsis), when the divinities who safeguard the deceased's soul are propitiated, involve holy words and food offerings such as round unleavened wheat bread (*dron*) and fruits that have been consecrated during a Yasna or worship ritual. On the fourth day (*caharom*), a legal heir to the deceased is recognized or appointed to oversee performance of subsequent rituals in memory of the deceased (among Parsis this sometimes occurs during the third day rites). On the 10th day (*dahom* or *Dahe*), on the 30th day (*siruz*), and on the first and later anniversaries (*salruz*) after the death, the Afrinagan Baj or liturgy of blessing is performed by priests at a fire temple. The memories and souls of deceased persons are commemorated collectively during the last 10 days of the Zoroastrian religious year — the Hamaspathmaedaya, Frawardigan/Farvardegan or Mukhtad period — during which the Afrinagan and Farokhshi rituals are performed to invoke the names of the dead and nourish their immortal souls with food offerings. Among Zoroastrians in Iran, souls of the deceased are also honored during an annual Porse Hamegani or memorial service.[13]

BELIEFS IN THE AFTERLIFE OF THE SOUL: JUDGMENT, HEAVEN, LIMBO AND HELL

Zoroastrian religious texts that discuss doctrines of an afterlife for each human soul include the Avestan-language Hadokht Nask ("Section on Worship," chapters 2 and 3) and the Pahlavi-language inscriptions of Kirdir and books such as the Arda Wiraz Namag, Menog i Khrad ("Book of the Spirit of Wisdom") and Bundahishn, and the New Persian-language Rivayats. These documents describe the basic set of tenets that most Zoroastrians follow with regard to the existence of a soul and its fate after death. Mazdean doctrine claims that each human has five parts: a corporeal body (*tanu/tan*) that unites with the earth upon death, a life force (*ushtana/ahu/gyan/jan*) that unites with the wind upon death, a mortal soul (*urvan/ruwan*) that unites with its immortal soul upon death, a prototype (*kehrpa/ewenag*) that unites with the sun upon death, and an immortal soul (*fravashi/frawahr*). Death is regarded as a focal point in the struggle between good and evil within each human. One medieval Zoroastrian text (Denkard, pp. 383-384) described death as an attack "upon an individual's essence, which is the soul, and upon the soul's instrument and garment — the body...evil strives to annihilate and defile an individual's essence, instrument, and garment." Within this religious worldview, the goal of evil is the pollution and destruction of the body so that the mortal and immortal souls may be exposed to evil as well. Hence, devotees are urged to remember that "the body is mortal, [but] the soul is eternal. Do good deeds for the soul...[as] the spiritual realm is what matters, not the material world" (Chidag Handarz i Poryotkeshan, l. 55).[14]

Zoroastrians believe that when an individual dies, the life force (*ushtana/jan*) leaves the body (*tan*) which then becomes an empty shell of matter — a corpse (*ristag*) that demonic forces attack and cause to decay. His or her mortal soul (*urvan*) also leaves the body at death, and sits near the head of the corpse for three days and nights — either at the funerary tower or at the burial ground (or at the crematorium). The soul of a righteous person is said to happily chant the Ushtauuaiti Gatha (Yasna 43), "according to our wish," while the soul of a sinful person wails the Kima Gatha or Kamnamaeza Haiti (Yasna 46), "to what land shall I go?" — each knowing its eventual destiny. Demons supposedly prey upon the soul during this period but are kept at bay by the oil lamp (or a fire) that the deceased individual's relatives have kindled. It is said that on the dawn of the fourth day, the soul of a good person inhales fragrant scents, while the soul of an evil person smells noxious orders. Sraosha, the divinity of obedience and prayer (and hence a messenger deity who carries invocations to Ahura Mazda), approaches the soul together with Vayu, the divinity of wind, and Verethraghna, the celestial spirit of victory. These three beneficial beings are opposed by three demonic creatures: Vizaresha, the ghoul of death; Asto-Vidhatu, the sunderer of bones; and Aeshma, the fiend of wrath. Despite such opposition, if the soul belonged to a good Zoroastrian, the three divinities lead it to the Bridge of the Accumulator (*Cinuuat-peretauu/chinwad-puhl*). If the soul belonged to a sinful Zoroastrian or to an unbeliever, the three demons fetter it and drag it to the Bridge of the Accumulator. This metaphysical transit point, which connects the material realm to the spiritual one, is said to begin in the north near hell and to end in the south at the entrance to heaven. Beneath the bridge, under the earth, is said to lie hell. Following long-established Indo-European and Indo-Iranian traditions, spiritual dogs guard the bridge.

A tribunal is convened at the bridge's base to determine the soul's holiness in an individual judgment. The divinities Mithra, who presides to assess whether the soul has kept its primeval covenant to do good while in the material world; Rashnu, the lord of equity; and Sraosha (in later tradition Mithra and Sraosha are occasionally replaced by Arshtat, a female divinity of rectitude; and Zamyad, an earth divinity) form this spiritual court. Rashnu is described as weighing each soul's good and bad deeds in the pans of a scale. If the soul's righteous acts outweigh its evil ones, the soul is greeted by its conscience (*daena/den*) in the form of a "beautiful maiden, radiant, fair, robust, beautiful" (Hadokht Nask 2:9), who personifies those pious actions. This good *daena,* together with other divinities, then escorts the saved soul across the bridge, which widens to permit easy passage to heaven where the soul will dwell until the end of time. If the soul's unrighteous acts outweigh its good ones, the soul is greeted by its conscience in the form of an "ugly hag, naked and deformed" (Hadokht Nask 3:9), who personifies those evil actions. This bad *daena,* together with other demons, then lugs the damned soul to the bridge, which narrows to a razor's edge, causing the soul and its conscience to fall off it into hell where the soul will dwell until the end of time. In cases where a soul's good and evil deeds are equal, it is consigned to limbo until the end of time.[15]

Heaven, known as *garo-demana/garodman* ("abode of song") or *wahisht* ("best place"), is depicted as a physical place — a realm of joy, peace and happiness; one full of light, warmth and all virtuous pleasures. In many respects, and not accidentally, paradise came to be envisioned as a beautiful garden. The term paradise originated in Old Iranian cultures and languages; for example, Avestan *pairi-daeza* (from *pairi* "round" plus *diz* "form"), where it designated a park surrounded by a wall. This Iranian word entered Greek as *paradeisos* ("park, pleasure grounds"), then became Latin *paradis(us),* and Old and Middle English *paradis* ("paradise"). In fully developed doctrine this spiritual abode, where righteous souls are believed to enjoy the company of the creator or chief god Ahura Mazda, the lesser divinities, and the souls of predeceased pious relatives and friends, is said to have four ascending regions — the levels of good thought, good speech, good action and the highest heaven or place of eternal profit (*hameshag sud gah*). Hell, known as *drujo-demana/druzman* ("abode of deceit") or *dushokh* ("worst place") is also depicted as a physical place — a realm of grief, conflict and despair; one filled with darkness, cold, stench, harmful insects and animals like scorpions and serpents. Hell, paralleling heaven, has four descending regions as well — the pits of bad thought, bad speech and bad action, followed by deepest hell. Here the demons, led by Angra Mainyu, the evil spirit par excellence, are said to gloat as they torment the newly arrived impious soul together with his or her predeceased bad relatives and friends in a gloomy, icy space. Fire, too, is occasionally described as a form of torment in hell. The Arda Wiraz Namag in particular contains especially graphic descriptions of the multifarious sufferings an evil soul can expect to encounter in the afterlife, much like medieval Christian and Muslim accounts of hell. Limbo, known as *nana* ("different place"), *misuuana gatauu* ("place of the mixed") or *hamestagan* ("place of the equally weighing ones"), is thought to be located between earth and heaven. It is described as a place where souls are suspended, each in isolation, experiencing nothing at all — neither joy nor pain, neither warmth nor cold, neither light nor darkness, neither good nor evil.

Because their doctrines claim that Ahura Mazda does no harm, Zoroastrians believe that the rewards of heaven, sufferings of hell and paralysis of limbo are not divine recompense. Rather, devotees feel that each soul earns its own fate in the afterlife through deeds while alive. So, in order to invigorate Zoroastrians to be pious during their lifetimes, illustrations of a soul's fate, including its trial at the Bridge of the Accumulator, are plentiful in manuscripts of the Arda Wiraz Namag, as are fanciful scenes purporting to depict the rewards and pleasures of heaven, the sufferings in hell and the loneliness of limbo. Careful direction of each and every action while alive so as to accomplish the most good, and thus fulfill the soul's covenant with god, is considered especially essential because Zoroastrians, by and large, do not subscribe to the notion of reincarnation: each individual has but one chance at ensuring that his or her mortal soul (*urvan*) reaches heaven after death. Only during the past few centuries, under the influence of Hinduism in India, have a few Parsis picked up a belief in reincarnation — a concept still abhorrent to most Zoroastrians who feel that it violates their notion of a primeval covenant with god. Zoroastrian descriptions of the afterlife had a powerful effect on other Near Eastern monotheistic religions during late antiquity. Islam absorbed not only Zoroastrian notions of heaven, hell and limbo, but the entire scheme involving individual judgment at a bridge of separation. Christianity also assimilated the Zoroastrian belief in the soul's afterlife, both directly and through Islam.[16] The conditions experienced by a soul after its body's demise, however, constitute only a temporary state. Mazdean doctrine preaches the concept of a universal eschatology that is expected to occur at the end of time.

BELIEFS IN UNIVERSAL ESCHATOLOGY: RESURRECTION, FINAL JUDGMENT AND RENOVATION

As previously mentioned, Zoroastrian sacred history consists of a cosmogonical and eschatological myth, based upon the Indo-Iranian creation beliefs of the earliest votaries, that were elaborated during the medieval period and preserved in the Bundahishn. This sacred history is believed to culminate during the present age of humanity, one in which a mixture (*gumezishn*) of good and evil exists in the material world. The reduction of Zoroastrianism to the status of a minor religious community was incorporated into the faith's sacred history and explained in terms of a steady increase in evil and pollution that heralds the advent of the final days (dramatically described in Bundahishn 33:20-26). As previously noted, social strife, personal calamity, and pollution of both body and soul are all viewed as originating from the evil spirit. Hence, it is believed that strife and calamity will increase with each passing century, until finally "in that basest of times death and pollution will become so widespread that [wherever] a person walks he [or she] will be walking on impurity" (Zand i Wahman Yasht 4:28).[17]

Those years of evil, pollution and suffering, in Zoroastrian belief, will be followed by two millennia during which three saviors — Ukhshyatereta, Ukhshyatnemah and Astvatereta or Saoshyant — would be born, one every 1000 years, to purify the world and its inhabitants. Finally, in the religious year 11,973, the eschaton supposedly will commence when the final savior Saoshyant resurrects the dead. This resurrection, performed by Saoshyant at Ahura Mazda's command, results in each human's mortal and immortal souls returning to earth from heaven, hell or limbo and gaining a final body (*tan i pasen*) once god "requests [return of] the bones from the spirit of the earth, the blood from the water, the hair from the plants, and the life-force from the wind" (Bundahishn 34:5). As other Pahlavi sources suggest, since Ahura Mazda created the creatures in perfection at the beginning of time, so can he restore them to life, purity and wholeness at the end of time. This argument was attributed by Zadspram, a 9th-century magus, to the creator deity himself: "Ahura Mazda said, 'I was able to create those creatures when they were not [in existence], and now that they have existed, and are dismembered, it is easier to restore them'" (Wizidagiha 34: 6). The eschaton is thus perceived as an act that reverses death and impurity.

Thereafter, Ahura Mazda will descend to earth with the other deities, it is held, and the final savior will separate the righteous individuals from the evil ones at a final assembly of all humans. This is the site of a final universal judgment. At that assembly, called the gathering of Isatvastra/Isadwastar after the prophet Zarathushtra's eldest son, each person will recognize his or her relatives and friends, and the pious will rejoice in their goodness while the sinful will lament their evil deeds. The stars will fall from space on to the earth, the mountains will be leveled and molten metal will be extracted from them. Each sinner, having already suffered in hell after death, will be purified once more of his or her transgressions and impurities by means of an ordeal involving passage through the molten metal. A mythical bovine named Hadhayash will be ritually sacrificed afterwards, and its fat mixed with a mythical white haoma to produce an elixir that will grant immortality of body and soul to all human beings who consume it. Ahura Mazda, the Amesha Spentas and the minor divine beings will then annihilate all the minor demons and noxious creatures. The evil spirit Angra Mainyu himself will be rendered innocuous and forced to scuttle out of creation and back to hell. Finally, hell will be sealed shut with molten metal, safeguarding the spiritual and corporeal worlds from evil, impurity and pollution forever: "The evil spirit and [the demon of] lust, their weapons shattered, will be made powerless by the Gathic incantation; and they will scuttle out into the darkness and gloom through that passage in the sky by which they [had] penetrated [the world]...molten metal will flow into hell, and all the stench and pollution that was in hell will be burned by that molten metal and become pure. The passage through which the evil spirit penetrated [into the material world] will be sealed [forever] with that molten metal" (Bundahishn 34:30-31). According to Zoroastrian eschatology, once the separation (*wizarishn*) of evil from good has been accomplished, Ahura Mazda will renovate or "make excellent" (*frasho-kereti/frasha-gird*) the universe in the year 12,000: "The renovation will take place in the world, [and the beings in] the material world will become immortal forever" (Bundahishn 34:32). Human history will then end, eternity will recommence in absolute purity and perfection, and humanity will dwell in happiness on a refurbished flat earth warmed by sunlight and not experiencing nightfall or cold.

Thus, according to the Zoroastrian worldview, human history is actually a 12,000-year linear progression of sacred history. Human history or the period of finite time (*zaman i kanaragomand*), also termed the "time of the long dominion" (*zaman i dagrand khwaday, zurwan i dagrand khwaday*), which is when aging, death, individual judgment and assignment to heaven, hell or limbo occurs, is bounded at its commencement and conclusion by infinite time (*zaman i akanarag, zurwan i akanarag*) when events are believed to function in absolute accordance with the will of Ahura Mazda, producing only beneficial effects. Zoroastrian beliefs involving death and the afterlife are part of a religious system in which good and evil, purity and pollution, life and death are not to be permitted to cycle infinitely. Each occurs within a fixed period of 12,000 years after which a final renovation grants salvation to all human souls and confers an immortal, youthful body upon everyone — so that all persons, whether Zoroastrian or not while first alive, can exist thereafter in joy and peace with their relatives, friends and the rest of humanity.[18] Through religious explanations of the process of aging and the occurrence of death, the Zoroastrian faith seeks to provide its followers with a purpose for existence — to combat evil — plus hope for the future — life after death — thus attempting to alleviate fears connected with the cessation of life and to make the transition from living to dying more bearable.

Notes

1. Details on the processes and consequences of conversion are discussed in Jamsheed K. Choksy, *Conflict and Cooperation: Zoroastrian Subalterns and Muslim Elites in Medieval Iranian Society* (New York: Columbia University Press, 1997), pp. 69-109.
2. General introductions to Zoroastrianism, its founder and sacred texts are found in Mary Boyce, *Zoroastrians: Their Religious Beliefs and Practices* (London: Routledge and Kegan Paul, 1979), pp. 17-24, 30-38; Jamsheed K. Choksy, *Purity and Pollution in Zoroastrianism: Triumph over Evil* (Austin: University of Texas Press, 1989), pp. 1-20; and Robert C. Zaehner, *The Teachings of the Magi: A Compendium of Zoroastrian Beliefs* (New York: Oxford University Press, 1976), pp. 17-28.

3. For more details on dualism in Zoroastrianism see Shaul Shaked's *Dualism in Transformation: Varieties of Religion in Sasanian Iran* (London: School of Oriental and African Studies, 1994), which is the basic study on permutations undergone by this doctrine during late antiquity and the early Middle Ages. Jamsheed K. Choksy, "Doctrinal Variation within Zoroastrianism: The Notion of Dualism," in *Proceedings of the Second International Congress of the K.R. Cama Oriental Institute, 1995* (Bombay: K.R. Cama Oriental Institute, 1996), pp. 96-110, analyzes both the rise of universal dualism and the constant tensions throughout the faith's history between dualism and monism.
4. On this notion of ritual or religious pollution see Choksy, *Purity and Pollution in Zoroastrianism,* pp. 10-22, 141-143.
5. The Zoroastrian creation story is discussed in more detail by Zaehner, *The Teachings of the Magi,* pp. 29-51, 67-79, who provides translations from Zoroastrian texts. Choksy, *Purity and Pollution in Zoroastrianism,* pp. 111-137, analyzes the importance of cosmological beliefs on life cycles and rituals.
6. Consult John R. Hinnells, "The Flowering of Zoroastrian Benevolence: Parsi Charity in the Nineteenth and Twentieth Centuries," in *Papers in Honour of Professor Mary Boyce, Acta Iranica 24* (Leiden: E.J. Brill, 1985), pp. 261-326, for specific examples.
7. On events in England refer to John Hinnells, *Zoroastrians in Britain* (Oxford: Clarendon Press, 1996), pp. 106-137. Regular accounts of developments among the associations on the North American continent are published in *FEZANA Journal.*
8. In orthodox settings, the cleansing consists of scrubbing the corpse first with bull's urine (*gaomaeza/gomez*) and then with water (*ab*). The ritual significance of *gaomaeza* is discussed in detail by Choksy, *Purity and Pollution in Zoroastrianism,* pp. 116-119. Among Zoroastrians in Australia, Europe and North America, contemporary predilections have resulted in widespread use of water alone during the purification.
9. The ritual importance of specially marked-off spaces is elucidated in Jamsheed K. Choksy, "Zoroastrian Notions of Sacred Space," in *Proceedings of the First International Avesta Conference* (Wiesbaden: Otto Harrassowitz, 1998). For the societal standing of professional corpse bearers, which Zoroastrians feel is menial owing to the constant contact with death that such individuals have, see Choksy, *Purity and Pollution in Zoroastrianism,* pp. 107-110. The passage on sacred words or *manthra* acting as defenses against evil and death is from Dhanjishah M. Madan, ed., *Denkard* (Bombay: Society for the Promotion of Researches into the Zoroastrian Religion, 1911), p. 519.
10. Karl Hoffmann, "Av. daxma-," *Zeitschrift für vergleichende Sprachforschung* 79, 3-4 (1965), p. 238. Photographs of the exterior and drawings of the interior of funerary towers may be seen in Josef Bauer, *Symbolik des Parsismus,* Symbolik der Religionen, vol. 18 (Stuttgart: Anton Hiersemann, 1973), pp. 125-128, figs. 97-100.
11. The *Padyab-Kusti* ritual and its associate prayers are described in Choksy, *Purity and Pollution in Zoroastrianism,* pp. 53-62.
12. Mary Boyce and Frantz Grenet, *A History of Zoroastrianism,* vol. 3 (Leiden: E.J. Brill, 1991), pp. 83, 98, 102, 105, 192-193. Photographs of medieval Zoroastrian ossuaries are found in Bauer, *Symbolik des Parsismus,* pp. 109-110, figs. 82-83.

13. More details of the funeral ritual are found in Jivanji J. Modi, *The Religious Ceremonies and Customs of the Parsees,* 2nd ed. (Bombay: British India Press, 1937, reprinted by the Society for the Promotion of Zoroastrian Religious Knowledge and Education, 1986), pp. 49-82, 354-384; Mary Boyce, *A Persian Stronghold of Zoroastrianism* (Oxford: Clarendon Press, 1977, reprinted by the University Press of America, 1989), pp. 41-44, 148-163, 211-226; "Corpse," *Encyclopaedia Iranica,* vol. 6 (Costa Mesa, CA: Mazda, 1993), pp. 279-286; "Death," *Encyclopaedia Iranica,* vol. 7 (Costa Mesa, CA: Mazda, 1996), pp. 179-181; and Hinnells, *Zoroastrians in Britain,* pp. 264-265.
14. The citation on the body's mortality and the soul's immortality is from the 9th-century Pahlavi book entitled *Chidag Handarz i Poryotkeshan* ("The Select Counsels of the Ancient Sages"), edited by Maneck F. Kanga (Bombay: Dorab H. Kanga, 1960).
15. The basic scriptural account, Hadokht Nask, chapters 2 and 3, was translated by Maneck F. Kanga, "Hadokht Nask," *Noor-e-Dastagir* 1 (1983), pp. 13-15. A contemporary edition of the Arda Wiraz Namag, edited and translated by Fereydun Vahman, is *Arda Wiraz Namag: The Iranian 'Divina Commedia,'* Scandinavian Institute for Asian Studies Monograph Series, vol. 53 (London: Curzon Press, 1986). The inscriptions of Kirdir were studied most recently by Philippe Gignoux, *Les quatre inscriptions du mage Kirdir: textes et concordances,* Studia Iranica, cahier 9 (Louvain: Peeters, 1991); and P. Oktor Skjærvø, "Kirdir's Vision: Translation and Analysis," *Archaeologische Mitteilungen aus Iran* 16 (1983), pp. 269-306. The most fundamental study of Zoroastrian beliefs in an afterlife, focusing on all the relevant texts, is Cursetji Pavry, *The Zoroastrian Doctrine of a Future Life: From Death to the Individual Judgment,* 2nd ed. (New York: Columbia University Press, 1929).
16. On the issue of Iranian influences on medieval Christian notions of the afterlife and especially on Dante's beliefs consult Asin Palacios, *Islam and the Divine Comedy* (London: private edition, 1926).
17. *Bundahishn,* edited by Tahmuras D. Anklesaria (Bombay: British India Press, 1908); and "Exegesis on the Hymn to Vohu Manah" or *Zand i Wahman Yasht,* edited by Behramgore T. Anklesaria (Bombay: K.L. Bhargava, 1957).
18. The most elaborate descriptions of Zoroastrian eschatology are preserved in Bundahishn 33:1-34:33, to which the biblical book of Revelation (20:1-21:27) can be compared. A valuable analysis of Zoroastrian eschatological notions is found in Marijan Nolé, *Culte, mythe et cosmologie dans l'Iran ancien: Le problème zoroastrien et la tradition mazdéenne* (Paris: Presses Universitaires de France, 1963).

Conclusion

Krishna, the Manifestation of God for the Hindus, once said, "Abandoning all duties, come to Me alone for shelter, be not grieved, for I shall release thee from all evils" (*Bhagavad Gita* XVII, 66). This is the promise of Moses, Buddha, Zoroaster, Jesus, Muhammad and Baha'u'llah. Moreover, Krishna, like Buddha and other Manifestations of God, promised:

> Whenever there is a decline in righteousness, and rise in unrighteousness, O Bharata; then I send forth Myself for the protection of good, for the destruction of the wicked, and for the establishment of righteousness. I come into being from age to age (*Bhagavad Gita* IV, 7-8).

Our book is a simple attempt to help people understand that God has never left humanity alone, even at the hour of death. Buddha and all of the Manifestations of God taught that at the hour of death, only religious practice will be of help. In our attempts to understand the beliefs of different religions about death and the afterlife, we opened our hearts to the common threads that run through every major religion in the world.

Whether it be the Torah, the Christian Gospel, the Qur'an or the Baha'i Sacred Writings, the different faiths maintain that human thought or good behavior leads to happiness and/or heaven and that evil thought or behavior leads to pain, torment and/or separation from God (hell). One attains salvation, nearness to God or individual serenity through prayer, study of religious teachings and engaging in good works. It is clear from studying most of the religious groups in this book that these works should be done for God's sake to benefit one's fellow human beings. Also, it seems important for the devotees of the different religions to have faith in their prophets' teachings as doors to eternal life. Hell — whether it be the literal fiery state believed in by some branches of Islam and Christian fundamentalist groups, or the eight hot and cold hells of some Buddhists, or the spiritual torment of being alienated from the Creator either in this lifetime or the next — involves turning one's back on God's infinite love.

God has given each person a free will and the potential to independently investigate the truth. Most people have a tendency to "get with the program" and automatically accept their parents' belief systems. Also, many clergy apply social pressure to induce people to conform to their faith without questioning doctrine. Certainly, throughout history there have been priests and divines who have promoted superstitions and delivered hateful comments about denominations inside and outside their own religion. Some of these clerics have lived with and thrived on fear of any group perceived to have beliefs that are different from theirs. Such irrational emotions can be countered to some degree by the provision of factual information, devoid of sensationalism, about what different religions believe about death and the afterlife. And it is our hope that in this book we have succeeded in doing just that.

Questions and Answers about Death and Afterlife

1. IS THERE A HEAVEN, AND IF SO, WHAT IS IT LIKE?

Assemblies of God

Heaven is a real place, a pleasant place. Jesus Christ is present there. God manifests His throne and rules in a special way there.

Baha'is

Though beyond any complete comprehension to anyone in the temporal world, heaven designates spiritual proximity to God, not a physical place. Because spiritual development continues after physical life, heaven is not a fixed point of achievement, but part of an eternal spiritual evolution of the soul.

Baptists

Heaven is a place where the redeemed go to receive the reward of eternal companionship with God. It is depicted as being filled with mansions and golden streets. A new heaven and new earth will be formed after the final judgment.

Buddhists

There are numerous heavens, hierarchically arranged and inhabited by joyous, long-lived, but ultimately mortal beings known as "gods" and "demi-gods." There are also heaven-like realms, usually called Pure Lands, where the Enjoyment Body — an exalted body composed of light — of an enlightened being resides. This heaven is itself made of light that arises from that being's enlightened wisdom: it has no independent existence without his or her presence there.

Christian Science

Christian Science teaches that heaven is a state of consciousness that acknowledges the present power and perfection of God and one's permanent unity with God. Thus heaven is not reserved for a distant place or time, but describes a state that may be experienced right here and now.

Churches of Christ

Heaven is the dwelling place of God and the future residence of the righteous. It is a realm of peace and love. Much of the Biblical description of heaven is metaphorical and, therefore, its features are not now known by humans.

Church of Jesus Christ of Latter-day Saints

There are three "degrees of glory" (I Corinthians 15). All are places of continuing growth and progress. The highest of these is the "Celestial Kingdom." Those who attain this level will live with God and Christ and with their own families. (Mormon Temple marriages are "for time and all eternity" rather than "till death do us part.")

Hindus

The most ancient sacred texts of the Hindus, the Vedas, speak of the journey of the "soul" to the heavenly realm of the ancestors. The body of the deceased is "purified" and the soul conveyed to heaven by the fire of the cremation. On arrival there it receives a subtle body in which it can enjoy pleasures like those on earth and enjoy the rewards of his or her good deeds. Heaven was conceived as a "place" somewhat similar to life on earth, but without sickness, old age and death. Heaven is presided over by Yama, the first man to die and find the road to the celestial world and later identified as the messenger or god of the dead. Later texts describe two paths that the departed soul may take: the path of the ancestors, which leads to rebirth and the path of the gods, which leads to liberation (from rebirth). For those who take the path of the ancestors, heaven is a temporary place for the soul to enjoy the fruits of his or her good actions performed while on earth. When their merit is exhausted, their desires drag them back to earth and to rebirth. The ancient texts of the Upanishads and the Bhagavad Gita identify the "attainment" of the "heavenly realm" with spiritual knowledge and virtuous conduct.

Islam

Heaven is described as a "Garden" having several layers (usually seven) with the highest being directly under God's throne. Souls are content; they eat, drink and arc able to gaze into the face of God.

Judaism

Heaven is a place where anxiety and travail are ended. Some sages have said that quiet, peaceful intellectual activity takes place and the mysteries of life are solved there. A praiseworthy life is of greater importance to the Jew than is seeking Heaven.

Lutherans

Lutherans generally believe that there is a heaven but are not given to speculative theology as to what the nature of heaven might be like.

Presbyterians

Heaven is dwelling in perfect holiness and joy with God; little is said about the nature of the next world because both heaven and hell are indescribable.

Quakers

Friends believe heaven constitutes a renewed creation, a "peaceable kingdom" with dimensions greater but not wholly unlike those experienced in earthly existence. Although it is cloaked in a mystery, the Spirit gives a foretaste of heaven's glory.

Roman Catholics

"Heaven" designates a condition rather than a place: eternal fullness of life, supreme happiness flowing from intimacy with God.

Seventh-day Adventists

Heaven is being in the presence of God. It is the dwelling place of God and will ultimately be located in the renewed earth.

Unitarian Universalists

This faith accepts a scientific view of life and sees life as lived in the here and now rather than in the hereafter. It is not known whether or not there is an afterlife.

United Methodists

Most believe heaven exists and is characterized by being in the presence of God. (As with most of the other groups, among the United Methodists there are those who literally expect streets of gold and those who interpret heaven and hell more symbolically.)

Unity

Heaven is a state of consciousness in which the soul is attuned to the harmonious arrangement of divine ideas in Divine Mind. Divine ideas are not mere intellectual concepts; they are the living attributes, energies or patterns of God, including love, wisdom, order and joy. Thus those who are conscious of the presence and nature of Spirit can experience heaven on earth and in whatever other dimensions of experience there may be.

Zoroastrians

There is a heaven and it is called *garo-demana* ("the house of song") or *wahisht* ("best place"). Heaven is regarded as a paradisiacal location where souls dwell in peace and joy, enjoying warmth and pleasure until the resurrection.

2. WHO WILL BE SAVED?

Assemblies of God

All will be saved who place active faith in Jesus Christ, accepting Him as their Lord and Savior, their assurance of future resurrection.

Baha'is

Salvation is not a single experience, but a process of becoming secure in one's efforts to recognize the reality of God and to follow His guidance. Whoever turns toward the light of truth and sincerely strives for this truth will achieve salvation. More specifically, Baha'is believe that two things are incumbent on every person — to recognize the Divine Manifestations when they appear and to obey their law and guidance for our lives. Baha'is believe that because Baha'u'llah is the most recent of these Manifestations, it is especially important for mankind to recognize Baha'u'llah and to follow His teachings.

Baptists

Those will be saved who believe in Jesus Christ. Baptism is not required for salvation, but it is the visible sign of the emergence from spiritual death.

Buddhists

"Saved" is not an entirely appropriate word for Buddhism because the emphasis there is on achieving liberation or enlightenment by one's own efforts. However, Mahayana does speak of receiving significant help to this end through the blessings of those already enlightened. According to Hinayana, anyone who, motivated by a wish to leave cyclic existence (*samsara*), gains insight into impermanence and selflessness will be free. Mahayana maintains that anyone, male or female, lay or clergy, who aspires to enlightenment out of a loving and compassionate wish to be of maximal help to others and who achieves wisdom realizing the selflessness taught in their philosophies, will be enlightened as a Buddha.

Christian Science

Universal salvation is an important element of Christian Science theology, based on the conviction that all creation is, in truth, the expression of God. Salvation is experienced progressively as this fact is recognized, established in consciousness and made the basis for daily life.

Churches of Christ

The saved are those who hear the proclamation of the Gospel, believe and confess that Jesus is the Christ, the son of God, repent of their sins and are baptized (immersed) for the forgiveness of sins.

Church of Jesus Christ of Latter-day Saints

Salvation, in the sense of being resurrected, comes as a gift to all men through the atonement of Christ. However, exaltation (or the privilege of living in the Celestial Kingdom with God) comes through our works and our obedience to the laws and ordinances of the Gospel.

Hindus

Being "saved" in the Hindu tradition means essentially being saved from spiritual ignorance. Everyone has the potential and the duty to be saved or rather to achieve their own salvation in this sense. Hindu scriptures articulate a variety of paths and means by which each person may lead a life that develops spiritual wisdom or understanding (divine knowledge) and love of God. A key element is the cultivation of dispassion from one's base instincts and desires. Attachment to one's body and this worldly life leads to suffering and to delusion about the true nature of our Self.

Islam

Those who live ethically and have faith in God's "oneness" will be saved. There are five clearly stated responsibilities required to be judged worthy of heaven. These include: verbal testimony of belief in God and Muhammad, praying, fasting, paying alms-tax and at least one pilgrimage to the holy city of Mecca.

Judaism

Entrance to Heaven is gained by righteous deeds and an ethical living pattern. Even so, anyone can repent until the end of life and be saved.

Lutherans

Those will be saved to whom God extends the gift of salvation.

Presbyterians

Those who have loved God, purity and other people will be saved. Salvation comes through faith in Christ. Believers must witness to others and engage in good works. Faith without works is not saving.

Quakers

All will be saved who respond faithfully to the Light of Christ within, accepting God's redeeming grace and seeking to live within God's will, which is supremely revealed in Jesus Christ.

Roman Catholics

No person, however holy, earns salvation, which can only be received as a pure gift bestowed upon the undeserving. Salvation comes only through Jesus, normally mediated through baptism and active membership in his church. Nonbelievers, especially those who help the needy, can also be saved through Jesus. To be a Christian means set apart for service, commissioned to share God's Good News with the whole world.

Seventh-day Adventists

Those who are obediently faithful will be saved. Care and discipline of the body are helpful on the path to salvation. The resurrected righteous pass a millennium in heaven and then dwell forever with the Lord in the purified and renewed earth, free from all sorrow, pain and sin.

Unitarian Universalists

Salvation of all souls was the original concept on which Universalism was founded. Modern Unitarian Universalism has not altered this assumption.

United Methodists

The United Methodist understanding speaks of salvation both now and hereafter. While living, sinners can be saved by turning from a life of sin to a life of holiness. Life everlasting is the gift of salvation that continues after death. Such salvation is available to all and whoever responds to God's grace through Jesus Christ may be saved.

Unity

Ultimately every soul will be saved, for salvation is assured by the Infinite Love and Grace of God. Life is like a school in which souls learn spiritual truths at their own pace. The teacher is omniscient, infinite Wisdom, which cannot fail.

Zoroastrians

Those who will be saved are the souls of Zoroastrians who followed the creed of good thoughts, good words and good deeds, who struggled against forms of evil and whose pious actions outweighed their improper ones while alive.

3. IS THERE A HELL, AND IF SO, WHAT IS IT LIKE?

Assemblies of God

Hell is a place of fire and darkness. Its inhabitants are full of remorse and frustrations, cut off from faith, hope and love. But this is not the final state. After the final judgment the unsaved will be placed in the lake of fire for eternity.

Baha'is

Just as "heaven" designates turning toward God or proximity to God, "hell" designates the spiritual condition of those who willfully reject this divine reality, whether in this life or in the next. Hell is thus not a place but a spiritual condition of remoteness.

Baptists

Most Southern Baptists believe in a place of punishment as it is described in the Bible, characterized by outer darkness, fire, torment and isolation.

Buddhists

There are eight hot and cold hells, each associated with a particular type of suffering. These tortures are described in detail in order to develop compassion for the beings there as well as to create an incentive not to engage in the types of non-virtuous behavior that will cause one to end up there. As with the heavens, one remains there for a very long period, but is eventually reborn elsewhere.

Christian Science

To a Christian Scientist hell, like heaven, is not a place but a state of consciousness. It is based on the hypothesis that intelligence, substance and life exist apart from God.

Churches of Christ

There is a literal hell. The characteristics of hell set forth in the scriptures are to some extent metaphorical and its features are not known except for eternal fire.

Church of Jesus Christ of Latter-day Saints

Persons who obtain a lower degree of glory may experience a form of hell in their regret or in the knowledge of what they could have achieved. Outer darkness, or the absence of any glory, will occur only in the rare instances of those who knowingly deny the Holy Ghost.

Hindus

Like heaven, hell too is a relative plane of existence and souls are led there to suffer the consequences of their sins or unrighteous actions on earth. In due course these souls are born once again on earth to take up the threads of their spiritual evolution. Though hell is not described in the earliest Hindu literature, it is described in detail in the later (especially Puranic) literature where numerous terrible hells are mentioned along with the various actions or behaviors that lead to one or another of these hells. In other contexts, our sense-perceived world and a life of spiritual ignorance are depicted as hellish in the sense that it is full of suffering.

Islam

Hell is described as a fire having seven levels. The lowest crackles and roars with fierce boiling water, scorching wind and wailing, wretched souls.

Judaism

The assumption is that God's caring nature rules out a sadistic punishment. The nature of hell is a mystery left alone by the Jew.

Lutherans

Traditional Lutheran belief suggests that there is a hell. As with heaven, Lutherans have not been inclined to speculate as to what the nature of hell might be.

Presbyterians

Hell is a place apart from God, filled with everlasting suffering and misery.

Quakers

Yes. Its reality testifies to both God's judgment of evil and to God's mercy in releasing the creation from bondage to it. Hell is a consequence of rebellion against God.

Roman Catholics

"Hell" designates a condition of self-chosen, permanent alienation from God who bestows all blessings.

Seventh-day Adventists

It is the punishment and destruction of the finally impenitent wicked at the end of history.

Unitarian Universalists

As with the good, what evil people do is compensated for in this life.

United Methodists

Hell is separation from God, the absence of fulfillment and communion with God and others.

Unity

Hell is a state of consciousness in which the soul is not attuned to the presence and goodness of Spirit. The suffering of this state is anxiety, fear, confusion, anger and other feelings that emerge from beliefs in separation from God. Hell is not a permanent place or experience, for the Grace of God works in many ways to bring the soul out of hell and into heaven.

Zoroastrians

There is a hell called *drujo-demana* ("abode of deceit") or *dushokh* ("the worst place"). It is a cold, dark place full of pain and suffering where souls dwell in torment until the resurrection.

4. WHO GOES TO HELL?

Assemblies of God

All who do not change their attitudes toward Jesus Christ and accept Him as their personal savior and Lord will go to hell.

Baha'is

In the sense that hell is not a physical place, one does not "go to it," and because it is a spiritual condition resulting from willful rejection of God's guidance, it can occur during the earthly experience as well as in the afterlife experience. Thus, those who experience the pain of this remoteness are those who willfully reject the truth and continue doing so, though forgiveness and reformation are never beyond attainment, whether in this life or the next.

Baptists

The wicked who have not been "born again" are consigned to hell.

Buddhists

Any type of nonvirtuous action, if powerful enough, can result in birth in a hell. Words, thoughts or deeds motivated by strong hatred are particularly likely to have this result.

Christian Science

From the standpoint of Christian Science, the concept of hell arises from thoughts that are contrary to the divine will and nature. Most people entertain such thoughts at one time or another and some people seem to dwell on them. But Christian Science teaches that eventually everyone will recognize and accept divine Truth.

Churches of Christ

The unrighteous will be punished in hell forever. Everyone who does not accept the salvation offered by God and live according to his rules will be cast into hell.

Church of Jesus Christ of Latter-day Saints

Outer darkness, or the absence of any glory, will occur only to those who knowingly deny the Holy Ghost.

Hindus

Those who have lived lives contrary to the teachings of the scriptures experience punishment in hell after death. The degree of punishment and length of time in hell are determined by the type and extent of the evil or unrighteous behavior.

Islam

Sinners who do not follow basic responsibilities of ethical living go to Hell. Denying the one God leads to sure damnation. Many believe sinners will eventually be pardoned and the fire will be extinguished forever.

Judaism

The unrepentant sinner will be punished. All humans are accountable before God for their misdeeds. The nature of the punishment should reflect divine justice, compassion and wisdom.

Lutherans

According to traditional belief, the devil and all who do not receive the gift of salvation go to hell.

Presbyterians

Hell receives those who have loved self, sin and evil.

Quakers

Impenitent sinners who have defied God's spirit striving within them will not be reunited with him.

Roman Catholics

God intends and works for the salvation of everyone. Unbelievers unknowingly accept or reject Jesus as their Savior by caring or refusing to care for the needy.

Seventh-day Adventists

The impenitent wicked are judged, punished and will finally perish completely; and it will be as though they had never existed.

Unitarian Universalists

No one "goes" to hell; people create their own hells here on earth.

United Methodists

There is fear, but not assurance, that people who do not respond positively to God's act of love in Jesus Christ go to hell. God will be the judge.

Unity

Hell is not a place that anyone goes to; it is a state of consciousness that anyone can be in and get out of. False beliefs in separation from God cause the unpleasant consciousness of "hell." Once those false beliefs are overcome, through hearing the Truth and prayer, people can get out of the "hell" state of mind and enter into more pleasant states of consciousness.

Zoroastrians

The souls of impious Zoroastrians and of all nonbelievers go to hell.

5. WHAT HAPPENS AT THE END OF TIME AND/OR AT A JUDGMENT DAY?

Assemblies of God

At the end of time, following a period of 1000 years of peace under Christ's rule, Satan will be released for a time. Then the wicked will be judged, cast into the lake of fire and God will bring into being a new heaven and a new earth where there will be no more death.

Baha'is

As this term is usually discussed, it designates the period immediately after the coming of a new Revelator, a new Manifestation, when the followers of the previous religions are tested ("judged"), as were the Jews at the time of Christ, then Christians at the coming of Muhammad and the Muslims with the coming of Baha'u'llah. The particular judgment alluded to in the New Testament refers to this present time in history when all people are challenged to recognize the essential unity of God's prophets and the oneness of humankind.

Baptists

Judgment is inevitable and occurs at death, but the final judgment occurs at the second coming of Christ at the end of the age, at which time the saved will go to be with Christ eternally and the wicked will be cast into Hell for eternity.

Buddhists

There is no end of time, there is only a cyclical process of world systems arising, abiding and ceasing. The beings in those systems do not cease to exist when their world disappears, they are simply reborn in another world system. There is no time foreseen when all the 100 billion world systems, each containing 100 billion worlds, will disappear.

Christian Science

Christian Scientists do not look to a culminating event to either reward good or to punish or correct wrongs. Rather, individual acknowledgment of and obedience to God progressively transforms character until the individual realizes he or she has never left God's presence. "Judgment" in this sense is not relegated to a time or place, but occurs continually during the course of one's life. The transformation of society is seen as an outgrowth of individual change and occurs in the same manner.

Churches of Christ

When Christ returns it will not be to set up a kingdom on earth, but to collect all those raised for the great judgment. Each person will appear before the judgment bar of God and his fate will be sealed. Those who have responded to the Gospel and lived consonant with the commands of God will enter heaven. The unrighteous will be cast into the fires of hell.

Church of Jesus Christ of Latter-day Saints

The resurrection is followed by continued progression in one of the three degrees of glory. We lived, as spirits, before this life with our Heavenly Father. The growth we experience in mortality and our resurrection into perfected bodies are part of our preparation to return to His presence and continue our eternal progress.

Hindus

In the Hindu view, the universe is endless. However, there are vast cycles of time (divided into four "ages" or *yugas*) when all that is in the universe is dissolved and then recreated or "manifested." This manifestation and dissolution are also known as the outbreathing and inbreathing of Brahman, the Supreme Being. We are presently in the last or most dissolute age (*Kali Yuga*) of the present cycle which eventually will be followed by a "golden age." On an individual level, it is the law of karma that "judges" each person for every action has a consequence that will inevitably work itself out in a person's life (or afterlife). Liberation from the cycle of rebirth implies extinguishing the effects of karma.

Islam

Moral chaos occurs. Cosmic events signify the coming of the Judgment Day. Nothing but God will remain. The Day of Judgment is terrifying even for the good.

Judaism

God will never again destroy the world. The coming of the Messiah will herald a peaceful age the likes of which the world has never known.

Lutherans

Traditional Lutheran belief holds that Jesus will return, the dead will be raised and a day of judgment will be held, with the just (i.e., the recipients of the gift of salvation) going to heaven and the unjust to hell for eternity.

Presbyterians

Doctrinal statements have seldom dealt with this question. Most say they do not know what will happen, but there will be a Day of Judgment.

Quakers

Friends believe in a Second Coming of Christ to complete the work of God's redemption of the world and in a Final Judgment to mark God's triumph over evil and the beginning of a new realm of reality. Quakers are more concerned, however, with witnessing, by word and deed, God's kingdom now than speculating about its future.

Roman Catholics

Immediately at death, God solemnly ratifies definitive acceptance or rejection of the salvation offered everyone. The Kingdom comes to individuals at the particular judgment, but God's grand salvific purpose of total renewal for all creation will be realized only at final or general judgment.

Seventh-day Adventists

The righteous dead will be resurrected and together with the righteous living will be glorified and taken to Heaven, but the unrighteous will die. After remaining dead for 1000 years, they will rise, be judged and destroyed in Hell. Afterwards, the earth, made new, will become the eternal home of the righteous.

Unitarian Universalists

No one knows, but a loving God would not condemn any person to eternal damnation.

United Methodists

Some believe in a specific day Christ will come again, judge and assign some to heaven and some to hell. Others believe judgment coincides with response to God's grace and continues from this life to the next.

Unity

Consciousness that life is eternal is the end of time, that is, the end of belief in the concept of absolute time with beginning and end. Physics has proved that time is not absolute, that time is a concept relative to space and motion. Spiritual teachings have long held that God is eternal and so transcends time. To the degree that we are consciously one with God, we transcend time and find eternal life. "Judgment Day" is every day in the sense that every day involves experiences that are consequences of previous actions.

Zoroastrians

There will be a resurrection of all souls, both Zoroastrian and non-Zoroastrian, a final universal judgment, the salvation of all souls, the vanquishing of evil, the renovation of the material world, and the restoration and reunification of human bodies with their souls.

6. DOES YOUR FAITH BELIEVE IN RESURRECTION, AND IF SO, WILL THE BODY OR SPIRIT RISE?

Assemblies of God

The resurrection of the body occurs.

Baha'is

Resurrection is spiritual, not physical. As it is alluded to in the scriptures, "resurrection" refers to the spiritual transformation of the planet.

Baptists

The body is resurrected in a glorified and perfected state to dwell with the Lord. The final judgment is preceded by this resurrection.

Buddhists

No future time of resurrection is foreseen; each person's consciousness leaves his or her body at death and takes rebirth soon thereafter, unless and until Enlightenment (Buddhahood) is achieved.

Christian Science

Christian Scientists think of resurrection as the way of life, both before and after the crucifixion, that Christ Jesus exemplified. They seek to follow his example by a daily spiritualization of thought that restores the conscious awareness of God's presence — the presence of Life, Truth and Love — and of man as God's spiritual, perfect image and likeness. Because Christian Scientists regard the body fundamentally as thought, they believe that as thought grows more spiritual, the body is increasingly freed of disease and limitation.

Churches of Christ

When Jesus Christ returns to earth there will be a resurrection of the dead, both righteous and wicked. The resurrection will be of a spiritual body, not the body of flesh and blood.

Church of Jesus Christ of Latter-day Saints

Yes. The spirit, which has awaited the resurrection in a Spirit World, reunites with a perfected physical body.

Hindus

No. Hinduism does not use the terminology of resurrection but rather of "liberation" (*moksha*) of the soul through self-knowledge or individual enlightenment. The soul is imperishable.

Islam

Descriptions of afterlife are of highly physical pains and pleasures.

Judaism

Yes. Reform Jews believe only in resurrection of the soul. Other Jews believe in the resurrection of both body and soul.

Lutherans

The traditional Lutheran view is that of the resurrection of the body.

Presbyterians

Although disagreement exists, most Presbyterians believe in the resurrection of a new body. Beliefs differ widely about the nature and timing of this event.

Quakers

Friends believe in a resurrection of the whole person — body, mind and spirit. The last enemy is death and through Christ's resurrection we are assured of our own. We believe that life after death offers continuing personal identity and interpersonal fellowship, the dimensions of which are hinted at by joys found in God's creation and within the community of faith.

Roman Catholics

Bodily resurrection means eternal life as full and integral persons, sharing the perfected existence already enjoyed by the risen Jesus. Christian theology distinguishes between full resurrection at End Times and perfected life with God immediately upon death.

Seventh-day Adventists

The glorified body will be resurrected for the life to come. This occurs at Christ's second coming. The glorified body has no defects or disfigurements but possesses continuity with the present body.

Unitarian Universalists

Because bodily decay occurs rapidly following death, from the scientific point of view, bodily resurrection is not possible. The spirit may continue somehow or in some form.

United Methodists

Resurrection of the dead is of the body and spirit, the recognizable and lovable person.

Unity

Resurrection is understood to mean "rising up again." Any experience of "rising up" in consciousness of omnipresent life, as in being healed of serious physical or emotional illness, is a resurrection in a metaphorical sense. Literally coming back to life is a resurrection, as in the story of Lazarus in the Gospel of John and in contemporary reports of "near death experiences." Life is eternal, so a soul's transition from this world into another dimension could also be considered a resurrection. We do not teach a literal physical resurrection of all souls at the end of time.

Zoroastrians

Both the body and the soul of each human will rise and be united at the final resurrection.

7. WHAT HAPPENS AFTER DEATH TO PEOPLE WHO ARE NOT OF YOUR FAITH?

Assemblies of God

Other Christians after death are immediately in paradise with Christ. People of other faiths awake in Hades (hell).

Baha'is

God does not judge people according to what they call themselves, but rather according to the lives they have lived, how sincerely they have strived to follow God's plan for their lives.

Baptists

Those who have consciously rejected Christ are thought to be damned, but God only is the judge. The incompetent and unenlightened are left in God's hands.

Buddhists

All people are the same in this regard: depending on their own actions in this or former lifetimes, they take rebirth in a good or bad situation. Except for persons highly developed spiritually, this is not a matter over which one has any control.

Christian Science

In Acts 10:34, Peter is quoted as declaring, "God is no respecter of persons." Christian Scientists maintain that God is no respecter of human races, creeds or cultures, either. All are His children and He loves all equally. The significant issue is, to what degree do His children recognize Him and their own true nature? To the extent that one's relation to God is understood, the individual knows his or her true identity as this beloved child. Christian Scientists understand that death is neither a help nor a deterrent to experiencing true identity, no matter what one's religious affiliation.

Churches of Christ

There is one faith according to the Scriptures. God will determine who belongs to that one faith.

Church of Jesus Christ of Latter-day Saints

All people go to the Spirit World (spoken of in II Peter, chapters 3 and 4) where they await the resurrection. Those who have not had the chance to learn of Christ and of His Gospel while on this earth will have that opportunity in the Spirit World.

Hindus

In the Hindu view all spiritual paths lead to the same goal, which is God consciousness and eternal union or communion with God. This is the destiny of every soul. Hindus view their teachings and religious truth in general as universal and applicable to all, irrespective of anyone's religious views and affiliations. Tolerance and respect for diverse points of view are encouraged.

Islam

Most Sunnis believe non-Muslims can achieve salvation and reach the Garden, but only after a period of purgation.

Judaism

There is tolerance for other religions. Anyone who fulfills the basic commandments of proper relationships with others has nothing to fear after death.

Lutherans

The determining factor is whether people have received the gift of salvation from God. Not all who profess to be Christians, according to traditional Lutheran theology, are recipients of this gift. Nor is it restricted to those who claim to be Christians. There has been considerable softening of this doctrine in the course of the centuries.

Quakers

Friends believe that God accepts into his eternal kingdom all persons who in faith follow the Light within them. We believe that atonement offered in Christ is effective for all such persons, however they articulate their faithful response. Together with Augustine, we say, "God is greater in our thoughts than in our words and in reality than in our thoughts."

Presbyterians

All who believe in Christ have a heavenly home. Presbyterians disagree about the fate of non-believers. Most leave non-Christians in the hands of a loving God.

Roman Catholics

"Afterlife" doesn't mean just a continuation of present earthly existence. Eternal happiness doesn't come as a reward earned by an elite few who did and said the right things to cajole blessings from a reluctant deity. Nor is it a gift limited to members of one particularly religious group. Life in God's Kingdom comes as a purest gift needing only grateful acceptance. It corresponds to creation's deepest longings and reflects divine selfless love. Humans will share his being so completely that they become as much like him as possible, while remaining themselves.

Seventh-day Adventists

This is left to God's judgment. No human can judge another's heart or his or her relationship to God.

Unitarian Universalists

There are no religious distinctions following death.

United Methodists

The ultimate place of other faiths and of those who have not been exposed to Christianity is left to God's judgment.

Unity

God's love is universal; one's particular faith does not matter in God's eyes. There is a diversity of spiritual paths because there is diversity among human beings; different people have different temperaments, inclinations, experiences and needs.

Zoroastrians

Their souls are consigned to hell until the final resurrection, at which time they are purified of their error and then saved.

8. IS THERE A PURGATORY OR LIMBO AFTER DEATH?

Assemblies of God

We do not believe that there is Purgatory or Limbo after death.

Baha'is

Inasmuch as there is an infinite variety of spiritual conditions, there are, we can assume, an infinite variety of individual experiences after death, not just a positive or a negative one. Consequently, there may be some spiritual conditions that would comply with purgatorial or so-called limbo states.

Baptists

No. The dead are souls waiting for the resurrection of the body, but they go either to heaven or hell immediately at death.

Buddhists

Hinayana maintains that the consciousness exits the body and immediately enters its next place of rebirth, for example, the mother's womb. Mahayana says that one may linger in an intermediate state, usually no longer than 49 days, before taking rebirth. During this period one has only a mental body, no physical form; however, one has all five senses and is able to travel as if magically through walls and instantaneously arrive where one wishes to go until finally one's passage is obstructed, in accordance with one's karma, by the next place of rebirth.

Christian Science

"Probation After Death" is the subject of one of the Bible Lessons studied by students of Christian Science. This reflects the importance in Christian Science of the idea that life continues after death. Christian Science also teaches the necessity of understanding the true nature of Life as God and that death, as the Bible indicates, will be overcome as individuals accept the facts of being and live according to them.

Churches of Christ

The place of the dead awaiting the great judgment is Hades. It is divided into two sections: Paradise, the abode of the faithful, and Tartarus, the realm of unbelievers and evildoers. Purgatory and Limbo are not found in scripture and for that reason are nonexistent.

Church of Jesus Christ of Latter-day Saints

When this life ends, our spirits leave our bodies and go to the Spirit World where they continue to progress and await the resurrection and judgment.

Hindus

One strand of Hinduism compares dying to falling asleep and the afterdeath experiences to dreams — of heaven and hell. In this dreamlike state, which is another plane of existence, the soul experiences rewards or punishment for its past actions. No new actions may be initiated in this state. Its duration is variable and from our point of view immeasurable. When the soul awakes after this sleep it finds itself reborn on earth as a human being. According to the ancient ritualistic strand of Hinduism, after death the soul remains in limbo until its "body" is ritually reconstructed by the deceased's living relatives. This takes about 10 days. Those for whom the proper rites were not performed or who died untimely deaths (through accident or murder) are thought to remain as unhappy "ghosts" who may hover around their relatives, potentially causing havoc, until placated and released.

Islam

There is a place where souls wait after death for the day of resurrection. Muslims speculate about what this is like. Good souls are allowed visions of God and the wicked also are allowed to see what awaits them, then both return to the grave. Even after the Judgment Day, some remain in limbo.

Judaism

Purgatory has deep origins in Jewish literature and has been described in different ways, but this has never become an influential Jewish doctrine.

Lutherans

Most of the medieval beliefs related to purgatory were not continued by the Lutheran movement.

Presbyterians

One of our creeds says, "The souls of believers are at their death made perfect in holiness and do immediately pass into glory." The wicked immediately enter the torments of hell. Some believe souls will sleep until resurrection. Others believe souls may come to know Christ in an intermediate state.

Quakers

We find no biblical warrant for a belief in an intermediate state.

Roman Catholics

Part of official Catholic doctrine, purgatory is a condition (rather than a place) of transition and adaptation for those entering heavenly beatitude, a passage at once painful and joyful into purified fullness of life with God. By contrast, limbo was never part of required belief and is now generally rejected as a well-meaning answer to a wrong question.

Seventh-day Adventists

Death is a sleep of total unconsciousness until the second coming of Christ. Souls do not live before the Resurrection. There is no purgatory.

Unitarian Universalists

As with heaven and hell, the scientific view sees purgatory or limbo as being improbable. They are not places.

United Methodists

Generally, there is no belief in purgatory because it alludes to salvation by works and United Methodists believe in salvation by grace and faith.

Unity

We have no teaching on this point. There may be some Unity people who believe in a concept of gradual self-perfection of the soul, but most do not believe in limbo or purgatory as they are usually understood.

Zoroastrians

Yes, a limbo is believed to exist for souls whose good and evil deeds are equivalent. The state of limbo ends with the final resurrection.

9. WILL WE RECOGNIZE FRIENDS AND RELATIVES AFTER DEATH?

Assemblies of God

There will be recognition of friends and relatives after death.

Baha'is

Yes. We will recognize them and commune with them and other souls with whom we have been associated in life.

Baptists

Yes, we will be reunited with our loved ones.

Buddhists

In the intermediate state we can see our living friends and relatives, but they cannot see or hear us. Those who have died before us will have taken rebirth themselves; we do not meet them. However, there is some likelihood of being reborn in situations where we continue relationships with persons from the past, though neither they nor we may be aware of this previous connection.

Christian Science

Yes, when, through spiritual growth, one comes to the same plane of consciousness as those who have already passed the experience of death.

Churches of Christ

It is now commonly believed that we will recognize friends and relatives after death.

Church of Jesus Christ of Latter-day Saints

Yes.

Hindus

Ancient Hinduism speaks of the departed being united with his or her ancestors after death. Later Hinduism speaks of this reunion as being temporary for each soul is in a unique stage of its evolution and must tread its own path, which may include sojourns in heaven and hell, immediate rebirth, or immediate union with God.

Islam

Some traditions believe families are reunited in the Garden. The Qur'an does not discuss this.

Judaism

Yes. It is a fervent hope of pious believers that husband and wife, parents and children and all close relatives will be reunited in loving togetherness after death.

Lutherans

Yes.

Presbyterians

Creeds do not deal with this, but most believe we will know our loved ones. Relationships will be lifted to a higher level and family will be superseded.

Quakers

We will recognize those whom we've cared about in life and we will have an enhanced capacity to love them. Friends believe that a creation renewed in righteousness offers added dimensions for interactive love. And 50 billion galaxies attuned to the purposes of God's Kingdom should offer sufficient venue for creative thought and activity!

Roman Catholics

Biblical teaching indicates a radically transformed existence in afterlife that is both continuous and discontinuous with life as we know it now. Friends and relatives will recognize each other, but in a situation of changed relationships. Because the entire community of the saved will know an intimacy beyond anything achieved on earth, private groupings in families and friendships have no place.

Seventh-day Adventists

Yes, we will recognize those we have known and will be reunited with them, nevermore to part (after the second coming).

Unitarian Universalists

Not in a physical sense.

United Methodists

Yes, we will know friends and relatives in the afterlife and may know and love them more perfectly than on earth.

Unity

We have no teaching on this point. Most Unity people probably believe in some kind of ongoing relationship with loved ones after death.

Zoroastrians

Yes, we will recognize friends and relatives in heaven or in hell or limbo, depending on where the soul goes, and also at the final judgment and after the renovation of the world.

10. IS CREMATION ALLOWED BY YOUR FAITH?

Assemblies of God

Cremation is not encouraged, but God can and will bring together whatever is necessary for resurrection of the body.

Baha'is

No. Because the body has been the temple of the spirit in the physical plane of existence, it should be treated with appropriate respect.

Baptists

Cremation is allowed but not encouraged.

Buddhists

Cremation is generally preferred. In Tibet, however, the body is often left on a charnel ground to feed wild animals.

Christian Science

The choice of cremation is left up to the individual.

Churches of Christ

Cremation is permitted, but not widely practiced. Because so few are cremated, most persons who are members of the Churches of Christ feel very uncomfortable about the prospect. The majority of members of the Churches of Christ live in regions where cremation is infrequent.

Church of Jesus Christ of Latter-day Saints

Yes, but not encouraged.

Hindus

Yes. Cremation is the most common method of disposal of the body. Fire is considered sacred and purifying and it is regarded as a messenger between the mundane and the divine world. Young children and ascetics, however, are normally buried or immersed in a river.

Islam

Cremation is not practiced because Muslims understand that the agonies of the fire are for God alone to prepare for the sinful.

Judaism

Cremation is not allowed by traditional Jews because it interferes with the return of the body to its natural state. Reform Jews permit it, but not very many reform Jewish families request it.

Lutherans

Yes, but not widely practiced.

Presbyterians

Yes, although it is neither encouraged nor discouraged.

Quakers

Customs vary among Friends; some prefer burial, some cremation.

Roman Catholics

Disposal of the body in no way affects afterlife or final-day resurrection. Anything is permitted so long as proper reverence is observed. Donation of organs is a fitting final expression of Christian neighbor love.

Seventh-day Adventists

There is no objection to cremation, although it is not commonly done. Resurrection is not dependent on a physically intact body.

Unitarian Universalists

Cremation is an increasingly favored method of disposal of the body. It is less costly than a traditional funeral and allows a more convenient scheduling of the preferred memorial service.

United Methodists

Yes.

Unity

Cremation is a permitted practice.

Zoroastrians

Not until recent times and even now not by the orthodox.

11. WHAT HAPPENS TO PEOPLE WHO COMMIT SUICIDE?

Assemblies of God

The destiny of people who commit suicide is left to God. He is merciful to those who do so because of mental illness.

Baha'is

Suicide is forbidden and those who commit suicide will, no doubt, regret this action in the afterlife; however, they are not beyond redemption because of this act nor should they be considered to be faithless or no longer members of the religion because of this violation of Baha'i law.

Baptists

They can go to heaven if they have established a relationship of forgiveness with God in this life and ask for forgiveness for this final sin.

Buddhists

Because the mind just prior to death is a particularly powerful determinant of how one will be reborn, anyone who dies in a distressed mental state is more likely to have an unfortunate rebirth. Thus, someone who commits suicide and dies in an anguished or depressed state is apt to be propelled to a similarly unhappy situation subsequently.

Christian Science

Death is never a friend, never a solution to any one of life's challenges. Seeking to escape through death is only to deepen one's misapprehension of the nature of Life, God. Suicide does not change God's love for the individual, but it renders the individual that much less able presently to accept God's love, be nourished by it and so be equipped to overcome the problems he or she faces.

Churches of Christ

Most persons argue that one should not decide the time of death. That is the prerogative of God. Therefore suicide is a violation of God's desires. But it is generally thought that God may show mercy to suicides as to others who violate his ways.

Church of Jesus Christ of Latter-day Saints

It would depend on the circumstances. Christ is the Judge.

Hindus

Life is sacred and suicide is generally condemned by Hindu lawgivers. Those who commit suicide will experience the negative consequences of this act in the afterlife.

Islam

The Qur'an itself contains no passages that can unequivocally be interpreted as prohibiting suicide. The theologians and authorities on tradition, however, condemn suicide as a grave sin. The person who takes his or her own life is considered to be doomed to the Fire, and according to tradition, must repeat for all eternity the act by which life was taken.

Judaism

For most of Jewish history, suicide was a major offense, the punishment for which was denial of normal burial and mourning. In modern times, it has become acknowledged that suicide is often the result of mental imbalance, so the stringency of the burial rule has been relaxed.

Lutherans

Lutherans generally regard most cases of suicide as the result of illness, rather than as a freely chosen act for which there is moral accountability. In cases in which suicide is viewed as a sin, it is generally believed that God's mercy is sufficient to forgive this sin, as well as all other sins. Lutheran theology holds that forgiveness is entirely a gift of grace, rather than something which is contingent upon confession and penance or anything else that the individual in question might do.

Presbyterians

Although our doctrinal statements have not dealt with the subject of suicide, most Presbyterians believe that suicide is not an unpardonable sin and that one who takes his own life is not, at that moment, of entirely sound mind. One who commits suicide will be judged, not merely by the one act that terminated his life, but by the overall faith that prevailed in his heart.

Quakers

Quakers believe that all taking of life is wrong, including suicide, but God is a righteous and merciful judge who is able to discern the thoughts and intents of the heart.

Roman Catholics

Suicide is now generally attributed to unbearable stress rather than rejection of God. Victims are accordingly not refused regular Christian burial.

Seventh-day Adventists

Judgment is left to a loving God. The life as lived is more important than this one act.

Unitarian Universalists

Suicide is usually due to unbearable stress and we should offer love and compassion to suicides and their survivors.

United Methodists

United Methodists view suicide as they do other misfortunes — as an error or sin. Suicide is not an unforgivable sin. All wrongs, errors and sins are viewed in the light of God's intention for life, abundant in the light of God's mercy and forgiveness through Jesus Christ. Suicide victims are commended to God's love and forgiveness and Christian ministry addresses problems that lead to suicide and seeks to aid persons who contemplate taking their lives.

Unity

That is not for us to judge. God is wise, just and merciful, so whatever the consequences of suicide are, we have faith that those consequences will ultimately work for good.

Zoroastrians

The souls of those who commit suicide stay suspended in limbo until after the final resurrection, then they are absolved of their evil deeds and saved.

12. DOES YOUR FAITH BELIEVE IN THE CONCEPT OF REINCARNATION?

Assemblies of God

We do not believe in reincarnation.

Baha'is

No. We believe that the human soul takes its beginning at conception and exists eternally from that point, but it has only one period during which it associates through a physical body.

Baptists

No.

Buddhists

Yes. From the belief in beginningless reincarnation it follows that we have been in every possible relationship with everyone else. Most significantly, everyone has been a great friend and even our own mother at some time in the past; hence, it is appropriate to have compassion and concern for them, no matter what their present situation is or how they now behave toward us.

Christian Science

No. Reincarnation is based on the view that matter defines and contains life. Christian Science teaches that since each life is the expression of God, it must be exclusively and eternally spiritual.

Churches of Christ

In scripture each individual is provided one lifetime in which to decide for or against God. For that reason reincarnation is foreign to the explicit vision of life as a boot camp for what awaits beyond the great judgment.

Church of Jesus Christ of Latter-day Saints

No. Mormons do, however, believe in a premortal existence during which we lived with our Heavenly Father. Man progresses eternally and mortality is one phase in that progression.

Hindus

Yes. Most Hindus accept the idea that each person has been and will be physically reborn many times during the course of a soul's evolution. Death is an interlude between one life and another. Liberated (or enlightened) souls do not return to this plane of existence. Others are reborn in a condition determined by the net effects of their past behavior. Memory of past lives does not normally survive physical rebirth.

Islam

No. The Qur'an clearly states that we have one life on earth.

Judaism

No. As a whole, Judaism has never subscribed to the belief in reincarnation. Some groups and sects have considered it, but it has never been a mainstream Jewish belief.

Lutherans

No.

Presbyterians

No. Reincarnation is vigorously denied because it is believed to be contrary to the Christian concept of salvation and God's respect for the individuality of each person.

Quakers

No.

Roman Catholics

Life and death are essential to Christian and therefore Catholic belief. Life comes as a gift that can't be earned but only accepted, made possible by Jesus' total act of love through his death followed by resurrection. The New Testament speaks of rebirth, of entry into a radically new and different form of existence quite beyond present comprehension. Reincarnation implicitly contradicts basic Catholic teaching.

Seventh-day Adventists

We are given only one life; it is a time of probation that ends at death and there is no second chance.

Unitarian Universalists

Reincarnation may be believed in by some of our members because there is no creedal prohibition.

United Methodists

Most United Methodists do not believe in reincarnation. The insistence on "the present age" in following Jesus, seeking perfection and serving human needs is a strong emphasis of United Methodism and a belief in repeated lives weakens the appeal to respond in this moment.

Unity

Our founders believed in reincarnation, as do most Unity people, but belief or disbelief in reincarnation is not a point of creed or dogma in Unity.

Zoroastrians

Only in recent times has the notion of reincarnation entered Zoroastrianism, but it is an insignificant notion that is adhered to by only a very small percentage of the community.

Index